Penguin Education X34

International Finance

Penguin Modern Economics Readings

International Finance

Selected Readings

Edited by R. N. Cooper

Penguin Books

Penguin Books Ltd, Harmondsworth,
Middlesex, England
Penguin Books Inc., 7100 Ambassador Road,
Baltimore, Maryland 21207, U.S.A.
Penguin Books Australia Ltd, Ringwood,
Victoria, Australia

First published by Penguin Books Ltd

Made and printed in Great Britain by
Richard Clay (The Chaucer Press) Ltd,
Bungay, Suffolk
Set in Monotype Times

Contents

Part Three **Government Policy and Balance-of-Payments Adjustment**

Part Four **International Liquidity and International Capital Movements**

Introduction

The readings included in this volume are all of sufficiently high calibre to speak for themselves. In that sense they need no introduction. Still, it may be helpful to indicate the place of each in the discipline of international monetary economics as it has developed over the years, and especially since the 1930s. The context in which each was written aids understanding the essay and also indicates why – apart from intrinsic merit – it was included in this volume. This introduction, therefore, will offer a few remarks about the subject of international monetary economics and then will indicate where each of the essays fits into the evolution of the subject.

Some of the readings require a greater knowledge of economics than others to be fully understood, but all should be suitable for university students of international economics. Some represent original contributions to the subject, while others are included because of their clear presentation of previous pioneering works – and of course the process of clarification often results in original discovery. Some of the selections do not represent fully accepted doctrine, and their practical conclusions can be expected to be modified in the course of further work; these essays therefore represent the 'state of the art' at the present time. The paucity of empirical content is symptomatic of the field, not merely of the selection for inclusion here.

The theory of international trade, like most economic theory, is principally concerned with the shift from one position of economic equilibrium to another as a result of some change in tastes, technology, or economic policy. The focus is on the characteristics of the new equilibrium. International monetary economics, in contrast, has been more concerned with the *process* of adjustment back to equilibrium than with the characteristics of the new equilibrium – indeed the new equilibrium is often the same as the initial one. But economic theory has been generally less successful in describing and analysing processes of adjustment than in characterizing equilibrium positions. As a result, international monetary economics has often been plagued with one or another of two problems: either it is trivial in its simplicity, or it involves specific assumptions about the nature of adjustment, and this latter fact places its generality under suspicion. In this respect it shares the difficulties arising from the failure, so far, to integrate monetary theory into the main corpus of economic theory in a meaningful and practically relevant way.

The difficulty is illustrated by the fact that the comparative static analysis by David Hume, written in 1752 and applying the quantity theory of money to the problem of international adjustment, so dominated the field that Jacob Viner could write nearly two centuries later: 'The "classical" theory of the mechanism of international trade, as developed from Hume to J. S. Mill, is still, in its general lines, the predominant theory. No strikingly different mechanism has yet been convincingly suggested . . .'.[1] Imbalances in international payments lead to changes in the domestic money supply which in turn lead to changes in the price level which in turn lead to equilibrating adjustments in the level of exports and imports; and the process continues until external balance is restored. It seemed for many years that little more was to be said. But the flowering of international monetary economics during the past thirty years denies this. Renewed vigour in the discussion is closely related to the 'Keynesian revolution' in economic thinking, a revolution which broadly speaking combined three quite different but related elements, not all due to Keynes himself: better conceptualization and improved measurement of national economic aggregates such as the gross national product; better understanding of the short-run determination of these aggregates; and assignment to governments of responsibility for maintaining aggregate incomes and output at acceptable levels, rather than leaving their determination exclusively to 'market forces'. This transformation in economic thinking shifted the attention of many economists from preoccupation with long-run equilibrium positions to the process of adjustment and to the possibility of prolonged economic *dis*equilibrium (for example in the labour market); and increasing attention to macro-economic policy also heightened sensitivity to the national balance of pay-

1. Jacob Viner, *Studies in the Theory of International Trade*, London, George Allen and Unwin, 1937, p. 291.

ments as a possible constraint on the achievement of other economic objectives.

The readings that follow reflect this evolution in thinking. They are grouped under four headings, although several essays include material that could fall comfortably under two or more headings. The first four selections are primarily concerned with 'automatic' adjustment to imbalances in international payments under a regime of fixed exchange rates and in the absence of policy interference with the process. Each provides a somewhat different hypothesis about the main features of the adjustment process. The next six readings are concerned with changes in exchange rates and the role that exchange rates may play in preserving or restoring international equilibrium. Following these are four readings that view maintenance of external equilibrium as a problem for economic policy, one national economic objective among several. They are addressed to the possibilities for achieving international balance without compromising other economic objectives. Finally, the last two readings are concerned, respectively, with the problem of international liquidity and with the changing nature of international capital movements.

The first selection is a brief excerpt from Hume, whose theory, as noted above, dominated the international adjustment for so long. It places almost exclusive emphasis on relative changes in national price levels, and relies on those changes to affect trade flows. In Reading 2 Robert Triffin takes sharp issue with the 'textbook' description of the actual working of the gold standard in the nineteenth century, a version based largely on Hume with some adjustments to allow for fractional reserves in the banking system. Triffin argues that in reality there was far greater parallelism in the movement of national price levels than could be accounted by the standard theory, which required divergent movements between surplus and deficit countries; that the principal burden of adjustment to imbalances in payments fell on countries of the 'periphery', producers of raw materials for the growing industries of Europe, countries which experienced adverse movements in the terms of trade whenever Britain tightened money and which often relied on changes in exchange rates to restore balance; and that imbalances among European countries did not cause great difficulty largely because they were not allowed to arise, monetary policy being largely in harmony. Triffin also discusses the evolution of international reserves, and this can be regarded as historical background for more recent discussions of international liquidity, represented here in the last part of Reading 14 and in Reading 15.

Swings in Britain's terms of trade, triggered by changes in domestic monetary conditions, represent quite a different adjustment mechanism than Hume's 'price-specie-flow' mechanism, as it is sometimes called. Hume's theory would have required *adverse* movements in the terms of trade of a deficit country – or at best no change at all. Triffin conjectures that Britain, by tightening credit, could induce a favourable movement in its terms of trade, and since it was a heavy purchaser of food and materials abroad, this change could reduce a deficit – but at the expense of the primary producing countries of the world. These countries in turn often used changes in exchange rates to correct their payments imbalances. But to be complete this description implies that the counterpart surpluses of Britain's deficits were always found in the primary producing countries, not in the manufacturing countries of Europe (although, to be sure, many European countries were important exporters of primary products into the second half of the century). Hence changes in the terms of trade reduced both deficit and surpluses.

Yet Triffin probably places undue emphasis on the harmonious movement of national monetary policy as a force preventing payment imbalances from arising among manufacturing countries. This harmony was more likely *ex post* than *ex ante*, being 'forced' on countries by the strong economic interdependencies among them. In other words, the observed parallelism may reflect the adjustment process at work rather than conscious attempts to avoid international disturbance, and this is the more likely when a third version of the adjustment process is recognized – changes in the level of income.

Johnson's 1956 essay (Reading 3) describes clearly and precisely the operation of these income changes in response to a hypothetical transfer payment from one country to another, and he contrasts these effects with the 'classical' adjustment mechanism. He also applies his analysis to the problem of exchange stability, a topic that more properly belongs in the following section.

Allowance for the direct effects on income, and of changes in income in turn on the trade balance, marked the most important addition to Hume's automatic adjustment mechanism based on monetary and price level effects. Hume was concerned with long-run equilibrium and assumed that, in the long run, economic resources would be fully employed. But if one allows for temporary (though perhaps prolonged) unemployment or under-employment of resources, financial transfers between countries or shifts in the pattern of international demand or costs will change real incomes directly, quite apart from the effects on the money supplies in each country. Since some portion of incomes is typically spent on foreign products, changes in income will alter trade levels by an amount governed by the income changes and the marginal propensities to import in the affected countries. This addition to the theory of international adjustment was a direct outgrowth of the Keynesian revolution noted above, in which full employment (implying unchanged total income in a stationary economy) ceased to be taken for granted; but hints of this process can be found in earlier writings. This element in the adjustment process was explicitly renounced by most countries in the 1940s, when government accepted responsibility for maintaining full employment.

Ingram (Reading 4) draws attention to still a fourth dimension of the adjustment process under a 'gold standard' regime, where by this is meant any system in which domestic money and international money are, in effect, indistinguishable to private residents. These conditions were largely satisfied in the nineteenth century, when gold and silver circulated freely both within and between countries. But they are also satisfied with respect to economic regions *within* a country, with its common currency, and it is interesting to speculate why we are not concerned about balance of payments adjustment between these regions. Ingram, generalizing from his study of the balance of payments relations between Puerto Rico and the United States, argues persuasively that *equilibrating* long-term capital movements play a central role in the adjustment process. (Puerto Rico is both within the customs area of the United States and part of the same monetary system, but with the advantage for research that data are available on merchandise trade with the United States.) A region in deficit experiences an outflow of cash, and this outflow tightens money in the deficit region. To replenish their cash balances, residents of the deficit area sell financial assets, either from their existing holdings or in the process of new borrowing. If such assets are widely acceptable, they can be sold at little or no loss in value to residents of the surplus regions, particularly since the latter, by virtue of their payments surpluses, now have cash holdings in excess of their requirements. This sale of assets 'finances' the deficit and can continue so long as the deficit region can generate assets acceptable in the surplus regions. Ingram is so impressed with the smoothness of Puerto Rican adjustment *vis-à-vis* the United States that he urges institutional changes in financial relations to facilitate the same kind of adjustment among all industrial countries.

Ingram's hypothesis falls short of being a complete solution to the process of international adjustment, however, for the 'perfect mobility' of capital will be eroded if the deficit continues for long. The deficit region will exhaust its holdings of generally acceptable assets, and creditors will become increasingly doubtful about taking up new claims on the region. Two related long-run effects may, however, bring about full adjustment. The funds borrowed from 'abroad' may be channelled into the creation of new productive capacity, and savings from the income so generated will permit larger exports and/or smaller imports. Alternatively, the decline in net worth implied by selling financial assets outside the region may exert a dampening effect on spending in the deficit area, thus lowering imports. The latter effect may also generate local unemployment – a problem taken up below in consideration of 'optimal' currency areas. Ingram's approach implies the complete loss to the region of the use of monetary policy to influence domestic economic activity. Fleming shows this more formally in Reading 13.

The dilemma which can arise, and which frequently has arisen, for national policy-makers faced with domestic unemployment and a balance of payments deficit, or domestic inflation and a balance of payments surplus, has led many economists to urge greater use of exchange rates to eliminate external imbalances. *Flexible* rates have actually been tried on a wide scale only in the period immediately following the First World War and again in the mid-thirties – neither with very encouraging results, but both under very difficult circumstances. Haberler's Reading (5) is a brief primer on the formal conditions required for a currency depreciation to improve the trade balance and on the relationship between the demand and supply of foreign exchange, the demand and supply of imports and exports, and the domestic demand and supply of commodities. In effect, he relates commodity markets to the foreign exchange market.

The usefulness of devaluation as a corrective measure was attacked on two very different fronts in the late forties and early fifties, shortly after exchange rate changes had been institutionalized in the Articles of Agreement of the International Monetary Fund. The first line of attack started with the important and valid point that a deficit in the current account of a country's balance of payments implied that its total expenditures on goods and services exceeded its total income. Elimination of the current account deficit therefore required bringing total expenditure and total income into correspondence. The 'elasticities approach' to devaluation, such as that set out by Haberler, was rightly criticized on the grounds that as defined the elasticities assumed that money income remained constant, whereas devaluation will typically change money income and indeed successful devaluation *requires* a change in money incomes and/or expenditure. The contrasting 'absorption approach' focused on the manipulation of aggregate income and expenditure to correct imbalances in current payments, with devaluation as such having little direct role to play in the process. In the ensuing debate some ground was given by both sides, and the resulting syntheses can be found reflected partly in Reading 6 by Tsiang, and, with focus on policy, in Reading 11 by Johnson. Tsiang attempts to show the role played by monetary and income factors in determining the effect of devaluation on the trade balance.

Reflecting a widespread habit of economists, Tsiang confines his analysis to *small* changes in exchange rates in the neighborhood of equilibrium. A more realistic analysis must relax both of these assumptions, since devaluation usually takes place in the presence of a large *im*balance in current account and by the time it is undertaken a small devaluation is not appropriate. One important illustration of the results that can emerge under these more common conditions, but which are ruled out under the assumptions of Tsiang's analysis, can be mentioned: a devaluation which is successful in improving the balance of trade in goods and services may also have a *de*flationary impact on the domestic economy. This possibility, pointed out by Hirschman in 1949 but subsequently neglected, is in fact likely to obtain for devaluations in many less developed countries. It arises because import prices measured in domestic currency will increase after devaluation, and so will total expenditure on imports, *in domestic currency*, if the elasticity of demand for imports is less than unity. Devaluation thus acts like an increase in excise taxes on imported goods. The resulting reduction in income may more than offset the increase in income arising from higher exports if the foreign elasticity of demand for imports is less than unity and if imports exceed exports even after the devaluation – a condition typically met in capital-importing countries. In this case the income effects of devaluation will reinforce the price effects in improving the trade balance, in contrast to the usual assumption that devaluation-induced *increases* in income will weaken the trade effects of devaluation.

The second attack on devaluation rested on an empirical claim that the relevant elasticities were too small to make devaluation an effective instrument for influencing the external balance. While theoretical work had focused on the minimal conditions required for devaluation to improve the trade balance, of which the Marshall–Lerner condition that the sum of import and export demand elasticities must exceed unity is one result, devaluation would typically require much higher elasticities than these to be an effective policy since devaluations often have undesirable side effects (e.g. as an impetus to increases in money wages), and these effects can be expected to become disproportionately more dangerous as the size of the devaluation increases. Money illusion (a willingness to accept a small decline in real income when it comes in the form of higher prices, but not in the form of lower money wages), for example, can be expected to diminish with larger increases in prices. Thus the elasticities must typically be much higher than those indicated by the minimum required for 'stability', and the theoretical point that elasticities too low for currency depreciation to improve the trade balance imply that currency appreciation would reduce the imbalance is, for practical purposes, irrelevant.

It was argued both on *a priori* grounds and on the basis of statistical estimates that the relevant elasticities were too low. But some of the factors pointing to low price elasticities prevalent in the late forties, such as the widespread use of import quotas, are now far less common (except in less developed countries). Statistical estimates of price elasticities typically drew on the atypical experience of the thirties, and in any case these estimates were subject to a downward bias arising from the methods of estimation. In Reading 7 Harberger sums up the evidence for moderate to high price elasticities.

In the absence of firm estimates of price elasticities in any particular case, it is difficult to assess the degree of over- or undervaluation of a currency. Economists instinctively look to comparisons of national price levels, and Balassa (Reading 8) reviews the so-called purchasing power parity doctrine and provides some new empirical evidence bearing on its validity as a technique for evaluating exchange rates.

In general, however, there is no widely applicable method for determining in practice what is the appropriate exchange rate for any country. This deficiency, combined with the tendency for officials to delay changing the exchange rate despite growing evidence that a change is needed, and to rely instead on many *ad hoc* interferences with international transactions, has led many economists to favour the use of flexible exchange rates, rates that would vary continuously with the pressures of supply and demand in the exchange market. Any fixed exchange rate, even if correct initially, is bound to become out of line in the course of time, and either it will have to be changed or other corrective measures will have to be taken. But discrete changes in exchange rates are thought to be disruptive. They tend to be delayed too long, giving rise both to unproductive (but not necessarily unrewarding) currency speculation and to resort to other, less efficient devices for correcting payments imbalances.

'Greater flexibility' in exchange rates can mean many things:

1. freely floating rates, without any official intervention
2. freely floating rates with official intervention only to

'stabilize' the market but not to influence trend movements in exchange rates

3. fixed parities, but permitted to move slowly, say by one or two per cent a year, in response to basic supply and demand pressures (the 'crawling peg')

4. fixed parities, but with a wide band around them within which exchange rates are determined largely or wholly by market forces

5. fixed parities, but with frequent changes in parities.

Fellner's Reading (9) makes the case for supporting a combination of the third and fourth versions of greater flexibility in exchange rates, in an attempt to combine the best features of flexibility with some of the restraining and stabilizing features of fixed parities. It is the outgrowth of an effort within a multinational group of international economists to find some measure of agreement on the working of the international monetary system. While of widely differing ideological views and with marked differences in their diagnoses of the ailments of the international monetary system, most members agreed that the present system of fixed parities with narrow margins for flexibility and infrequent changes in parity reflected a bad compromise among a number of alternative systems.

If flexible exchange rates are so superior to alternative arrangements, why are they not also appropriate between regions within a country, or indeed even for individual cities? Obviously at some point the inconvenience of dealing in many currencies, and the real costs associated with attempting to overcome the inconveniences, would outweigh the gains which proponents of flexible rates see arising from them. The benefits alleged for flexible rates are the avoidance of under-utilization and other inefficiencies in the use of resources that arise under alternative processes of adjustment. If these costs of adjustment are in fact low, then the argument for flexible rates is greatly weakened. Ingram emphasized the importance of high *capital* mobility in facilitating adjustment and argued that this high flexibility was more likely to be achieved if *no* change in exchange rates were possible, i.e. if in effect there were a common currency. Smooth adjustment might also be expected to depend heavily on high *labour* mobility, such that labour released in deficit regions readily migrate to regions where demand for labour is high. If factor mobility is high, adjustment costs will be low.

In Reading 10 McKinnon emphasizes still a third factor in determining an 'optimal currency area' within which fixed and unchangeable exchange rates should prevail, viz. each region's degree of economic openness in terms of goods and services. With imports heavily represented in the cost of living and other expenses, fluctuating exchange rates might induce residents to hold their financial assets outside the region with a view to stabilizing the real purchasing power of their assets, thereby depriving the area of investment corresponding to some of its saving. Regions closely linked by strong ties of trade might therefore reasonably prefer fixed exchange rates. Without high labour mobility, however, such a region still might find itself 'adjusting' to disequilibrium in the balance of payments through higher unemployment and downward pressure on incomes.

The third group of readings shifts the focus explicitly to policy choices. They differ from the preceding readings (Fellner excepted) in asking not how the international payments system works but what are the possible and optimum combinations of policies to deal with external disequilibrium with a minimum cost to other economic objectives. In Reading 11 Harry Johnson lays out a general framework for analysis of policies that distinguishes, on the one hand, between disturbances requiring a once-for-all adjustment in the *stock* of reserves and disturbances which give rise to a continuous (flow) change in reserves. To deal with the latter, in turn, he distinguishes between expenditure-reducing policies, which affect the level of domestic demand, and expenditure-switching policies, which influence the source (domestic or foreign) of demand. Overall monetary and fiscal policies fall into the former category, while changes in exchange rates, in tariffs, or in direct controls over trade and other international transactions fall into the latter.

Corden's Reading (12) builds on this distinction between expenditure-reducing and expenditure-switching policies and indicates diagrammatically the impact of various policy measures on the trade balance and on the level of domestic expenditure. He makes explicit the focus on *two* policy objectives, full employment and equilibrium in the balance of payments, and he brings out clearly the proposition that some combination of expenditure-reducing and expenditure-switching policies will generally have to be used to assure attainment of both objectives.

In Reading 13 Fleming is concerned with a rather different problem, strictly speaking not involving the balance of payments at all. He asks how the impact on domestic demand of the two principal macro-economic policy instruments, fiscal and monetary policy, is affected by alternative systems of exchange rates in the presence of interest-sensitive, international capital movements. He finds that as the interest-sensitivity of international capital movements increases, the impact of fiscal policy is weakened under a regime of flexible exchange rates and the impact of monetary policy is weakened under a regime of fixed exchange rates. In the former case, an increase in government expenditure will, *ceteris paribus*, increase interest rates and attract capital inflows from abroad. This inflow will cause the currency to appreciate, thereby worsening the trade balance and offsetting to that extent the stimulative effect of the initial increase in government expenditure. In the latter case, a given volume of open market sales by the central bank will simply attract inflows of funds from abroad and this will diminish the impact of 'tighter money' on domestic interest rates; and conversely for open market purchases. If capital movements are interest-sensitive, however, open market operations can have a powerful effect on the balance of payments. Fleming's analysis is relevant to the 'assignment' of policy objectives to different authorities, a topic taken up by Johnson in Reading 14.

Fleming's analysis applies to a single country and assumes that events in the rest of the world will be unaffected by what the country in question is doing. This assumption is very convenient, and it is not unrealistic for a country that is small relative to its trading partners taken as a group. But his conclusions may have to be modified when the country is large enough to influence the *world* level of demand and of interest rates. In that case domestic monetary policy will affect the level of interest rates abroad, and hence possibly the level of activity abroad; and this in turn will affect the current account of the first country's balance of payments even under a régime of fixed exchange rates. If domestic investment is sufficiently *in*sensitive to monetary policy, under certain conditions prevailing abroad, the effectiveness of monetary policy on domestic activity in the first country will increase relative to fiscal policy, as the interest-sensitivity of capital increases, by operating through the current account of the balance of payments. This outcome, which reverses Fleming's conclusion, is perhaps unlikely; but it is possible.

Reading 14, by Harry Johnson again, does allow for some repercussions in the rest of the world. It also addresses the question of the 'policy mix' from the dual points of view of efficiency and stability, under a regime of fixed exchange rates. Johnson points out that using monetary policy to influence the balance of payments (by attracting capital inflows, for example) in order to compensate for a current imbalance may lead to an inefficient allocation of the world's capital among countries, since the current account balances so 'financed' result in the transfer of real resources from one country to another. He also points out that using monetary policy in this way does not facilitate real balance of payments adjustment, and may on the contrary worsen the degree of imbalance if the maintenance of high demand, resulting in current account deficits financed by capital inflows (or in smaller surpluses financed by smaller capital outflows than would otherwise have occurred), leads to higher increases in wages and other factor costs. He fails to mention, on the other hand, that the continued flow of capital between countries will affect the wealth of the residents both of surplus and of deficit countries, and that the steady increase in the wealth of countries in surplus may lead to an increase in consumption, including consumption of imports, while the reverse will take place in the countries in balance of payments deficit. These portfolio adjustments, which have been largely neglected in balance of payments analysis, may however require a long time before producing pronounced effects.

The second part of Johnson's reading more properly belongs to the last group of selections, since it deals with the overall demand and supply of international reserves rather than with balance of payments adjustment policies for individual countries. In it he describes the problem with which both academic economists and, more recently, financial officials have been concerned for nearly a decade – that demand for additional international reserves exceeds the net supply (after private uses) of new gold. The gap has been filled primarily by the U.S. dollar, which thereby became a 'reserve currency'. (See Triffin's Reading 2 for factual background on the evolution of credit money.) But the implied lending to the United States has become unacceptable to a number of countries, and, beyond that, the stability of the payments system may be threatened by reliance on new dollar liabilities that grow more rapidly than U.S. gold reserves.

Creation of man-made reserve assets would solve this problem, but that raises the question of how such reserves, which unlike gold do not absorb real resources in their creation, should be distributed among countries. The distribution of purchasing power arising from the creation of money at the national level is partially determined by the fact that national governments maintain a monopoly over the minting of coinage and the issuing of currency notes, so the 'seignorage' – the difference in value between the cost of the coins and notes and their monetary value – accrues to the national government. (How the gains from central bank open market operations are distributed is a more complicated question.) The various possibilities for distributing the 'seignorage' on international issue are discussed by Johnson and, in the following reading, by Machlup.

Machlup also considers the question of 'backing' for a new, man-made international reserve asset, and he contrasts the principles underlying the present International Monetary Fund with those which would underlie a true credit-creating international central bank.

Finally, in Reading 16 Ragnar Nurkse provides long-term perspective on the changing nature and function of international capital movements – not in the context of balance of payments, but in terms of transfers of resources from capital-exporting countries to the rest of the world. This reading thus opens a basically different field of inquiry from the preceding ones, but one which overlaps them at several points. It has in common with Readings 14 and 15, raised there in connexion with distributing new reserve assets, concern with the prospects and possibilities for transferring real resources in adequate amounts to the poor countries of the world.

It should be noted that Nurkse's reading was written before the great upsurge of private capital outflows from the United States (and, gross, from other industrial countries as well), but most of what he says remains intact despite this sharp change since the mid-fifties. These outflows have gone largely to Canada (a 'region of recent settlement' in Nurkse's classification) and to Europe, where growing markets and greater receptivity towards rapid economic change have created strong attractions to American management and capital. The movement of capital to less developed countries, apart from those well endowed with natural resources, has devolved largely on governments, in the form of foreign assistance programmes.

Taken as a group, these readings pose the problems of contemporary macro-economic policy in a world of open economies, where the balance of payments must be taken into account as a restraint on the attainment of other objectives, and where the gold standard mechanism of adjustment is rejected as too costly under modern conditions. Most of the essays are addressed to the problems facing the economically advanced countries, but many of the principles apply to less developed countries as well. None, however, is addressed to the peculiar problems of less developed countries, where foreign exchange considerations often exert a powerful influence on plans and prospects for economic development. To treat that complex topic adequately would require another volume.

Part One The Adjustment Mechanism under Fixed Exchange Rates

The four readings in Part One introduce the problem of balance of payments adjustment among countries – or regions within a country – and suggest four different 'mechanisms of adjustment' to imbalances between economies that have the same currency or – what comes to nearly the same thing – have currencies that are linked rigidly to one another through fixed exchange rates.

David Hume's reading is the classic statement of the relationship between a nation's price level, its stock of money, and its balance of international payments. In the second reading Robert Triffin advances his own interpretation of payments adjustment during the nineteenth century, one that draws attention to Britain's influence over its own terms of trade. The next reading, by Harry Johnson, outlines a third mode of adjustment, in the context of the celebrated transfer problem. An outgrowth of the Keynesian revolution, this mechanism focuses on the changes in real income, upward in the recipient (surplus) country and downward in the paying (deficit) country. Finally, James Ingram points to the potential importance of the mobility of funds and urges greater emphasis on equilibrating movements of capital between countries.

1 D. Hume

Of the Balance of Trade

Excerpts from D. Hume (1752), 'Of the balance of trade', *Essays, Moral, Political and Literary*, vol. 1, Longmans Green, London, 1898, pp. 330–41, 343–5.

It is very usual, in nations ignorant of the nature of commerce, to prohibit the exportation of commodities, and to preserve among themselves whatever they think valuable and useful. They do not consider, that, in this prohibition, they act directly contrary to their intention; and that the more is exported of any commodity, the more will be raised at home, of which they themselves will always have the first offer.

It is well known to the learned, that the ancient laws of Athens rendered the exportation of figs criminal; that being supposed a species of fruit so excellent in Attica, that the Athenians deemed it too delicious for the palate of any foreigner. And in this ridiculous prohibition they were so much in earnest, that informers were thence called *sycophants* among them, from two Greek words, which signify *figs* and *discoverer*. There are proofs in many old acts of parliament of the same ignorance in the nature of commerce, particularly in the reign of Edward III. And to this day, in France, the exportation of corn is almost always prohibited; in order, as they say, to prevent famines; though it is evident, that nothing contributes more to the frequent famines, which so much distress that fertile country.

The same jealous fear, with regard to money, has also prevailed among several nations; and it required both reason and experience to convince any people, that these prohibitions serve to no other purpose than to raise the exchange against them, and produce a still greater exportation.

These errors, one may say, are gross and palpable: But there still prevails, even in nations well acquainted with commerce, a strong jealousy with regard to the balance of trade, and a fear that all their gold and silver may be leaving them. This seems to me, almost in every case, a groundless apprehension; and I should as soon dread, that all our springs and rivers should be exhausted, as that money should abandon a kingdom where there are people and industry. Let us carefully preserve these latter advantages; and we need never be apprehensive of losing the former.

It is easy to observe, that all calculations concerning the balance of trade are founded on very uncertain facts and suppositions. The custom-house books are allowed to be an insufficient ground of reasoning; nor is the rate of exchange much better; unless we consider it with all nations, and know also the proportions of the several sums remitted; which one may safely pronounce impossible. Every man, who has ever reasoned on this subject, has always proved his theory, whatever it was, by facts and calculations, and by an enumeration of all the commodities sent to all foreign kingdoms.

The writings of Mr Gee struck the nation with an universal panic, when they saw it plainly demonstrated, by a detail of particulars, that the balance was against them for so considerable a sum as must leave them without a single shilling in five or six years. But luckily, twenty years have since elapsed, with an expensive foreign war; yet is it commonly supposed, that money is still more plentiful among us than in any former period.

Nothing can be more entertaining on this head than Dr Swift, an author so quick in discerning the mistakes and absurdities of others. He says, in his *Short View of the State of Ireland*, that the whole cash of that kingdom formerly amounted but to 500,000*l.*; that out of this the Irish remitted every year a neat million to England, and had scarcely any other source from which they could compensate themselves, and little other foreign trade than the importation of French wines, for which they paid ready money. The consequence of this situation, which must be owned to be disadvantageous, was, that, in a course of three years, the current money of Ireland, from 500,000*l.* was reduced to less than two. And at present, I suppose, in a course of thirty years it is absolutely nothing. Yet I know not how, that opinion of the advance of riches in Ireland, which gave the Doctor so much indignation, seems still to continue, and gain ground with every body.

In short, this apprehension of the wrong balance of trade, appears of such a nature, that it discovers itself, wherever one is out of humour with the ministry, or is in low spirits; and as it can never be refuted by a particular detail of all the exports, which counterbalance the imports, it may here be proper to form a general argument, that they may prove the impossibility of this event, as long as we preserve our people and our industry.

Suppose four-fifths of all the money in Great Britain to be annihilated in one night, and the nation reduced to the same condition, with regard to specie, as in the reigns of the Harrys and Edwards, what would be the consequence? Must not the price of all labour and commodities sink in proportion, and everything be sold as cheap as they were in those ages? What nation could then dispute with us in any foreign market, or pretend to navigate or to sell manufactures at the same price, which to us would afford sufficient profit? In how little time, therefore, must this bring back the money which we had lost, and raise us to the level of all the neighbouring nations? Where, after we have arrived, we immediately lose the advantage of the cheapness of labour and commodities; and the farther flowing in of money is stopped by our fulness and repletion.

Again, suppose, that all the money of Great Britain were multiplied fivefold in a night, must not the contrary effect follow? Must not all labour and commodities rise to such an exorbitant height, that no neighbouring nations could afford to buy from us; while their commodities, on the other hand, became comparatively so cheap, that, in spite of all the laws which could be formed, they would be run in upon us, and our money flow out; till we fall to a level with foreigners, and lose that great superiority of riches, which had laid us under such disadvantages?

Now, it is evident, that the same causes, which would correct these exorbitant inequalities, were they to happen miraculously, must prevent their happening in the common course of nature, and must for ever, in all neighbouring nations, preserve money nearly proportionable to the art and industry of each nation. All water, wherever it communicates, remains always at a level. Ask naturalists the reason; they tell you, that, were it to be raised in any one place, the superior gravity of that part not being balanced, must depress it, till it meet a counterpoise; and that the same cause, which redresses the inequality when it happens, must for ever prevent it, without some violent external operation.[1]

Can one imagine, that it had ever been possible, by any laws, or even by any art or industry, to have kept all the money in Spain, which the galleons have brought from the Indies? Or that all commodities could be sold in France for a tenth of the price which they would yield on the other side of the Pyrenees, without finding their way thither, and draining from that immense treasure? What other reason indeed is there, why all nations, at present, gain in their trade with Spain and Portugal; but because it is impossible to heap up money, more than any fluid, beyond its proper level? The sovereigns of these countries have shown, that they wanted not inclination to keep their gold and silver to themselves, had it been in any degree practicable.

But as any body of water may be raised above the level of the surrounding element, if the former has no communication with the latter; so in money, if the communication be cut off, by any material or physical impediment, (for all laws alone are ineffectual) there may, in such a case, be a very great inequality of money. Thus the immense distance of China, together with the monopolies of our India companies, obstructing the communication, preserve in Europe the gold and silver, especially the latter, in much greater plenty than they are found in that kingdom. But, notwithstanding this great obstruction, the force of the causes abovementioned is still evident. The skill and ingenuity of Europe in general surpasses perhaps that of China, with regard to manual arts and manufactures; yet are we never able to trade thither without great disadvantage. And were it not for the continual recruits, which we receive from America, money would soon sink in Europe, and rise in China, till it came nearly to a level in both places. Nor can any reasonable man doubt, but that industrious nation, were they as near us as Poland or Barbary,

1. There is another cause, though more limited in its operation, which checks the wrong balance of trade, to every particular nation to which the kingdom trades. When we import more goods than we export, the exchange turns against us, and this becomes a new encouragement to export; as much as the charge of carriage and insurance of the money which becomes due would amount to. For the exchange can never rise but a little higher than that sum.

would drain us of the overplus of our specie, and draw to themselves a larger share of the West Indian treasures. We need not have recourse to a physical attraction, in order to explain the necessity of this operation. There is a moral attraction, arising from the interests and passions of men, which is full as potent and infallible.

How is the balance kept in the provinces of every kingdom among themselves, but by the force of this principle, which makes it impossible for money to lose its level, and either to rise or sink beyond the proportion of the labour and commodities which are in each province? Did not long experience make people easy on this head, what a fund of gloomy reflections might calculations afford to a melancholy Yorkshireman, while he computed and magnified the sums drawn to London by taxes, absentees, commodities, and found on comparison the opposite articles so much inferior? And no doubt, had the *Heptarchy* subsisted in England, the legislature of each state had been continually alarmed by the fear of a wrong balance; and as it is probable that the mutual hatred of these states would have been extremely violent on account of their close neighbourhood, they would have loaded and oppressed all commerce, by a jealous and superfluous caution. Since the union has removed the barriers between Scotland and England, which of these nations gains from the other by this free commerce? Or if the former kingdom has received any increase of riches, can it reasonably be accounted for by any thing but the increase of its art and industry? It was a common apprehension in England, before the union, as we learn from L'abbe du Bos,[2] that Scotland would soon drain them of their treasure, were an open trade allowed; and on the other side the Tweed a contrary apprehension prevailed: With what justice in both, time has shown.

What happens in small portions of mankind, must take place in greater. The provinces of the Roman empire, no doubt, kept their balance with each other, and with Italy, independent of the legislature; as much as the several counties of Great Britain, or the several parishes of each county. And any man who travels over Europe at this day, may see, by the prices of commodities, that money, in spite of the absurd jealousy of princes and states,

2. *Les Intérêts d'* Angleterre *Malentendus.*

has brought itself nearly to a level; and that the difference between one kingdom and another is not greater in this respect, than it is often between different provinces of the same kingdom. Men naturally flock to capital cities, sea-ports, and navigable rivers. There we find more men, more industry, more commodities, and consequently more money; but still the latter difference holds proportion with the former, and the level is preserved.[3]

Our jealousy and our hatred of France are without bounds; and the former sentiment, at least, must be acknowledged reasonable and well-grounded. These passions have occasioned innumerable barriers and obstructions upon commerce, where we are accused of being commonly the aggressors. But what have we gained by the bargain? We lost the French market for our woollen manufactures, and transferred the commerce of wine to Spain and Portugal, where we buy worse liquor at a higher price. There are few Englishmen who would not think their country absolutely ruined, were French wines sold in England so cheap and in such abundance as to supplant, in some measure, all ale, and home-brewed liquors: But would we lay aside prejudice, it would not be difficult to prove, that nothing could be more innocent, perhaps advantageous. Each new acre of vineyard planted in France, in order to supply England with wine, would make it requisite for the French to take the produce of an English acre, sown in wheat or barley, in order to subsist themselves; and it is evident, that we should thereby get command of the better commodity.

There are many edicts of the French king, prohibiting the planting of new vineyards, and ordering all those which are

3. It must carefully be remarked, that throughout this discourse, wherever I speak of the level of money, I mean always its proportional level to the commodities, labour, industry, and skill, which is in the several states. And I assert, that where these advantages are double, triple, quadruple, to what they are in the neighbouring states, the money infallibly will also be double, triple, quadruple. The only circumstance that can obstruct the exactness of these proportions, is the expense of transporting the commodities from one place to another; and this expense is sometimes unequal. Thus the corn, cattle, cheese, butter, of Derbyshire, cannot draw the money of London, so much as the manufactures of London draw the money of Derbyshire. But this objection is only a seeming one: For so far as the transport of commodities is expensive, so far is the communication between the places obstructed and imperfect.

lately planted to be grubbed up: So sensible are they, in that country, of the superior value of corn, above every other product.

Mareschal Vauban complains often, and with reason, of the absurd duties which load the entry of those wines of Languedoc, Guienne, and other southern provinces, that are imported into Brittany and Normandy. He entertained no doubt but these latter provinces could preserve their balance, notwithstanding the open commerce which he recommends. And it is evident, that a few leagues more navigation to England would make no difference; or if it did, that it must operate alike on the commodities of both kingdoms.

There is indeed one expedient by which it is possible to sink, and another by which we may raise money beyond its natural level in any kingdom; but these cases, when examined, will be found to resolve into our general theory, and to bring additional authority to it.

I scarcely know any method of sinking money below its level, but those institutions of banks, funds, and paper-credit, which are so much practised in this kingdom. These render paper equivalent to money, circulate it throughout the whole state, make it supply the place of gold and silver, raise proportionably the price of labour and commodities, and by that means either banish a great part of those precious metals, or prevent their farther increase. What can be more short-sighted than our reasonings on this head? We fancy, because an individual would be much richer, were his stock of money doubled, that the same good effect would follow were the money of every one increased; not considering, that this would raise as much the price of every commodity, and reduce every man, in time, to the same condition as before. It is only in our public negotiations and transactions with foreigners, that a greater stock of money is advantageous; and as our paper is there absolutely insignificant, we feel, by its means, all the ill effects arising from a great abundance of money, without reaping any of the advantages.[4]

4. We observed in Essay III. [not included here] that money, when increasing, gives encouragement to industry, during the interval between the increase of money and rise of the prices. A good effect of this nature may follow too from paper-credit; but it is dangerous to precipitate matters, at the risk of losing all by the failing of that credit, as must happen upon any violent shock in public affairs.

Suppose that there are 12 millions of paper, which circulate in the kingdom as money, (for we are not to imagine, that all our enormous funds are employed in that shape) and suppose the real cash of the kingdom to be 18 millions: Here is a state which is found by experience to be able to hold a stock of 30 millions. I say, if it be able to hold it, it must of necessity have acquired it in gold and silver, had we not obstructed the entrance of these metals by this new invention of paper. *Whence would it have acquired that sum?* From all the kingdoms of the world. *But why?* Because, if you remove these 12 millions, money in this state is below its level, compared with our neighbours; and we must immediately draw from all of them, till we be full and saturate, so to speak, and can hold no more. By our present politics, we are as careful to stuff the nation with this fine commodity of bank-bills and chequer-notes, as if we were afraid of being over-burthened with the precious metals.

It is not to be doubted, but the great plenty of bullion in France is, in a great measure, owing to the want of paper-credit. The French have no banks: Merchants bills do not there circulate as with us: Usury or lending on interest is not directly permitted; so that many have large sums in their coffers: Great quantities of plate are used in private houses; and all the churches are full of it. By this means, provisions and labour still remain cheaper among them, than in nations that are not half so rich in gold and silver. The advantages of this situation, in point of trade as well as in great public emergencies, are too evident to be disputed.

The same fashion a few years ago prevailed in Genoa, which still has place in England and Holland, of using services of China-ware instead of plate; but the senate, foreseeing the consequence, prohibited the use of that brittle commodity beyond a certain extent; while the use of silverplate was left unlimited. And I suppose, in their late distresses, they felt the good effect of this ordinance. Our tax on plate is, perhaps, in this view, somewhat impolitic.

Before the introduction of paper-money into our colonies, they had gold and silver sufficient for their circulation. Since the introduction of that commodity, the least inconveniency that has followed is the total banishment of the precious metals. And after the abolition of paper, can it be doubted but money will return, while these colonies possess manufactures and commodities, the only thing valuable in commerce, and for whose sake alone all men desire money.

What pity Lycurgus did not think of paper-credit, when he wanted to banish gold and silver from Sparta! It would have served his purpose better than the lumps of iron he made use of as money; and would also have prevented more effectually all commerce with strangers, as being of so much less real and intrinsic value.

It must, however, be confessed, that, as all these questions of trade and money are extremely complicated, there are certain lights, in which this subject may be placed, so as to represent the advantages of paper-credit and banks to be superior to their disadvantages. That they banish specie and bullion from a state is undoubtedly true; and whoever looks no farther than this circumstance does well to condemn them; but specie and bullion are not of so great consequence as not to admit of a compensation, and even an overbalance from the increase of industry and of credit, which may be promoted by the right use of paper-money. It is well known of what advantage it is to a merchant to be able to discount his bills upon occasion; and every thing that facilitates this species of traffic is favourable to the general commerce of a state. But private bankers are enabled to give such credit by the credit they receive from the depositing of money in their shops; and the bank of England in the same manner, from the liberty it has to issue its notes in all payments. There was an invention of this kind, which was fallen upon some years ago by the banks of Edinburgh; and which, as it is one of the most ingenious ideas that has been executed in commerce, has also been thought advantageous to Scotland. It is there called a Bank-credit; and is of this nature. A man goes to the bank and finds surety to the amount, we shall suppose, of a thousand pounds. This money, or any part of it, he has the liberty of drawing out whenever he pleases, and he pays only the ordinary interest for it, while it is in his hands. He may, when he pleases, repay any sum so small as twenty pounds, and the interest is discounted from the very day of the repayment. The advantages, resulting from this contrivance, are manifold. As a man may find surety nearly to the amount of his substance, and his bank-credit is equivalent to ready money, a merchant does hereby in a manner coin his houses, his household furniture, the goods in his warehouse, the foreign debts due to him, his ships at sea; and can, upon occasion, employ them in all payments, as if they were the current money of the country. If a man borrow a thousand pounds from a private hand, besides that it is not always to be found when required, he pays interest for it, whether he be using it or not: His bank-credit costs him nothing except during the very moment in which it is of service to him: And this circumstance is of equal advantage as if he had borrowed money at much lower interest. Merchants, likewise from this invention, acquire a great facility in supporting each other's credit, which is a considerable security against bankruptcies. A man, when his own bank-credit is exhausted, goes to any of his neighbours who is not in the same condition; and he gets the money, which he replaces at his convenience.

After this practice had taken place during some years at Edinburgh, several companies of merchants at Glasgow carried the matter farther. They associated themselves into different banks, and issued notes so low as ten shillings, which they used in all payments for goods, manufactures, tradesmen's labour of all kinds; and these notes, from the established credit of the companies, passed as money in all payments throughout the country. By this means, a stock of five thousand pounds was able to perform the same operations as if it were six or seven; and merchants were thereby enabled to trade to a greater extent, and to require less profit in all their transactions. But whatever other advantages result from these inventions, it must still be allowed that, besides giving too great facility to credit, which is dangerous, they banish the precious metals: and nothing can be a more evident proof of it, than a comparison of the past and present condition of Scotland in that particular. It was found, upon the recoinage made after the union, that there was near a million of specie in that country: But notwithstanding the great increase of riches, commerce, and manufactures of all kinds, it is thought, that, even where there is no extraordinary drain made by England, the current specie will not now amount to a third of that sum.

But as our projects of paper-credit are almost the only expedient, by which we can sink money below its level; so, in my opinion, the only expedient by which we can raise money above it, is a practice which we should all exclaim against as destructive, namely, the gathering of large sums into a public treasure, locking them up, and absolutely preventing their circulation. The fluid, not communicating with the neighbouring element, may, by such an artifice, be raised to what height we please. To prove this, we need only return to our first supposition, of annihilating the half or any part of our cash; where we found, that the immediate consequence of such an event would be the attraction of an equal sum from all the neighbouring kingdoms. Nor does there seem to be any necessary bounds set, by the nature of things, to this practice of hoarding. A small city, like Geneva, continuing this policy for ages, might engross nine tenths of the money of Europe. There seems, indeed, in the nature of man, an invincible obstacle to that immense growth of riches. A weak state, with an enormous treasure, will soon become a prey to some of its poorer, but more powerful neighbours. A great state would dissipate its wealth in dangerous and ill-concerted projects; and probably destroy, with it, what is much more valuable, the industry, morals, and numbers of its people. The fluid, in this case, raised to too great a height, bursts and destroys the vessel that contains it; and mixing itself with the surrounding element, soon falls to its proper level. [. . .]

From these principles we may learn what judgment we ought to form of those numberless bars, obstructions, and imposts which all nations of Europe, and none more than England, have put upon trade; from an exorbitant desire of amassing money, which never will heap up beyond its level, while it circulates; or from an ill-grounded apprehension of losing their specie, which never will sink below it. Could any thing scatter our riches, it would be such impolitic contrivances. But this general ill effect, however, results from them, that they deprive neighbouring nations of that free communication and exchange which the Author of the world has intended, by giving them soils, climates, and geniuses, so different from each other.

Our modern politics embrace the only method of banishing money, the using of paper-credit; they reject the only method of amassing it, the practice of hoarding; and they adopt a hundred contrivances, which serve to no purpose but to check industry, and rob ourselves and our neighbours of the common benefits of art and nature.

All taxes, however, upon foreign commodities, are not to be regarded as prejudicial or useless, but those only which are founded on the jealousy above-mentioned. A tax on German linen encourages home manufactures, and thereby multiplies our people and industry. A tax on brandy increases the sale of rum, and supports our southern colonies. And as it is necessary, that imposts should be levied, for the support of government, it may be thought more convenient to lay them on foreign commodities, which can easily be intercepted at the port, and subjected to the impost. We ought, however, always to remember the maxim of Dr Swift, That, in the arithmetic of the customs, two and two make not four, but often make only one. It can scarcely be doubted, but if the duties on wine were lowered to a third, they would yield much more to the government than at present: Our people might thereby afford to drink commonly a better and more wholesome liquor; and no prejudice would ensue to the balance of trade, of which we are so jealous. The manufacture of ale beyond the agriculture is but inconsiderable, and gives employment to few hands. The transport of wine and corn would not be much inferior.

But are there not frequent instances, you will say, of states and kingdoms, which were formerly rich and opulent, and are now poor and beggarly? Has not the money left them, with which they formerly abounded? I answer, If they lose their trade, industry, and people, they cannot expect to keep their gold and silver: For these precious metals will hold proportion to the former advantages. When Lisbon and Amsterdam got the East-India trade from Venice and Genoa, they also got the profits and money which arose from it. Where the seat of government is transferred, where expensive armies are maintained at a distance, where great funds are possessed by foreigners; there naturally follows from these causes a diminution of the specie. But these, we may observe, are violent and forcible methods of carrying away money, and are in time commonly attended with the transport of people and industry. But where these remain, and the drain is not continued, the money always finds its way back again, by a hundred canals, of which we have no notion or suspicion. What immense treasures have been spent, by so many nations, in Flanders, since the revolution, in the course of three long wars! More money perhaps than the half of what is at present in Europe. But what has now become of it? Is it in the narrow compass of the Austrian provinces? No, surely: It has most of it returned to the several countries whence it came, and has followed that art and industry, by which at first it was acquired. For above a thousand years, the money of Europe has been flowing to Rome, by an open and sensible current; but it has been emptied by many secret and insensible canals: And the want of industry and commerce renders at present the papal dominions the poorest territory in all Italy.

In short, a government has great reason to preserve with care its people and its manufactures. Its money, it may safely trust to the course of human affairs, without fear or jealousy. Or if it ever give attention to this latter circumstance, it ought only to be so far as it affects the former.

2 R. Triffin

The Myth and Realities of the So-called Gold Standard

R. Triffin (1964), 'The myth and realities of the so-called gold standard', *The Evolution of the International Monetary System: Historical Reappraisal and Future Perspectives*, Princeton University Press, pp. 2–20. [This study also appears in R. Triffin, *Our International Monetary System: Yesterday, Today and Tomorrow*, Random House, 1968, ch. 1.]

The monetary traditions and institutions of the nineteenth century provided a remarkably efficient mechanism of mutual adjustment of national monetary and credit policies to one another, essential to the long-term maintenance of exchange-rate stability between national currencies.

The reasons for this success, and for the breakdown of the system after the first world war, are very imperfectly reflected in most of our textbooks. Most of all, however, overconcentration on the mechanism of *intercountry* adjustments fails to bring out the broader forces influencing the *overall pace* of monetary expansion on which individual countries were forced to align themselves.

The Mechanism of Adjustment among Countries

Textbook abstract

Starting from an initial position of balance-of-payments equilibrium, the emergence of a fundamental deficit is generally described in terms of divergent movements of exports – downward – and imports – upward – in the deficit countries, with opposite, and equally divergent, movements in the surplus countries.

The money flows associated with the international settlement of such imbalances, if not offset by domestic 'neutralization' policies, should then tend to prompt downward price readjustments in the deficit countries, and upward readjustments in the surplus countries. This would restore a competitive price and cost pattern among them, and bring their balances of payments back into equilibrium.

These 'automatic' adjustment forces were strengthened and speeded up by central banks through the so-called 'rules of the game'. Discount-rate policy and open-market interventions would raise interest rates and tighten credit in the deficit countries, while lowering interest rates and expanding credit in the surplus countries. This would both cushion balance-of-payments and monetary transfers in the short term, by stimulating compensatory capital movements from the surplus to the deficit countries, and accelerate the desirable downward readjustment of prices and costs in the latter countries and their upward readjustment in the first.

The 'rules of the game' were widely violated after the first world war. The surplus countries adopted 'neutralization' policies which increasingly concentrated upon the deficit countries the burdens of adjustment previously distributed between surplus and deficit countries alike. At the same time, the development of stronger resistance to downward price and wage adaptations – particularly as a result of the growing strength of the trade unions – blocked the price-adjustment mechanism in the deficit countries, transferring its impact to fluctuations in economic activity and employment. The resulting social and political strains gradually became unbearable, particularly during the world depression of the 1930s, and induced governments to abandon the harsh gold-standard disciplines in favor of fluctuating exchange rates and/or trade and exchange restrictions.

Historical abstract

This highly simplified digest of the theory of international adjustment under the actual gold standard certainly meets the first test of an economic theory, i.e. the test of logical consistency. Does it meet equally well the second test by which a theory should be judged, i.e. its conformity to the major facts calling for explanation?

It undoubtedly fits *some* of the facts. Comparative price – or exchange-rate – movements obviously play a role in the fluctuations of balances of payments on current account, and are themselves influenced by the tightening or expansion of money flows arising both from international settlements and from domestic policies or lack of policies.

Other facts, however, must also be taken into account if we are to develop a general and politically meaningful theory of balance-of-payments adjustments.

1. First of all, the most cursory look at international trade statistics reveals an enormous degree of parallelism – rather than divergent movements – between export and import fluctuations *for any one country*, and in the general trend of foreign-trade movements *for the various trading countries*. Over the eighty years from 1880 to 1960, all significant increases or decreases in the exports of Western Europe were marked by *parallel* increases, or decreases, *for the eleven major trading countries of the world* in 91 per cent of the cases, and by *simultaneous* increases, or decreases, of *exports and imports for each country*, taken separately, in 88 per cent of the cases. These proportions fall to 77 and 73 per cent, respectively, for fluctuations of one year only, but rise to 95 and 92 per cent for fluctuations of more than a year's duration, and to 98 and 100 per cent for movements extending over more than four years.[1]

2. Equally impressive is the overall parallelism – rather than divergence – of price movements, expressed in the same unit of measurement, between the various trading countries maintaining a minimum degree of freedom of trade and exchange in their international transactions. In spite of wide differences and fluctuations in the composition of each country's exports, the indices of export unit values – measured in current dollars – for the same eleven countries over the period 1870–1960 moved in the same direction in 89 per cent of the observed fluctuations, and in opposite direction in only 11 per cent of the cases.[2]

This solidarity of national price movements – when measured in a common unit of account – is not incompatible, of course, with sharp divergences in national price levels, offset by opposite divergences in exchange-rate fluctuations. One does find indeed

1. The above percentages are derived from 287 observations of national increases or decreases for eleven countries (the United States, the United Kingdom, France, Germany, Italy, Belgium, the Netherlands, Switzerland, Sweden, Austria, and Canada), in the course of seventeen upward or downward movements of more than one per cent in Western European exports, in the period 1880–1960. The estimates used in these calculations are those of Maddison (1962), pp. 179–81.

2. Based on estimates from Maddison (1962), pp. 189–90.

that any large variations in the evolution of national prices are invariably offset, more or less rapidly, by exchange-rate fluctuations, and vice versa. Such variations were, however, eschewed – except in wartime – by most industrial countries in the nineteenth century, but were relatively frequent in the countries of the so-called 'periphery', and particularly in Latin America.

3. Thirdly, downward wage adjustments rarely reached any sizable amplitude, even in the nineteenth century, among the countries which maintained exchange-rate stability, and it may be doubted whether they would have proved much more acceptable at that time, economically, politically, and socially, than they are today. Wherever substantial inflation had been allowed to develop, international cost competitiveness was nearly invariably restored through devaluation rather than through downward price and wage adjustments.

Standard statistical series for the United States, the United Kingdom, France, and Germany show only four or five instances of actual declines in any broad-based indices of money wages during the fifty years preceding the first world war. Such declines were, moreover, usually confined to one or a few percentage points only. They were far exceeded, in post-gold-standard days, by the much sharper wage drops of the 1920–22 recession – 37 per cent in the United Kingdom – and of the first years of the great depression – 22 per cent in the United States and Germany.[3]

4. The 'neutralization' policies stigmatized by Ragnar Nurkse as another major cause – alongside of increasing price and wage rigidity – of the downfall of the gold standard (Nurkse, 1944, pp. 66–8) were by no means a postwar innovation. Using exactly the same techniques of measurement as Nurkse, Arthur I. Bloomfield found that 'central banks in general played the rules of the game just as badly before 1914 as they did thereafter!'[4] It might be noted in passing, however, that Nurkse's method defines as neutralization the cases where fluctuations in a central bank's domestic portfolio offset only a fraction – no matter how

3. See, for instance, Bureau of the Census (1960), pp. 90–92; Mitchell (1962), pp. 343–5; and France (1939), pp. 443–4.

4. Bloomfield (1959), p. 50. The evidence of neutralization, measured by Nurkse's formula, was present in 60 per cent of total observations, in the period 1880–1913, coinciding exactly with Nurkse's results for the 1922–38 period.

small – of the changes in its international assets. In many cases, however, there remained a *positive* correlation between the latter and changes in the central bank's sight liabilities. The impact of the latter changes upon the country's money supply would most often be magnified, in turn, several times by the operation of the private banking system under customary cash and liquidity requirements. Nurkse's 'neutralization' policies, therefore, could still permit a *multiple* impact of international gold – or foreign-exchange – movements upon money supply, as contrasted with the mere one to one impact which would have resulted under the pure gold-coin system of monetary circulation assumed in the most abstract formulations of gold-standard theory (Triffin, 1947, pp. 52–3).

5. The impact of discount rates on *cushioning* capital movements and on *corrective* changes in cost competitiveness was also far less general and uniform than is usually assumed.

The first seems indeed to have been particularly effective for the well-developed money and capital markets of the major creditor countries and financial centers, and most of all in the case of the United Kingdom. Discount and interest-rate changes could accelerate, or slow down, the normal, or average, pace of capital exports, and had to be resorted to frequently by the Bank of England to defend its very slender gold reserves. The much higher reserve levels of the Bank of France enabled it, on the other hand, to cushion temporary deficits out of its own reserves, with much rarer recourses to discount-rate changes. Most of all, however, capital-importing countries were far less able to influence in the same way the pace of their capital imports, these being primarily determined by the ease or stringency prevailing in the major financial centers.

The impact of Britain's international surpluses and deficits on British bank reserves was cushioned, moreover, by the ample use of sterling balances as cash reserves by overseas banks, particularly throughout the British Empire. Surpluses and deficits between Britain and its Empire – and even, to some extent, with other countries – merely led to a reshuffling of British bank deposits, rather than to an overall expansion or contraction in their amount and to correlative gold inflows or outflows.

Finally, the enormous role played by the London discount

market in the financing of the food and raw-materials exports of the less developed countries probably imparted to the Bank of England's discount-rate policy an influence on British terms of trade – and balance of payments – which has escaped the attention of economic theorists. Increases in discount rates did – as is usually pointed out – tend to reduce British prices and costs, improving the competitiveness of British exports in world markets and of home-made import-substitute goods on the domestic market. What is forgotten, however, is that the tightening of the London discount market also affected, most directly and overwhelmingly, the ease with which inventories of staple foods and raw materials could be financed, thus forcing also a quicker liquidation and attendant price declines in Britain's chief import goods. Such declines could be expected to be far larger than those in the less sensitive and volatile prices of British industrial exports. Thus, the favorable impact of discount-rate increases on British competitiveness (lowering British prices in relation to foreign prices in competing industrial nations) would be reinforced in its balance-of-payments effects by a simultaneous improvement of Britain's terms of trade (i.e. by decreases in the prices of foreign suppliers of complementary goods to Britain, larger than the decreases in British export prices to them). See Triffin (1947, pp. 60–63), and Kenen (1960, pp. 59–62).

6. The importance of international capital movements, and of their fluctuations, is often obscured by the disproportionate emphasis often placed on comparative price and cost fluctuations as the major factor in balance-of-payments disequilibria and their correction. Attention is thereby centered on the current-account items of the balance of payments, and tends to suggest that most disturbances arose in this area and had to be corrected promptly by the restoration of equilibrium between receipts and expenditures on current – or even merely merchandise – account.

In fact, however, international capital movements often did cushion – and even stimulate – vast and enduring deficits, or surpluses, on current account without calling for any correction whatsoever, except in an extremely long run indeed. Developing countries, such as the United States, Canada, Argentina, Australia, etc., could maintain, over an average of years, large and persistent deficits on current account, financed by correspondingly large, persistent, and growing capital imports from the more advanced countries of Western Europe. Rough estimates, compiled by the United Nations (1949, p. 2), place at about $40.5 billion, on the eve of the first world war, the gross long-term foreign investments of the principal creditor countries of Western Europe, and at $3.5 billion those of the United States. Of this $44 billion total, $12 billion had been invested in Europe itself, $6.8 billion in the United States – which was still a net debtor country at the time – $8.5 billion in Latin America, $6.0 billion in Asia, $4.7 billion in Africa, $3.7 billion in Canada, and $2.3 billion in Australia and New Zealand.

The lion's share of these investments was that of the United Kingdom ($18 billion), followed by France ($9 billion), and Germany ($5.8 billion). The United Kingdom had indeed been running persistent and growing surpluses on current account for more than a century, without any tendency whatsoever toward equilibrium. On the contrary, these surpluses rose continually from about $35 million a year, on the average, over the years 1816–55 to more than $870 million a year in the last years before the first world war (1906–13). Nobody could ever dream of explaining this favorable balance – and its fluctuations – in terms of the cost-competitiveness adjustment mechanism depicted in the textbooks, since it arose primarily from Britain's earnings on its swelling foreign-investment portfolio, and coincided with large and increasing *deficits* on merchandise account – close to $670 million a year over the period 1906–13 – offset themselves, for the most part, by net receipts on services and remittances account.

These current-account surpluses were nearly fully absorbed by Britain's investments abroad, which rose over the same period from an average of less than $30 million a year in 1816–55 to more than $850 million a year in 1906–13, and indeed more than a billion dollars a year in the last three prewar years, i.e. about a third of the British export level at the time, and 10 per cent of net national income (Imlah, 1958, pp. 70–75).

Foreign investments on such a scale undoubtedly accelerated economic development and helped at times relieve balance-of-payments pressures in the recipient countries. In the case of the United States, for instance, net capital inflows from Europe – primarily Britain – financed large and growing deficits on current account throughout most of the nineteenth century. They reached a peak of close to $300 million in 1888, tapering off afterwards, and shifting to net capital exports around the turn of the century, as the United States finally turned from chronic deficits to equally chronic surpluses on current account (Bureau of the Census, 1960, pp. 562–6).

7. The cyclical pattern of international capital movements, however, had a very different impact upon the capital-exporting and the capital-importing countries.

A mere slowdown of capital exports could help relieve, in the first countries, any pressures on central-bank – and private-bank – reserves arising from unfavorable developments in other balance-of-payments transactions. In the British case, for instance, capital exports dropped year after year, from their 1872 peak of roughly $480 million to $60 million in 1877, recovered again to $480 million in 1890, and declined once more in the following years to $110 million in 1898, rising nearly uninterruptedly afterwards to $250 million in 1904, and booming to $400 million in 1905, $570 million in 1906, to reach finally close to $1,100 million in 1913 (Imlah, 1958, pp. 73–5).

The borrowing countries, on the other hand, were far less able to control the rate of their capital imports which tended, on the whole, to swell in boom times and dry up in hard times, contributing further to the economic instability associated with their frequent dependence on one or a few items of raw material or foodstuff exports, themselves subject to wide quantity and/or price fluctuations. All in all, therefore, the balance of payments of the countries of the so-called 'periphery' would be assisted, over the long run by the large capital imports available to them from the financial markets of industrial Europe, but these countries would pay for this dependence through perverse fluctuations in the availability of such capital and in their terms of trade over the cycle. The exchange-rate instability of most underdeveloped countries – other than those of colonial or semi-colonial areas tightly linked to their metropolitan country's currency and banking system – finds here one of its many explanations.[5]

5. Another, closely connected with the main topic of this study, lies in the retention of a silver standard long after the effective abandonment of silver or bimetallic standards in Europe and the United States.

8. Another important qualification of the traditional theory of balance-of-payments adjustments relates to the international timing of reserve movements and discount-rate changes. The textbook explanation suggests that rate increases were undertaken by the deficit countries in order to relieve a drain of their reserves to the surplus countries. As noted by Bloomfield, however:

the annual averages of the discount rates of twelve central banks [England, Germany, France, Sweden, Finland, Norway, Denmark, Belgium, Switzerland, the Netherlands, Russia, and Austria-Hungary] reveal the . . . interesting fact that, in their larger movements at least, the discount rates of virtually all the banks tended to rise and fall together. . . . To some degree, and certainly for many of the banks, this broad similarity reflected competitive or 'defensive' discount rate changes. . . . But a more important explanation lies in the fact that discount rates in most . . . of the individual countries tended . . . to show a positive correlation, though generally not a very marked one, with domestic business cycle fluctuations. Since, as is well known, major cyclical fluctuations tended to be broadly synchronous in all countries, discount rate movements thus generally tended to exhibit a broad parallelism over the course of the world cycle – although there were, of course, many dissimilarities with respect to short-term movements in the various countries (Bloomfield, 1959, pp. 35–7).

This importance of parallel movements, associated with the international business cycle – as against divergent movements between surplus and deficit countries – brings us back to the first two points made above (pp. 40–41) and to the comparative neglect of this parallelism in textbook discussions centered nearly exclusively on intercountry balance-of-payments adjustments.

Reinterpretation and conclusions

1. The nineteenth-century monetary mechanism succeeded, to a unique degree, in preserving exchange-rate stability – and freedom from quantitative trade and exchange restrictions – over a large part of the world.

2. This success, however, was limited to the more advanced countries which formed the core of the system, and to those closely linked to them by political, as well as economic and financial ties. The exchange rates of other currencies – particularly in Latin America – fluctuated widely, and depreciated

enormously, over the period. This contrast between the 'core' countries and those of the 'periphery' can be largely explained by the cyclical pattern of capital movements and terms of trade, which contributed to stability in the first group, and to instability in the second.

3. The adjustment process did not depend on any tendency toward equilibrium of the national balances of payments on current account. Vast and growing capital movements cushioned over many years, up to a century or more, correspondingly large and increasing surpluses – and deficits – on current account.

4. The preservation of exchange-rate stability depended, however, on the impact of international monetary settlements – of the combined current and capital accounts – upon domestic monetary and credit developments. Large or protracted deficits or surpluses had to be corrected, residually, by a slowdown or acceleration of bank-credit expansion sufficient to bring about – through income and/or price and cost adaptations, and their impact on exports and imports – a tenable equilibrium in overall transactions, and a cessation of persistent drains in the deficit countries' stock of international money (i.e. gold and silver initially, and increasingly gold alone as all major countries shifted from the silver or bimetallic standard to the gold standard).

5. This residual harmonization of national monetary and credit policies, depended far less on *ex post* corrective action, requiring an extreme flexibility, downward as well as upward, of national price and wage levels, than on the *ex ante* avoidance of substantial disparities in cost competitiveness and in the monetary policies which would allow them to develop.

As long as stable exchange rates were maintained, national *export* prices remained strongly bound together among all competing countries, by the mere existence of an international market not broken down by any large or frequent changes in trade or exchange restrictions. Under these conditions, national price and wage levels also remained closely linked together internationally, even in the face of divergent rates of monetary and credit expansion, as import and export competition constituted a powerful brake on the emergence of any large disparity between internal and external price and cost levels.

Inflationary pressures could not be contained within the

domestic market, but spilled out *directly*, to a considerable extent, into balance-of-payments deficits rather than into uncontrolled rises of internal prices, costs, and wage levels.[6] These deficits led, in turn, to corresponding monetary transfers from the domestic banking system to foreign banks, weakening the cash position of domestic banks and their ability to pursue expansionary credit policies leading to persistent deficits for the economy and persistent cash drains for the banks. (Banks in the surplus countries would be simultaneously subject to opposite pressures, which would also contribute to the harmonization of credit policies around levels conducive to the re-equilibration of the overall balance of payments.)

Central banks could, of course, slow down this adjustment process by replenishing through their discount or open-market operations the cash reserves of the commercial banks. As long as exchange controls or devaluation were effectively ruled out from their horizon, however, they would themselves be responsive to similar pressures, arising from the decline in the ratio of their own reserves to liabilities. While their liabilities were internal, and thus easy to expand, their reserves were – and still are today – limited to international assets over which they had no direct control.

6. These pressures for international harmonization of the pace of monetary and credit expansion were indeed very similar in character to those which continue today to limit divergent rates of expansion among private banks within each national monetary area.

They were further reinforced, as far as central banks were concerned, by the fact that a substantial portion of the domestic monetary circulation itself was in the form of commodity money – gold and silver – wholly or partly international in character, rather than in credit money. Expansionary credit policies were thus accompanied by an outflow of gold and silver assets from the coffers of central banks into internal circulation and commercial banks' reserves, as well as to foreign countries. This movement of specie into internal circulation was all the more

6. This is still true today, in the absence of major changes in exchange rates and/or trade and exchange restrictions. See Triffin and Grubel (1962), pp. 486–91.

pronounced, as the lowest denomination of paper currency was usually much too high – often equivalent to several times the level of monthly wages – to be usable in household and wage payments. Central-bank credit expansion was therefore limited not only by *foreign* deficits and gold losses, but also by *internal* gold and silver losses, very much as commercial banks' credit and deposit expansion may be limited today by the drain on their paper-currency reserves. While the latter can be replenished by central-bank credit, central banks themselves did not have access to any gold or silver 'lender of last resort'.

The overall pace of advance of commercial banks' credit and deposit-money creation in a national economy was and remains subject today to the policies of the central bank. Similarly, the *overall* pace of credit creation by the central banks *as a group* was limited, in the nineteenth century's international economy, by their ability to increase *simultaneously* their international reserves.

7. This latter observation brings once more into the limelight a most important question left unanswered by the theory of balance-of-payments adjustment among countries: granted the need for mutual harmonization of national monetary policies among the gold-standard countries, what were the factors determining the *international pace* on which such alignments did take place? The question is all the more significant in view of the size and parallelism of major fluctuations in national price, export, and import levels over the period 1815–1914 as a whole.

The International Pace of Adjustment

A gentle reminder of the apostles of gold money

1. The gold standard is often credited with having reconciled, to an unprecedented degree, price stability with a high rate of economic growth over the nineteenth century. Contemporary advocates of a return to gold rarely miss the opportunity of quoting, in this respect, Gustav Cassel's observation that 'the general level of prices in 1910 was practically the same as in 1850'.[7]

7. See Cassel (1930), p. 72. The calculation is based on the Sauerbeck–Statist index of wholesale prices, and carried back to 1800 on the basis of Jevons' index. See also Kitchin (1930), pp. 79–85.

This stability is then attributed to the safeguards erected against inflation by the small size of new gold production and monetary gold increases in relation to existing stocks, and, more generally and optimistically, to the response elasticity of new gold production to any substantial decreases or increases in the price level: price declines or increases would be kept in check by their impact on gold-mining costs and profitability, and the resulting stimulation or slowdown of new gold production and monetary expansion.

2. As pointed out by Cassel himself, however, price fluctuations were by no means inconsiderable in the nineteenth century. Increases and decreases of 30 to 50 per cent, or more, accompanied the famous Kondratieff cycles (Kondratieff, 1926), and have been attributed by many writers – including Cassel – to fluctuations in gold production, following new mining or refining discoveries.

The evidence of long-term stability – or rather reversibility – of prices seen in the return of the 1910 index to its 1850 level is, to say the least, extremely misleading. Such an arbitrary choice of dates would allow us, for instance, to demonstrate equally well the 'stability' of the price level over the period from 1913 to the early thirties, since the precipitous fall of prices during the Great Depression brought back both the U.S. and the U.K. price indices down to approximately their 1913 level in 1931–2!

The starting point of Cassel's comparison – 1850 – is taken close to the very bottom of a long depression during which prices had fallen by 50 per cent or more, while the end year – 1910 – comes at the end of a fifteen-year upward trend during which the index used by Cassel had risen by more than 30 per cent.

Making the same comparison from peak to peak, or from trough to trough, we would find a rather pronounced downward long-run trend of wholesale prices in all major countries (Table 1). Prices declined, for instance, by 25 per cent in the United States from 1814 to 1872, and by 25 per cent again from 1872 to 1913, adding up to a cumulative 44 per cent decline over the century, from 1814 to 1913. In the United Kingdom, price declines of 30 per cent from 1814 to 1872, and 20 per cent from 1872 to 1913 also add up cumulatively to a similar 44 per cent decline for the century as a whole.

3. The influence of fluctuations in gold production upon these broad price trends seems far more plausible than the supposed inverse relationship from commodity prices to gold production. The significance of any such relationship as may have existed

Table 1
Wholesale Price Indices, 1814–1913

	U.S.	*U.K.*	*Germany*	*France*	*Italy*
Indices (1913 = 100)					
1814	178	178	129	132[1]	
1849	80	90	71	96	
1872	133	125	111	124	
1896	67	76	71	71	74
1913	100	100	100	100	100
Changes (in %)					
1814–1849	−55	−49	−45	−27[2]	
1849–1872	+66	+39	+56	+31	
1872–1896	−50	−39	−36	−43	
1896–1913	+49	+32	+41	+41	+35
1814–1913	−44	−44	−22	−24[2]	

Notes:
(1) 1820
(2) since 1820

Sources:
1. *For the United States:*
   (a) Warren and Pearson index until 1890
   (b) BLS index since 1890
2. *For the United Kingdom:*
   (a) Gayer, Rostow, and Schwartz index until 1849
   (b) Rousseaux index from 1844 to 1871
   (c) Board of Trade index since 1871
3. *For Germany, France, and Italy: Annuaire Statistique*, pp. 513–15 of 1951 edition (Paris, 1952).

was certainly dwarfed by the gold avalanche unleashed by the discovery of new gold fields and the improvement of mining and refining techniques, both after 1848 and after 1888. On both occasions, current production just about doubled, over twenty-four or twenty-five years, the gold stock accumulated over the previous three-and-a-half or four centuries. The yearly rate of growth in the estimated *monetary* gold stocks – after deduction for hoarding, industrial, and artistic uses – rose abruptly from 0.7 per cent in the first half of the nineteenth century to 4.3 per cent over the years 1849–72, declined precipitously to only 1.3 per cent in 1873–88, and rose again to 3.2 per cent in 1889–1913.

4. The neat mechanistic explanation derived by some authors from this broad parallelism between gold production and long-run trends in commodity prices fails, however, to give a full account of the complex factors involved in the process of nineteenth-century economic growth. The Kondratieff long waves were certainly influenced also to a major degree by the clustering and spread of technological discoveries and innovations in production, transportation, etc., by the vast migrations from old to new settlement areas, and – last but not least – by the preparation, waging, and aftermath of wars. These powerful influences, brilliantly analyzed by Schumpeter (1934, 1939) among others, obviously cannot be reduced to any mechanistic monetary explanation. It would be equally absurd, on the other hand, to deny that monetary and banking developments also had a role – even if primarily permissive, rather than initiating – on the acceleration or retardation of price trends and production growth. Schumpeter himself insisted abundantly on the role of bank credit in the process of capitalistic development.

One might well wonder, indeed, whether the unprecedented stability of the major currencies in terms of gold – and exchange rates – in the nineteenth century was not due to the spectacular growth of bank money or 'credit money' – in the form of paper currency and bank deposits – rather than to the residual, and fast declining, role of gold and silver 'commodity money'. Certainly, full dependence of the monetary system on gold and silver, in pre-nineteenth-century days, to the exclusion or near-exclusion of credit or paper money, did not prevent wide inflationary excesses – through debasement of the coinage – and wide fluctuations in exchange rates. The pound sterling lost three-fourths of its gold value and the French franc more than nine-tenths, from the middle of the thirteenth century to the end of the eighteenth century.

5. It is rather ludicrous to reflect that the vast literature devoted to the so-called nineteenth-century gold standard is practically devoid of any quantitative estimates of the enormous changes that modified, out of all recognition, the actual structure of the volume of money, or means of payments, as between gold, silver, currency notes, and bank deposits, between the end of the Napoleonic wars and the outbreak of the first world war.

Yet, according to the League of Nations estimates, paper currency and bank deposits already accounted in 1913 for nearly nine-tenths of overall monetary circulation in the world, and gold for little more than one-tenth. Comprehensive estimates for earlier periods are practically nonexistent and can only be pieced together from disparate sources, the reliability of which is most difficult to assess. Yet, some broad facts and orders of magnitude can hardly be in doubt. Bank currency and demand deposits probably constituted less than a third of total money supply at the beginning of the nineteenth century, but close to nine-tenths by 1913. Silver exceeded gold in actual circulation by about two or three to one until well into the second half of the century, but dropped considerably behind in the latter part of the period, the previous proportion being just about reversed by 1913. Increases in credit money – paper currency and demand deposits – accounted, in the major and more developed countries, for two-thirds or more of total monetary expansion after the middle of the century, and more than 90 per cent from 1873 to 1913.

These facts can hardly be reconciled with the supposed *automaticity* still ascribed by many writers – particularly in Europe – to the so-called nineteenth-century gold standard. The reconciliation of high rates of economic growth with exchange-rate and gold-price stability was made possible indeed by the rapid growth and proper management of bank money, and could hardly have been achieved under the purely, or predominantly, metallic systems of money creation characteristic of the *previous* centuries. Finally, the term 'gold standard' could hardly be applied to the period as a whole, in view of the overwhelming dominance of silver during its first decades, and of bank money during the latter ones. All in all, the nineteenth century could be far more accurately described as the century of an emerging and growing credit-money standard, and of the euthanasia of gold and silver moneys, rather than as the century of the gold standard.

Monetary expansion and international reserves before the First World War

A more precise assessment of the nature of the nineteenth-century international monetary mechanism and of its relation to production and price fluctuations must await the development of better monetary and reserve statistics than are now available, not only for the world as a whole, but even for the major countries which formed the basic core of the so-called gold standard.

The task should not prove impossible, if two limitations are accepted from the start. The first relates to the dearth of meaningful and reasonably reliable statistics for many countries. This should not prove too damaging for an appraisal of the international monetary mechanism in the few major countries which formed in the nineteenth century – and still form today – the core of the system. I have assembled some rough estimates of this sort, running back to 1885, for eleven such countries (the present so-called Group of Ten, or Paris Club, plus Switzerland). They accounted in 1885 and 1913 for 60 to 80 per cent of the world money supply and monetary reserves. Earlier estimates – back to 1815 – are for three countries only – the United States, the United Kingdom, and France – but accounted for about half the world money and reserves in 1885 and 1913, and for about two-thirds to three-fourths of the eleven core countries.[8] Table 2 gives further indications in this respect, revealing an encouraging parallelism between the estimates in the three groups.

The second limitation lies in the incompleteness and lack of full comparability of available data even for the major countries. Yet, this could hardly be more damaging than similar – and often far worse – limitations on the validity of other nineteenth-century estimates, in the field of national accounting for instance. They certainly remain, moreover, very minor in relation to the broad orders of magnitude involved in the enormous shifts in the monetary structure revealed by the tables. [Not reproduced here. For

8. World totals, however, are somewhat incomplete and particularly unreliable.

further data, sources, and qualifications, see the original source – *editor*.] In any case, imperfect as they are bound to be, such estimates are essential to an understanding of the nineteenth-

Table 2

Comparative Evolution of Money and Reserve Structure, 1885 and 1913

	Three countries[1]		*Eleven countries*[2]		*World*	
End of	*1885*	*1913*	*1885*	*1913*	*1885*	*1913*
(in billions of U.S. dollars)						
I. Money Supply	**6.3**	**19.8**	**8.4**	**26.3**	**14.2**	**33.1**
a. Gold	1.4	2.0	1.8	2.7	2.4	3.2
b. Silver	0.7	0.6	1.0	1.2	3.0	2.3
c. Credit money	4.1	17.2	5.6	22.4	8.8	27.6
i. Currency[3]	*1.6*	*3.8*	*2.3*	*5.9*	*3.8*	*8.1*
ii. Demand deposits	*2.6*	*13.3*	*3.3*	*16.5*	*5.0*	*19.6*
II. Monetary Reserves	**1.0**	**2.7**	**1.5**	**4.0**	**2.0**	**5.3**
a. Gold	0.6	2.1	0.9	3.2	1.3	4.1
b. Silver	0.4	0.6	0.6	0.8	0.7	1.2
III. Total Gold and Silver	**3.1**	**5.4**	**4.3**	**7.9**	**7.4**	**10.8**
a. Gold	2.0	4.1	2.7	5.9	3.7	7.3
b. Silver	1.1	1.2	1.6	2.0	3.7	3.5
(in % of money supply)						
I. Money Supply	**100**	**100**	**100**	**100**	**100**	**100**
a. Gold	23	10	21	10	17	10
b. Silver	11	3	12	5	21	7
c. Credit money	66	87	67	85	62	83
i. Currency[3]	*25*	*19*	*27*	*22*	*27*	*25*
ii. Demand deposits	*41*	*67*	*39*	*63*	*35*	*59*
II. Monetary Reserves	**16**	**14**	**18**	**15**	**14**	**16**
a. Gold	9	11	11	12	9	12
b. Silver	7	3	7	3	5	4
III. Total Gold and Silver	**49**	**27**	**51**	**30**	**52**	**33**
a. Gold	32	21	32	22	26	22
b. Silver	17	6	19	8	26	11

Notes:

1. United States, United Kingdom, and France
2. United States, United Kingdom, France, Germany, Italy, Netherlands, Belgium, Sweden, Switzerland, Canada, and Japan
3. Including subsidiary (non-silver) coinage, except in last column.

century international monetary mechanism, and far better than the implicit and totally unwarranted assumptions that underlie most of past and current theorizing about the so-called gold standard.

With these qualifications in mind, the following observations can be derived from these tables:

1. Although the 1816–48 estimates are particularly venturesome, there can be no doubt about the very slow growth of monetary gold stocks – just about nil, if we can trust the estimates – and of total money supply – about 1.4 per cent a year – over this period. Monetary expansion was sustained, not by gold accretions, but by an approximate doubling of silver stocks, accounting for about two-thirds of the total increase in the money supply, and for the remaining third by the incipient increase in internal credit monetization.[9]

2. The gold avalanche of the next twenty-four years produced an average increase of 6.2 per cent yearly in the total stock of monetary gold. This rate of growth declined sharply, to about 1.4 per cent a year, from 1873 to 1892, but recovered to about 3.7 per cent in the last twenty years preceding the outbreak of the first world war.

These enormous fluctuations in gold-stock increases were significantly smoothed down by concurrent adaptations in the functioning of the monetary and banking system. The yearly rate of growth of money supply declined only from 4.2 per cent in 1849–72 to 3.3 per cent in 1873–92, and recovered to 4.3 per cent, on the average, in the period 1893–1913.

This smoothing down was due, to a minor extent, to the partial offsetting of gold fluctuations by opposite fluctuations in the monetary silver stocks. These contracted substantially in the two periods of fastest gold expansion, but more than doubled during the leaner gold years from 1873 through 1892. Far more significant is the dwarfing of gold and silver stock changes by the spectacular growth of credit money, which fed more than 70 per cent of total money increases over the years 1849–72, and about to 34 per cent (see Table 3).

3. Credit money – i.e. paper currency and bank deposits – did not, however, normally circulate beyond the national borders of the issuing country and banking institutions. Exchange-rate stability thus depended on their ready convertibility – directly by

9. The latter being measured, indifferently, by the excess of money supply increases over the increase of monetary gold and silver stocks, or by the excess of credit money increases over the increase of monetary reserves.

Table 3

Composition of Money and Reserve Increases, 1816–1913: United States, United Kingdom, and France

	1816–1913	*1816–48*	*1849–72*	*1873–92*	*1893–1913*
(*in millions of U.S. dollars*)					
I. Money Increases	**18,791**	**581**	**2,688**	**3,863**	**11,659**
a. Gold	1,673	−55	913	81	734
b. Silver	287	379	−167	132	−57
c. Credit money	16,831	257	1,942	3,650	10,982
i. Currency and coin	*3,551*	*44*	*1,044*	*461*	*2,002*
ii. Demand deposits	*13,280*	*213*	*898*	*3,189*	*8,980*
II. Reserve Increases	**2,675**	**81**	**215**	**1,046**	**1,333**
a. Gold	2,097	62	218	379	1,438
b. Silver	578	19	−3	667	−105
III. Total Gold and Silver Increases	**4,635**	**405**	**961**	**1,259**	**2,010**
a. Gold	3,770	7	1,131	460	2,172
b. Silver	865	398	−170	799	−162
IV. Internal Credit Monetization (I − III = Ic − II)	**14,156**	**176**	**1,727**	**2,604**	**9,649**
(*in % of money increases*)					
I. Money Increases	**100**	**100**	**100**	**100**	**100**
a. Gold	9	−9	34	2	6
b. Silver	2	65	−6	3	—
c. Credit money	90	44	72	95	94
i. Currency and coin	*19*	*8*	*39*	*12*	*17*
ii. Demand deposits	*71*	*37*	*33*	*83*	*77*
II. Reserve Increases	**14**	**14**	**8**	**27**	**11**
a. Gold	11	11	8	10	12
b. Silver	3	3	—	17	−1
III. Total Gold and Silver Increases	**25**	**70**	**36**	**33**	**17**
a. Gold	20	1	42	12	18
b. Silver	5	69	−6	21	−1
IV. Internal Credit Monetization	**75**	**30**	**64**	**67**	**83**
(*% absorption of new gold into*)					
I. Reserves	56	886	19	82	66
II. Circulation	44	−786	81	18	34

the issuing banks, or ultimately through a national central bank – into the foreign currencies required, or into metallic currencies or bullion of international acceptability. Silver bullion lost its previous role in this respect around 1872, and silver-coin settlements remained acceptable only among the countries of the Latin Monetary Union. Silver, however, was no longer 'full-bodied' money, as the commercial value of silver coins fell well below their nominal value.[10] Gold thus emerged increasingly as the primary guarantor of international exchange stability even for the countries which remained on a so-called 'limping' bimetallic standard.

Three factors explain the maintenance of stable exchange rates in the face of growing issues of *national* credit moneys, side by side with fast declining proportions of *international* gold and silver moneys.

The first is the *de facto* harmonization of the national rates of monetary and credit expansion among the gold-standard countries. This harmonization itself, however, depended, as pointed out above (pp. 42–3), on the reaction of the issuing banks to the fluctuations in their reserve ratio arising from cyclical movements in internal circulation, as well as from external settlements of balance-of-payments disequilibria.

The *overall* pace of expansion, in turn, could not but be strongly influenced by the ability of the national banking systems to accumulate sufficient gold reserves to guarantee the convertibility of their national credit money issues into the gold through which foreign currencies could be acquired at stable exchange rates. The maintenance of relatively fast rates of monetary expansion after 1848 was thus conditioned by two further factors which the tables bring clearly into light.

The first was the spectacular spurt in gold production that followed the discovery of new gold fields and improved mining and refining techniques, and was of course predominantly accidental in character.

10. The valuation of silver at nominal par in the tables thus *understates* the importance of credit money, since silver coinage included in effect a substantial credit money component. Its acceptance at par among the countries of the Latin Union demonstrates the feasibility of international credit money settlements, even under the very imperfect arrangements negotiated to this effect among the countries of the Latin Union.

The second lay in the resiliency and adaptability of monetary and banking institutions, and the enormous economy of the precious metals which resulted from their increasing transfers from actual circulation in the public to the reserve coffers of commercial banks and of national central banks – or Treasury in the case of the United States.[11] The proportion of monetary gold and silver stocks absorbed in centralized monetary reserves rose from about 10 per cent in 1848 to 16 per cent in 1872, 41 per cent in 1892, and 51 per cent in 1913.[12] Even more significant is the relative proportion of new gold accretions absorbed by central reserves, on the one hand, and by the public and banks on the other. During the first gold avalanche of 1849–72, 81 per cent of the new gold was dispersed among the public and banks, only 19 per cent being accumulated in reserves. These proportions were nearly exactly reversed in the leaner gold years from 1873 through 1892, 82 per cent of the new gold feeding the increase of central reserves, with a multiple impact on overall money creation. When gold production rose again at a faster pace in the period 1893–1913, the proportion absorbed by central reserves declined to 66 per cent, while that of private holdings rose from 18 to 34 per cent (see Table 3).

These spectacular changes in the structure of money and reserves thus contributed powerfully both to the maintenance of relatively fast rates of monetary expansion, and to a considerable smoothing out of money supply fluctuations in relation to fluctuations in the available gold stocks.

11. The reserve estimates of the tables refer to the centralized holdings of central banks and treasuries only. The gold and silver components of money supply estimates include, therefore, gold and silver held by other issuing banks and commercial banks, thus overstating once more the metallic component of money supply in the modern sense of the word – coin, currency, and demand deposits in the hands of the public – and understating the proportion of credit money in circulation outside banks.

12. The proportion of gold alone temporarily dropped from 31 per cent in 1848 to 20 per cent in 1872, rising later to 35 per cent in 1892, and 51 per cent in 1913. The 1848–72 decline, however, was more than compensated by the increased absorption into centralized reserves of silver which could still be regarded at that time as a valid reserve component. After 1872, the movements of gold alone are more significant than those of gold and silver combined.

4. There was nothing inherently stable, however, in a process of monetary creation so heavily dependent on the accidents:

(a) of gold and silver discoveries and production rates;

(b) of uncoordinated – and largely irrational – national decisions regarding the adoption, retention, or abandonment of silver, gold, or bimetallism as the basic monetary standard; and

(c) of compensatory adaptations in banking structure, the scope of which would inevitably taper off over time, especially when central banks could no longer replenish their own reserves from the dwindling – relatively, if not yet absolutely – amounts of gold still in circulation.

In any case, the slow evolution which had adjusted gradually the international monetary system of the nineteenth century to the economic requirements of peacetime economic growth, but had also changed it out of all recognition between 1815 and 1913, was brutally disrupted by the outbreak of the first world war. The ensuing collapse of the system ushered in half a century of international monetary chaos, characterized by widespread exchange-rate instability and/or trade and exchange controls, with only brief interludes of nostalgic and vain attempts to fit upon the twentieth-century economy the monetary wardrobe of the nineteenth-century world.

References

Bloomfield, A. I. (1959), *Monetary Policy under the International Gold Standard: 1880–1914*, Federal Reserve Bank of New York.

Bureau of the Census (1960), *Historical Statistics of the United States*, Washington.

Cassel, G. (1930), 'The supply of gold', in *Interim Report of the Gold Delegation of the Financial Committee*, Geneva.

France (1939), *Annuaire Statistique* – 1938, Institut National de la Statistique et Etudes Economique, Paris.

Imlah, A. H. (1958), *Economic Elements in the Pax Britannica*, Harvard University Press.

Kenen, P. B. (1960), *British Monetary Policy and the Balance of Payments*, Harvard University Press.

Kitchin, J. (1930), 'The supply of gold compared with the prices of commodities', in *Interim Report of the Gold Delegation of the Financial Committee*, Geneva.

Kondratieff, N. D. (1926), 'The waves of economic life', *Review of Economic Statistics*, November 1935. (Abridged in English by W. Stolper.)

MADDISON, A. (1962), 'Growth and fluctuations in the world economy', *Banca Nazionale del Lavoro Quarterly Review*, June.

MITCHELL, B. R. (1962), *Abstract of British Historical Statistics*, Cambridge.

NURKSE, R. (1944), *International Currency Experience*, League of Nations.

SCHUMPETER, J. A. (1934), *The Theory of Economic Development*, Harvard University Press.

SCHUMPETER, J. A. (1939), *Business Cycles*, Harvard University Press.

TRIFFIN, R. (1947), 'National central banking and the international economy', *International Monetary Policies*, Federal Reserve System, Washington.

TRIFFIN, R., and GRUBEL, H. (1962), 'The adjustment mechanism to differential rates of monetary expansion among the countries of the European Economic Community', *Review of Economics and Statistics*, November.

UNITED NATIONS (1949), *International Capital Movements during the Inter-war Period*, New York.

3 H. G. Johnson

The Transfer Problem and Exchange Stability

H. G. Johnson (1958), 'The transfer problem and exchange stability', *International Trade and Economic Growth*, Allen and Unwin, pp. 169–90. (*Note:* This paper first appeared in *Journal of Political Economy*, 1956, vol. 64, no. 3, pp. 212–5, in a slightly shortened form.)

The transfer problem bulks large in the literature of international trade theory, both because international economic relations have abounded in transfer problems of various kinds and because the problem offers an attractive opportunity for the application of new theoretical techniques. My purpose here is not to survey the literature (see Viner, 1937, ch. 6; Samuelson, 1952 and 1954; Haberler, 1955), but to offer a straightforward and (it is hoped) simplified exposition of the theory of transfers in modern terms, based largely on recent literature but extending and unifying it in certain respects. In addition, it will be argued that transfer theory has a wider application than might appear at first sight and that, in particular, it can be applied directly to the problem of exchange stability.

In the context of modern international trade theory, the transfer problem can be posed in either of two ways – as a *real* problem or as a *monetary* problem. More precisely, it can be approached either on the classical assumption that the economic system works so as to maintain equality between income and expenditure at the level corresponding to full employment of resources in each country, or on the Keynesian assumption that the economy of each country is characterized by a perfectly elastic supply of labour and commodities at a fixed wage and price level,[1] so that output and income are determined by aggregate effective demand. In this paper the problem will be discussed from both approaches.

On either set of assumptions, classical or Keynesian, the

1. It is possible, but unnecessarily complicating, to assume a perfectly elastic supply of labour at a fixed money wage and an imperfectly elastic supply of output, as Keynes did in the *General Theory*. An analysis of this case may be found in Meade (1951).

transfer problem can be separated into two problems for analysis. The first is whether the process by which the transfer is financed in the transferor country and disposed of in the transferee will affect each country's demand for imports (at unchanged prices) sufficiently to create the trade surplus and deficit necessary to effect the transfer. The financing and disposal of the transfer will tend to reduce the transferor's demand for goods and increase the transferee's demand for goods; both effects will tend to improve the balance of trade of the transferor and worsen that of the transferee, and the changes may fall short of, or exceed, the amount of the transfer. Unless the changes in trade balances are exactly equal to the amount of the transfer, there will remain a balance-of-payments disequilibrium which must be corrected by some adjustment mechanism. In the classical model the adjustment mechanism is assumed to be a change in the terms of trade of the countries, brought about by price deflation and inflation;[2] in the Keynesian model the adjustment mechanism may be assumed to be either deflation and inflation of effective demand or a terms-of-trade change brought about by devaluation. In either model an alternative method of adjustment would be the tightening and relaxation of trade restrictions.

The second part of the transfer problem is whether the adjustment mechanism will be effective in restoring equilibrium. This problem really raises two subsidiary questions, one of direction and one of magnitude of influence. Taking the classical mechanism of a change in the terms of trade as an example, there is, first, the question whether a small deterioration in a country's terms of trade will tend to improve or to worsen its trade balance – the stability problem. Second, on the assumption that the balance would be improved by a small deterioration in the terms of trade, there is the question whether the trade balance can be improved sufficiently by this means to achieve a surplus of a given size. The same two questions arise with respect to the Keynesian mechanism of demand deflation and inflation, and also with respect to the use of trade controls of various kinds. It is obvious that the second question is an empirical one on which

2. Strictly speaking, what must change is the double-factoral rather than the commodity terms of trade, since with non-traded goods the commodity terms of trade can change in either direction as the price level changes.

theory can render little assistance, since it would always be possible to specify a surplus too large to be achieved by any method of adjustment. The question of direction of effect is, however susceptible of theoretical analysis, and conditions for the mechanism to work in the right direction can be established.

To summarize, the transfer problem has two theoretical facets: whether the transfer will be undereffected or overeffected as a consequence of the process by which it is financed and disposed of (that is, the direction in which the adjustment mechanism will be required to operate) and whether the adjustment mechanism will operate in the direction of restoring equilibrium. This chapter is concerned mainly with the first of these problems, and the argument will assume that the adjustment mechanism will suffice. A large part of the answer to the second problem will, however, be provided by applying the results of the argument on the first problem to the general problem of exchange stability, and to the problem of the effect of various kinds of governmental intervention in trade on the trade balance.

The argument which follows makes the usual simplifying assumptions, namely, that the world consists of two countries, A and B, producing two commodities or commodity bundles, A-goods and B-goods, these being the commodities exported by A and B, respectively. It is assumed that A is the transferor and B the transferee.

The Classical Transfer Problem[3]

On classical assumptions, the question whether the transfer would be undereffected or overeffected at constant prices is extremely simple to deal with, since the assumption of automatic full employment implies that the transfer must be financed and disposed of in such a way as to reduce aggregate expenditure by the transferor and increase aggregate expenditure by the transferee by the amount of the transfer and thus rules out any multiplier effects. The transferor's balance of trade is improved both by the reduction in its expenditure on imports and by the

3. This section reproduces, in a somewhat simpler form, the argument of Johnson (1955). That note and some of the additional argument of the present section owe much to Samuelson's two masterly articles (1952 and 1954).

increase in the transferee's demand for its exports. The total improvement, expressed as a proportion of the transfer, will be equal to the sum of the proportions of the expenditure changes in the two countries which fall on imports – more precisely, the sum of the proportions of the expenditure changes by which the receipts of the exporting country change. The transfer will be undereffected or overeffected, and the terms of trade will be required to change against, or in favour of, the transferor, according to whether the sum of these proportions is less or greater than unity. This general rule may be translated into several equivalent forms, by use of the fact that the proportion of the expenditure change which does not fall on imports must fall on exportable goods. The most convenient of these forms to work with is that the transfer will be undereffected or overeffected according to whether the sum of the proportions of expenditure change falling on the countries' export goods is greater or less than unity.

This rule, however, does not establish anything very interesting (beyond the demonstration that either result is possible), since nothing has been said about what determines the proportions of expenditure change. In general, these would depend on the nature of the transfer and the assumed conditions of international trade; as there is no reason for identifying the effects of the financing and disposal of a transfer with the effects of any other kind of economic change, nothing more can, in strictest generality, be said. Nevertheless, it is customary in the literature (and defensible in many cases) to identify the effects of the transfer on expenditure with those of an income tax and a subsidy. On this assumption the proportions of expenditure change can be related to the countries' marginal propensities to spend on exportables or importables, the precise relation depending on the assumed conditions of international trade. Three cases may be distinguished.

1. *Free trade, no transport costs*

In this case all expenditure on imports constitutes receipts for the exporting country, and the proportions of expenditure change are equal to the marginal propensities to spend. The transfer criterion is therefore whether the sum of the marginal propensities to spend on exportables is greater or less than unity.

2. *Tariffs, no transport costs*

Tariffs introduce a difference between the price paid by residents of a country for imports and the receipts of the foreign exporters. In conformity with classical assumptions, the tariff proceeds cannot be allowed to disappear from circulation but must be assumed to be spent by someone. The simplest assumption is that they are redistributed as an income subsidy and spent like any other increment of income, in which case part of the initial change in expenditure on imports associated with the transfer will wind up as a change in expenditure on exportables (out of redistributed tax proceeds). Consequently, the proportions of expenditure change falling on exportables will be larger than the marginal propensities to spend on exportables, and the transfer criterion is accordingly whether the sum of the marginal propensities to spend on exportables is greater or less than a critical value which will be less than unity.[4]

3. *Transport costs, no tariffs*

In this case also there will be a difference between the price paid by residents for imports and the price received by the exporters,

4. Let C and M be the marginal propensities to spend on exportables and imports and t be the proportion of the final price of imports taken in taxes. Then total expenditure at market prices will change by:

$$1 + tM + (tM)^2 + \ldots = \frac{1}{1 - tM}$$

times the amount of the transfer, and the proportion of the transfer by which expenditure on exportables changes will be:

$$\frac{C}{1 - tM} = \left(1 + \frac{tM}{1 - tM}\right) C$$

Since the transfer will be undereffected or overeffected according to whether the sum of these proportions is greater or less than unity, i.e. according to whether:

$$\left(1 + \frac{t_a M_a}{1 - t_a M_a}\right) C_a + \left(1 + \frac{t_b M_b}{1 - t_b M_b}\right) C_b \gtrless 1$$

the critical value of the transfer criterion will be:

$$C_a + C_b = 1 - \frac{t_a M_a C_a}{1 - t_a M_a} - \frac{t_b M_b C_b}{1 - t_b M_b}$$

The right-hand side of this expression must be less than unity, since t, M, and C are all positive fractions.

the difference representing the transport costs. To the extent that transport of exports utilizes the exported good, the transport costs will constitute receipts for the exporting country. In the extreme case where transport utilizes only the exported good, all expenditure on imports will be (direct, or indirect) receipts for the exporting country, the proportions of expenditure change will be equal to the marginal propensities to spend, and the transfer criterion will be the same as in the no-impediments case (3, above). But to the extent that transport utilizes the exportable good of the importing country, transport costs constitute an indirect demand for that good; consequently, the proportions of expenditure change falling on exportables will be larger than the (direct) marginal propensities to spend on exportables, and the critical value for the transfer criterion will be something less than unity, as in the previous case.[5]

The transfer criteria derived in the three cases just examined suggest a reference to a question which has concerned many writers on the transfer problem, namely, whether, even though the classical proposition that the terms of trade *must* turn against the transferring country is erroneous, there nonetheless remains a presumption in favour of this conclusion. Fundamentally, this is a meaningless question, since only ignorance can come from ignorance and no satisfactory basis exists for assessing the likely magnitudes of the marginal propensities to spend which enter into the criteria, short of measuring them in particular cases, when no question of presumption would arise.[6] An argument

5. Let k be the proportion of the price of imports representing transport cost incurred in the importer's exportable commodity; then the proportion of the transfer by which expenditure on exportables changes is $C + kM$, and the critical value of the transfer criterion is:

$$1 - k_a M_a - k_b M_b, \quad \text{which is less than unity.}$$

6. Statistical estimates of marginal propensities to import in the interwar period (1924–38) have produced results for some countries well above the average of ½ required by the criteria. For example, T. C. Chang (1951), p. 37, found six agricultural countries with marginal propensities to import ranging from 0·52 to 0·73, though in all but one case (Denmark, 0·54) the estimates are based on relatively short series. More recently J. J. Polak (1954), ('Summary of results', opposite p. 156) has obtained the following estimates: for the whole period, Denmark, 0·73; Norway, 0·67; for the 1920s Finland, 0·93; New Zealand, 0·65; Indonesia, 0·62; Union of South Africa, 0·57. While these estimates do not correspond very precisely with the theoretical concepts employed here (imports generally being valued

from 'equal ignorance' might, however, be drawn on the following lines: given only that the sum of the marginal propensities to spend on imports and exportables is unity, equal ignorance would suggest no presumption that the average marginal propensity to spend on exportables is either greater or less than $\frac{1}{2}$. Thus in the no-impediments case there would be no presumption in favour of the classical conclusion; but there would be such a presumption in the cases of tariffs and of transport costs incurred in the exportable good of the importing country, since in these cases the transfer would be undereffected if the average marginal propensity to spend on exportables were exactly $\frac{1}{2}$. In the latter case the presumption would be reinforced by the fact that, if these transport costs absorbed half the delivered price of imports on the average, the transfer would necessarily be undereffected for any positive values of the marginal propensities to spend on exportables.[7]

A less controversial, more 'positive', approach to the classical presumption is to examine what it implies about the countries involved in the transfer. For this purpose it is convenient to use an alternative form of the transfer criterion, namely, that the transfer will be undereffected if the extra physical quantity of A-goods purchased (directly or indirectly) out of an increase in income in A is greater than it is in B;[8] that is, the transfer will be

---

c.i.f., which excludes tariffs but may include invisible receipts of the exporting country) and their application is complicated by the presence of many countries and many commodities, they are not inconsistent with the possibility that in some cases a transfer might be overeffected.

7. On the assumption that $k_a + k_b = 1$, the criterion of n. 5 becomes $k_aC_a + k_bC_b$, which is necessarily less than $C_a + C_b$.

8. One formulation of the rule developed in the first paragraph of this section is that the transfer will be undereffected or overeffected according to whether the proportion of expenditure change in the transferor which falls on exportables is greater or less than the proportion of expenditure change in the transferee which falls on the transferor's exportables. Since the latter deducts tariffs and transport costs from the delivered price and adds back in transport cost incurred in the exported good, which amounts to measurement at factor cost in the transferor, deflation by factor cost gives the criterion stated in the text. Further, it follows that, since the sum of the proportions of expenditure change measured in this way must equal unity for each country, the condition respecting A-goods, as stated previously, implies the reverse for B-goods.

undereffected if the countries are biased (at the margin) towards the purchase of their exportables.

In the free-trade, no-transport-cost case the prices facing consumers are the same in both countries. Consequently, the classical presumption requires either that the countries differ in tastes and are biased towards consumption of their exportables or that, tastes being identical, the goods differ in degree of necessity and the country with the higher income per head produces the more 'luxurious' goods for export. In the case of tariffs and of transport costs the relative prices facing consumers differ, each commodity being relatively cheaper in the exporting than in the importing country. Consequently, if the economies were on identical consumption indifference curves before the transfer, each would have an *average* bias in *direct consumption* towards the purchase of its exportable commodity; and if *average* preferences are assumed to coincide with *marginal* preferences – which implies unitary income-elasticities of demand – *direct consumption* will display the marginal bias required by the classical presumption. To put the point the opposite way so far as *direct* consumption is concerned, tastes must be biased towards imported goods or marginal preferences must be so biased either because the latter behave contrarily to average preferences or because the country with the higher income per head produces the more necessary commodity, if the classical presumption is to be invalid. But indirect consumption must also be considered. In the case of tariffs without transport costs, indirect consumption out of tariff proceeds is assumed to behave in the same way as direct consumption, leaving the foregoing argument unaffected. In the case of transport costs and free trade, the bias towards direct consumption of exportables induced by the difference in prices is reinforced if transport costs are incurred entirely in the exportable good of the importing country and mitigated – perhaps outweighed – if transport costs are incurred entirely in the imported good. The effects of transport costs incurred in both goods are too complex to be analysed here, though analogy with the tariff case indicates that, in the case of identical pretransfer indifference curves and unitary income – elasticities, a necessary condition for invalidation of the classical presumption is that transport is more 'import-intensive' than is marginal consumption expenditure in the importing country.

Before concluding this section, it is appropriate to consider briefly the effects of relaxing some of the simplifying assumptions. The possibility of varying home production of the imported good makes no difference, since this is conditional on the price ratio between the goods changing, which in turn depends on the criteria derived previously. The introduction of non-traded goods does alter the criteria, since changes in demand for such goods must be classed either as changes in (virtual) demand for exportables or as changes in (virtual) demand for imports, according to whether they are more substitutable in production and consumption for one or the other.[9] In both these cases, however, the direction of change of the commodity terms of trade is not uniquely determined by whether the transfer is undereffected or overeffected at constant prices. The introduction of more countries also alters the criterion, since the balances of payments of the two countries are no longer equal and opposite in sign. From the transferor's point of view, the transfer will be undereffected or overeffected (at pretransfer prices) according to whether the sum of the proportions of the transfer by which the transferor's expenditure on imports is reduced, and the transferee's expenditure *on the transferor's exports* (not on imports in general) is less or greater than unity. Again, the movement of the commodity terms of trade is not decided by whether the transfer is undereffected or overeffected.

The Keynesian Transfer Problem (see also Johnson, 1953)

For the analysis of the transfer problem in Keynesian terms, it is assumed that output in each country is in perfectly elastic supply at a fixed domestic-currency price level, so that output, income, and employment are determined by the aggregate demand for output. It is also assumed that each country fixes its exchange rate and level of interest rates by appropriate monetary action, though its policy in this respect may change in the event of a

9. If it can be assumed that non-traded goods are substitutes for exports, this strengthens the classical presumption that the terms of trade turn against the transferor; but contrary cases are conceivable (Samuelson, 1954, pp. 288–9).

continuing balance-of-payments disequilibrium, and that, apart from accommodating financial transactions between monetary authorities, international capital movements are independent of the levels of national incomes.

These assumptions permit the derivation of multiplier equations relating changes in the national incomes of the countries and in the balance of payments between them to the various autonomous changes in demands for goods and transfers which may occur. The equations may be written as follows:

$$Y_a = I_a + c_a Y_a + M_b + m_b Y_b \qquad \mathbf{1a}$$
$$Y_b = I_b + c_b Y_b + M_a + m_a Y_a \qquad \mathbf{1b}$$
$$B_a = M_b + m_b Y_b - M_a - m_a Y_a - T \qquad \mathbf{1c}$$

where Y_a, Y_b, and B_a are the total changes in the two countries' national incomes and in country A's balance of payments (all measured in international currency units): I_a and I_b are autonomous changes in the countries' demands for their own outputs; M_a and M_b are autonomous changes in their demands for each other's outputs; T is an autonomous change in capital movements from A to B; c_a and c_b are the marginal propensities to spend on the purchase of domestic output; and m_a and m_b are the marginal propensities to spend on imports. It is assumed in what follows that all marginal propensities, including the marginal propensities to save (represented below by s_a and s_b) are positive, an assumption which suffices to guarantee stability of the system. It should also be remarked that while the system is set up in the symbols of a simple Keynesian system (implying the absence of government, business, and transport sectors and the utilization of goods only for direct consumption), it can be extended simply by redefinition of symbols to represent aspects of more complicated economic systems, such as the presence of direct and indirect taxes (other than export duties, which would require modification of the balance-of-payments equation), the dependence of government and business expenditure on taxation and sales receipts, and the use of domestic and imported goods in the production process.[10]

10. Let P represent the total change in sales proceeds at market prices, I and M autonomous changes in purchases of domestic and foreign output at these prices, h the proportion of a change in sales proceeds by which purchases of domestic output are further increased, and f the proportion

The transfer problem in the Keynesian case differs from that in the classical (real) case in two respects. First, there is no reason to assume that the process of financing and disposal of the transfer leads to changes in aggregate expenditure in the two countries equal to the amount of the transfer – the funds may come out of dissaving or go into saving. Second, any changes in expenditure brought about by the financing and disposal of the transfer will have multiplier repercussions on the balance of trade between the countries. The problem in this case is therefore whether, when all multiplier effects have been taken into account, the changes in demands for goods which result from the financing and disposal of the transfer are less or more than sufficient to improve the transferor's balance of trade by the amount of the transfer – that is, whether the transferor's balance of payments worsens or improves as a consequence of the transfer.

To analyse this problem, it is necessary merely to substitute for the various autonomous changes in demands in the multiplier equations the proportions of the transfer by which the demands for domestic and foreign goods are reduced in the transferor and increased in the transferee. In doing so, however, it is most convenient to work with the changes in demand for imports and in saving associated with the transfer, using the property that the transfer must alter the demand for home goods, the demand for imports, or the accumulation of assets through saving. Representing the changes in demand for imports and in saving directly due

---

by which purchases of foreign output are further increased. We may define h and f to include induced governmental expenditure from tax receipts, business expenditure from undistributed profits, and purchases of output for use in the production process, as well as final consumers' expenditure from disposable income. Then the multiplier equation for A, for example, may be written $P_a = I_a + h_a P_a + M_b + f_b P_b$. But since, for small changes, the change in national income at factor cost will be some given proportion of the change in sales proceeds, $Y = kP$, the multiplier equations based on sales proceeds may be rewritten in the standard form by defining:

$$c = 1 - \frac{1 - h}{k}, \quad m = \frac{f}{k}$$

and:

$$s = \frac{1 - h - f}{k}$$

Consequently, it is unnecessary to assume, as is generally done, that imports are used only in final consumption to avoid input–output complications.

to the financing or disposal of the transfer, expressed as proportions of the amount transferred, by m' and s', respectively, the multiplier equations yield the following solutions for the resulting changes in incomes and country A's balance of payments:

$$Y_a = \frac{1}{s_a}(B_a + s_a'T) \quad \text{2a}$$

$$Y_b = -\frac{1}{s_b}(B_a + s_b'T) \quad \text{2b}$$

$$B_a = \left(m_a' + m_b' - \frac{m_a}{s_a}s_a' - \frac{m_b}{s_b}s_b' - 1\right) \times \frac{s_a s_b}{\Delta}T \quad \text{2c}$$

where $\Delta = s_a s_b + s_a m_b + s_b m_a$. From this it follows that the transfer will be undereffected or overeffected according to whether $m_a' + m_b'$ (the sum of the proportions of the transfer by which expenditure on imports is altered by the financing and disposal of the transfer) is less or greater than:

$$\frac{m_a}{s_a}s_a' + \frac{m_b}{s_b}s_b' + 1$$

(1 plus the sum of the proportions of the transfer by which saving is altered – expenditure *not* changed – by the financing and disposal of the transfer, each weighted by the ratio of the marginal propensity to import to the marginal propensity to save in the country concerned).

The criterion just established, like that established earlier for the classical model, permits the transfer to be either undereffected or overeffected, according to the magnitudes of various parameters. This result is contrary to the findings of Metzler (1942) and Machlup (1943, ch. 9), whose analyses led to the conclusion that the transfer would necessarily be undereffected in the case under discussion (that is, on the assumption of positive marginal propensities to save in both countries).[11] This conclusion ran contrary to the findings of the classical analysis, a point of which

11. Metzler (1942) showed that the transfer would be overeffected if one country had a negative marginal propensity to save (in his analysis, a marginal propensity to invest higher than the marginal propensity to save) – a possibility allowed by the stability conditions – and if in that country the financing of the transfer altered demand for home output to the same extent. Machlup (1943, p. 181) showed that the transfer would be exactly effected if the transferor had a zero marginal propensity to save.

Metzler, in particular, made much. However, the contradiction is attributable to the adoption of special assumptions, namely, that the financing and disposal of the transfer does not directly affect the demand for imports and that it changes the demand for domestic goods either by the amount of the transfer or not at all.[12] (In terms of the present system, the *m*'s were assumed to be zero, and the *s*'s to be either zero or unity,[13] which, with positive marginal propensities to save, insures that the transfer cannot be effected.) If, instead of these rather unrealistic assumptions, one version of the assumption of the classical analysis is chosen – that the transfer is accompanied by equal changes in expenditure in the two countries, divided in some way between domestic goods and imports – the criterion becomes the same as that for the classical case: the transfer will be undereffected or overeffected according to whether the sum of the proportions of the transfer by which import demands are changed is less or greater than unity. This is the assumption adopted by Meade (1951). One of its consequences is that the behaviour of incomes is determined by whether the transfer is undereffected or overeffected; it is obvious that this should be so, since the assumption reproduces the classical model, with the exception that switches of demand from one country's output to the other's influence outputs instead of prices.

The Meade-classical assumption, however, like the assumption of Machlup and Metzler, is only a special case. In general, there would seem to be less reason in a Keynesian model than in the classical model for identifying the direct effects of the transfer on demand with those of any other economic change. But if the usual assumption of the classical analysis is chosen – that the transfer affects demands in the same way as any other change in

12. In the case of Metzler, this description refers to the mathematical analysis. Metzler's verbal argument identifies the effects of the transfer with those of other income changes – a case discussed in the next paragraph – rather than a change in demand for domestic output. As will be shown later, the two assumptions yield the same conclusions about the effects of the transfer on the balance of payments.

13. Machlup (1943, p. 183) allows *s*′ in the receiving country to be positive but less than unity; he also discusses the possibility of the transfer affecting the demand for imports directly, without realizing that this might permit the transfer to be effected by the income-effects alone.

income – with the difference that it also affects saving (that is, $m' = m$ and $s' = s$), the transfer cannot be effected if the marginal propensities to save are positive,[14] since the equation for the change in the transferor's balance of payments reduces to:

$$B_a = -\frac{s_a s_b}{\Delta} T \qquad 3$$

For this particular case, it is obviously unnecessary to investigate the influence of tariffs and transport costs, since the effects of the transfer on the balance of payments are unambiguous, while the 'classical presumption' is a certainty. In the general case, analysis of these problems is possible, but too cumbersome to be worth pursuing here.

In concluding this section, it would be appropriate to comment on a paradox suggested to the writer by P. A. Samuelson, namely why, when the transfer is treated as an income change, the Keynesian analysis gives a definitely negative answer, whereas in the classical case the answer depends on the marginal propensities to buy foreign goods. To begin with, it may be pointed out that the transfer criterion for the Keynesian case can be made precisely the same as that for the classical case, by redefining the 'proportion of the transfer by which expenditure on imports changes' to allow for the indirect effect on import demand of the failure of the transfer to be fully reflected in a change in

14. The results on this assumption are the same as on the Machlup–Metzler assumption, so far as the balance of payments is concerned, though the effects on income are different. This is not surprising, since the effects of the transfer in this case are the same as if the transfer financing led to an equal change in the demand for domestic output in each country, except that the first round of income change in each is wiped out. The conclusion that the transfer cannot be effected in this case can be generalized to any number of countries (see Johnson, 1956).

The econometric model of the world economy constructed by Neisser and Modigliani (1953) can be applied to throw some statistical light on the extent to which the transfer might be undereffected in practical cases. Their Table 15 (p. 93), which calculates the effects of income changes on trade balances in 1928, allowing for all repercussions on national incomes, implies that a transfer between England and Germany would improve one country's trade balance and worsen the other's by about 32 per cent of the amount transferred, while a transfer between the United Kingdom and the United States would alter the former's trade balance by about 30 per cent, and the latter's by only about 11½ per cent, of the amount transferred.

expenditure. This effect is represented in equation (2c) by the deduction from the direct effects of the transfer on import expenditure m' of the quantities $\frac{m}{s}s'$, which stand for the effects on import demand of the changes in income that would result from the missing changes in expenditure, if trade were kept balanced so that the closed-economy multipliers $\left(\frac{1}{s}\right)$ applied. If the terms $m' - \frac{m}{s}s'$ are taken as the proportions of the transfer by which expenditure on imports changes, then the Keynesian transfer criterion is the same as the classical, namely whether the sum of these proportions is greater or less than one. But where the transfer is treated as an income change, it so happens that the indirect effect exactly offsets the direct effect of the transfer on import demand, so that the total effect is zero.

There is in the Keynesian analysis, however, a more fruitful analogue to the 'sum of the proportions of expenditure changes falling on imports' criterion of classical analysis, which runs in terms of the proportions in which changes in saving are divided between holdings of domestic and of foreign assets; and the definiteness of the Keynesian answer turns out to be a consequence of the assumptions stated at the beginning of this section, that international capital movements are independent of the levels of national incomes, which implies that all changes in saving consequent on the transfer go into or come out of domestic assets. If this assumption is relaxed to permit changes in saving to be divided between domestic and foreign assets, as they would be on the other assumptions of the model, the balance of payments multiplier equations presented above become:

$$(1c)' \; B_a = M_b + (m_b + k_b s_b)Y_b - M_a - (m_a + k_a s_a)Y_a + (k_a' s_a' + k_b' s_b' - 1)T$$

$$(2c)' \; B_a = \left(m_a' + m_b' - \frac{m_a}{s_a}s_a' - \frac{m_b}{s_b}s_b' - 1\right)(1 - k_a - k_b) \times \frac{s_a s_b}{\Delta}T + (k_a' - k_a)s_a'T + (k_b' - k_b)s_b'T$$

$$(3)' \; B_a = (k_a + k_b - 1)\frac{s_a s_b}{\Delta}T$$

where k represents the proportion of a change in saving which is devoted to the purchase of foreign assets [and, in (3)′, $k = k'$]. It follows from (3)′ that, if the transfer is treated as an income change, it will be undereffected or overeffected according as the sum of what may be described as 'the marginal foreign investment ratios' is less or greater than unity; in other words, the transfer will be undereffected if there is a bias (at the margin) in each country towards investment in domestic assets – such as would result from additional ignorance and uncertainty about foreign conditions, or from exchange control, but not from difference in yields as such – and vice versa. In the more general case represented by (2c)′, if (as seems a reasonable simplification) the possibility of differences between the marginal foreign investment ratios applying to the initial and the induced effects of the transfer on savings is ignored, the transfer will be undereffected unless *either* the criterion discussed in earlier paragraphs is satisfied (for which a necessary but not sufficient condition is a marginal bias towards expenditure of transfer finance on foreign goods) *or* there is a marginal bias towards the purchase of foreign assets – but not if both occur together. More simply, unless there is some sort of marginal bias in the division of savings between domestic and foreign assets, no presumption is possible as to whether or not the transfer will be effected. Thus the division of savings between domestic and foreign assets plays a role in the Keynesian analysis analogous to that played by the division of expenditure between domestic and foreign goods in the classical analysis. This analogy will not, however, be pursued further here; nor will the remainder of the argument take account of the possibility that savings may be invested in foreign assets.

Applications of Transfer Theory: The Exchange Stability Problem

Transfer theory has generally been developed and applied in the analysis of such standard problems as reparations payments and international flows of long-term capital. It has, however, a far wider application in the field of balance-of-payments theory, since any actual balance-of-payments disequilibrium involves a transfer in some form from the surplus to the deficit country (or countries), and the problem of rectifying the disequilibrium can be framed as the problem of creating a transfer of equal amount in the opposite direction. Hence transfer theory can be applied to the analysis of methods for overcoming balance-of-payments disequilibria – whether automatic mechanisms of adjustment or planned governmental policies. For example, the analysis of the classical transfer problem shows that in a 'full-employment' world the deficit country does not necessarily have to turn its terms of trade against itself to correct the deficit and that the deterioration of the terms of trade will be less (or the improvement greater), the more the deflation of expenditure in the deficit country and the inflation of expenditure in the surplus country fall on imports rather than on exportable goods. The Keynesian transfer analysis shows that (with positive marginal propensities to save in both countries) changes in income taxation sufficient to yield changes in budget surpluses or deficits (at the initial income levels) equal to the initial balance-of-payments deficit will not suffice to remedy the disequilibrium, though changes in government expenditures of this amount may do so.[15]

The examples just cited involve adjustment mechanisms directed in the first instance at aggregate incomes and expenditures; a more interesting application is to the effects of changes in relative price levels on the balance of payments. Such changes in relative prices may be brought about either by deflation or inflation of domestic currency prices at a fixed exchange rate or by alterations in the exchange rate with domestic currency prices remaining unchanged. The latter case is the one more usually treated in contemporary theoretical analysis. The problem is formulated *either* in terms of the effects of devaluation on the trade balance *or* in terms of the stability of the foreign exchange market, the formulation depending on whether or not it is assumed that the monetary authorities intervene in the market to peg the rate of exchange.[16] In either case the central theoretical problem concerns

15. The Keynesian transfer analysis also shows that the gold-standard mechanism of adjustment (deflation and inflation of expenditure brought about by the effects of gold movements on interest rates) did not *necessarily* work by creating unemployment in the deficit country, as has often been alleged. This proposition requires a further assumption about the distribution of expenditure changes between importable and exportable goods.

16. In the 'classical' cases, analysis of devaluation must also assume some policy or process whereby the altered relations between national in-

the conditions under which a relative reduction in export prices would tend to improve a country's trade balance. This problem, which may be described generically as 'the exchange stability problem', also arises as a phase of the transfer problem, as the latter has been posed in the introduction to this reading.

The exchange stability problem can readily be formulated in terms of transfer theory, and the criteria which determine whether the transfer will be undereffected or overeffected can be transformed into criteria for exchange stability. For simplicity of exposition, it will be assumed (in addition to the assumptions of the preceding sections) that trade is initially balanced and that there are no barriers to trade.

A reduction in the price of A-exportables relative to B-exportables carries with it a transfer from A to B equal in amount, so far as A is concerned, to the increase in the cost of A's initial volume of imports and, so far as B is concerned, to the reduction in the cost of B's initial volume of imports. With initially balanced trade and a small price change, these two measures of the transfer will be approximately equal. The transfer is 'financed' and 'disposed of' through the effects of the relative price change, which will have income and substitution effects on the demands of the countries for their own and each other's goods. Alternatively, the price change will affect the two countries' aggregate expenditures and expenditures on imports, these expenditures being evaluated at the pretransfer prices because the effects of the price change on values are approximately subsumed in the

---

come and expenditure in the two countries inherent in a change in the trade balance are effected. This introduces an important complication, since the total effect of a devaluation will depend on the effect of the assumed policy or process on the trade balance as well as on the effect of the relative price change; and the effect of the supporting policy may be so strong as to reverse the effect devaluation by itself would tend to have on the trade balance. For example, if devaluation by A increased the demand for A's goods at the expense of B's, and the sum of the marginal propensities to spend on imports exceeded unity, restoration of equilibrium between aggregate demand and supply for each country's goods would require inflation of expenditure in A and deflation of expenditure in B, which would more than offset the effect of A's devaluation and leave A's trade balance worse than before. This complication is ignored in the following argument, which is concerned chiefly with exchange stability.

transfer itself. For what follows, it is important to notice that if expenditure measured in exportables is constant in the face of an altered price of imports, expenditure measured at the initial price of imports alters by the amount of the change in the cost of imports, that is, by the amount of the transfer.[17]

The exchange stability problem is the problem whether the effects of the price change on expenditures will be sufficient to effect the transfer implicit in the price change itself. In the classical case the assumption that all income is spent insures that the transfer is accompanied by equal changes in the two countries' expenditures (valued at pretransfer prices). The transfer will be overeffected or undereffected and the exchange market stable or unstable[18] according to whether the sum of the proportions of the transfer by which the two countries' expenditures on imports change is greater or less than unity. These proportions are equal to the price elasticities of demand for imports of the countries,[19] so that the market is stable or not according to whether the sum of these elasticities is greater or less than unity.[20]

17. Let $E = C + pM$ be aggregate expenditure, measured in exportables, where C and M are quantities of exportables and imports consumed, and p is the price of imports in terms of exports. Then the effect of a change in the price of imports (dp) is:

$$dE = \frac{\delta C}{\delta p}\,dp + p\frac{\delta M}{\delta p}\,dp + M\,dp.$$

The first two terms on the right amount to the change in expenditure measured at the initial price of imports, the third is the change in the cost of the initial quantity of imports. These two changes will be equal in magnitude and opposite in sign if $dE = 0$.

18. In a real model, the exchange rate has no independent existence; what is really under discussion is the stability or instability of the underlying real equilibrium of international trade.

19. The change in expenditure on imports, valued at the pretransfer price, is:

$$p \cdot \frac{\delta M}{\delta p} \cdot dp = \eta_m\left(-pM\frac{dp}{p}\right)$$

where:

$$\eta_m\left(= -\frac{p}{M}\frac{\delta M}{\delta p}\right)$$

is the elasticity of demand for imports. Since the implicit transfer is $-pM(dp/p)$, the change in expenditure on imports expressed as a proportion of the transfer is η_m.

20. This is, of course, the familiar Marshall–Lerner criterion. Since the elasticity of demand for importables consists of the sum of the marginal

In the Keynesian case the transfer analogy leads to the conclusion that the exchange market will be stable or unstable according to whether the sum of the elasticities is greater or less than

$$1 + s_a' \frac{m_a}{s_a} + s_b' \frac{m_b}{s_b}$$

where m and s, as before, represent the marginal propensities to save and to import of the subscript country; s_a' represents the proportion of the transfer by which saving from the pretransfer level of income is reduced (expenditure at pretransfer prices not reduced) in A by the increase in the price of A's imports; and s_b' represents the proportion of the transfer by which saving from the pretransfer level of income is increased (expenditure at pretransfer prices not increased) in B by the decrease in the price of B's imports. Alternatively, the s''s represent the effect of a decrease in the price of imports on saving or an increase in the price of imports on expenditure, from the initial income, divided by the initial value of imports.[21]

It was in the latter version that the exchange stability criterion for the Keynesian case was first published by Laursen and Metzler (1950), who saw correctly that any difference from the classical criterion hinged on the presence or absence of a terms-of-trade effect on aggregate expenditure and argued from the statistical evidence that (in the 'short run' of the cycle) a rising

---

propensity to spend on importables and the 'compensated' or 'constant-utility' elasticity of demand, argument on the lines of the last part of the first section of this reading shows that instability requires both a marginal bias towards the consumption of exportables and a low degree of substitutability between importable and exportable goods in consumption in the two countries. In the case in which both countries produce both goods, instability also requires a low degree of substitutability in production in the two countries.

It should be observed also that, though the argument of this section assumes the absence of trade impediments, the exchange stability criterion is unaltered by the introduction of tariffs or of transport costs incurred in the imported good, since the expenditure change in these cases depends only on the elasticity of final demand for imports.

21. This follows from the fact that the contrasting signs of the savings changes, as defined, cancel the contrasting signs of the price changes and that the change in saving is equal and opposite to the change in expenditure.

proportion of real income is saved to the conclusion that an increase in the price of imports would increase expenditure, thus making the critical sum of the elasticities of import demand greater than unity. Their conclusion has recently been disputed by White,[22] on the grounds that time lags make the long-run behaviour of the savings ratio relevant and that in the long run the ratio is constant.

Prior to the publication of Laursen and Metzler's work, Harberger published an analysis of the problem,[23] in which the apparatus of formal value theory was employed to determine the effect of an increase in import prices on saving. Harberger assumed that saving, measured in exportable goods, is a function of real income only, changes in prices inducing no substitution between saving and consumption; that the marginal propensity to save for changes in real income due to changes in the terms of trade is the same as that for changes in output at constant prices; and that the effects of a change in the terms of trade on real income may be approximated by the change in the cost of the initial value of imports. On these assumptions each s' in the preceding formula becomes equal to the corresponding s, and the criterion of exchange stability becomes whether the sum of the elasticities of import demand is greater or less than one plus the sum of the marginal propensities to import.

All three of the assumptions by which Harberger derived this elegant result have recently been subjected to criticism. Day (1954) has argued that saving and imports may be substitutes, since imports may be consumers' durables yielding a flow of satisfaction comparable to the interest on savings. Spraos (1955) has

22. See White (1954). I agree with the authors' 'Reply' in the same issue; but the evidence for, and theoretical explanations of, the constancy of the savings ratio in the long run are relevant to the present discussion of the exchange stability problem. In my review of Meade's *The Balance of Payments* (Johnson, 1951) I derived a stability criterion identical with that of Metzler and Laursen and adopted their conclusion about the direction of the terms-of-trade effect; the argument of that review is therefore open to the same sort of criticism that White expressed.

23. See Harberger (1950). Harberger erroneously attributed the difference between his results and those of earlier writers to the variability of production; in fact, this is merely a necessary condition, the fundamental explanation lying in the introduction of a non-zero effect of the terms of trade on saving.

shown that, if this is so, the Harberger criterion overestimates the critical value of the elasticities, though he is sceptical of the importance of such substitution. Pearce has shown that Day overlooks the effects of a change in the price of imports on the real value of interest and that, when this is recognized, no presumption as to the direction of substitution between imports and saving is possible (see Spraos, 1955). Spraos has argued convincingly that the marginal propensity to save from a change in real income due to a change in import prices is likely to be substantially greater than the marginal propensity to save from a change in output at constant prices, thus making the Harberger criterion an underestimate. Both Spraos and Pearce have shown that Harberger's assumptions imply the presence of money illusion, since they ignore the effect of the increased price of imports in reducing the real value of saving.[24] Spraos attempted to correct for this by raising the approximation of the real income loss to allow for an estimate of the loss of real value of saved (unspent) income, but, as Pearce shows, this preserves elements of money illusion in the savings function by leaving money rather than real savings a function of real income and by ignoring the effect of the price change on the real value of accumulated saving and consequently on the incentive to save.

If substitution effects between imports and saving and the 'Pigou effect' of import prices on savings are both ignored and if (following Spraos) it is assumed that saving is intended to be spent on imports and exportables in the same ratio as current consumption expenditure, the Harberger analysis can be reworked on the assumption that real, rather than money, saving is a function of real income, to yield this result:

$$s' = \frac{\bar{s}}{1-\bar{s}}(\epsilon_s - 1) \qquad 4$$

24. Harberger can be defended against this criticism by a careful reading of his argument. His 'saving' is described as 'hoarding' and is defined as the excess of income over expenditure; with initially balanced trade, current saving in this sense and presumably accumulated saving also are zero. On this reading (which would make all expenditure consumer expenditure) a positive marginal propensity to save ('hoard'), whether in money or in real terms, is sufficient to make the critical value of the stability criterion greater than the classical unity.

where $\bar{s}$ is the average propensity to save and ϵ_s is the income elasticity of demand for (real) saving.[25] This reworking reconciles the Harberger approach with that of Metzler and Laursen and confirms the latter in deducing the effect of devaluation on expenditure from the relation between the savings ratio and income. It assumes, however, that imports are demanded for consumption only. If some imports are required for investment and investment expenditure is fixed in real, rather than money, terms (an assumption supported by the assumption of fixed interest rates), a reduction in import prices affects money saving both by increasing consumers' real income and by reducing the cost of investment imports. The preceding result is then altered to:

$$s' = m_c \frac{\bar{s}}{1 - \bar{s}} (\epsilon_s - 1) + m_i \qquad \mathbf{5}$$

25. Let the initial volume of domestic output be Y and the initial quantities of domestic and foreign output consumed be C and M, respectively, these quantities being measured in units such that the initial domestic prices are unity. On the assumptions stated previously, real income, Y_r, may be measured by output deflated by a price index, so that:

$$Y_r = Y \div \frac{C + pM}{C + M},$$

where p represents the (real) price of imports, initially unity; and real saving, S_r, is a function of real income only and its money value (value in terms of domestic output) is:

$$S = S_r \cdot \frac{C + pM}{C + M}$$

Hence the change in money saving due to a reduction in the price of imports, expressed as a proportion of the initial value of imports, is:

$$\begin{aligned} s' = -\frac{1}{M}\frac{\delta S}{\delta p} &= \frac{1}{M}\left(\frac{YM}{C + M}\frac{\delta S_r}{\delta Y_r} - \frac{S_r M}{C + M}\right) \\ &= \frac{S_r}{C + M}(\epsilon_s - 1) \\ &= \frac{\bar{s}}{1 - \bar{s}}(\epsilon_s - 1) \end{aligned}$$

where:

$$\bar{s} = \frac{S}{Y} = \frac{Y - C - M}{Y}$$

and:

$$\epsilon_s = \frac{Y_r}{S_r}\frac{\delta S_r}{\delta Y}$$

where m_c and m_i are the proportions of the initial volume of imports devoted to consumption and investment, respectively. This last result suggests that, though the Harberger–Metzler and Laursen finding that the critical value of the sum of the elasticities of import demand is greater than unity implies a questionable assumption about the behaviour of the savings ratio, it can be supported by the introduction of investment imports.

References

CHANG, T. C. (1951), *Cyclical Movements in the Balance of Payments*, Cambridge.

DAY, A. C. L. (1954), 'Relative prices, expenditure, and the trade balance: a note', *Economica*, vol. 21, no. 82, pp. 64–9.

HABERLER, G. (1955), *A Survey of International Trade Theory*, Princeton University Press.

HARBERGER, A. C. (1950), 'Currency depreciation, income and the balance of trade', *Journal of Political Economy*, vol. 58, no. 1, pp. 47–60.

JOHNSON, H. G. (1951), 'The taxonomic approach to economic policy', *Economic Journal*, vol. 61, no. 244, pp. 812–32.

JOHNSON, H. G. (1953), 'The reparations problem: a correction', *Economic Journal*, vol. 63, no. 251, pp. 724–5.

JOHNSON, H. G. (1955), 'The transfer problem: a note on criteria for changes in the terms of trade', *Economica*, vol. 22, no. 86, pp. 113–21.

JOHNSON, H. G. (1956), 'A simplification of multi-country multiplier theory', *Canadian Journal of Economics and Political Science*, vol. 22, no. 2, pp. 244–6.

LAURSEN, S., and METZLER, L. A. (1950), 'Flexible exchange rates and the theory of employment', *Review of Economics and Statistics*, vol. 32, no. 4, pp. 281–99.

MACHLUP, F. (1943), *International Trade and the National Income Multiplier*, Philadelphia.

MEADE, J. E. (1951), *The Theory of International Economic Policy*, vol. I. *The Balance of Payments*, London, and its *Mathematical Supplement*.

METZLER, L. A. (1942), 'The transfer problem reconsidered', *Journal of Political Economy*, vol. 50, no. 3, pp. 397–414. (Reprinted in 1949 in *Readings in the Theory of International Trade*, Philadelphia.)

NEISSER, H., and MODIGLIANI, F. (1953), *National Incomes and International Trade*, Urbana, Illinois.

POLAK, J. J. (1954), *An International Economic System*, London.

SAMUELSON, P. A. (1952), 'The transfer problem and transport costs', *Economic Journal*, vol. 62, no. 246, pp. 278–304.

SAMUELSON, P. A. (1954), 'The transfer problem and transport costs', *Economic Journal*, vol. 64, no. 254, pp. 264–89.

SPRAOS, J. (1955), 'Consumers' behaviour and the conditions for exchange stability', *Economica*, vol. 22, no. 86, pp. 137–47. (See also I. F. Pearce's, 'A note on Mr Spraos' paper', ibid., pp. 147–51.)

VINER, J. (1937), *Studies in the Theory of International Trade*, New York.

WHITE, W. H. (1954), 'The employment-insulating advantages of flexible exchanges: a comment on Professors Laursen and Metzler', *Review of Economics and Statistics*, vol. 36, no. 2, pp. 225–8. (See also the authors' 'Reply' in ibid.)

4 J. C. Ingram

Some Implications of Puerto Rican Experience

J. C. Ingram (1962), 'Some implications of Puerto Rican experience', *Regional Payments Mechanism: The Case of Puerto Rico*, University of North Carolina Press, pp. 113–33.

Absence of a Balance-of-payments 'Problem'

The close similarity between an international payments system and the United States–Puerto Rican payments system has been emphasized in this study. This raises a further question: Why do balance-of-payments 'problems' similar to those between nations not arise between the United States and Puerto Rico? In its economic planning the Commonwealth government rarely ever considers the possibility of any payments difficulties, and most observers assume that balance-of-payments problems cannot arise.[1] In an open economy such as Puerto Rico's, with no exchange controls and a small 'foreign-exchange reserve', this view demands an explanation.

We have seen that the close links between Puerto Rico and the United States are reflected in the mechanism of income adjustment. Changes in expenditure in Puerto Rico cause changes in income and imports that quickly affect the balance of payments. Indeed, so sensitive is this mechanism that increases in Puerto Rican expenditures must in a sense be 'covered' by external funds before they can be made. Before the Puerto Rican banking system can expand loans, the banks must possess external funds (or assets capable of quick conversion into external funds) equal to the amount of additional loans to be made. Bank managers probably do not think about the problem in these terms, and of course their actual operations involve daily changes in asset portfolios, deposit liabilities, and mainland clearings which obscure the essential determinants of lending power, but we have seen

1. '. . . the island can no more have a balance-of-payments problem than can an individual State of the union.' Federal Reserve Bank of New York (1960), p. 71.

that an increase in local loans generates changes in income and imports that quickly result in adverse external clearings approximately equal to the increase in loans.

The rapid expansion of total loans and deposits of Puerto Rican banks has been made possible by the net inflow of external capital – by the willingness of the rest of the world to hold real property and long-term claims in Puerto Rico. Without such an inflow of capital, it would be necessary for Puerto Rico to develop an export surplus on current account in order to support an increase in domestic loans and deposits.

In a sense, then, we can say that Puerto Rico has no external payments 'problems' because her money supply is automatically determined by the market – the capital market and the market for goods and services. In other words, the Puerto Rican money supply is an outcome of market forces; it is not subject to conscious determination by the Commonwealth government, and that government has so far recognized and accepted its lack of autonomy in monetary policy. Not only does it lack the right to issue coin and currency (as required by the United States Constitution under present political arrangements concerning Puerto Rico), but it also makes no effort to manipulate commercial bank reserve requirements or in other ways to influence the volume of bank deposits. Consequently, it exercises no direct influence on the structure of interest rates in Puerto Rico.

These characteristics of the monetary relations between Puerto Rico and the United States suggest a further explanation for the easy and untroubled payments system that exists. The Puerto Rican economy is unlikely to be subject to the kind of instability and panic movements of capital that afflict international payments systems because the capital markets of the two regions are tightly integrated. There are many 'points of contact' between the two economies. Thus Puerto Rican banks hold sizable amounts of their assets in United States securities and other claims which are readily marketable in the United States, and so do private firms and individuals. The ready market for Commonwealth government securities in New York also serves as a 'point of contact'. Common stock in Puerto Rican firms is not traded in great amounts in the New York market, but this is largely because such stock is closely held. Puerto Ricans, of course, hold some United States stocks and bonds. Mortgages and other forms of financial assets are marketable in mainland markets, and both banks and firms have lines of credit upon which they can draw in case of need. Banks can discount customers' paper with their mainland correspondents, while the branches of external banks can rely upon home offices for assistance. Use of a common currency in the two regions is also a point of strength, since outflows of currency provide their own exchange, so to speak. Such 'points of contact' serve virtually to guarantee that, at least in the short run, payments between Puerto Rico and the mainland are not in danger of interruptions and uncertainties arising from the exchange or transfer process.

The development of a mainland market for Puerto Rican mortgages is a good illustration of the importance of institutional factors and of the way in which 'local' financial claims may be transformed into 'generalized' claims acceptable and readily marketable in the external world (Ingram, 1959). This particular illustration also involves the federal government as a supra-regional authority. Because housing mortgages in Puerto Rico are eligible for mortgage insurance under the Federal Housing Administration, it was possible for local lenders (commercial banks and other firms) to make mortgage loans for residential construction and then to sell the mortgages to mainland buyers. Although such transactions first involved F.H.A.-insured mortgages, they were later extended to conventional mortgages as well. A large majority of mortgages financed in Puerto Rico have in fact been sold to United States buyers, and those remaining in the portfolios of local lenders can readily be sold.

Thus a large part of Puerto Rican financial claims are readily marketable in the external (mainland) financial market. Furthermore, this is more than a legal possibility; it is an actual operating practice. One can say, then, that Puerto Rican firms and the Commonwealth government can undertake anything they can finance in the New York market! We have seen that the Commonwealth government has foregone autonomy with respect to monetary policy, but this does not mean that that government cannot engage in deficit financing. As a matter of fact, outlays have regularly exceeded ordinary revenue, with the excess financed by bond issues in New York. Such bonds are sold on a competitive basis, although Puerto Rico does have the advantage (over an independent nation) that her bonds are exempt from federal income tax. This exemption of course reduces the cost of borrowing.

Through a circuitous route we come back, in a sense, to monetary policy. Through its fiscal operations the Commonwealth government does affect the insular money supply. If it borrows more heavily in New York, some portion of the 'external funds' remains to support a larger volume of bank deposits. In practice, however, fiscal operations are undertaken with other objectives than monetary policy in mind. As mentioned above, changes in the money supply are simply an outcome, a by-product, and not a goal of policy. Furthermore, the Commonwealth government can do little or nothing to influence the structure of interest rates on claims that are traded in the integrated capital market. It must be a 'price taker' as far as interest rates are concerned, given the quality of the security. It is in this sense that autonomy has truly been surrendered.

The Commonwealth government may in the future take a more active role in monetary policy. The Government Development Bank could begin to function as a central bank in a modest way. It could engage in open-market operations on a limited scale; it could vary collateral requirements against government deposits; and it could be given power to vary reserve requirements of Commonwealth chartered banks. However, it is likely that the government will be extremely cautious in this area. Sensitive aspects of confidence are involved, and confidence, once shaken, is not easily restored. Another possibility is that Puerto Rico will formally become part of a Federal Reserve district. This would best insure continuance of the present passive role in monetary policy.

Implications for International Monetary Policy

In discussions of the international monetary system and its stability, great emphasis is placed on 'foreign exchange reserves'. For example, the gold and dollar reserves of the United Kingdom are carefully watched and their level is treated as a vital factor in the maintenance of convertibility at a given exchange rate. In the Puerto Rican case, by contrast, no one gives much thought to the size of 'external exchange reserves', and certainly the economic quantity most closely analogous to the United Kingdom reserve concept is not regarded as important in the maintenance of a smooth payments system. The reason, as we have seen, is that a wide variety of other financial claims can easily be sold abroad to increase the supply of external exchange. In the United Kingdom, on the other hand, there is a much sharper distinction between domestic and external financial instruments and claims. Emphasis is placed on the quantity of spot foreign exchange, or of assets very close to actual foreign monies such as gold and short-term treasury bills, available to monetary authorities. It is recognized that other financial claims (such as common stocks, corporate bonds, and long-term government bonds) are traded internationally, but the concern about convertibility is a concern about convertibility of *money* and the very close 'near-monies'. In the last few years there has indeed been a growing recognition of what might be called the convertibility of short-term securities, and it is understood that interest rates on such securities cannot vary widely without inducing a flow of transactions that tend to reduce the spread.

However, this wider concept of convertibility does not extend far into the medium-term and long-term financial instruments, nor do the actual practices of financial institutions warrant it. The risk of exchange-rate fluctuations is the major reason that a sharp line of demarcation between 'domestic' and 'international' (or 'local' and 'generalized') claims continues to exist. (Custom, lack of knowledge, and institutional inertia are other reasons.) In the absence of this risk, there is little reason to expect United Kingdom bonds to sell at a 6.5 per cent yield while United States bonds of similar maturities sell at a 3.8 per cent yield. In the case of Puerto Rico, there is no exchange-rate risk, and the concept of convertibility has extended beyond the near-monies and into the longer-term securities. Not only is $1.00 in Puerto Rico exchangeable for exactly $1.00 in New York (in a monetary sense of spot convertibility at a fixed exchange rate of unity) and a treasury bill selling at $982 in Puerto Rico also worth $982 in New York, but in addition a wider range of claims (in quality and maturity) sell for roughly equal prices (and yields) in the two markets.[2] Consequently, a shift in the external payments position of Puerto Rico is immediately accompanied by a flow of transactions in a wide range of financial instruments that serve to offset it. Thus, in sharp contrast to the United Kingdom, virtually the entire stock of financial claims in Puerto Rico can be regarded as an 'external exchange reserve'; there is no reason for exclusive preoccupation with the amount of demand claims on foreigners at any moment.

This analysis has implications for some issues of international monetary policy and especially for institutional arrangements to be worked out for member nations of a common market. Current proposals to modify the international monetary system, such as those made by Triffin and Bernstein (Triffin, 1960; Bernstein, 1960), place great emphasis on the size of foreign-exchange reserves and on the maintenance of convertibility of spot money and the very short-term near-monies. Triffin wants to 'internationalize' exchange reserves in order to remove the danger of 'hot money' movements from one currency to another. Bernstein proposes a kind of multilateral clearing agreement sponsored by the International Monetary Fund and designed to enable a single nation to receive help from others when its currency is under attack. Both of these proposals seek merely to alleviate stresses that arise when convertibility of spot money is threatened by loss of confidence in exchange-rate stability or by some change (presumably temporary) in economic conditions. Essentially, they seek to preserve the sharp separation of claims into 'domestic' and 'international' claims, and thus to permit a nation to determine for itself the structure of interest rates on its stock of 'domestic' claims. They recognize that in certain near-monies such a separation is no longer feasible and that short-term interest rates in the leading financial centers are linked together, but the assistance they render is to neutralize and expand exchange reserves. They do nothing to increase the number of 'points of contact' or to make the total stock of claims in a nation a potential source of foreign exchange.

Other proposals and practices attempt more directly and explicitly to separate 'domestic' and 'international' claims. The

2. This is not to say that interest-rate differences do not arise as a result of differences in risks, imperfections of the market, and the like.

proposal to widen the permitted range of fluctuation of a nation's exchange rate from the present 1 per cent to 5 or 10 per cent would, by increasing the risk of exchange-rate loss, widen the potential range of interest-rate differentials on short-term as well as long-term claims. If the pound sterling could vary from $2.66 to $2.94 (a 5 per cent range around the par of $2.80), then no reasonable differential in the United Kingdom–United States bill rates would pull funds to London without forward-exchange cover (if the spot pound were about par). For example, if *no* variation in the spot rate were allowed, and if the market had complete confidence in the rigidly fixed rate of $2.80 = £1, then any differential in bill rates would be erased by capital movements. If a 1 per cent exchange-rate variation were allowed, the interest-rate differential for three-month bills could be as much as 4 per cent. That is, even if the market had complete confidence in the limits ($2.828 and $2.772), the buyer of United Kingdom treasury bills could lose as much as 4 per cent (annual basis) as a result of an exchange rate change. If a 5 per cent variation in the exchange rate were allowed, the interest-rate differential would have to be 20 per cent. Of course, the forward-exchange market would normally set much smaller limits to the interest-rate differential,[3] but it is nevertheless true that exchange-rate flexibility encourages a separation of national financial markets. It preserves a distinction between domestic and international financial claims. Exchange controls on capital movements are also designed to separate 'domestic' from 'international' claims. Finally, administrative measures such as those taken by West Germany in 1960 – prohibition of interest payments on foreign-owned demand deposits, restrictions on foreign borrowing by banks and their customers – also seek to weaken the link between domestic and external interest rates. None of these administrative measures is very successful, however.

Our analysis of the Puerto Rican payments system suggests that, if nations desire to minimize payments pressures and related problems, they should seek to unify rather than separate the markets for 'domestic' and 'international' claims. They should take actions to extend convertibility into the longer-term financial

3. Furthermore, as the spot rate approached the limits of the widened range, smaller interest-rate differentials would again become effective.

instruments and to create a situation in which a claim of a certain maturity and risk sells at approximately the same yield (price) everywhere. Some types of claims will inevitably remain 'local' in character, just as they do in Puerto Rico, but the range of 'generalized' claims can certainly be greatly extended.

This suggestion means that the entire structure of interest rates in different nations would be linked together and become similar. It is often argued that this would require a supra-national body capable of determining world monetary policy and that it would mean a loss of monetary autonomy in each nation. Of course, it would mean that a nation could not fix its structure of interest rates as it chose. But a nation would still possess some control over its money supply and fiscal operations. The principal restraint would be that in financing a government deficit (or an increase in business expenditures) it would have to pay the 'going' rate of interest for the type of security offered.

Our argument is that present arrangements produce the worst results in two respects. First, efforts of nations to keep their interest rates below the going rates are a source of balance-of-payments problems for them. Such nations may try to maintain convertibility of spot monies and certain types of near-monies, but they deliberately introduce longer-term securities that are not 'convertible' in the sense that they sell for the same yield as similar securities elsewhere. Not only is the nominal yield of such securities lower than that for comparable securities elsewhere, but in addition the holder bears a risk of exchange-rate change. This risk widens the perceived yield spread between domestic and foreign securities. Holders of the lower-yielding domestic securities will tend to shift towards higher-yielding foreign securities, and this shift must be checked by some form of exchange control. Thus the monetary authorities are under pressure to try to separate domestic and foreign markets for medium and long-term securities in order to preserve the yield structure of the domestic market. However, the constant inducement to shift into foreign securities, the opportunities to shift from long- to short-term domestic securities, and the ingenuity of traders faced with statutory controls, all combine to hold a steady pressure on the spot exchange rate. There is at best an uneasy equilibrium in the market for foreign exchange.

Second, institutional barriers to capital movements and the risk of exchange-rate changes serve to rob some nations (notably the United Kingdom) of the benefits of an interest-rate structure that is higher than that of external money markets. Such countries would benefit from measures that would link their capital markets more closely to external capital markets – such measures as rigidly fixed exchange rates, elimination of exchange controls, and elimination of institutional barriers to the easy flow of claims. Under present circumstances, a nation may raise its structure of interest rates considerably above those of its major trading partners (as the United Kingdom has done) only to find that the separation of its domestic capital market from foreign capital markets operates to prevent an increase in foreign purchases of its securities over a wide range of maturities. Foreign purchases tend to be concentrated in short-term securities where exchange controls are not present and where the exchange-rate risk can be covered in the forward exchange market. The higher long-term interest rates thus have their principal effect on the balance-of-payments position through indirect, slower-acting influences on domestic economic activity, rather than directly through increased foreign capital inflow. Because foreign holdings of short-term claims tend to be liquidated if and when the interest rate differential (allowing for cost of forward-exchange cover) declines, foreign purchases of such claims do not supply a permanent corrective solution. Failure to forge what we have called 'points of contact' between the domestic and foreign capital markets thus exacts a penalty in instability and chronic payments pressures.

So far, nations continue to be ambivalent on this issue. There has been a vigorous movement toward convertibility of money and a recognition of intimate interconnections of short-term securities (what we have called convertibility of near-monies), but at the same time there has been a disposition to retain separate national interest-rate structures for longer-term securities and a tendency to resist a full integration of capital markets. However, the tendency of a system of fixed exchange rates and spot convertibility is toward greater 'international solidarity of capital markets' (Morgenstern, 1959). When this tendency is resisted, problems arise; if it were welcomed and encouraged, these problems would be abated.

It may be objected that the essential point of the foregoing discussion is simply that if there were complete confidence in the maintenance of convertibility at a fixed rate and no legal barriers to capital movements, such movements would become quite sensitive to interest-rate differentials. Since confidence cannot be legislated, the discussion is fruitless. Our argument is that, while the matter can be put in these terms, such a formulation does not lead to a solution. The habit of thinking of two largely separate groups of financial claims – foreign-exchange reserves and mobile short-term securities, and a large mass of 'domestic' claims – reduces the prospects that many interlocking points of contact will be forged between a nation's capital market and external capital markets. We saw that Puerto Rico has many such points of contact. As a result, the volume of gross capital flows is very large. Our estimates in Chapter II [not included here] indicated that such flows were three times the value of total imports of goods and services, and twice as large as gross insular product. Changes in the relative structure of interest rates that influence the motivations for these capital-account transactions could enable substantial shifts in the net flow to be accommodated. (We maintain that adoption of policies deliberately designed to lead toward a tighter integration of international capital markets would result in a lessening of pressures on traditional foreign-exchange reserves and in alleviation of balance-of-payments crises.)

This discussion applies particularly to nations whose economies are linked closely together in world markets. We have in mind especially economic relations among members of the European common market and between the United States and Canada. It is in this context that the above remarks are most relevant. In these areas great strides have been taken toward the integration of markets for goods and services and toward freedom of certain types of factor movements. For external residents, convertibility on current account and freedom of short-term capital transactions (in some cases) have been accepted. Yet the implications of these moves for the further integration of capital markets seem not to be understood. There is still a tendency to maintain separate national markets in which an individual nation can adopt its own monetary policy in the sense of fixing its own interest-rate structure.[4] Not even the failure of exchange restrictions to control short-term capital movements has had the effect on policy one would have expected.

One consequence of the reluctance of nations to move toward full integration of capital markets is a tendency to seek solutions for payments pressures in enlarged international reserves. Emphasis is usually placed upon the cover for short-term liabilities to external residents. To protect the spot exchange rate from shifts to funds from one national currency to another, various schemes have been put forward to enlarge the stock of international reserves and to make this stock available to the country whose currency is under attack. Given the drive toward other aspects of economic integration, however, these schemes do not meet the real issue. The clue lies in their almost exclusive emphasis upon *external* liabilities. If full convertibility of spot monies is allowed (as in the United States and as approximated in some European countries), holders of the entire stock of money in a country may conceivably seek to convert their holdings into another currency. Furthermore, holders of any assets, long- or short-term, may seek to sell the assets to obtain money that will then be eligible for conversion. Attempts to meet such a threat by enlarging international reserves would be futile. There is little prospect of creating a sufficient volume of official reserves to allow conversion of any significant fraction of domestic claims into foreign monies. The real solution must be to let asset prices fall in the country concerned until they become attractive to foreign buyers (and domestic holders), at which point any further sales for the purpose of obtaining money to use in buying foreign exchange would be matched by sales of foreign exchange as foreigners begin to buy the assets in question.

Of course it is true that external holders are more likely to

4. No doubt the interwar experience is responsible for the tenacity with which governments cling to autonomy in this respect. Keynes's oft-quoted speech to the House of Lords (23 May 1944) is characteristic: '. . . we intend to retain control of our domestic rate of interest, so that we can keep it as low as suits our own purposes, without interference from the ebb and flow of international capital movements or flights of hot money.' Reprinted in Harris (1947), p. 374.

shift funds from domestic into foreign currency than are domestic holders, but this is a matter of degree. Furthermore, behavior patterns can change in this respect. As investment institutions, corporate treasurers, and even individuals become more sophisticated and knowledgeable about international financial transactions, their responses to price and interest differentials will probably become more sensitive. There is evidence that they have already learned much about the market for short-term securities. Further steps toward economic integration, as are contemplated in the common market, are likely to lead to more knowledge about the securities of different nations and to closer contacts through the financial markets.

A considerable amount of financial integration has already occurred in Europe. We cannot discuss this matter in detail, but a few remarks may be pertinent. Direct investment has been *de facto* free since December 1957, when O.E.E.C. (Organization for European Economic Co-operation) countries agreed to allow all payments 'in connection with the making and the liquidation of direct investments' (O.E.E.C., 1961, p. 32). The right to refuse permission is retained, but it is rarely used. Portfolio investment has been liberalized but not yet freed. In addition to changes in governmental regulations, there have been private and institutional developments that contribute to integration of capital markets. For example, European stock exchanges are attempting to work out standard procedures for security transactions and to increase the flow of information about corporate operations.[5] They recognize that the traditional scarcity of published information about company accounts hinders the movement of securities. Stocks are being listed on two or more exchanges; bonds are being issued more frequently in external capital markets.

The Bank for International Settlements (1960, p. 14) has called attention to the increasing financial integration of Europe and its consequences. Speaking of the years 1957 to 1960, the bank's *Annual Report* stated: 'There seems to have been a tendency for

5. Representatives of eighteen stock exchanges in thirteen countries met in London in October 1961 to discuss ways to facilitate freer movements of securities throughout Western Europe. *The Economist* (14 October 1961), pp. 161–2.

long-term rates [of interest] gradually to move together – a tendency which, on account of the greater freedom of long-term capital movements between countries, can perhaps be expected to continue.'

If governments take steps to encourage or even allow the integration of capital markets, this tendency will continue. One consequence, we argue, is that payments pressures in the usual sense will be diminished. The role of conventional exchange reserves will be smaller, and more of the adjustment process will be accomplished through capital transactions in a wide range of securities.

We have also argued that this easy flow of capital will be facilitated by rigidly fixed exchange rates. The basis for this argument is primarily institutional, not theoretical. Banks, insurance companies, and other institutional investors are more likely to be willing to hold securities of several nations under a fixed rather than under a variable exchange rate system. And, what may be even more pertinent, they are more likely to be *permitted* such diversification by regulatory authorities in the case of fixed rates. It is true that the forward exchange market would conceivably provide almost the same assurance of reconversion into domestic currency, but there are formidable practical difficulties to the development of such a forward exchange market. For example, if a French insurance company buys a thirty-year German bond, it must make forward exchange contracts for sixty semi-annual interest payments in addition to a contract for the final redemption value of the bond. If its situation changes and it disposes of the bond before maturity, some of these contracts would have to be bought out or re-negotiated. At the very least, the necessity to cover with forward exchange contracts would reduce flexibility. Another problem concerns perpetual bonds and common stocks. How could the buyer hedge his foreign-exchange risk in these cases?

Our proposal requires that nations undertake to fix their exchange rates permanently at a given level. With the reminder that we are discussing a group of nations with a considerable degree of economic integration, such as the common market group, we shall comment briefly on the methods that might be used to fix exchange rates in this fashion. With respect to fiscal operations of governments, each nation must finance any excess of expenditures over ordinary revenues by issuing securities of suitable maturities and yields to make them salable in external capital markets. As a corollary, the prices of outstanding government securities must move to whatever levels are necessary to make them salable (marginally) in external markets. A government can still engage in deficit financing, but it must pay an interest rate high enough to compete with other issues in world capital markets. New issues of government securities might still be sold largely in the domestic market, just as in the United States the bonds of state governments are sometimes purchased by institutions and individuals within that state, although the yields must still be competitive. Similarly, in the private sector some securities would acquire the character of 'generalized claims', whether because of a governmental guarantee (as with F.H.A.-insured mortgages) or international reputation of a company (as with A.T. & T. [American Telephone and Telegraph] bonds, to take just one example), and these securities would sell for similar prices and yields in several national capital markets. Other types of claims, such as personal loans and localized debts, would continue to vary in yields from one country to another.

When the demand for foreign exchange increased, banks would be obliged to sell part of their assets in external financial markets or to discount securities with foreign banks in order to raise additional foreign exchange. Alternatively, they could simply sell securities in the domestic financial market. Such sales would marginally depress prices and raise yields of the whole range of 'generalized claims' and thereby induce an increase in the supply of foreign exchange. Once the prices of securities had been equalized in domestic and external markets, very small changes in price would be sufficient to induce the necessary response.

The changes in institutions and governmental policies that would be necessary to make this system work would take some time to become effective. The transitional process would be easiest if several countries moved to adopt it at the same time, and most difficult if a single country adopted it. We shall not discuss the political aspects of the system, but these are obviously of great significance. (The reader can imagine the Congressional response had the United States Treasury begun in 1958–60 to sell refunding issues in Europe at yields necessary to attract buyers, perhaps even denominating the issues in foreign currencies.)

In order to encourage the development of numerous contacts between domestic and foreign financial markets, it would be desirable to encourage commercial banks to arrange their own facilities for settling checks drawn upon them and deposited in foreign banks. Commercial banks could arrange matching correspondent balances, set up lines of credit, work out procedures for discounting claims, and include internationally marketable claims among their assets. It goes without saying that banks should not be hampered by exchange controls on such transactions – nor, for that matter, should other traders. Other financial institutions should be encouraged to hold a wider variety of securities of different nations. In capital-short regions, where interest rates on local claims were relatively high, a mechanism would probably develop whereby these claims would be marketed in regions with more abundant capital, much as has been done for residential mortgages by mortgage companies in the United States.

Such an extension of convertibility into a wide variety of securities would reduce the concentration of pressure on the central bank and on the exchange reserves (narrowly defined) of a nation. A large part of the entire stock of claims within a national economy would become a potential source of foreign exchange. It is this broadening of the range of convertibility that could free a nation from the preoccupation with official exchange reserves that has dominated recent discussions of the international monetary system. Our argument is that this present emphasis on official short-term claims on (and liabilities to) foreigners, with its tendency to lead to a search for ways to preserve the separation of domestic and external financial markets, conflicts with the trend toward economic integration and hampers movement toward a fundamental solution to international payments problems.

These proposals for a more complete integration of financial markets raise questions about the role of central banks in such a system. Some writers have said that financial integration will require close coordination of national monetary authorities and perhaps even the creation of a supra-national monetary authority. We shall not attempt a detailed discussion of this matter, but a few remarks need to be made. First, as already mentioned, a given central bank would be unable to fix the nation's interest-rate structure at a level that differed much from levels elsewhere. Although some may regard this as a drastic surrender of autonomy, it can be argued that in nations whose economies are closely integrated the central banks do not have this power anyway. As the United Kingdom has learned, domestic interest rates cannot be set by domestic economic considerations alone. Even the United States is finding that a low long-term interest rate will lead to foreign bond issues in New York and thus accentuate balance-of-payments difficulties. It is now generally recognized that short-term rates cannot be fixed in disregard of comparable rates elsewhere. Under the present system, nations suffer the disadvantages of interdependence of interest-rate structures but do not enjoy the benefits of sensitive, equilibrating capital movements.

Second, central banks would still have some important functions to perform. They could do much to facilitate equilibrating flows of capital, and they could assist commercial banks in setting up clearing mechanisms. Their own asset portfolios could be used to generate a supply of (or demand for) foreign exchange. Through open-market operations the central bank could induce a flow of funds in the desired direction. Some scope for determination of the national money supply would also remain. The central bank could bring about marginal changes in domestic interest rates – it could slightly increase such rates in order to attract external funds, thus increasing the domestic money supply. It could also establish a system to market local claims in external markets, and by varying the volume of such transactions, it could exert some influence on the availability of credit. Variations in required reserve ratios could also furnish some degree of control.

Third, a nation would still be able to influence domestic economic activity through fiscal policy. Provided that an excess of outlays over ordinary revenues was financed by debt instruments salable in world markets, deficit financing would be feasible. Through fiscal policy the money supply would also be affected. A nation could undertake anything it could finance in the world capital market, just as Puerto Rico can undertake anything it can finance in the New York capital market. These matters need not be determined for the entire group of nations by a central authority, but each nation would be subject to a monetary discipline.

Fourth, there still remains the question of the method through which the international interest rate structure would be determined. Ideally, an international monetary authority would determine the appropriate overall supply of money and level of interest rates. Such an authority does not now exist, however, and these matters are resolved in some way by the actions of separate national authorities. We may argue that the proposals made here do not change the present method of determination in any fundamental sense. They may create more pressures for the development of an international body, but assuming that it will not be established under the present system, the proposed system can operate under existing arrangements just as well as can the present system. In other words, the problem of regulating a world monetary policy does not arise as a result of the integration of financial markets. It was there all the time. We conclude that the proposals made here do not absolutely require the creation of a supra-national monetary authority to which national autonomy would be surrendered. The need for such an authority would be no more imperative than it is under the present system, but the need might be more clearly seen.

What we propose essentially involves the creation and acceptance of a one-price system for claims. Economic integration of national economies is usually understood to involve movement toward free trade in commodities, one result of which is a one-price system for commodities, after allowing for transport costs. So far, however, nations have tried to couple one-price commodity markets with a variable-price market for claims. This creates a great many strains, as might be expected. After all, transactions in claims are usually several times as large as transactions in commodities. In the Puerto Rican case, we estimated that gross capital movements were three times the value of gross imports. Claims of similar quality (maturity, interest rate, degree of risk) are almost perfect substitutes for each other.

They are available in standard units, they are easily identifiable, and costs of transfers are small. Consequently, the demand for claims held by any one country would be highly elastic. If international transactions in claims were free from all controls, the demand and supply of foreign exchange would also be highly elastic. Such high elasticities would make for easy adjustment to any change in circumstances.

We do not argue that financial integration in the above sense would solve all problems of balance-of-payments adjustment. Difficult and painful adjustments would still be necessary, especially in the long run. Short-run payments pressures should be greatly eased, however, and attention could be shifted from the problems of short-term liquidity and the volume of international reserves to the more basic problems of resource allocation and economic efficiency. Freedom of capital movements might help to solve these problems, but we do not claim it would be sufficient. Depressed areas remain a problem even in a single country.

References

BANK FOR INTERNATIONAL SETTLEMENTS (1960), *Thirtieth Annual Report*, Basle.

BERNSTEIN, E. M. (1960), *International Effects of U.S. Economic Policy*, Study Paper 16, Joint Economic Committee, 86th Cong., 2nd Sess., 25 January 1960.

FEDERAL RESERVE BANK OF NEW YORK (1960), *Monthly Review*, April.

HARRIS, S. E. (1947), *The New Economics*, Alfred A. Knopf, New York.

INGRAM, J. C. (1959), 'State and regional payments mechanisms', *Quarterly Journal of Economics*, vol. 73, pp. 619–32. (See also 'Reply' in ibid., vol. 74, pp. 648–52.)

MORGENSTERN, O. R. (1959), *International Financial Transactions*, Princeton University Press.

ORGANIZATION FOR EUROPEAN ECONOMIC CO-OPERATION (1961), *Liberalization of Current Invisibles and Capital Movements*, Paris.

TRIFFIN, R. (1960), *Gold and the Dollar Crisis*, Yale University Press.

Part Two **Adjustment through Changes in Exchange Rates**

In contrast to Part One, all the readings in Part Two are concerned with the effect of changes in exchange rates. Such changes in theory offer a means of adjustment to payments imbalances in many ways preferable to the 'mechanisms of adjustment' considered in Part One.

The opening reading, by Gottfried Haberler, is a systematic account of the relationship between changes in exchange rates and changes in the demand for and supply of imports and exports. In the next reading Tsiang attempts to link the type of analysis expounded by Haberler to aggregative monetary developments at the time of a devaluation. The two following readings, by Arnold Harberger and Bela Balassa, respectively, are concerned with empirical aspects of the relationships between prices and exchange rates. Fellner advocates a system of limited flexibility in exchange rates. The final reading in Part Two, by R. I. McKinnon, raises and attempts briefly to answer the question: under what circumstances should exchange rates *not* fluctuate among countries?

5 G. Haberler

The Market for Foreign Exchange and the Stability of the Balance of Payments: a Theoretical Analysis

G. Haberler (1949), 'The market for foreign exchange and the stability of the balance of payments: a theoretical analysis', *Kyklos*, vol. 3, pp. 193–218.

I. The Problem Stated

The present article presents a more systematic and more comprehensive treatment than can be found in the literature of a subject which has received much attention in recent years. The problem is a twofold one. First, we shall discuss how to derive demand and supply curves of one currency in terms of another, for example, of dollars in terms of francs, from the underlying demand and supply curves for exports and imports. Secondly, stability conditions in the market for foreign exchange will be stated in terms of the elasticities of those underlying curves.

These are matters of great practical importance, which arise continuously in current policy discussions. For example, whenever it is urged that the currency of a country should be depreciated, the objection is raised that the elasticities of demand for exports and imports of the country in question are such that a depreciation could not be expected to lead to an improvement of the balance of payments. The extreme position taken by many recent writers that a depreciation would actually deteriorate the balance of payments of a country (i.e. would lead to, or accelerate, an outflow of gold), is equivalent to the assertion that the market for foreign exchange (of dollars in terms of francs) is in unstable equilibrium.

Here, however, no attempt at application will be made. We shall present the theoretical skeleton without putting much descriptive, empirical flesh around the bare bones. Two countries or, what is the same, one country against the rest of the world will be considered, and we shall abstract from possible dynamic complications, for example, from the possibility that a change in the exchange rate may lead to anticipatory and speculative purchases or to speculative capital movements.

II. Stable and Unstable Equilibria in the Market for Foreign Currency

Many writers have applied ordinary demand and supply analysis to the foreign exchange market (Machlup, 1949).

So long as the demand and the supply curve (of dollars in terms of francs) has its 'ordinary' shape, that is to say, so long as the demand curve is negatively inclined (slopes down from left to right) and the supply curve is positively inclined (slopes up from left to right), the equilibrium is stable. The following example will make that clear. Suppose we start from an equilibrium in which demand and supply for dollars is equal; now the demand curve shifts to the right so that at the old rate demand for dollars exceeds supply. There is a balance of payments deficit and the Central Bank will lose gold. If now the price of dollars is raised, that is, if the franc depreciates, the excess demand will be eliminated and equilibrium restored.

If, however, the supply curve is negatively inclined, the equilibrium may become unstable. This will be the case, if the supply curve is less steep than the demand curve. If we are near the point where demand and supply are equal, this can be also expressed by saying equilibrium is unstable, provided the elasticity of supply is greater than the elasticity of demand.

In Figure 1, the point R is one of unstable equilibrium. Suppose demand for dollars increases, the demand curve shifts from D to D'. Then we get an excess of demand over supply (a deficit) of the magnitude RR'. If the Central Bank, after losing some gold, decided to raise the price of dollars in order to stop the drain on its reserve, it would find that it has made things worse: At a higher price the deficit (the horizontal difference between the S- and D- or D'-curves) is greater, that is to say, gold will flow out at an accelerated rate: Equilibrium could, however, be restored by reducing the price of dollars to P'. An omniscient Central Bank would do just that although it would require a rather unorthodox policy, namely, an appreciation of the currency of the deficit country. But the free price mechanism could not achieve that result; it would drive the exchange rate in the wrong direction. (The reader can easily verify that the situation will be stable, if the *S*-curve is steeper than the *D*-curve. Suppose, for example, that in Figure 1 the *S*-curve is the demand schedule and the *D*-curve is the supply schedule. If the supply schedule shifts from *D* to *D′*, there will be an excess of supply (balance of payments surplus) of *RR′* at the rate *P*. The price of dollars will fall and equilibrium restored at *R″*.)

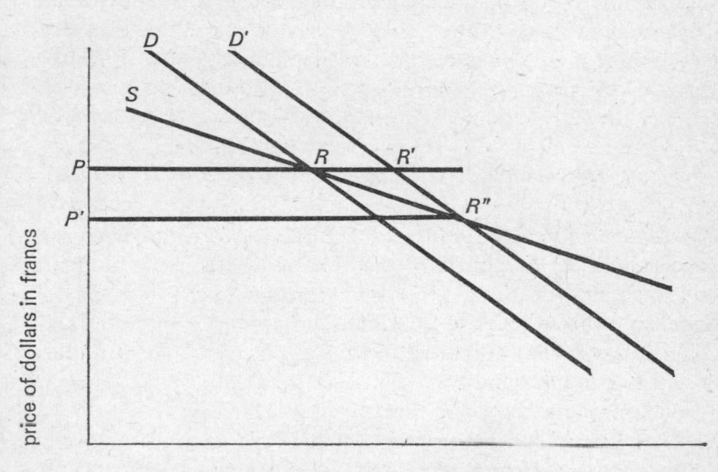

Figure 1

The question whether such a situation is at all likely to arise will be discussed later. But it may be mentioned that as a short-run possibility, unstable equilibria in the exchange market have been mentioned in earlier literature.[1]

It should also be observed that in order to establish the probability that the maintenance of equilibrium in the balance of payments by means of exchange rate variations may encounter

1. See, e.g. Graham (1929), p. 221. Dynamic instability due to speculation and destruction of confidence in the currency or through the setting up of inflationary or deflationary spirals is probably more important than the static type of instability in which we are interested here.

serious difficulties, it is not necessary to assume outright instability. It would be sufficient for that purpose to demonstrate that demand and supply curves are steep (inelastic). For in that case small displacements of the curves, that is to say, small deficits or surplusses would require large variations in the exchange rate. This would be decidedly inconvenient especially because it may imply large changes in the terms of trade.

It is, therefore, of great importance to have an idea of the approximate shape of the curves. Some insight will be gained, if we analyse how the shape of the demand and supply of dollars in terms of francs is determined by the shape of demand and supply curves of exports and imports.

III. Demand and Supply of Imports and Exports in Terms of Home and Foreign Currency

The shape of demand and supply curves of foreign currency is determined by the nature of the underlying transactions. Thus, the demand for foreign currency for the purpose of paying interest on fixed interest securities held abroad is of zero elasticity, if the debt is expressed in foreign currency and of unitary elasticity, if the liability is expressed in domestic currency although payable abroad in foreign currency.

Let us now concentrate on demand and supply for foreign currency arising from the export and imports of goods and services which is obviously related to, and derived from, the supply and demand at home and abroad of imports and exports. This derivation we shall now investigate (Robinson, 1937; Jöhr, 1947).

We are given two demand and supply diagrams, one for exports, the other for imports. There is evidently a separate diagram for each commodity exported and imported. But we assume that we have constructed a sort of average or aggregate curve; in other words, we have demand and supply curves of a 'representative bale' of imports and exports. Because our curves represent averages over a variety of goods and services, it is permissible to assume that the supply curves have their normal shape, that is, are positively sloped.[2]

2. A few exceptions would not be fatal so long as the average has its normal shape. For further justification of this assumption, see section VI, page 121.

We have to deal with two currencies, foreign and domestic, francs and dollars. So long as no change in the exchange rate is contemplated, we can use the same curves, whether the price of exports or imports is expressed in one or the other currency. But when we wish to study the influence of a change in the exchange rate, we had better draw two pairs of diagrams. Diagrams I and II in Figure 2 show demand and supply for exports and imports with prices expressed in terms of foreign currency (dollars); in diagrams III and IV prices are expressed in terms of domestic currency (francs).

The *D*- and *S*-curves picture the original situation before a change in the exchange rate has taken place. They are, therefore, identical in the upper and lower part of Figure 2.

Now let the domestic currency depreciate in terms of the foreign currency. Throughout the present article (up to section VIII), we assume that nothing else happens, specifically that in each country the supply curve of exports and the demand curve of imports, *in terms of the respective home currencies*, remain unchanged.

This is a serious restriction. It excludes not only speculative changes resulting from anticipated further changes of the exchange rate but also shifts of the curves induced by the inflow and outflow of funds which result from the change in the exchange rate. Such shifts are, of course, an integral part of the balance-of-payments mechanism. But whether and how they come into play, depends largely on the impact-effect of the depreciation which we study in the present paper. The justification of this assumption will be further discussed in section VIII, page 127.

Let us now ask the question how, under these assumptions, a depreciation of the home currency (franc) in terms of the foreign currency (dollar) will influence prices, quantities, and values of exports and imports. It is clear that the quantity of imports will fall and the quantity of exports will rise. But as far as prices and values are concerned, we must now carefully specify whether they are to be expressed in foreign or domestic currency, for what is true of one may not be true of the other. For example, export and import prices will rise in terms of the domestic currency but fall in terms of the foreign currency. Under certain conditions it is possible that the balance of trade will improve in terms of one currency and deteriorate in terms of the other currency upon a depreciation.[3]

We now analyse the various changes systematically in terms of the diagrams in Figure 2. Let us see first what happens in terms

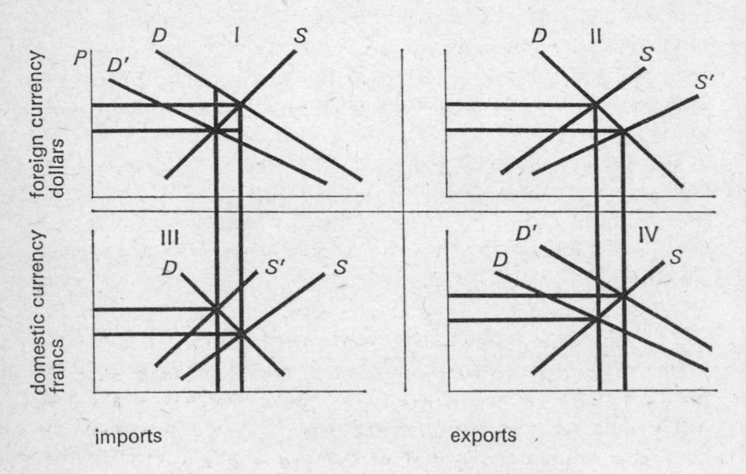

Figure 2 Demand and supply curves of exports and imports

of the foreign currency (diagrams I and II of Figure 2). The foreign supply curve of imports remains unchanged. But the domestic demand curve for imports expressed in foreign currency shifts down from *D* to *D′*. Each point of the *D*-curve is vertically reduced in the proportion of the depreciation of the currency. In francs the *D*-curve remains unchanged, but that

3. See section VII, page 125. It depends on the problem on hand whether one is interested in value of exports and imports in terms of the domestic or of the foreign currency. The usual balance-of-payments problem is the task of eliminating a deficit of gold or dollars. Hence what matters is the value of exports and imports in terms of the foreign money. On the other hand, if we are interested during a depression in the stimulating effect of a depreciation on the domestic economy, export and import values in home currency are relevant. For example, Mrs Robinson's discussion (1937), is conducted entirely in terms of home currency, because she is interested in the domestic employment situation.

means that in dollars the demand price for each quantity is less than it was before. On the export side the foreign demand curve remains unchanged, while the domestic supply curve shifts down – for the foreigner in dollars our supply prices are lowered in proportion of the depreciation of the franc.

It follows that the price of imports and exports in terms of foreign currency falls (except if the import supply curve or the export demand curve were perfectly elastic or if the import demand curve or export supply curve were entirely inelastic).[4]

The value of imports in foreign currency falls (except if the demand curve were entirely inelastic). The value exports, however, will rise, fall, or remain unchanged, depending upon the elasticity of foreign demand: If the elasticity is unity, it remains unchanged; if it is greater than unity, it will rise; if it is less than unity, it will fall.

In terms of domestic currency, the situation is different. The import demand curve remains unchanged but the supply curve shifts up, foreign goods becoming more expensive in home currency because of the appreciation of the foreign currency. The export supply curve in the exporting country's currency remains unchanged, while the foreign demand curve shifts up in terms of our currency.

It follows that import prices and export prices in domestic currency will rise (excepting again some extreme positions in which the price remains unchanged).

How the value of imports in terms of domestic currency will be affected depends upon the elasticity of demand; if this elasticity is unity, the value remains unchanged; if it is greater than one, the value of imports will fall, if it is smaller than one, the value will rise. The value of exports, on the other hand, will definitely go up (except if the foreign demand were entirely inelastic).

Let us summarize the results with respect to import and export values: In foreign currency the value of a country's imports will fall in consequence of a depreciation; but whether the value of exports rises or falls depends on the elasticity of the foreign

4. Remember that an inelastic (vertical) curve cannot shift downward or, expressed differently, that it shifts into itself.

demand for home exports. In terms of home currency, it is the other way round: The value of exports will rise, while the value of imports may rise or fall, depending upon the elasticity of home demand for imports.

IV. Demand and Supply of Foreign Currency as Derived from Demand and Supply of Exports and Imports

From the four diagrams in Figure 2 can be derived demand and supply curves of foreign currency in terms of the domestic currency or of domestic currency in terms of foreign currency. The two types of curves, (a) demand and supply curves of exports and imports in terms of domestic or of foreign currency and (b) the demand and supply curves of one currency in terms of the other, must not be confused.

Take, first, imports in terms of foreign currency which we call $ (diagram I in Figure 2). The shapes of the *D*- and *S*-curves evidently determine the shape of the demand curves for dollars in terms of home currency which we call francs. The following relations can be easily deduced from the figure: The amount of $ demanded is represented by the rectangle under the intersection of the supply and demand curves corresponding to a given rate of $ in francs. Hence, the elasticity of demand for $ will be greater, the more rapidly this area shrinks upon a given appreciation of $ as represented by a downward shift of the *D*-curve. It follows that given the *S*-curve, the elasticity of the demand for $ will be the greater, the greater the elasticity of the *D*-curve. Suppose, for example, that the elasticity of demand is infinite (the demand curve being horizontal), then the price of imports will fall by the full amount of the depreciation and the value of imports (demand for dollars) will be reduced considerably. If, on the other hand, the elasticity of demand is zero (vertical straight line), there will be no fall in the price and no reduction in the value of imports, i.e. the demand for dollars is completely inelastic.

On the other hand, given the *D*-curve, the influence of the elasticity of the *S*-curve on the elasticity of demand for $ is more complicated. It depends upon the elasticity of the *D*-curve. If the elasticity of the *D*-curve is unity, the elasticity of demand for $ is unity (i.e. the same amount of francs is spent on imports whatever the value of the $ in francs, irrespective of the elasticity of the S-curve). If the elasticity of the D-curve is greater than unity, the elasticity of demand for $ will be the greater, the greater the elasticity of the S-curve.[5] If the elasticity of the D-curve is less than unity, the elasticity of demand for $ will be the greater the smaller the elasticity of the S-curve.[6]

The second diagram in Figure 2 yields a supply curve of $. As the $ appreciates in francs, the S-curve shifts down and the rectangle under its intersection with the D-curve represents the supply of $. It follows at once that the $ value of exports will increase upon a depreciation of the franc, i.e. that the supply curve of $ will be positively inclined, if the elasticity of foreign demand for our exports is greater than unity. The $ value of exports will fall upon a depreciation of the franc, i.e. the supply curve of $ will be negatively inclined, if the elasticity of foreign demand for our exports is less than unity. The numerical value of the elasticity of supply of $ (whether negative or positive) will be the greater, the greater the elasticity of the S-curve (home supply of exports). If the D-curve has unit elasticity, the supply

5. The following consideration leads to that result: Suppose the S-curve were more elastic than the one drawn in the diagram. Then it would cut the D'-curve above and to the left of the point shown. If the elasticity of the D-curve is greater than unity, the area under the more elastic S-curve is smaller than the area under the less elastic S-curve.

6. Using the usual notation of η for demand elasticities and ϵ for supply elasticities and denoting by subscripts x and m that the elasticities relate to demand or supply of exports and imports, respectively, and by the subscripts $ and fr. that the elasticities relate to demand and supply of dollars and francs, respectively, the precise relationship is as follows:

$$\eta_{\$} = \eta_m \frac{\epsilon_m + 1}{\eta_m + \epsilon_m} = \frac{\epsilon_m + 1}{\dfrac{\epsilon_m}{\eta_m} + 1}$$

(In this formula η is taken as a positive number, as it is usually done.) From this formula the rules formulated in the text can be easily derived. It also follows that if $\epsilon_m = \infty$, $\eta_{\$} = \eta_m$. This is seen from the fact that $\frac{\epsilon_m + 1}{\epsilon_m + \eta_m}$ tends to unity as ϵ_m approaches infinity. (This formula is similar to that of Mrs Robinson (1937). She derives it, however, for domestic currency only and her notation is a little different: She writes ϵ for demand, and η for supply elasticities and she uses subscripts f and h denoting whether demand or supply is foreign or domestic. Thus our η_m corresponds to her ϵ_h, our ϵ_m to her η_f, and so on.)

curve of \$ has zero elasticity, i.e. is a vertical straight line whatever the elasticity of the *S*-curve.[7]

Similar rules can be derived for the demand and supply curves of the home currency from diagrams III and IV of Figure 2.[8]

V. Depreciation and the Balance of Payments

We proceed now to formulating the condition under which a change in the exchange rate will have its 'normal' effect on the balance of payments, i.e. will improve the balance of payments of the depreciating country and weaken the balance of the appreciating country.

This condition is usually expressed in terms of elasticities of demand for imports and of demand for exports. It is now often referred to as the 'Lerner condition', although it has been mentioned by Marshall and formulated with even greater precision later by Mrs Robinson (Lerner, 1944, p. 348; Marshall, 1923, p.

7. In the notation of the preceding footnote the relationship is as follows:

$$\epsilon_{\$} = \epsilon_x \frac{\eta_x - 1}{\eta_x + \epsilon_x} = \frac{\eta_x - 1}{\dfrac{\eta_x}{\epsilon_x} + 1}$$

from which the rules in the text easily follow.

8. The formulae are as follows:

$$\epsilon_{\text{fr.}} = \epsilon_m \frac{1 - \eta_m}{\eta_m + \epsilon_m}$$

$$\eta_{\text{fr.}} = \eta_x \frac{\epsilon_x + 1}{\epsilon_x + \eta_x}$$

From the second formula it follows that if $\epsilon_x = \infty$, $\eta_{\text{fr.}} = \eta_x$ (because the fraction becomes unity when ϵ_x approaches infinity). Since demand for francs constitutes supply of dollars and supply of francs constitutes demand for dollars, the corresponding elasticities are related. Concretely, as shown in the following section,

$$\eta_{\text{fr.}} + \epsilon_{\$} = 1 \quad \text{and} \quad \epsilon_{\text{fr.}} + \eta_{\$} = 1$$

This can be easily verified by inserting for $\eta_{\$}$, etc., the expression stated above. It should be emphasized that these are relationships by definition. The demand curve for francs in terms of dollars presents the same material as the supply curve of dollars in terms of francs, only differently arranged. On the other hand, demand for francs and supply of francs or, differently expressed, demand for dollars and demand for francs are independent of one another, although there may exist indirect causal relations between them in the sense that a change of one may influence the other.

354; Robinson, 1937; Brown, 1942, pp. 57–75; Polak, 1947, p. 178).

The Lerner condition is that: 'the sum of the elasticity of (home) demand for imports *plus* the elasticity of (foreign) demand for exports' should be greater than unity. If that sum is equal to unity, a change in the exchange rate will leave the balance of payments unchanged. If that sum is smaller than unity, a depreciation will make the balance unfavorable and an appreciation will make it more favorable. The reasoning is as follows:

> the elasticity of (foreign) demand for exports is less than unity, say one third, the quantity bought (exported) will increase only one-third as much as the price falls and the value of exports will fall. Suppose the price of exports falls (upon a depreciation) 3 per cent. This will result in an increase in exports of 1 per cent (one-third of the fall in price) so that the value of exports will fall about 2 per cent. Now suppose the elasticity of (home) demand for imports to be two-thirds (so that the sum of the two elasticities is equal to one), thus the increase of about 3 per cent of the price of imports will result in a decrease in the amount bought [imported], and in their value, of 2 per cent (two-thirds of the change in price because the elasticity of demand for imports is two thirds). The values of imports and exports move together and the import balance is the same (Lerner, 1944, p. 378).

The last sentence should really read: 'The values of imports and exports change in the same proportion and if exports and imports were equal to begin with, the balance would not change, that is to say, would remain zero.' If exports and imports are not equal to begin with, an equal proportional change in exports and imports would change the absolute size of the balance (Robinson, 1937). It follows that Lerner's condition has to be modified, if exports and imports are not equal. But let us defer discussion of that aspect of the problem until later (section VII, page 125).

Professor Lerner also assumes that exports and imports are supplied at constant cost, i.e. that the supply curves of imports and exports are infinitely elastic. If supply elasticities are different, a much more complicated condition obtains, because in that case a depreciation of 3 per cent would not result in a proportional change of import and export prices.

Before we go into those complications, let us consider another interpretation of the Lerner condition, which has been suggested by Dr A. Hirschman (1949). Instead of referring to the sum of the elasticity of demand for exports and imports (the *D*-curves in Figure 2), reference may be made to the sum of elasticity of (home) demand for the foreign currency and of (foreign) demand for the home currency. The two types of demand curves, viz. for imports and exports on the one hand and for one currency in terms of the other currency, on the other hand, must be carefully distinguished. As we have seen above, only if supply elasticities are infinite (under constant cost) is the elasticity of demand for imports equal to the elasticity of (home) demand for foreign currency, and the elasticity of (foreign) demand for our exports equal to the elasticity of (foreign) demand for our currency.

If we interpret the Lerner condition in this way (as the sum of the elasticity of demand for francs and the elasticity of demand for $), it is not necessary to assume that the elasticity of supply of exports and imports is infinite. The supply elasticities enter into the determination of the elasticities of demand for currency and need not be further considered.[9] Lerner's condition can now be written $\eta_{fr.} + \eta_{\$} > 1$. Now let us reflect that demand for francs in terms of $ implies an offer or supply of $ for francs. Similarly, demand for $ implies an offer or supply of francs. In other words, from the demand curve for francs can be derived the supply curve of $, and from the demand curve for $, the supply curve of francs.[10]

In order to convert a demand curve for francs into a supply curve of $ we have, evidently, to plot for each point on the demand curve, the rectangle under the demand curve (that is, price times quantity which constitutes amount of $ offered at that price) against the price of $ in francs. The price of $ in francs is the reciprocal of the price of francs in $, which is shown on the ordinate of the demand curve for francs.

Figure 3 will make this relationship clear. Point *A* on the demand curve corresponds to Point *A* on the supply curve, the

9. For that reason, the 'condition' in terms of demand for currencies is less informative and more truistic than in terms of demand for import and export goods.

10. Machlup (1949, p. 367) says that every undergraduate ought to know how that is to be done. But experience shows that he is too optimistic in making that assumption.

ordinate (price) of *A* on the supply curve being the reciprocal of the price at *A* on the demand curve. Point *B*, where the elasticity of demand is unity, corresponds to Point *B* on the supply curve, where the supply elasticity is zero. Point *C* on the demand curve,

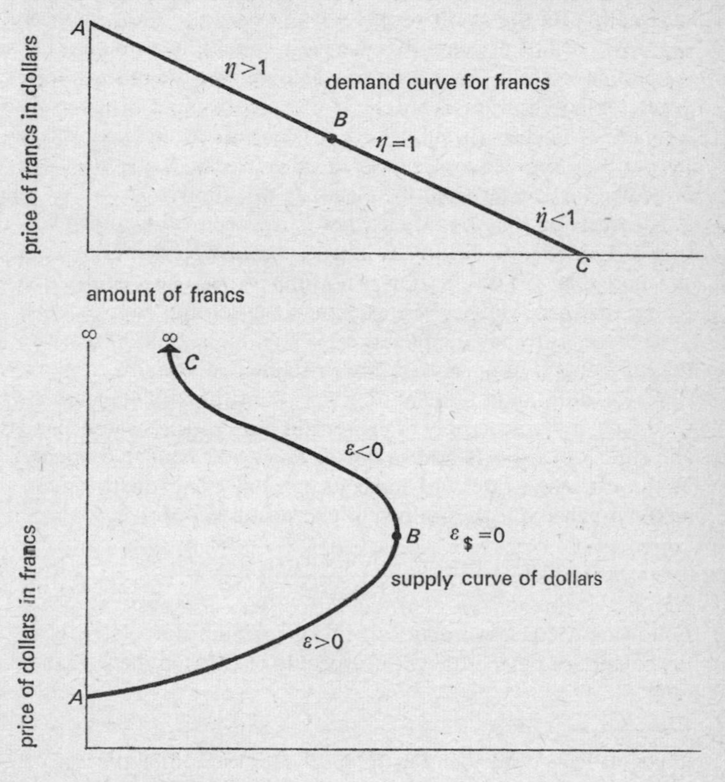

Figure 3

where the price of francs in \$ approaches zero, corresponds to Point *C* on the supply curve, where the price of \$ in francs rises to infinity. The figure shows that when $\eta = 1$, $\epsilon = 0$, when $\eta > 1$, ϵ is negative and when $\eta < 1$, ϵ is positive.[11]

11. Since we follow the usual procedure of taking η as positive (although the slope of the demand curve is conventionally called negative), we have

There is, thus, a simple relation between the elasticity of demand and the elasticity of the corresponding supply (Pigou, 1931, p. 88; Viner, 1937, pp. 539–40). It is $\eta + \epsilon = 1$. We can, therefore, rewrite the Lerner condition $\eta_{fr.} + \eta_{\$} > 1$, and by substituting for the $\eta_{\$}$ the term $1 - \epsilon_{fr.}$ we get $\eta_{fr.} - \epsilon_{fr.} > 0$, or $\eta_{fr.} > \epsilon_{fr.}$. It thus appears that Lerner's condition is nothing but the familiar stability condition to which we referred in section II, page 108: equilibrium is stable, if the supply curve is positively inclined; or in case the supply curve is negatively inclined, if it is steeper than the demand curve, in other words, if the elasticity of demand is greater than the elasticity of supply.

The question may be asked what is the use of this reformulation of Lerner's condition? It is true, the new formula does not say more than the old. Still, it is useful inasmuch as it helps us to realize that instability in the exchange market implying perverse influence of currency depreciation, is possible even if all markets for exports and imports each are in stable equilibrium.

We get additional information if we substitute for the elasticities of demand and supply of currencies the elasticities of demand and supply of exports and imports. The result is this: A change in the exchange rate will have its normal effect on the international balance if the following expression is positive:[12]

$$\frac{\eta_m\eta_x(1 + \epsilon_m + \epsilon_x) + \epsilon_m\epsilon_x(\eta_m + \eta_x - 1)}{(\eta_x + \epsilon_x)(\eta_m + \epsilon_m)}$$

Following Metzler we may call this expression the 'elasticity of the balance of payments' with respect to changes in the exchange rate.

---

to use the same convention for the supply elasticity. It follows that ϵ is positive when the supply curve is negatively inclined and negative when it is positively inclined.

12. The formula was written in this form by Metzler (1948), p. 226, but was first derived in slightly different form by Mrs Robinson (1937). Stable equilibrium requires:

$$\eta_{fr.} > \epsilon_{fr.} \text{ that is: } \eta_x\frac{\epsilon_x + 1}{\epsilon_x + \eta_x} > \epsilon_m\frac{\eta_m - 1}{\eta_m + \epsilon_m} \quad \text{or} \quad \eta_x\frac{\epsilon_x + 1}{\epsilon_x + \eta_x} - \epsilon_m\frac{\eta_m - 1}{\eta_m + \epsilon_m} > 0$$

After multiplication and rearrangement this expression reduces to the one in the text. The same result is obtained by using the condition $\eta_{\$} > \epsilon_{\$}$.

It should be observed that η_x, η_m, ϵ_x and ϵ_m are all taken positive.

From the formula it follows that if the sum of the demand elasticities for exports and imports is greater than unity ($\eta_m + \eta_x > 1$) the situation is stable. But even if $\eta_m + \eta_x$ were smaller than unity, the situation would be still stable, if the supply elasticities are sufficiently small. As Metzler points out, if one of the two supply elasticities is zero, the above expression is positive which implies that the situation is stable.[13]

VI. Export Supply and Import Demand versus Total Supply and Total Demand

From a practical point of view, it is not sufficient that the exchange market should be stable, that what Metzler aptly calls 'the elasticity of the balance of payments' should be positive, but also that the elasticity should be fairly large. For if it were positive but small, large changes in the exchange rate would be required to correct small deficits, which would be decidedly inconvenient, especially because such changes may imply changes in the real terms of trade.

How large the elasticity of the balance of payments of, say, some of the large trading nations actually is, is, of course, an empirical question of great complexity. Theorists of international trade have almost always assumed that it is large. Marshall was very emphatic on that point.

> All such suggestions [that there might be unstable equilibria] derive their origin from the sport of imagination rather than observable facts. For they assume the total elasticity of demand of each country to be less than unity, and on the average to be less than one half, throughout a large part of its schedule. Nothing approaching to this has ever occurred in the real world: it is not inconceivable, but it is absolutely improbable.[14]

13. See Metzler (1948), p. 227. Thus the Lerner condition (if related to the demand for exports and imports rather than to the demand for currencies) is a sufficient but not a necessary condition. It also follows that the situation will be stable if either $\eta_{\text{fr.}}$ or $\eta_{\$}$ is greater than one. All these rules can be easily deduced from Figure 2.

14. Metzler (1948), pp. 353–4. This quotation is appropriate in this connection, although Marshall's famous 'reciprocal' demand-and-supply curves are in real terms and must not be confused with our curves which are in terms of money.

Statistical studies, on the other hand, which have been undertaken in recent years seem to indicate that the elasticity is often not very large.

We cannot at this point enter into a thorough discussion of these empirical investigations. Only a few general considerations will be discussed which establish a strong presumption that Marshall was right and which at the same time show why the statistical findings referred to above, are probably unreliable or even outright spurious.

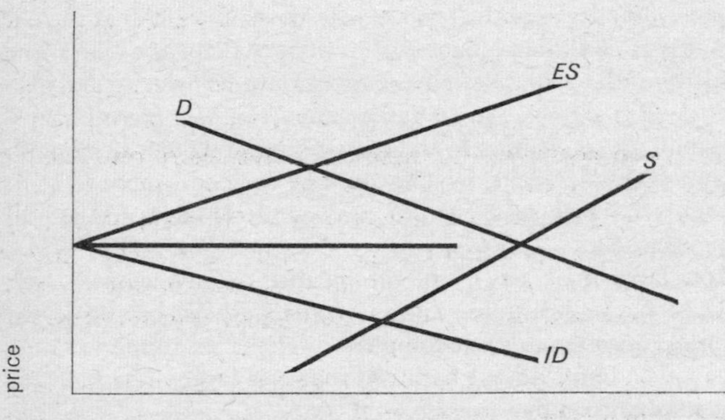

Figure 4 Ordinary demand and supply curves, *D* and *S*, for a single commodity in a particular country

The first very important point is the following. It must be kept in mind that the import demand curves and export supply curves in Figure 2 are not what may be called 'pure' or 'primitive' demand and supply curves. In all cases where an export commodity is also consumed in the exporting country and an import commodity also produced in the importing country, the export supply as well as the import demand curve is derived from pure or primitive domestic demand and supply curves.

In Figure 4, in order to derive the import demand and export supply curves, we simply have to plot against each price the difference between home demand and home supply. The abscissa of each point on the import demand curve, *ID*, is the excess of home demand over home supply. Import demand thus depends not only on domestic demand but also on domestic supply. Similarly, the abscissa of each point on the export supply curve, *ES*, is the excess of home supply over home demand.

It is clear from the diagram that whenever there is domestic production competing with imports, and domestic consumption competing with exports, the elasticity of import demand and export supply is much greater than the elasticity of 'pure' home demand and supply.[15] The reason is that a lower price of imports stimulates imports not only by increasing consumption but also by checking domestic production. And a higher export price stimulates exports not only by expanding production, but also by reducing home consumption.

The fact that even on the import demand side supply changes are involved, makes the time factor so very important. Supply is likely to be comparatively inelastic in the short run, and to become much more elastic in the longer run.[16] Hence import demand and export supply curves are the more elastic the longer the reaction time which is allowed. This time factor makes statistical measurement of demand reactions very difficult and may be largely responsible for the discrepancy between statistical results and theoretical expectations.

Another closely related fact is that the list of actual import and export commodities cannot be treated as given once for all. At least in the somewhat longer run it is not a datum but a variable. The dividing line between import, export, and domestic goods varies not only because of economically unexplained ('autonomous') changes in the basic data such as technology of production and transportation, consumers' tastes, etc., but also in

15. Only in the exceptional case that the home supply curve has a positive slope, is it possible (although by no means necessary) that the import demand curve is more elastic than home demand. But it should be observed that even if the elasticity of home supply is zero (the supply curve being a vertical straight line) the elasticity of import demand would be greater than the elasticity of home ('pure') demand. This can be seen from the fact that in this case the import demand curve is parallel to the home demand curve, but is situated to the left of it; it has the same slope but a greater elasticity than the home demand curve. See Yntema (1932, pp. 43–5), for a precise statement of the relation of the various elasticities.

16. Consumer demand may be also slow in reacting to price changes. But on the supply side such lags are certainly much more important, because technological changes are involved which necessarily take time.

response to price changes as an integral part of the adjustment mechanism. If foreign prices rise because of an appreciation of the currency, commodities which have not been exported so far, will enter the export list and commodities which were imported will drop out of the import list. The existence of non-traded, domestic goods which are, however, potential export and import commodities is due to the existence of transportation cost including import and export duties. Especially if all goods were traded, in a world of zero transportation cost, the shift of commodities from the export to the import side and *vice versa* would be an important factor which increases the elasticity of the balance of payments.[17] This is again a type of adjustment which takes time and is likely to cause great trouble to the statistician who wishes to measure the elasticity of international demand.

From what has been said, it follows that the danger of international demand being not sufficiently elastic is greatest in the case of highly specialized countries which have a near-monopoly in their principle export goods and are unable to substitute easily and to a large extent home-produced goods for imports. Agricultural countries, especially in the tropical zone, are most likely to be in that category. Brazil is probably as good an example as any. Coffee constitutes a large percentage of its own exports and of world exports. Consumer demand for coffee is probably fairly inelastic and there is no domestic production in the consuming countries to increase the elasticity of foreign demand for Brazilian coffee. The industrial countries in their mutual dealings are in a different position, because their economies are much more diversified, most of them having also a highly developed agriculture. A. Marshall, in a famous passage, emphasized this point.

It is practically certain that the demand for each of Ricardo's two countries for the goods in general of the other would have considerable elasticity *under modern industrial conditions* even if *E* and *G* were single countries whose sole trade was with one another. And if we take *E* to

17. See Graham (1932). Strange to say, however, Graham uses this fact as an argument for the rejection of the Marshall–Edgeworth 'reciprocal demand' curves. But Marshall and Edgeworth were aware of this factor and did make allowance for changes in the composition of exports and imports in the construction of their curves. Marshall (1923, appendix H) makes that quite clear.

be a large and rich commercial country, while *G* stands for all foreign countries, this certainly becomes absolute.[18]

VII. Exports and Imports Unequal

We have seen earlier that in case exports and imports and hence demand and supply of foreign currency resulting from those exports and imports are not equal, the condition for the balance of payments to react 'normally' (rather than perversely) to changes in the exchange rate must be modified. By normal reaction we mean (as before) that an appreciation of the foreign currency should improve the balance and a depreciation weaken it.

We must now carefully distinguish between the balance in terms of domestic and in terms of foreign currency. For it is clearly possible that depreciation of a currency may improve the country's balance in terms of the foreign money but make it worse in terms of the domestic currency. Suppose a country has an import surplus; in terms of foreign money, this surplus decreases by, say, 4 per cent upon a depreciation of the currency of 10 per cent. In domestic currency the new surplus will be larger than before.[19]

The way in which our stability condition has to be modified

18. See Marshall (1923, p. 176).

The demand and supply curves we have been using in this paper must, however, not be confused with the Marshallian so-called 'reciprocal demand and supply curves'. The difference is this: Our curves relate the quantities of imports and exports to prices *in terms of money* while Marshall's curves relate quantities ('representative bales') of exports to quantities of imports. Marshall's curves are, therefore, in the nature of total revenue curves, while ours are average revenue curves. More important is, however, the following difference: Marshall's curves are drawn under strict equilibrium assumptions. They picture the final outcome of the whole process of adjustment. The curves used in the present paper, in contrast, stay at the beginning of the equilibrium process. Since each point on a Marshallian curve pictures a potential equilibrium position of equality of exports and imports, the Marshallian apparatus is entirely unsuited for the purpose of investigating changing positions of disequilibrium.

19. This cannot happen in case of an export surplus. For if the export surplus increases in terms of the foreign currency upon a depreciation, it must increase even more in domestic money. What may happen in that case is that the balance deteriorates in terms of the foreign money and improves in terms of domestic money.

will be easily understood, if we formulate it in terms of the slopes of demand and supply curve. We have seen that the supply curve must be steeper than the demand curve. From Figure 5, it appears that this formulation can be applied, without change, to the case where exports and imports are unequal.

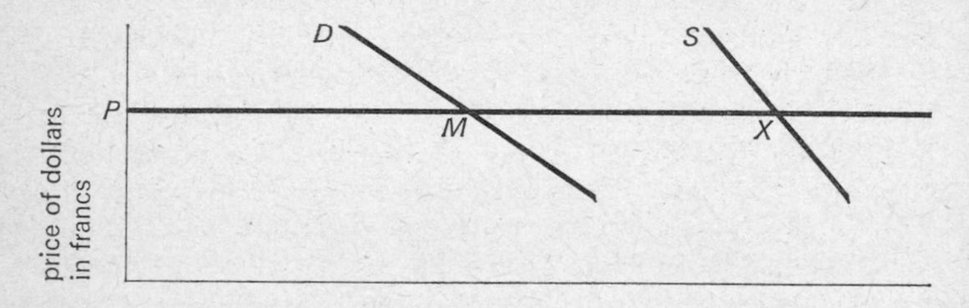

Figure 5

At the price P exports (supply of \$) is PX and exceeds imports (demand for \$) which is PM. The supply curve is steeper, therefore the export surplus increases, if the price of \$ increases – the criterion of a 'normal' reaction.

In terms of elasticities, however, the formula must be modified. For if demand and supply are not equal, the condition that the slope of the D-curve be greater than the slope of the S-curve, is no longer equivalent to the condition that $\eta_{\$} > \epsilon_{\$}$. But slopes can be easily expressed in terms of elasticities. Let D' be the slope of the demand curve and S' the slope of the supply curve. Then $D' = \eta_{\$} \cdot \frac{M}{P}$ and $S' = \epsilon_{\$} \cdot \frac{X}{P}$.[20] Our condition $D' > S'$ becomes $\eta_{\$} M > \epsilon_{\$} X$. Or if we translate the supply of \$ into a demand for francs, we have $\eta_{\$}\frac{M}{X} + \eta_{\text{fr.}} > 1$. If $X = M$, this expression reduces to Lerner's original formula.

Similarly, it can be shown that the condition for a depreciation to improve the balance in terms of the domestic currency is $\eta_{\$} + \eta_{\text{fr.}}\frac{X}{M} > 1$. Instead of elaborating further on the mathe-

20. X = exports, M = imports, both in \$.

matics (Hirschman, 1949), let us discuss a few economic implications of these rules.

Consider the condition for the balance to improve in terms of the foreign currency. This condition is relevant for the typical balance-of-payments problem, the problem of the 'dollar shortage'. As Mr Hirschman points out (1949), it appears from the formula that the more serious the disease, i.e. the larger the unbalance as measured by an excess of imports over exports, the better the chances that a depreciation will improve the balance. This follows from the fact that the larger M compared with X, the greater the weight attached to $\eta_{\$}$.[21]

One more word should perhaps be said of how to interpret 'exports' and 'imports'. Clearly those terms must include services proper such as transportation, tourist expenditures, commissions, and the like. For these items are affected by changes in the exchange rate in much the same way as exports and imports of goods.[22] Their elasticity with respect to changes in the exchange rate may be different from the elasticity of commodity exports and imports. But these individual elasticities are simply elements of the aggregate contributing to the average elasticity like that of any other individual export or import. Interest payments and receipts have to be included and, as we pointed out earlier, their elasticity with respect to changes in the exchange rate is easy to evaluate.

VIII. Shifts in Domestic Demand and Supply

As emphasized earlier, it has been assumed in this paper that in each country import demand and export supply curves in terms of the country's own currency remain unchanged. It is unlikely that this assumption will be entirely correct. As a rule, a change in the exchange rate will cause shifts in the domestic demand and supply curves, and we may distinguish two types of shifts. First there may be specific connections between individual export and

21. The medal has, however, another side: The larger the import surplus, the more vulnerable is the country to changes in the terms of trade or even to an equal rise in price of exports and imports.

22. Some of these items, such as commissions, banking services, and interest on certain types of short-term credit the volume of which varies with the volume of goods shipped, are likely to be closely correlated with the value of exports and imports.

import goods and their prices. For example, exports frequently contain imported raw materials or imports contain exported raw materials. This factor we can, however, eliminate by assuming that the demand and supply curves with which we operate relate to the domestic component of exports. In other words, we define exports of each commodity as *net* exports, i.e. net of the import content of those exports.[23] Another possibility is that particular imports and exports are competitive or complementary in consumption. This possibility can, however, probably be ignored when dealing with imports and exports in general.

The second reason why domestic demand and supply curves may shift in consequence of a depreciation is much more important and is monetary in nature. A depreciation of the currency is likely to result in an increase in total expenditures, in MV, implying a shift to the right of demand and supply curves; in other words, it is likely to have an inflationary or expansionary effect.

This is an important and rather complex matter which can be only lightly touched upon in the present paper, although it would deserve careful consideration.

We leave out of account at this point possible inflationary effects of a depreciation through the creation of the expectation that it is the first step in an inflationary process. Apart from that, there are two avenues through which the inflationary force of a depreciation will make itself felt.

Firstly there is the more or less automatic operation of balance-of-payments mechanism, of the 'foreign trade multiplier'. If the depreciation improves the balance of payments on current account, this in itself implies an increased flow in national expenditure and national income and a shift to the right of domestic demand and supply curves. If all this happens in a state of general depression and unemployment, approximately constant cost will prevail, that is supply curves will be nearly horizontal and only demand curves will shift; in that case not

23. The statistician who tries to measure the probable effect of, say, a depreciation of the currency or exports and imports will have to pay close attention to this matter. The import content of exports has been estimated for various countries. On the whole, it is quite small, even for a country like Great Britain which imports a large part of its industrial raw materials.

only money national income but also real national income and employment will rise. If it happens in a state of fairly full employment, supply and demand curves will be shifted to the right, prices and money incomes will rise, but real income and employment will be not or only little affected. Suffice it to say at this point, whether this multiplier effect comes into operation or not depends on whether the current balance is improved by the depreciation, which in turn depends, in the manner stated above, on the elasticities of demand and supply of exports and imports.

Secondly, this automatic expansion effect can be easily reinforced by monetary and wage policy, although it could (and on many occasions ought to) be counteracted by conscious policy.

If international demand is highly elastic and the balance of payments improves, it may be tempting to pursue a more liberal credit policy. Currency depreciation is often a means of creating a margin for more liberal credit or spending policies.

Similarly, wage policies are an extremely important factor. Suppose imports consist largely of wage goods and wage earners press through their unions immediately for higher wages when the cost of living goes up. In this case, even under conditions of depression and unemployment, will depreciation be quickly followed by price inflation.[24] But especially in a state of full or overfull employment, when the margin created by depreciations is quickly utilized, any favorable effect of a depreciation on the balance of payments may be nullified by a shift to the right of the demand for foreign currency.[25] Suppose any rise in the

24. It may be useful to consider an extreme case: Suppose that not only workers but all classes of a society are able to increase their money income immediately so as to offset any reduction in their living standard due to higher import prices. That would be tantamount to a refusal of society as a whole to permit an improvement in the balance of payments. For any such improvement implies that fewer goods are available for domestic use.

25. The situation is essentially different (a) under full employment and (b) in a depression with much unemployment. In the latter case, an improvement in the balance of payments does not imply that fewer goods are available for domestic use. The reason is that an improvement in the balance of payments will stimulate employment (multiplier effect). Hence more goods are available for exports *and* domestic use. Under full employment an improvement in the foreign balance implies a decrease of domestic supplies. Even if a depreciation does not improve the balance, it will

price of foreign currency is followed and compensated, or over-compensated, by additional inflation the impression can be easily created, that the exchange market is in neutral or even unstable equilibrium, that the sums of the two elasticities is unity or less than unity. This shows that in practice it is not easy to distinguish between movement along the curves and shifts of the curves.

To repeat what was said earlier, shifts of the monetary demand and supply curves of exports and imports resulting from income effects (multiplier effects) or from other types of repercussion are an integral part of the balance of payments mechanism. In this reading we must adhere to the assumption that aggregate domestic demand remains unchanged.[26] It should be also observed that this is an appropriate assumption in connection with the following question of policy: Would a currency depreciation be an effective measure for improving the balance of payments? Nobody can deny that any improvement would be undone by a sufficient dose of inflation. But would there be an improvement provided inflation is avoided? This is not only a legitimate but the most relevant question in that connection.

---

reduce the supply of goods at home because physical exports will increase and physical imports decrease.

It would be tempting to say that (under full employment) real national income is reduced by a depreciation irrespective of whether it improves the foreign balance or not. But I hesitate to use that expression, for the reason that 'real national income' is not co-extensive with 'volume of goods available for domestic use'. Suppose, for example, that imports of a country rise (or exports fall) and the deficit in the balance is financed by ioreign loans or sales of foreign assets. In that case (net) real income is not fncreased, although more goods are available for domestic use (consumption or investment). This is largely but not entirely a terminological matter. For the empirical question arises whether income effects on exports and imports attach to the one or the other magnitude.

26. It would not be appropriate to define our monetary curves so as to make allowances for some of these reactions. Professor Samuelson distinguishes 'between (1) the elasticity of real exports and imports with respect to a real change in the terms of trade and (2) the elasticity of the trade balance with respect to exchange variations' (Samuelson, 1948, p. 404). This is an important distinction, but it is insufficient, because it is not specified what kind of reactions are allowed for under (2). 'Elasticity of the trade balance', as Samuelson uses the term, is not an unambiguous concept unless specific assumptions with respect to monetary conditions and policies are made.

Another limitation which the foregoing analysis shares with all that has been written on the subject must be mentioned: Competitive conditions have been assumed throughout. In the currency market that is not a serious restriction. This statement may sound paradoxical in view of the fact that there is tight exchange control in the majority of countries. In reality there is, however, nothing paradoxical about the statement for the reason that our theory is concerned with what would happen if there was no public control of the exchange market. There can be no doubt that exchange markets would be highly competitive, even if the markets of individual export or import commodities are not.[27]

It, however, often happens that the market of individual export or import goods in a country is not strictly competitive. As a consequence, the construction of a demand curve for imports in general and of a supply curve of exports in general becomes a more complicated matter. This problem, which to my knowledge has never been treated in the literature, cannot be discussed at this point. But I venture the guess that no far-reaching modification of the theory would be required.

Summary

In this paper we were studying how the supply and demand for exports and imports determine supply and demand in the foreign exchange market. In particular, we wanted to discover the conditions under which a change in the exchange rate would have its 'normal' effect on the balance of payments. In other words, we were interested in the conditions of stability in the exchange market or, in still more technical language, in the condition under which the balance of payments has its 'normal' (i.e. positive) elasticity with respect to changes in the exchange rate.

By normal reaction we mean that a depreciation of a country's currency should improve the balance of payments and an appreciation should affect it adversely. If the opposite happens, we speak of abnormal or perverse behavior or of negative elasticity of the balance.

Starting with the market for foreign currency the condition for

27. Occasional exceptions may arise in cases where a large percentage of exports (or more rarely of imports) consists of a single commodity the supply of (or demand for) which is monopolistically controlled.

stability or normal behavior is that the supply curve of foreign currency is positively inclined, or if it is negatively inclined, that it be steeper than the demand curve. The condition can also be expressed in terms of elasticities, although it is really simpler in terms of slopes.

Since the supply curve of foreign currency can be translated into a demand curve of the home currency, the condition can be expressed in terms of elasticities of demand for foreign and for the home currency. Thus we get the well-known rule that the sum of these two demand elasticities must be greater than unity.

The demand and supply curves of foreign currency must be carefully distinguished from demand and supply curves of exports and imports.

Demand and supply curves of imports determine the demand curve for foreign currency. Demand and supply curves of exports determine the demand curve of home currency, or put differently, the supply of foreign currency. Hence the condition of normal reaction of the balance of payments with respect to changes in the exchange rate can be stated in terms of the elasticities of demand and supply of imports and exports.

This result must, however, be qualified in one important respect. It is true only, if the list of exports and imports remains unchanged. If that list changes, we have an additional factor. Concretely, if an appreciation of the foreign currency induces the exportation of goods that had not been exported so far, and eliminates goods from the import list, the demand curve for foreign currency will be turned counter-clockwise (its elasticity will increase numerically) and the supply curve will be turned clockwise (its elasticity will increase algebraically).[28] Thus the elasticity of the balance of payments with respect to rate changes will increase.

Demand and supply curves of exports and imports must not be mixed up with the underlying domestic demand and supply curves for the commodities involved. For example, the import demand curve, even for a consumer good is not a 'pure', consumer demand curve, but is the excess of home demand over home supply. It is clear that whenever an imported commodity is

28. That is to say, if it is negative, it will become smaller negative or positive; if it was positive, it will become greater positive.

also produced at home and an exported commodity also consumed at home, the import demand and import supply will be much more elastic than home demand and home supply, respectively.

Furthermore, it must be remembered that demand and supply of imports and exports are aggregated from demand and supply of individual import and export commodities.

We have, thus, a hierarchy of demand and supply curves, in three or four layers. First, there are what we call the 'pure' or 'primitive' demand and supply schedules for each commodity in each country. From these schedules export supply curves and import demand curves for each commodity are derived. Those curves are aggregated into composite demand and supply curves for exports and imports. From these aggregate curves, we derive then the demand and supply curve of foreign currency in terms of home currency (or the other way round). These various types of curves have to be carefully distinguished, if confusion is to be avoided. All these curves are in terms of money, domestic or foreign, and must not be confused with the Marshallian 'reciprocal demand and supply curves' which represent a relationship of exports and imports in real terms drawn up under rigid equilibrium assumptions.

The limitations of the theory here presented must be kept in mind. It is not intended to give a complete picture of the international balance-of-payments mechanism. It is only the first step toward such a theory. In a complete theory induced shifts of the monetary curves here assumed to be fixed (in home currency) would play an integral part.

References

Brown, A. C. (1942), 'Trade balance and exchange stability', *Oxford Economic Papers*, no. 6.

Graham, F. (1929), 'Self-limiting and self-inflammatory movements in exchange rates; Germany', *Quarterly Journal of Economics*, vol. 43.

Graham, F. (1932), 'The theory of international values', *Quarterly Journal of Economics*, vol. 46, pp. 581–616.

Hirschman, A. O. (1949), 'Devaluation and the trade balance – a note', *Review of Economics and Statistics*, vol. 31, pp. 50–53.

Jöhr, W. A. (1947), 'Soll der Schweizer Franken aufgewertet werden', *Überbeschäftigung und Frankenparität*, St Gallen.

Lerner, A. P. (1944), *The Economics of Control*, Macmillan, New York.

MACHLUP, F. (1949), 'The theory of foreign exchanges', in H. S. Ellis and L. A. Metzler, eds., *Readings in the Theory of International Trade*, Blakiston, Philadelphia.

MARSHALL, A. (1923), *Money, Credit and Commerce*, Macmillan, London.

METZLER, L. A. (1948), 'The theory of international trade', *A Survey of Contemporary Economics*, Irwin.

PIGOU, A. C. (1931), 'Demand and supply equations', in A. C. Pigou and D. H. Robertson, eds., *Economic Essays and Addresses*, London.

POLAK, J. J. (1947), 'Exchange depreciation and international monetary stability', *Review of Economics and Statistics*, vol. 29.

ROBINSON, JOAN (1937), 'The foreign exchanges', *Essays on the Theory of Employment*, New York, ch. 1. (Reprinted in H. S. Ellis and L. A. Metzler, eds., *Readings in the Theory of International Trade*, Blakiston, Philadelphia, 1949, pp. 83–103.)

SAMUELSON, P. A. (1948), 'Disparity in postwar exchange rates', in S. E. Harris, ed., *Foreign Economic Policy for the United States*, Cambridge, Mass.

VINER, J. (1937), *Studies in the Theory of International Trade*, New York.

YNTEMA, T. O. (1932), *A Mathematical Reformulation of the General Theory of International Trade*, Chicago.

6 S. C. Tsiang

The Role of Money in Trade-balance Stability; Synthesis of the Elasticity and Absorption Approaches

S. C. Tsiang (1961), 'The role of money in trade-balance stability: synthesis of the elasticity and absorption approaches', *American Economic Review*, vol. 51, pp. 912–36.

The spirited controversy between Alexander (1, 2) and Fritz Machlup (13, 14) on the relative merits of the relative prices (or elasticities) and aggregate spending (absorption) approaches to the problem of determining the effect of devaluation appears to have ended, for the time being, in a rather disappointing anti-climax. After having witnessed the mutual accusation of the rival approaches as consisting of implicit theorizing based upon purely definitional tautologies (13, pp. 268–71; 2, pp. 22–4), one feels somewhat let down by the compromise which Alexander now proposes (2, pp. 26–34): that the result obtained by the traditional elasticities approach may be treated as the 'initial' (or primary) effect of a devaluation to which a sort of 'multiplier' (normally less than unity), computed from the propensities to hoard, to import, etc., is to be applied to yield the final effect of the devaluation.

The extension of the elasticity approach by a superimposition of a multiplier analysis in this manner is essentially the same as what A. J. Brown had already done in 1942 (6, pp. 64–6; 3). Indeed, it was already indicated by J. Robinson (18, esp. p. 93) in her pioneering article on the foreign exchanges first published in 1937.

The superimposition of a multiplier upon the elasticities solution of the effect of a devaluation usually glosses over the following difficulty: Unless the supplies of exportable and domestic goods in both countries concerned are all infinitely elastic, so that prices in both countries (except prices of imports) will remain constant, the multiplier effect of the initial change in the trade balance will bring about further changes in relative prices, and hence further substitution between imports and domestically produced goods in both countries. Thus if the conventional elasticities solution is treated as a sort of multiplicand, to which a multiplier (or a damping coefficient) is to be applied to obtain the final effect, then the multiplier itself should again involve the relevant elasticities that are in the multiplicand. There can be no neat dichotomy of the final effect of a devaluation into a part that consists of the elasticities solution and another that consists of the multiplier (or absorption) solution. The total effect of a devaluation must be analysed in a comprehensive system in which changes in incomes, prices, and outputs are all taken into consideration. In fact, even before Alexander raised the outcry against the elasticities approach and proposed the substitution of the absorption approach, a number of attempts had already been made to analyse the effect of a devaluation with more or less comprehensive mathematical systems that allow for both income and price changes, notably those by Meade (15), Harberger (7), Laursen and Metzler (12), and Stuvel (22). If the controversy between the relative-prices and aggregate-spending approaches merely leads to a synthesis which had already been worked out before the controversy, what then has been gained by the debate?

If anything of enduring value has come out of Alexander's proposal of the absorption approach, it is the fact that the simple identity:

B	$\equiv$	Y	$-$	A
Trade Balance		National Income		Absorption or National Expenditure

which he pushed to the forefront in the analysis of the effect of a devaluation, has brought out in strong relief a fundamental fact, viz. that a negative trade balance necessarily implies national expenditure in excess of national income. This obvious truth was underscored by Machlup (13, pp. 272–3) who therefore emphasized the role played by credit creation in sustaining the excess expenditure in the case of a trade deficit (a negative B) and concluded that 'nothing can be said about the effects of a devaluation unless exact specifications are made regarding the supply of money and credit'. The highlighting of the monetary implications of a balance-of-payments deficit or surplus was also stressed by Johnson (10a, pp. 156–8) as the major contribution of the absorption approach. More recently, Michaely, in an attempt to reconcile the relative-prices and absorption approaches under the assumption of full employment, also naturally resorted to the 'real balance effect' of devaluation-induced price changes with the money supply kept constant (16). Thus as a by-product of Alexander's attack on the elasticities approach, the much neglected role played by the supply of money and credit in working out the effect of a devaluation and the stability of the trade balance is once more being recognized.[1]

The rediscovery of the significance of monetary factors, however, has not yet been reflected in the formulae and mathematical models for the analysis of the effect of a devaluation on the balance of trade. Not only did the conventional elasticities formulae of the effect of devaluation take no account of the monetary factors (since implicitly they generally assume a constant money income), but in the various attempts to combine the elasticities approach with a multiplier analysis (e.g. Brown, 6 and Allen, 3, and even in most of the more or less comprehensive models of Harberger, 7, Laursen and Metzler, 12, Stuvel, 22, and Jones, 11), the role of money and credit was also totally disregarded. In a quite recent attempt to marry the elasticity and the absorption approaches, Brems also did not include either the money supply or the rate of interest in his otherwise rather complicated mathematical model (5). Even Alexander himself tends to neglect the role of money; for in his discussion of the multiplier process engendered by the initial change in the trade balance, a process supposed to be determined by the propensities to hoard and to spend on imports and exportables, the monetary mechanism of income expansion was never brought in at all. It was only in his discussion of the cash balance effects at full employment that the money supply was briefly mentioned (2, p. 33).

In this respect, Meade's model for the analysis of the balance of payments stands out as a splendid exception; for he alone

1. Monetary factors were certainly not overlooked by classical economists, who regarded the contraction or expansion of the money supply under the gold standard as the automatic mechanism for the adjustment of the balance of payments. It is with the advent of the 'new economics' and the breakdown of the gold standard that monetary factors came to be disregarded in the discussion of the balance of trade and devaluation.

included the money supply and the rate of interest as variables in his model and always clearly stated the specific assumptions he made about monetary and fiscal policies. Unfortunately, however, Meade worked out the solution for the effect of a devaluation from his model only under the assumption of either a so-called 'Keynesian neutral economy' or that of a monetary policy that ensures 'internal balance'. Under the 'neutral economy' assumption, the monetary authorities are supposed to keep the supply of money infinitely elastic at a constant interest rate, so that the supply of money will passively adapt itself to whatever the demand for money might be at the constant interest rate (15, pp. 31, 49). This in effect obliterates all possible influences the supply of money and the interest rate might have on his solution for the effect of a devaluation. On the other hand, the assumption of a monetary policy that ensures 'internal balance' (i.e. a constant level of employment [15, pp. 33, 56–7]), coupled with the assumptions that money wage rates are exogenously given and that prices always equal marginal labor cost, in effect implies that money income is somehow effectively kept constant, provided money wage rates remain constant. This again eliminates all the positive influences the money supply and the interest rate might exert on the effect of a devaluation, as they are assumed to adjust themselves passively to the requirements of the policy objective of maintaining money income constant (15, pp. 68–72; Table 4, p. 150).

The purpose of this paper is to demonstrate the crucial role that could be played by monetary factors and thus to show in a more comprehensive way how relative prices and income–expenditure adjustments combine to determine the effect of a devaluation. To avoid further proliferation of models, each with the idiosyncrasies of its creator fully displayed in the choice of variables and notation system, I shall adopt Meade's simplified two-country, two-commodity model, which seems by far the most economically sound, and shall only make a slight modification to make good an omission (viz. that of the effect of changes in the terms of trade on aggregate expenditure) which has been much discussed since Harberger, Laursen, and Metzler pointed out its possible significance. I shall also trim his model of all non-essential policy variables, such as tariff rates and various shift variables, which he adopted to represent controlled or uncontrolled shifts in various functional relationships, so as to make the system intelligible to the reader without overtaxing his perseverance.

I. The Model

We shall adopt Meade's notation throughout so as to facilitate comparison between his results and ours. In Meade's notation, a subscript *a* refers to country *A* and a subscript *b* to country *B*. The subscript *ab* for a term indicates that it is the sum of a corresponding *A*-term and *B*-term (e.g. $\pi_{ab} = \pi_a + \pi_b$). Capital italic letters refer to total quantities; small italic letters to small increments (or differentials) of those qualities; and a bar over a term means a price corresponding to that term. The small Greek letters stand for functional relationships between the differentials (i.e. either partial derivatives or elasticities obtained from such partial derivatives). Thus:

Q_a = *A*'s product.
$\bar{Q}_a$ = the price of *A*'s product, which is put equal to 1 at the initial position by using the appropriate unit for Q_a.
H_a = volume of employment in country *A*.
$\bar{H}_a$ = the money wage rate in country *A*, which is put equal to 1 at the initial position by choosing the appropriate unit for H_a.
I_a = the physical volume of *A*'s imports, which constitute *B*'s exports.
D_a = domestic expenditures in *A* in terms of domestic currency.
R_a = the rate of interest in *A*.
M_a = the amount of money in *A*.

The corresponding terms for country *B* with the subscript *b* are similarly defined.

E = the rate of exchange expressed as the number of units of *A*'s currency per unit of *B*'s currency, which is again put equal to 1 at the initial position by choosing the appropriate unit for *B*'s currency.

$T =$ the balance of trade, i.e. the net excess of A's receipts from exports valued in A's currency.

It is assumed that [trade being balanced] at the initial position:

$$I_a\bar{Q}_bE = I_b\bar{Q}_a = I_a = I_b = I.$$

The differentials of these terms are represented by the corresponding small italic letters with the same subscripts, thus $dQ_a = q_a$, $d\bar{Q}_a = \bar{q}_a$, etc.

Meade's system as simplified for our purpose may be represented by the following system of equations in differentials. First, we have a pair of identities for the increments in domestic expenditures for the two countries:

$$d_a \equiv q_a - i_b + i_a + (Q_a - I)\bar{q}_a + I\bar{q}_b + Ie, \qquad 1$$

$$d_b \equiv q_b - i_a + i_b + (Q_b - I)\bar{q}_b + I\bar{q}_a - Ie, \qquad 2$$

which are obtained by differentiating the following definitional expenditure identities:

$$D_a \equiv \bar{Q}_a(Q_a - I_b) + \bar{Q}_bEI_a,$$

$$D_b \equiv \bar{Q}_b(Q_b - I_a) + \bar{Q}_a\frac{1}{E}I_b.$$

Next Meade gives us the two domestic expenditure functions in differentials:

$$d_a = (1 - \lambda_a)q_a - \rho_a r_a + D_a\bar{q}_a, \qquad 3$$

$$d_b = (1 - \lambda_b)q_b - \rho_b r_b + D_b\bar{q}_b. \qquad 4$$

where $(1 - \lambda_a)$ and $(1 - \lambda_b)$ are the partial derivatives of domestic expenditures with respect to domestic money incomes, and hence λ_a and λ_b are the marginal propensities to hoard, and ρ_a and ρ_b are the partial derivatives of domestic expenditures with respect to the interest rate in the two countries, respectively. The terms $D_a\bar{q}_a$ and $D_b\bar{q}_b$ are introduced to indicate that these expenditures functions are 'real functions' in the sense that domestic expenditure in real terms is a function of real income, so that a change in the general price level would bring about a proportionate change in money expenditures. Here for the sake of simplicity, Meade has taken the change in the price level of domestic products to represent the change in the general price level so that the effect of a change in the terms of trade on the price level and on the level of aggregate domestic expenditures is neglected.[2]

However, the effect upon domestic expenditure of a change in the terms of trade produced by a devaluation has been emphasized by both Harberger (7, pp. 50–55) and Laursen and Metzler (12, pp. 295–7) as having the effect of making the stability condition for the exchange rate more stringent. To assume away with Meade the effect of the terms of trade on domestic expenditure would, therefore, seem to gloss over a potentially significant factor. In fact, Meade has been strongly criticized by H. Johnson for this omission (10b, pp. 816–18 and 830–32). Actually, Meade could have allowed for the effect of a change in the terms of trade on domestic expenditure without making the aggregate expenditure functions too complicated to handle. For if we assume with Meade that the relationship between domestic expenditure and its determinants is a 'real' and not a 'money' relationship and that there is no money illusion (so that the money expenditure function is homogeneous of degree 1 in money income and all prices, including prices of imports), then

2. In effect, equations 3 and 4 are derived by differentiating aggregate expenditure functions of the type:

$$D_a = D_a\{Q_a\overline{Q}_a, \overline{Q}_a, R_a\} \quad \text{(i)}$$

which is supposed to be homogeneous of degree 1 in $Q_a\overline{Q}_a$ and $\overline{Q}_a$. By Euler's Theorem:

$$D_a = \frac{\partial D_a}{\partial(Q_a\overline{Q}_a)} \cdot Q_a\overline{Q}_a + \frac{\partial D_a}{\partial \overline{Q}_a}\overline{Q}_a$$

$$= (1 - \lambda_a)Q_a + \frac{\partial D_a}{\partial \overline{Q}_a} \quad \text{(ii)}$$

$$\therefore \quad \frac{\partial D_a}{\partial \overline{Q}_a} = D_a - (1 - \lambda_a)Q_a.$$

Substitute (ii) in the differentiation of (i), we get:

$$d_a = (1 - \lambda_a)q_a + D_a\bar{q}_a - \rho_a r_a.$$

Alternatively, equations 3 and 4 may be regarded as derived from expenditure functions of the form:

$$\frac{D_a}{\overline{Q}_a} = D_a{}^*\left\{\frac{Q_a\overline{Q}_a}{\overline{Q}_a}, R_a\right\} \quad \text{(iii)}$$

which, upon differentiation, yields directly the same result.

the two equations for changes in aggregate expenditures, taking into consideration the effect of the terms of trade, would be no more complicated than:

$$d_a = (1 - \lambda_a)q_a - \rho_a r_a + D_a\bar{q}_a - \lambda_a I(\bar{q}_a - \bar{q}_b - e) \qquad \textbf{3a}$$

and

$$d_b = (1 - \lambda_b)q_b - \rho_b r_b + D_b\bar{q}_b - \lambda_b I(\bar{q}_b - \bar{q}_a + e). \qquad \textbf{4a}$$

In view of the lively controversy over the possible effect of a change in the terms of trade upon aggregate domestic expenditure,[3] I shall try to derive equations 3a and 4a in the most unsophisticated and least controversial way. Let us suppose that in the absence of money illusion and dynamic price expectations, domestic expenditure in real terms is a function of domestic real income and the interest rate, i.e.:

$$\frac{D_a}{P_a} = D_a\left\{\frac{Q_a\bar{Q}_a}{P_a}, R_a\right\} \qquad \textbf{5}$$

where P_a is the general price level in country A, defined as:

$$P_a = \frac{D_a - I_a}{D_a} \cdot \bar{Q}_a + \frac{I_a}{D_a} \cdot \bar{Q}_b E, \qquad \textbf{6}$$

which is equal to 1 at the initial position, since $\bar{Q}_a = \bar{Q}_b = E = 1$. Equation 5 indicates that domestic money expenditure is homogeneous of degree 1 in money income and all prices.[4]

3. See, for example, (25, 21, 17, and 11). Although Laursen and Metzler have specifically discussed the effect of a change in the exchange rate upon domestic money expenditure, including investment as well as consumption, later participants in this discussion have concentrated exclusively on the effect upon consumption expenditure to the total neglect of the effect upon investment expenditure, as if the latter may be assumed to be fixed in money terms with a change in import prices. Actually, under the assumptions of no money illusion and no dynamic price expectations, there is as much reason to assume money expenditure on investment to be homogeneous of degree 1 in all prices and money income as to assume the same for money expenditure on consumption.

4. The money balances effect (or the Pigou effect) of a proportionate rise in money income and all prices may preclude the homogeneity of the money expenditure function. However, an increase in the relative scarcity of cash balances implies a rise in the marginal convenience yield of money balances and hence would lead to a rise in the interest rate, which is included as another determining variable of the expenditure function. The Pigou

Differentiating 5 and 6 and substituting, we get:

$$d_a - (D_a - I)\bar{q}_a - I(\bar{q}_b + e)$$
$$= (1 - \lambda_a)\left[q_a + Q_a\bar{q}_a - \frac{Q_a(D_a - I)}{D_a}\bar{q}_a - \frac{Q_aI}{D_a}(\bar{q}_b + e)\right] - \rho_a r_a.$$

Since at the initial position $Q_a = D_a$, therefore,

$$d_a = (1 - \lambda_a)q_a + D_a\bar{q}_a - \lambda_a I(\bar{q}_a - \bar{q}_b - e) - \rho_a r_a.$$

By a similar procedure, equation 4a may be obtained.[5] Equations 3a and 4a clearly indicate that the partial derivative of domestic expenditure with respect to a change in the terms of trade (an improvement is here to be treated as a positive change and a worsening a negative change) is equal to minus the marginal propensity to hoard times the initial amount of imports of the country concerned (i.e. $-\lambda_a I$ or $-\lambda_b I$).[6]

The two import functions are written by Meade in differentials as follows: For country A,

$$i_a = \pi_a d_a + [-(Q_a - I)\pi_a + I\epsilon_a]\bar{q}_a - I(\pi_a + \epsilon_a)(\bar{q}_b + e) \qquad 7$$
$$= \pi_a s_a - \pi_a Q_a\bar{q}_a + I(\pi_a + \epsilon_a)(\bar{q}_a - \bar{q}_b - e)$$

where π_a is A's propensity to import defined with reference to A's aggregate national expenditure instead of national income. ϵ_a is

---

effect of a proportionate rise in all prices is therefore taken care of in the term $\rho_a r_a$, and hence would not interfere with the homogeneity of the expenditure function in money income and all prices, exclusive of the interest rate.

5. A crucial assumption here is that $Q_a\bar{Q}_a = Q_a = D_a$ and $Q_b\bar{Q}_b = Q_b = D_b$ at the initial position which is implied in the assumption that trade is initially balanced.

6. This result agrees fully with those obtained by Harberger and Jones. Harberger, in whose model there is no investment, has shown that the effect of the terms of trade (an adverse change is treated as a positive change) is equal to the propensity to save times the initial amount of imports (7, pp. 52–3). Jones, by a more general and elegant method, has shown that the partial derivative of consumption expenditure with respect to a rise in import prices is equal to: (1 minus the ratio of the marginal propensity to consume to the average propensity to consume) times the initial amount of imports (11, pp. 78–9). Substituting total expenditure and the propensity to spend for consumption expenditure and the propensity to consume, respectively, and taking into account the assumption that in our model the average propensity to spend is 1 in the initial position (trade being initially balanced), their results can be readily converted to ours.

what he calls 'the expenditure compensated price elasticity of demand for imports in A' (or in other words, the elasticity of the pure substitution effect on A's import demand with respect to the relative price ratio between domestic products and imports). Hence $-(Q_a - I)\pi_a\bar{q}_a$ and $-I\pi_a(\bar{q}_b + e)$ are the familiar Slutsky–Hicksian income effect on A's demand for imports of a change in the price of A's domestic products and a change in A's import prices, respectively, and $I\epsilon_a(\bar{q}_a - \bar{q}_b - e)$ the pure substitution effect on A's import demand of the change in the relative price ratio in A between domestic products and imports.[7]

Similarly, for country B, we have:

$$i_b = \pi_b d_b - \pi_b Q_b \bar{q}_b + I(\pi_b + \epsilon_b)(\bar{q}_b - \bar{q}_a + e) \qquad 8$$

The income effect components of the effect on import demand of a change in domestic prices or import prices perhaps require

7. The Slutsky–Hicksian way of splitting off the income effect of a price change presumes that the effect on real income of a change in the price of a commodity, with money income fixed, is equal to the initial volume of that commodity purchased times the change in its price. In his criticism of Harberger, however, Spraos has rightly pointed out that in so far as there is a part of income which is neither spent on domestic products nor on imports, the loss in real income out of a fixed money income implied by, say, a rise in import prices is greater than the initial amount of imports consumed times the rise in import prices; for the loss in real value of the part of income that was initially not spent must also be compensated. Otherwise the demand function would imply some degree of money-illusion. In the present case, however, it is assumed that trade was initially balanced so that all income must have been spent initially either on imports or on domestic products. Hence, as Spraos himself has conceded, his objection would not apply to the present case (21, p. 144, esp. fn. 4).

Meade's import demand equations, i.e. 7 and 8, certainly cannot be accused of implying the presence of money illusion, because it can be shown that the partial derivatives of the demand for imports in these two equations satisfy Euler's theorem for a homogeneous equation of degree zero in all the determining variables; for from, say, equation 7 we have:

$$\frac{\partial I_a}{\partial D_a} = \pi_a; \quad \frac{\partial I_a}{\partial \bar{Q}_a} = [-(Q_a - I)\pi_a + I\epsilon_a]$$

and:

$$\frac{\partial I_a}{\partial(\bar{Q}_b E)} = -I(\pi_a + \epsilon_a).$$

Thus:

$$\pi_a D_a + [-(Q_a - I)\pi_a + I\epsilon_a]\bar{Q}_a - I(\pi_a + \epsilon_a)\bar{Q}_b E = 0,$$

since at the initial position $\bar{Q}_a = \bar{Q}_b = E = 1$, and $D_a = Q_a$.

a little further explanation. Since Meade has defined π_a as the partial derivative of imports with respect to domestic expenditure instead of national income, it might be thought that in formulating these import functions, Meade has not been consistent with his definition of the propensity to import. For it might be questioned that if π_a (or π_b) is defined as the marginal propensity to import with reference to aggregate money expenditures, should not the income effect on the demand for imports of a change in, say, domestic prices be written as $-(Q_a - I)\pi_a(1 - \lambda_a)\bar{q}_a$, since out of the equivalent implicit increase in money income only $(1 - \lambda_a)$ part of it will result in new expenditure and only π_a times the new expenditure concerned will be on additional imports? This inconsistency, however, is only apparent; for if the decrease in domestic prices should result in a net decrease in aggregate money expenditure (a net hoarding) equal to $\lambda_a(Q_a - I)$, its effect on import demand is already taken care of by the term $\pi_a d_a$. When aggregate money expenditure is included as a separate determining variable of import demand, therefore, we may assume, in formulating the income effect of a change in domestic prices (or in import prices), that all the implicit increase in income will be spent or that all the implicit decrease in income will be borne by a cut in expenditure.

Meade's definition of the propensity to import with reference to aggregate expenditure must be regarded as an improvement over the conventional one which related the demand for imports to domestic national income. For the demand for imports, in so far as they are finished products, as is tacitly assumed in this model, is clearly primarily a function of total expenditure and, hence, is correlated with national income only at one remove (i.e. through the correlation between income and expenditure). Since in the present model the relationship between income and expenditure is subject to the influence of both the interest rate and the terms of trade, the relationship between income and demand for imports may also be expected to change under the influences of these factors. Such influences on the functional relationship between income and import demand can only be taken into account when the propensity to import is defined as Meade did, i.e. with respect to expenditures instead of income.

Next we shall adopt Meade's equations for the changes in

domestic prices simplified by the assumption of constant money wages, viz.:

$$\bar{q}_a = \frac{1}{\eta_a}\frac{q_a}{Q_a} \qquad 9$$

$$\bar{q}_b = \frac{1}{\eta_b}\frac{q_b}{Q_b} \qquad 10$$

where η_a and η_b are the elasticities of supply of A and B's products, respectively, in terms of real labor cost (i.e. in terms of wage units).[8]

When full employment is reached, the expressions on the right-hand side of equations 9 and 10 would automatically become indeterminate forms, with q and η both approaching zero, and thus would leave it entirely to the other equations of the system to determine the changes in domestic prices with no change in domestic products (i.e. a zero q).

We shall also simplify the demand-for-money equations in Meade's model by getting rid of the assumed link between money

8. These are derived from the condition that the prices of domestic products in both countries must equal the marginal costs of those products, i.e.:

$$\bar{Q}_a = \bar{H}_a \frac{h_a}{q_a}, \qquad 11$$

$$\bar{Q}_b = \bar{H}_b \frac{h_b}{q_b}. \qquad 12$$

Differentiating equation 11, we get:

$$\bar{q}_a = \bar{H}_a d\left(\frac{h_a}{q_a}\right) + \frac{h_a}{q_a}\bar{h}_a = d\left(\frac{h_a}{q_a}\right)$$

since $\bar{H}_a$ is assumed constant and put equal to 1 at the initial position. By definition,

$$\eta_a = \frac{\frac{h_a}{q_a}}{Q_a}\frac{q_a}{d\left(\frac{h_a}{q_a}\right)}.$$

By equation 11, however, when $\bar{Q}_a$ and $\bar{H}_a$ are put equal to 1, h_a/q_a must also equal 1.

$$\therefore \quad \bar{q}_a = d\left(\frac{h_a}{q_a}\right) = \frac{1}{\eta_a}\frac{q_a}{Q_a}.$$

The derivation of equation 10 is exactly the same.

supply and gold or foreign exchange reserves, as there is hardly any country that mechanically follows this rule of the gold standard game. Thus we shall simply state that:

$$m_a = \xi_a(q_a + Q_a\bar{q}_a) - \zeta_a r_a \qquad 13$$

$$m_b = \xi_b(q_b + Q_b\bar{q}_b) - \zeta_b r_b \qquad 14$$

where ξ_a and ξ_b are redefined, as distinct from Meade's own usage, as the partial derivatives of the demand for money with respect to money income in countries A and B, respectively, and ζ_a and ζ_b are redefined as the partial derivatives of their demand for money with respect to domestic interest rates, respectively.

Finally, the balance-of-trade equation in differentials and in terms of A's currency may be stated as:

$$t = i_b - i_a + I\bar{q}_a - I(\bar{q}_b + e). \qquad 15$$

The eleven equations 1, 2, 3, 4, (or alternatively 3a and 4a as we have amended them) 7–10 and 13–15 should normally be sufficient to determine the eleven variables, d_a, d_b, $\bar{q}_a$, $\bar{q}_b$, i_a, i_b, r_a, r_b, and t. The variables m_a, m_b, and e will be treated as exogenous policy variables. In particular, when we want to examine the effect of a devaluation on the trade balance, we shall determine the value of t in terms of e and the parameters when all the other dependent variables have adjusted to the new situation.[9]

9. It should be noted that substituting equations 15 into equations 1 and 2 in turn, we get:

$$t = q_a + Q_a\bar{q}_a - d_a \qquad 1'$$

$$t = d_b - (q_b + Q_b\bar{q}_b) \qquad 2'$$

Furthermore, by substituting equations 3 into 1′ and 4′ into 2′, we get:

$$t = \lambda_a q_a + \rho_a r_a \qquad 3'$$

$$t = -\lambda_b q_b - \rho_b r_b \qquad 4'$$

and similarly, by substituting 3a into 1′ and 4a into 2′ we get:

$$t = \lambda_a q_a + \rho_a r_a + \lambda_a I(\bar{q}_a - \bar{q}_b - e) \qquad 3'\text{a}$$

$$t = -\lambda_b q_b - \rho_b r_b - \lambda_b I(\bar{q}_b - \bar{q}_a + e). \qquad 4'\text{a}$$

These equations facilitate the solution of t in terms of e, i.e. the ascertainment of the effect of a small devaluation on the trade balance, which we shall presently proceed to do.

Equations 1′ and 2′ indicate that the change in the trade balance must be equal to the change in the gap between national product and expenditure

II. Effect of a Devaluation

Internal balance assumed

As pointed out above, the effect of a devaluation was examined by Meade only under the assumption of either a Keynesian neutral monetary policy or a monetary policy that assures internal balance. The assumption of a monetary policy that ensures internal balance for both countries concerned implies that q_a and q_b are both zero. With the additional assumption that money wages are given, $\bar{q}_a$ and $\bar{q}_b$ may also be taken as zero. Thus equations 9 and 10 may be dropped and the rest of the equations greatly simplified. The solution for t/e obtained from equations 1, 2, 7, 8, and 15 is:

$$\frac{t}{e} = \frac{dT}{dE} = \frac{(\pi_{ab} + \epsilon_{ab} - 1)I}{1 - \pi_a - \pi_b} \qquad \mathbf{16}$$

where:

$$\pi_{ab} = \pi_a + \pi_b \quad \text{and} \quad \epsilon_{ab} = \epsilon_a + \epsilon_b.$$[10]

The solution is different from the Marshall–Lerner formula in that it has a denominator of $1 - \pi_a - \pi_b$. This is solely due to the fact that the propensities to import are defined here with respect to aggregate expenditures instead of incomes, so that the effect on the demand for imports of changes in aggregate ex-

---

(absorption). Equations 3′ and 4′, or 3′a and 4′a, further tell us that the improvement in the trade balance must equal the increase in hoardings, which are either income-induced, or interest-induced, or terms-of-trade-induced – the last-mentioned item being shown only in 3′a and 4′a. These equations, however, provide only partial solutions for the effect of devaluation on the trade balance; for q_a, q_b, r_a, r_b, $\bar{q}_a$, and $\bar{q}_b$ will all be affected by e, and the total effect on t will depend on how they in their turn are affected. This is, however, as far as the absorption approach can carry us. To obtain a full solution for the effect of a devaluation, the elasticity approach must be called in.

10. From equations 1′ and 2′ in footnote 9, we can see directly that, when internal balance is maintained in both countries,

$$t = -d_a = d_b.$$

Substitute this result into equations 7, 8, and 15, we get the result as in equation 16.

penditures cannot be excluded even though incomes in both countries are, by assumption, kept constant.[11]

For stability of the exchange rate, it is necessary that t/e should be positive, i.e. that a devaluation should bring about an improvement in the balance of trade. Since the denominator $(1 - \pi_a - \pi_b)$ can normally be assumed to be positive, the stability-condition for the exchange rate is the same as that implied in the Marshall–Lerner formula, viz. that the sum of the elasticities of demand for imports in both countries (including both the income effect and the substitution effect) should be greater than unity.

Also note that under Meade's assumption of internal balance, the introduction of the terms-of-trade effect on aggregate expenditure would make no difference at all in the effect of a devaluation on the trade balance. In other words, substituting equations 3a and 4a for 3 and 4 in the above system of nine equations would yield exactly the same solution for t/e as equation 16. This is because the additional effect on expenditure of a change in the terms of trade would be automatically compensated by monetary policy which is assumed to offset any tendency of deviation from full employment.[12]

Under such an implicit assumption of internal balance, the influence of monetary factors is not observable at all from the equation for the effect of a devaluation, because changes in monetary factors are assumed to happen implicitly. It is therefore rather uninteresting for the study of the role played by monetary factors.

11. It can be shown that when the propensities to import of both *A* and *B* are defined with respect to their respective money incomes, as is usually done, so that the import demand functions may be written as:

$$i_a = \pi_a{}^* q_a + I(\pi_a{}^* + \epsilon_a)(\bar{q}_a - \bar{q}_b - e) \qquad \text{7a}$$

and,

$$i_b = \pi_b{}^* q_b + I(\pi_b{}^* + \epsilon_b)(\bar{q}_b - \bar{q}_a + e) \qquad \text{8a}$$

the denominator would disappear.

12. In fact the solution 16 for t/e can be derived without reference to equations 3 and 4. The substitution of 3a and 4a for 3 and 4, respectively, merely affects the monetary changes that will be required for the maintenance of internal balance.

Keynesian neutral monetary policy

The alternative policy assumption made by Meade is that of a neutral policy combination, under which, in addition to the assumed absence of direct government efforts to influence imports, exports, and domestic expenditures by commercial and fiscal policies, the domestic rate of interest is specifically assumed to be kept constant by the monetary authorities by maintaining the supply of money and credit infinitely elastic at the existing rate of interest. According to Meade, this neutral monetary policy is the type generally assumed in 'what may be called Keynesian analysis'. Indeed, it is tacitly taken for granted by all economists who apply the multiplier analysis to international trade without any explicit mention of monetary factors at all.

To distinguish this type of neutral monetary policy from the more orthodox type of neutral money policy, we shall call the former the Keynesian neutral monetary policy. The latter will be called the orthodox neutral monetary policy, which, in the absence of long-run growth of population and real productive capacity of the economy, may be described simply as the monetary policy that keeps the money supply of the economy constant.

When Keynesian neutral monetary policy is assumed for both countries *A* and *B*, r_a and r_b are *ex hypothesi* zero and equations for the demand for money, i.e. 13 and 14, can be omitted altogether in the solution for the change in the balance of trade *t*. Using Meade's own domestic expenditure functions, i.e. 3 and 4, together with the other seven equations 1, 2, 7–10, and 15, the result obtained is:

$$\frac{t}{e} = \frac{dT}{dE} = \frac{\lambda_a \lambda_b(\pi_{ab} + \epsilon_{ab} - 1)I}{\Delta_1} \qquad 17$$

where

$$\Delta_1 = \lambda_a \lambda_b \left\{1 + \frac{\pi_a(1-\lambda_a)}{\lambda_a} + \frac{\pi_b(1-\lambda_b)}{\lambda_b} + (\pi_{ab} + \epsilon_{ab} - 1)\left(\frac{\Pi_a}{\lambda_a \eta_a} + \frac{\Pi_b}{\lambda_b \eta_b}\right)\right\} \qquad 18$$

and Π_a and Π_b are the proportions of national expenditures (hence of national incomes, since with initial balance assumed to be zero, national incomes and expenditures are identical) initially spent on imports in countries A and B, respectively.[13]

Again the stability of the exchange rate requires that $t/e > 0$. However, since it is by no means unlikely that either one or both of the two propensities to hoard (i.e. λ_a and λ_b) should be negative, we need to be more specific about this stability condition. For it has been pointed out by Samuelson that for an equation system such as the nine equations 1–4, 7–10, and 15, to be dynamically stable, it is necessary that Δ_1 (which is the determinant of the system with the sign reversed) be positive too.[14] Since it is impossible for the exchange rate to be stable when the whole system is dynamically unstable, we must conclude that it is necessary, for the stability of the exchange rate, that both equations 17 and 18 be positive.[15] This is what Samuelson calls 'the correspondence principle' which enables us to narrow down the necessary stability conditions in comparative static analysis with dynamic stability requirements.

We shall leave for later discussion the more complicated cases where one or both of λ_a and λ_b might be negative, and for the time being concern ourselves with the simple case where they are both positive. As long as λ_a and λ_b are both positive, equations 17 and 18 will both be positive when $(\pi_{ab} + \epsilon_{ab} - 1) > 0$. In other

13. The method of solution is simply successive substitution to eliminate all other variables than t and e. While the order in which these other variables are eliminated is quite immaterial, the particular procedure used was first to reduce the variables s, ds, and is to expressions in terms of the qs only, and then, making use of equations 3′ and 4′ in footnote 9, to solve for the qs. Then t can be readily solved as $t = \lambda_a q_a$, using 3′ in footnote 9 and assuming $r_a = 0$.

14. The number of equations being odd in this case, it is a necessary condition, for all the eigenvalues of the matrix of the system to be negative, that the determinant of the system be negative also (19, 20). For an excellent lucid exposition of this principle see, also Baumol (4, pp. 373–8).

15. This point was glossed over by Meade, who, after canceling out $\lambda_a \lambda_b$ from both the numerator and the denominator, observed that the denominator (with $\lambda_a \lambda_b$ canceled out) 'is certainly positive if $\epsilon_{ab} + \pi_{ab} > 1$, which we shall assume normally to be the case' (15, p. 50). This point appears also to have been overlooked by Stuvel who, after obtaining a similar expression for the effect of a devaluation on the balance of payments, asserted that it is only the sign of the whole expression that matters for stability, regardless of the sign of the denominator. See (22, ch. 4, esp. math. app., pp. 233–5).

words, the critical value for the sum of the elasticities of demand for imports in the two countries concerned is 1 in this Keynesian case of variable income, just as in the classical case of constant money incomes. The only difference is that the effect of devaluation will be much dampened by the changes in incomes and prices in both countries.

The terms-of-trade effect

Let us now allow for the terms-of-trade effect upon aggregate expenditures by substituting equations 3a and 4a for 3 and 4 in the above system of nine equations. The solution for t/e then becomes:

$$\frac{t}{e} = \frac{dT}{dE} = \frac{\lambda_a \lambda_b(\epsilon_{ab} - 1)I}{\Delta_2} \qquad \textbf{19}$$

where

$$\Delta_2 = \lambda_a \lambda_b \left\{\left[1 + \frac{\pi_a(1 - \lambda_a)}{\lambda_a} + \frac{\pi_b(1 - \lambda_b)}{\lambda_b}\right]\left(1 + \frac{\Pi_a}{\eta_a} + \frac{\Pi_b}{\eta_b}\right) + (\epsilon_{ab} - 1)\left(\frac{\Pi_a}{\lambda_a \eta_a} + \frac{\Pi_b}{\lambda_b \eta_b}\right)\right\} \qquad \textbf{20}$$

[16]

Again Samuelson's correspondence principle would require that for the stability of the exchange market it is necessary that both equations 19 and 20 be greater than zero.

Again assuming for the time being that λ_a and λ_b are both positive, the crucial stability condition is now $(\epsilon_{ab} - 1) > 0$, i.e. the sum of the components of the pure substitution effect alone in the two elasticities of demand for imports must be greater than 1.

A comparison of equations 17 and 19 therefore confirms the findings of Harberger as well as Laursen and Metzler that when the effects of the terms of trade on aggregate expenditures are taken into consideration, the stability condition for the exchange rate becomes more stringent. The crucial stability condition implied in equation 19, when λ_a and λ_b are both assumed to be positive, i.e. $(\epsilon_{ab} - 1) > 0$, although apparently much simpler,

16. The method of solution adopted here is again successive elimination, and the particular procedure is first to reduce the $\bar{q}$s, ds, and is to expressions in terms of the qs only and then solve for the qs. The solution for t can then be obtained from those for q_a and q_b.

is in fact identical to the stability conditions obtained by Harberger and Laursen and Metzler.[17] This simpler form, however, shows more clearly the true magnitude of this bugbear, which, according to Laursen and Metzler, might require the crucial value of the sum of the two elasticities of demand for imports to 'exceed unity by a considerable amount' (12, p. 296). Equation 19 clearly shows that the result of allowing for the terms-of-trade effect on aggregate expenditures is merely to cancel out the components of the income effect in the crucial sum of the two elasticities of demand for imports. If the proportion of the national income spent on imports is high so that the terms-of-trade effect on expenditure may be expected to be of some significance, so also would be the income effect component in the elasticity of demand for imports which offsets it. Conversely, if the income effect component in the elasticity of import demand is negligible, then the terms-of-trade effect upon aggregate expenditure, that is supposed to cause difficulty, would also be of negligible significance. Therefore, the existence of the terms-of-trade effect upon aggregate expenditure is not likely to make the stability condition of the exchange rate so dangerously stringent as was at first suggested.

17. Harberger's stability condition is:

$$(\eta_1 + \eta_2) > (1 + c_1 + c_2),$$

where η_1 and η_2, the two elasticities of demand for imports, correspond to our $(\pi_a + \epsilon_a)$ and $(\pi_b + \epsilon_b)$, respectively; and c_1 and c_2, the two propensities to import, correspond to our π_a and π_b, respectively. Thus his condition can be easily converted to our form, viz. $(\epsilon_{ab} - 1) > 0$ (7, p. 53, esp. fn. 13).

Laursen and Metzler's condition is given in the form:

$$\{(1 - w_1)(1 - w_2)v_1(\eta_1 + \eta_2 - 1) - s_1 m_1(1 - w_2) - s_2 m_2(1 - w_1)\} > 0,$$

where w_1 and w_2 are the propensities to spend, and hence $(1 - w_1)$ and $(1 - w_2)$ correspond to our λ_a and λ_b; v_1, the initial volume of imports (assumed to be the same for both countries), corresponds to our I; η_1 and η_2 to our $(\pi_a + \epsilon_a)$ and $(\pi_b + \epsilon_b)$, respectively; m_1 and m_2 to our π_a and π_b, respectively; and s_1 and s_2 are partial derivatives of the aggregate expenditures with respect to the exchange rate for the two countries, respectively. In our notation, $s_1 = \partial D_a/\partial E$ and $s_2 = \partial D_b/\partial(1/E)$, which, according to equations (3a) and (4a) above, are respectively equal to $\lambda_a I$ and $\lambda_b I$. Thus written in our notation, Laursen and Metzler's condition becomes:

$$\{\lambda_a \lambda_b I(\pi_{ab} - \epsilon_{ab} - 1) - \lambda_a I \pi_a \lambda_b - \lambda_b I \pi_b \lambda_a\} = \lambda_a \lambda_b I(\epsilon_{ab} - 1) > 0,$$

which is exactly the same as implied in equation 19.

Instability of the Keynesian neutral monetary policy

This observation about the significance of the terms-of-trade effect upon aggregate expenditure, however, is rather a digression from our main purpose in this paper, which is to achieve a synthesis of the elasticity and the absorption approaches and to highlight the role played by monetary factors. More pertinent to the main purpose of this paper are the following facts about the effect of a devaluation, as may be observed from equations 17 and 18 or 19 and 20:

a. It is impossible to dichotomize the effect of a devaluation into two clear-cut components, viz. a relative-price effect and an absorption or multiplier effect which constitutes a damping coefficient to the former; for as soon as we abandon the usual assumption of constant costs and prices of domestic products in both countries, the multiplier process would again involve changes in relative prices and hence the relative-price effect on the trade balance.[18] It is quite naïve, therefore, to claim that the absorption approach is a superior new tool that could supersede entirely the relative-price approach.

b. The absorption approach is right in the case of a Keynesian neutral monetary policy in pointing out that unless there is a positive propensity to hoard in both countries, the balance of trade is unlikely to be stable even if the sum of the elasticities of demand for imports of the two countries is greater than 1. For if one of the propensities to hoard is negative while the sum of the elasticities of demand for imports is greater than 1, then equations 17 and 19 cannot be positive, when the necessary

18. If we make the usual simplifying assumption that the elasticities of supply of products of A and B are both infinite, i.e. $\eta_a = \eta_b = \infty$, so that prices of domestic products will remain constant, then equation 19, for instance, can be simplified to:

$$\frac{t}{e} = \frac{\lambda_a \lambda_b(\epsilon_{ab} - 1)I}{\lambda_a \lambda_b + \pi_a(1-\lambda_a)\lambda_b + \pi_b(1-\lambda_b)\lambda_b}. \qquad 21$$

In this case, it is indeed permissible to say that the relative-price effect determines the initial change in trade balance to which a damping coefficient, determined by propensities to hoard and import is to be applied. Too often, however, analyses of the effect of a devaluation stop with such simple cases.

condition for the dynamic stability of the system is satisfied, i.e. when Δ_1 or $\Delta_2 > 0$.

If one of the propensities to hoard is zero, t/e would be zero, which implies that the effect of a devaluation would be zero. If both λ_a and λ_b are negative, it might seem that it is not impossible for both equations 17 and 18, or 19 and 20, to be positive as required for stability, and hence for the exchange rate to be stable, provided the absolute values of the negative λ_a and λ_b are large enough relatively to π_a and π_b, respectively, and η_a and η_b are also large. This is, however, illusory; for it must be remembered that Δ_1 (or Δ_2) > 0 is only a necessary condition for the dynamic stability of the system. By direct economic reasoning, it can be shown that there can be no stability for the system if the marginal propensities to spend in both countries are greater than 1. For with marginal propensities to spend greater than 1 and the supplies of money infinitely elastic at constant interest rates as assumed under the Keynesian neutral monetary policy, both countries would be unstable in isolation. It is therefore impossible that the two countries would become stable when joined together in mutual trade, since there is no possibility for the instability of the one being compensated by the stability of the other.[19]

In the actual state of affairs, it is not at all unlikely that the marginal propensity to hoard, in the sense of 1 minus the marginal propensity to spend (on both investment and consumption), should be zero or negative. Thus it would appear that the stability of the exchange rate and the balance to trade is frequently in a very precarious state, even if the sum of the elasticities of demand for imports is well above 1.

We shall soon see, however, that only under the Keynesian neutral monetary policy that eliminates all the stabilizing influences of monetary factors is the stability of the exchange rate

19. There seems to be a possibility that, if one of the propensities to hoard is negative and at the same time the sum of the elasticities of demand for imports is smaller than its critical value, the necessary condition for the stability of the dynamic system as well as the exchange rate might be satisfied. I am not sure, however, whether the sufficient condition for dynamic stability can be satisfied by such a combination since I have not worked out fully the sufficient condition for dynamic stability. Furthermore it seems that in such cases, the relative speed of price and income adjustments will have to be taken into consideration.

so precarious. Under a different monetary policy, say, the orthodox neutral monetary policy, it would not be necessary at all for the stability of the exchange rate and the dynamic system that the propensity to hoard of either country be greater than zero.

c. Furthermore, even if the sum of the elasticities of demand for imports is well above 1 and the marginal propensities to hoard of both countries are greater than zero, the exchange rate would at best be in a sort of 'indifferent' or 'neutral' equilibrium under the Keynesian neutral monetary policy, as soon as full employment is reached in the devaluing country. For when full employment is reached in country A, η_a approaches 0 as a limit and equations 17 and 19 would also approach zero as a limit, i.e.:

$$\frac{dT}{dE} = \frac{t}{e} \rightarrow 0, \quad \text{as } \eta_a \rightarrow 0;$$

for Δ_1 and $\Delta_2 \rightarrow \infty$, as $\eta_a \rightarrow 0$. In other words, the effect of devaluation on the balance of trade would be zero.[20] Thus if a freely fluctuating exchange rate system is adopted in a country with full employment and a Keynesian neutral monetary policy, any slight chance imbalance in trade could cause violent depreciation of the currency as the exchange rate would be entirely indeterminate.[21]

20. The fact that the other country is fully employed is not a menace to the stability of the trade balance and exchange rate for a devaluing country. For under full employment, the elasticity of aggregate supply is likely to take on different values according to the direction in which aggregate demand is changing. The elasticity of aggregate supply is zero when confronted with an increase in aggregate demand, but it is not likely to be zero when confronted with a decrease in aggregate demand, particularly when money wages in the country concerned are rigid. Since the aggregate demand for the products of the country whose currency has relatively appreciated is likely to fall, the relevant elasticity of supply of its products is not likely to be zero, even when it is enjoying full employment.

21. So far we have assumed a balanced trade position as the starting point. It has been pointed out by A. O. Hirschman that if there is a trade deficit to start with, the necessary and sufficient condition for a devaluation to improve the balance of trade becomes easier to fulfill (9). However, in a sense, the condition for $dT/dE > 0$, assuming no initial trade deficit, is still the basic stability condition; for if $dT/dE > 0$ only when there is an initial trade deficit, but <0 when there is no initial deficit, then the country concerned may use devaluation to improve its balance of trade to some extent when it has an initial trade deficit, but it cannot use devaluation to eliminate

d. So far we have abstracted from money-wage changes due to trade union pressure and speculative capital movements. We have reached the conclusion that a full-employment economy with a Keynesian neutral monetary policy would imply instability in the balance of trade and the exchange rate without taking into consideration the possibilities of a wage–price spiral and a destabilizing speculative capital movement.

When these possibilities are taken into consideration, the instability implied in the Keynesian monetary policy will certainly be aggravated. I have shown elsewhere (23, 24) that the Keynesian monetary policy – i.e. the pegging of the interest rate at a fixed level with an infinitely elastic supply of money – provides precisely the monetary condition that is most conducive to the generation of a cumulative (self-aggravating) speculative capital movement; and that the instability of the French franc due to speculative capital flights in the twenties, a case which has been much cited as the evidence of the inherent instability of a floating exchange rate system, was really made possible and stimulated by the French monetary policy at the time of pegging the interest rate on the large amount of floating debt then in existence and being issued. Those economists with a Keynesian inclination, who decry the traditional reliance on exchange rate adjustment to restore the balance of payments, often forget that one of the chief reasons why devaluation may fail to improve the balance of trade, particularly in the postwar world of full or overfull employment, is precisely the monetary policy which they either take for granted or are actively advocating.

Orthodox neutral money policy

That monetary factors can play a vital stabilizing role in the exchange market can be clearly shown by substituting the orthodox

---

its deficit; for when its deficit gets smaller, further devaluation may begin to have an adverse effect on its trade balance. If $dT/dE > 0$ when there is an initial deficit, but equals 0 when trade is balanced, then theoretically it is not impossible for the country eventually to eliminate its initial trade deficit by keeping on devaluing its currency. But once the trade deficit is eliminated, the momentum of devaluation may carry it further and further; for then the exchange rate becomes indeterminate (being in an indifferent equilibrium).

neutral money policy as defined above for the Keynesian neutral monetary policy. Under the assumption of an orthodox neutral money policy, changes in money supply, i.e. m_a and m_b, may be put equal to zero, whereas interest rates would be permitted to change freely. The effect of a devaluation can then be obtained by solving the system of 11 equations, consisting either of 1, 4, 7–10, and 13–15 or 1, 2, 3a, 4a, 7–10, and 13–15, for t in terms of e after putting m_a and m_b equal to zero.

The result obtained with the first set of equations, i.e. the set of equations that do not allow for the terms-of-trade effect on aggregate expenditure, is:

$$\frac{t}{e} = \frac{dT}{dE} = \frac{\alpha\beta(\pi_{ab} + \epsilon_{ab} - 1)I}{\Delta_3} \qquad 22$$

where,

$$\Delta_3 = \alpha\beta\left\{1 + \frac{\pi_a(1-\alpha)}{\alpha} + \frac{\pi_b(1-\beta)}{\beta} + (\pi_{ab} + \epsilon_{ab} - 1)\left(\frac{\Pi_a}{\alpha\eta_a} + \frac{\Pi_b}{\beta\eta_b}\right)\right\} \qquad 23$$

$$\alpha = \lambda_a + \left(1 + \frac{1}{\eta_a}\right)\frac{\rho_a\xi_a}{\zeta_a} \qquad 24$$

and

$$\beta = \lambda_b + \left(1 + \frac{1}{\eta_b}\right)\frac{\rho_b\xi_b}{\zeta_b}.\text{[22]} \qquad 25$$

Equations 22 and 23 are of exactly the same form as 17 and 18 respectively; the only difference is that in 22 and 23 α and β are substituted for λ_a and λ_b of 17 and 18. The terms α or β may be regarded as consisting of two components: First, there is the usual marginal propensity to hoard directly induced by real-income changes (viz. λ_a or λ_b respectively). Secondly, we have the interest-induced marginal propensity to hoard brought about by changes in the interest rate resulting from changes in the demand for transaction balances in connection with changes in money income, viz.:

$$\left(1 + \frac{1}{\eta_a}\right)\frac{\rho_a\xi_a}{\zeta_a} \quad \text{or} \quad \left(1 + \frac{1}{\eta_b}\right)\frac{\rho_b\xi_b}{\zeta_b}$$

22. The procedure adopted here is again to reduce the $\bar{q}$s, rs, ds, and is to expressions in terms of the qs only and then solve for q_a and q_b. The solution for t is then obtained from those for q_a and q_b.

respectively. As long as the interest-elasticity of the demand for money is not infinitely large (in absolute value) and the interest elasticity of aggregate expenditure is not zero, the interest-induced marginal propensity to hoard is always positive. Moreover, there is a practical limit to the velocity of circulation of money, ζ_a or ζ_b would approach zero as the limit of the velocity of circulation is gradually approached.

Thus unless we start from a position deep down in the liquidity trap, the second component is bound eventually to overwhelm the first, regardless of whether the latter is positive or negative. The danger of instability due to a negative propensity to hoard (or a greater than unity propensity to spend), which is after all quite a normal phenomenon, will, therefore, be quite under control if an orthodox neutral monetary policy is adopted instead of the Keynesian neutral monetary policy.

Furthermore, and what is more important for the current world, full employment at home need not imply instability in the balance of trade and the exchange rate. For when full employment is reached in country A, and hence η_a approaches zero, t/e would not approach zero as under the Keynesian neutral monetary policy. For equations 22–5 indicate that, as $\eta_a \to 0$,

$$\frac{t}{e} \to \frac{(\pi_{ab} + \epsilon_{ab} - 1)I}{1 - \pi_a + \dfrac{\pi_b(1 - \beta)}{\beta} + (\pi_{ab} + \epsilon_{ab} - 1)\left(\dfrac{\Pi_a \zeta_a}{\rho_a \xi_a} + \dfrac{\Pi_b}{\beta \eta_b}\right)} \qquad 26$$

since

$$\alpha = \lambda_a + \left(1 + \frac{1}{\eta_a}\right)\frac{\rho_a \xi_a}{\zeta_a} \to \infty, \quad \alpha\eta_a \to \frac{\rho_a \xi_a}{\zeta_a}, \quad \text{as} \quad \eta_a \to 0.$$

The limit for t/e as $\eta_a \to 0$ will be greater than zero as long as the primary stability condition $\pi_{ab} + \epsilon_{ab} > 1$ is fulfilled. Thus full employment at home and a marginal propensity to spend equal to or greater than 1 are no threat to the stability of the balance of trade and the exchange rate under an orthodox neutral money policy.[23]

23. I have shown elsewhere (23, pp. 410–12) that so long as the interest elasticity of supply of money is zero (as is implied by the orthodox neutral monetary policy) and the interest elasticity of demand for money is fairly small, as it would be when the prevailing interest rate is well above the minimum set by the liquidity trap, it is highly unlikely that the speculative demand for foreign exchange will be unstable or self-aggravating.

The introduction of the effect of terms-of-trade changes on aggregate expenditures would make no difference to the substance of the above conclusions. In addition it may be shown that the significance for exchange rate stability of the terms-of-trade effect on expenditure is less under an orthodox neutral money policy than under a Keynesian monetary policy. For by substituting equations 3a and 4a for 3 and 4 in the system and putting m_a and m_b equal to zero as before, we get:

$$\frac{t}{e} = \frac{ab\left(\pi_{ab} + \epsilon_{ab} - 1 - \frac{\lambda_a \pi_a}{\alpha} - \frac{\lambda_b \pi_b}{\beta}\right) I}{\Delta_4} \qquad 27$$

where

$$\Delta_4 = \alpha\beta\Bigg\{1 + \frac{\pi_a(1-\alpha)}{\alpha} + \frac{\pi_b(1-\beta)}{\beta} + \left[\pi_{ab} + \epsilon_{ab} - 1 + \lambda_a(1-\pi_{ab}) - \frac{\pi_b(\lambda_a - \lambda_b)}{\beta}\right]\frac{\Pi_a}{\alpha\eta_a} + \left[\pi_{ab} + \epsilon_{ab} - 1 + \lambda_b(1-\pi_{ab}) - \frac{\pi_a(\lambda_b - \lambda_a)}{\alpha}\right]\frac{\Pi_b}{\beta\eta_b}\Bigg\}.[24] \qquad 28$$

Comparison of equation 27 with 22 again indicates that, as pointed out by Harberger, and Laursen and Metzler, if λ_a and λ_b are positive so that a worsening of the terms of trade has a stimulating effect on the aggregate spending of the country concerned, the terms-of-trade effect upon aggregate expenditure would make the stability condition for the exchange rate more stringent. On the other hand, comparison of equation 27 with 19 shows that the significance for exchange stability of the terms-of-trade effect on expenditure is clearly reduced under an orthodox neutral monetary policy. For whereas under the Keynesian neutral monetary policy the effect of the terms-of-trade changes on expenditure would exactly cancel out the income-effect components of the elasticities of demand for imports, thus making the stability condition $\epsilon_{ab} > 1$, under an orthodox neutral money policy it will normally fall short of doing this. Given that α and β are both positive, which is practically always ensured under such

24. The procedure adopted here is similar to the one used in the preceding case.

a monetary policy, the crucial stability condition for the balance of trade is now:

$$\left(\pi_{ab} + \epsilon_{ab} - 1 - \frac{\lambda_a \pi_a}{\alpha} - \frac{\lambda_b \pi_b}{\beta}\right) > 0. \qquad 29$$

Since α and β are normally greater than λ_a and λ_b, respectively, the influence of the terms-of-trade effect on expenditure will not be big enough to offset completely the income-effect components in the elasticities of import demands. Thus the terms-of-trade effect on expenditure appears to be a much exaggerated bugbear in the eyes of elasticity pessimists.

It also can be shown that under an orthodox neutral money policy full employment at home will cause no difficulty to exchange rate stability even if the terms-of-trade effect on expenditure is allowed for. For as $\eta_a \rightarrow 0$, equation 27 becomes:

$$\frac{t}{e} \rightarrow \frac{\left(\pi_{ab} + \epsilon_{ab} - 1 - \frac{\lambda_b \pi_b}{\beta}\right) I}{\Delta_5} \qquad 30$$

where

$$\Delta_5 = 1 - \pi_a + \frac{\pi_b(1-\beta)}{\beta} + \left[\pi_{ab} + \epsilon_{ab} - 1 + \lambda_a(1 - \pi_{ab}) - \frac{\pi_b(\lambda_a - \lambda_b)}{\beta}\right]\frac{\Pi_a \zeta_a}{\rho_a \xi_a} + [\pi_{ab} + \epsilon_{ab} - 1 + \lambda_b(1 - \pi_{ab})]\frac{\Pi_b}{\beta \eta_b}. \qquad 31$$

When λ_a is positive, the stability condition implied in equation 30, i.e.

$$\left(\pi_{ab} + \epsilon_{ab} - 1 - \frac{\lambda_b \pi_b}{\beta}\right) > 0$$

is certainly fulfilled, when that implied in equation 27 is fulfilled.

When $\lambda_a < 0$, it implies that the terms-of-trade effect on expenditure in country *A* will give a boost to, instead of detracting from, the stability of the balance of trade. Equation 30 would then merely indicate that when full employment at home is attained, this possible boost to stability would disappear. In any case, the stability condition

$$\left(\pi_{ab} + \epsilon_{ab} - 1 - \frac{\lambda_b \pi_b}{\beta}\right) > 0$$

is not substantially different from the traditional Marshall–Lerner stability condition of $(\pi_{ab} + \epsilon_{ab} - 1) > 0$.[25]

III. Concluding remarks

We conclude that the absorption approach to the analysis of the effects of devaluation has contributed to our understanding of the problem only in emphasizing the fundamental facts that a positive trade balance implies the presence of hoarding (non-spending) of incomes or credit contraction and that a negative trade balance implies the presence of dishoarding or credit expansion, and that a more comprehensive analysis, including in particular an analysis of the effect on income and expenditure, is needed than is implied in the classical elasticity approach. As an independent analytical tool, in substitution for the traditional elasticity approach, however, it is quite inadequate; for we have shown that not only is the primary effect of a devaluation determined by the elasticities, but the secondary damping factor also depends on the relevant elasticities, once domestic prices are recognized as liable to change with the changes in income.

The significance of monetary factors, the role of which is clearly indicated by the fundamental identity of the absorption

25. In fact a comparison of equations 22 and 23 with 17 and 18, or of 27 and 28 with 19 and 20, shows that the dampening influence of income variation on the effect of a devaluation is generally reduced by the adoption of an orthodox, instead of a Keynesian, neutral monetary policy.

In the extreme case, where the interest elasticity of demand for money is zero in both countries (i.e. $\zeta_a = \zeta_b = 0$, which implies that the velocities of circulation of money are constant in both countries), α and β would approach infinity. Then equations 22, 26, 27, and 30 would all become the same as 16; i.e.:

$$\frac{t}{e} = \frac{(\pi_{ab} + \epsilon_{ab} - 1)I}{1 - \pi_a - \pi_b},$$

which is the solution we obtained under the assumption of internal balance in both countries (see page 148).

Thus the neglect of the dampening influence of income variation by the neoclassical economists is probably due partly to their customary assumption of zero interest elasticity of demand for money (or constant velocity of circulation of money). Alexander's characterization of the neoclassical elasticity approach as pure tautological theorizing is, therefore, quite unjustified.

approach, is however entirely obliterated by the usual assumption of constant interest rates supported by infinitely elastic supply of or demand for money with respect to the interest rate, an assumption explicitly or implicitly made in practically all modern Keynesian analyses. Such a monetary assumption, however, would imply instability in the exchange rate as soon as full employment is reached at home, even without allowing for the destabilizing influence of speculative capital movements and the possibility of a wage–price spiral. To take for granted such a monetary policy may have been justified in the deep depression years of the thirties, but it is hardly appropriate in the current world of prosperity and high-level employment.

It is high time that we abandoned this ubiquitous underlying assumption in our aggregate analysis lest we should scare ourselves out of our own wits in 'discovering' dangerous instability lurking everywhere in our economy (notably for example, the supposed razor-edge instability of our growth path) and thus clamor for more and more government controls on our economic life.

References

1. S. S. Alexander, 'Effects of a devaluation on a trade balance', *International Monetary Fund Staff Papers*, vol. 2 (1952), pp. 263–78.
2. S. S. Alexander, 'Effects of a devaluation: a simplified synthesis of elasticities and absorption approaches', *American Economic Review*, vol. 49 (1959), pp. 23–42.
3. W. R. Allen, 'A note on the money income effect of devaluation', *Kyklos*, vol. 9 (1956), pp. 372–80.
4. W. J. Baumol, *Economic Dynamics*, New York, 2nd edn, 1959.
5. H. Brems, 'Devaluation, a marriage of elasticity and absorption approaches', *Economic Journal*, vol. 67 (1957), pp. 49–64.
6. A. J. Brown, 'Trade balances and exchange stability', *Oxford Economic Papers*, vol. 6 (1942), pp. 57–75.
7. A. C. Harberger, 'Currency depreciation, income and the balance of trade', *Journal of Political Economy*, vol. 58 (1950), pp. 47–60.
8. A. C. Harberger, 'Pitfalls in mathematical model building', *American Economic Review*, vol. 42 (1952), pp. 856–65.
9. A. O. Hirschman, 'Devaluation and trade balance – a note', *Review of Economics and Statistics*, vol. 31 (1949), pp. 50–53.
10a. H. G. Johnson, 'Towards a general theory of the balance of payments', *International Trade and Economic Growth*, ch. 6, London, 1958. [Reprinted here as Reading 11.]

10b. H. G. JOHNSON, 'The taxonomic approach to economic policy', *Economic Journal*, vol. 61 (1951), pp. 812–32.
11. R. W. JONES, 'Depreciation and the dampening effect of income changes', *Review of Economics and Statistics*, vol. 42 (1960), pp. 74–80.
12. S. LAURSEN and L. A. METZLER, 'Flexible exchange rates and the theory of employment', *Review of Economics and Statistics*, vol. 32 (1950), pp. 281–99.
13. F. MACHLUP, 'Relative prices and aggregate spending in the analysis of devaluation', *American Economic Review*, vol. 45 (1955), pp. 255–78.
14. F. MACHLUP, 'The terms of trade effects of devaluation upon real income and the balance of trade', *Kyklos*, vol. 9 (1956), no. 4, pp. 417–52.
15. J. E. MEADE, *The Theory of International Economic Policy*, vol. I. *The Balance of Payments, Mathematical Supplement*, London, 1951.
16. M. MICHAELY, 'Relative prices and income absorption approaches to devaluation: a partial reconciliation', *American Economic Review*, vol. 50 (1960), pp. 144–7.
17. I. F. PEARCE, 'A note on Mr. Spraos' paper', *Economica*, vol. N.S. 22 (1955), pp. 147–51.
18. J. ROBINSON, 'The foreign exchanges', *Essays in the Theory of Employment*, part 3, ch. 1, New York, 1937. (Reprinted in H. S. Ellis and L. A. Metzler, eds., *Readings in the Theory of International Trade*, Philadelphia, 1949, pp. 83–103.)
19. P. A. SAMUELSON, 'The stability of equilibrium: comparative statics and dynamics', *Econometrica*, vol. 9 (1941), pp. 97–120.
20. P. A. SAMUELSON, *Foundations of Economic Analysis*, Cambridge, 1947.
21. J. SPRAOS, 'Consumers' behaviour and the conditions for exchange stability', *Economica*, vol. N.S. 22 (1955), pp. 137–47.
22. G. STUVEL, *The Exchange Stability Problem*, Oxford, 1951.
23. S. C. TSIANG, 'A theory of foreign exchange speculation under a floating exchange system', *Journal of Political Economy*, vol. 66 (1958), pp. 399–418.
24. S. C. TSIANG, 'Floating exchange rate system in countries with relatively stable economies: some European experiences after World War I', *International Monetary Fund Staff Papers*, vol. 7 (1959), pp. 244–73.
25. W. H. WHITE, 'The employment-insulating advantages of flexible exchange rates: a comment on Professors Laursen and Metzler', *Review of Economics and Statistics*, vol. 36 (1954), pp. 225–8.

7 A. C. Harberger

Some Evidence on the International Price Mechanism

A. C. Harberger (1957), 'Some evidence on the international price mechanism', *Journal of Political Economy*, vol. 65, pp. 506–21.

Introduction

The nations of the world, I believe, have learned the bitter lesson of the 1930s. Gone is the passive, or even perverse, behavior of monetary and fiscal authorities, which permitted the great slump of the 1930s to occur and to be transmitted from country to country through the international multiplier mechanism. In its stead are a determination in each country to prevent the occurrence of an initiating slump and an international effort, institutionalized in the International Monetary Fund, to lessen the degree to which balance-of-payments difficulties will frustrate the independent pursuit of full-employment policies by individual countries.

If major cycles do not occur in important countries, the main future changes in international demand are likely to be caused by shifts in the pattern of comparative advantage among relatively fully employed economies. These shifts will cause balance-of-payments difficulties for some countries, but strong efforts will be made to prevent adjustment through declining incomes. Adjustment there must be, however, and, if adjustment by income changes is ruled out, then the price mechanism or trade restrictions or both must be called into play.

The power of the price mechanism to bring about necessary adjustments in the balance of payments therefore takes on great importance. This article seeks to draw inferences about the power of the price mechanism from a number of recent econometric contributions to the field of international trade.

Direct Measurements of Price Elasticities Using Interwar Data

The tragic story of the 1930s is set down in the recent works of Polak (1953) and of Neisser and Modigliani (1953). Both studies make clear the extent to which levels of income the world over depended upon levels of demand in international trade. Polak fitted eighteen functions explaining changes in levels of national income in different countries during the interwar period. In each of these the level of exports was the major determining variable, and the coefficients of correlation were, in all but five cases, 0.95 or greater. Neisser and Modigliani do not attempt a statistical explanation of fluctuations in incomes, but their tables show the effects of changes in one country's income upon the incomes of other countries, assuming that trade balances are brought into equilibrium by an income-adjustment process. Their computations suggest that the reduction of one country's income by $1.00 may have caused the reduction of other countries' incomes by as much as $2.80 (Neisser and Modigliani, 1953, table 29, p. 128).

While the main mechanism of adjustment documented by Polak and by Neisser and Modigliani appears today to be obsolete, their studies do not afford very fruitful insights into the price mechanism. In both studies, relative price was typically included as a variable in relating changes in imports to other factors, but only rarely was it statistically significant. Out of twenty-four import functions fitted by Polak, relative price was found to be a statistically significant explanatory variable in only four. Neisser and Modigliani, even though they broke down the import statistics into major commodity groups, found price to be significantly related to imports in only three out of nineteen cases. The few statistically significant price elasticities were numerically small. Polak's highest estimated price elasticity was −0.40, while Neisser and Modigliani's was −0.26.[1]

On the export side, the picture is only slightly different. Polak

1. The results cited from Neisser and Modigliani refer to the 'structural equations' that appear in their model of the world economic system. In their later treatment of manufactured goods imports as a special category, they estimated the elasticity of demand to be greater than unity for the United States, the United Kingdom, and Sweden.

found price to be a statistically significant explanatory variable in thirteen out of thirty export demand functions, with elasticities ranging from −0.16 to −1.56. Neisser and Modigliani found price significant in ten out of thirty-seven cases, with elasticities ranging from −0.19 to −1.27. Both sets of estimates were mainly for exports of particular categories of goods. Neisser and Modigliani, however, also presented estimates of the elasticities of demand for total exports, obtained by aggregating over commodity groups for each country. The range for these estimates is from −0.06 to −0.66.

Taken at face value, these two sets of results suggest that the price mechanism has rather limited power to bring about adjustments in international trade. The authors, however, are reluctant to draw this conclusion (Polak, 1953, p. 65; Neisser and Modigliani, 1953, p. 96).

Since problems of measuring price coefficients in studies of international demand have been discussed elsewhere in detail (Orcutt, 1950; Harberger, 1953), it will suffice here to give a brief summary of the difficulties.

I

During the interwar period, for most countries income fluctuations were very large compared with changes in relative prices. Even comparatively modest variations in marginal propensities to import (or in income elasticities) would lead to a situation in which, statistically, there was substantial variation in import magnitudes that was 'unexplained' by income changes when constant marginal propensities or income elasticities were imposed on the data. To ask for a high partial correlation coefficient relating imports to prices in such cases amounts to asking that price variations 'explain' a good share of the error arising from fitting a single constant income parameter.

II

Most of the relations that have been fitted use least squares, treating quantity as the dependent variable. This biases the price coefficient toward zero if there are errors in the price data or if the country whose demand is being studied faces a rising supply curve of the commodity in question.

III

The reactions to price changes that are most relevant for the study of international adjustment mechanisms occur, by and large, when the import prices of a country or its export prices move in roughly parallel fashion, as, for example, in the case of a devaluation. These reactions can be estimated by studying the price reactions in individual commodities and averaging the elasticities that result or by concentrating on those times when the price movements of the different imported or exported commodities were similar. When an average of price changes is related to an average of quantity changes and the components of the averages move in widely different ways, a hodge-podge elasticity is obtained which, at its worst, may be meaningless and which in most cases will be biased toward zero.

IV

Price elasticities tend to be higher in the long run than in the short run; time-series analysis over relatively short periods thus does not fully reflect the long-run effectiveness of price changes.

These weaknesses, recognized both by Polak and by Neisser and Modigliani, warn us against accepting at face value the poor showing of price variables in their studies. Yet no listing of tendencies toward downward bias can show that price elasticitics are, in fact, large. For this we need evidence, not just arguments.

The search for appropriate evidence is not easy. The traditional technique of time-series analysis has been found wanting, and we are reduced to rummaging around in the welter of data and information on international trade and to find bits and pieces that will help shed more light on the price mechanism and how it works. It is likely that some of the bits and pieces will be inconclusive and that each will be subject to weaknesses of its own. Yet one can hope that amassing the results of independent experiments will lessen the degree of our uncertainty. When all or most of a set of uncertain and imprecise pieces of evidence point in the same direction, we have the sort of situation where ignorance turns into hunch, hunch into belief, and, ultimately, belief into knowledge.

A Prewar–Postwar Comparison

By the mid-1950s the world economy had pretty substantially recovered from World War II. The 'equilibrium' that had been reached was not the long-run norm, but I suspect that it was about as close to the long-run norm as the 'equilibrium' of the late 1930s and probably as close as we are likely to get in a constantly changing world. Between the late 1930s and the mid-1950s, two major sets of changes had taken place that might affect the levels of imports of various countries. One was in the long-term growth of real incomes, and the other was in the pattern of relative prices. Both sets of changes were substantial, and I suspect that together they account for most of the changes that occurred in the import picture.

If we compare the mid-1950s with the late 1930s, we observe a certain change in the quantity of imports of each country. To explain this change, we must look to the changes in both real income and the relative prices of imports. Unless we know how much of the change in imports was caused by income movements, we cannot find out how much was caused by price movements. Let us therefore assume that the income coefficients obtained from Polak's study were fairly reliable. By applying these coefficients to the changes in income between the late 1930s and the mid-1950s, we can estimate what part of the change in imports was attributable to income movements. I shall boldly attribute to price movements whatever part of the change in import demand is not 'explained' by income movements in this way.

I have done this by using Polak's estimated import demand functions for eight major countries. In each case an income elasticity of import demand was obtained by dividing Polak's estimate of the marginal propensity to import by the average propensity to import in the base year. This income elasticity was then applied to the percentage change in real national income between the base year and 1954, to obtain the percentage change in the quantity of imports to be attributed to the change in income. Imports in 1954 were predicted (on the basis of income change alone) by applying this last percentage to the base-year import quantity. The percentage by which actual imports

Table 1

Computation of Price Elasticity of Import Demand

	United Kingdom	*Nether-lands*	*United States*	*Canada*	*Australia*	*New Zealand*	*South Africa*	*Sweden*
Base year	1938	1938	1937	1937	1938	1937	1938	1938
Marginal propensity to import (Polak)	0.18	0.48	0.045	0.32	0.23	0.47	0.40	0.28
Average propensity to import (base year)	0.19	0.30	0.044	0.20	0.155	0.29	0.28	0.22
Income elasticity of import demand	0.95	1.60	1.00	1.60	1.48	1.65	1.43	1.30
Percentage increase in real income to 1954	29	31	100	137	70	66	79	31
Base-year index of import quantity[1]	127	118	93	60	32	91	191	94
Predicted 1954 index of import quantity[1]	163	178	186	192	66	190	407	133
Actual 1954 index of import quantity[1]	124	196	119	141	54	152	286	134
Actual minus predicted 1954 imports as percentage of predicted	−24	10	−34	−27	−18	−20	−30	0.7
Percentage increase in relative price of imports	43	44	36	13	23	10	40	15
'Implied' price elasticity of import demand	−0.56	0.23	−0.95	−2.12	−0.78	−2.00	−0.75	0.05

exceeded predicted imports was the percentage change in imports attributed to price movements. The calculations are outlined in Table 1. The data were obtained from *International Financial Statistics*, except that the Department of Commerce series on deflated gross national product was used to estimate real income change for the United States. The general price index used for most countries was an arithmetic average of the wholesale price index and the cost-of-living index.

The data of Table 1 give no more than a hint that Polak's results may understate the effect of the price mechanism. Though a well-defined income elasticity of import demand could conceivably be applicable in situations of cyclical change where the economic structure is fairly stable, I have qualms about applying such an elasticity to a situation of economic development and growth, where, almost by definition, the economic structure is changing.[2] The growth in a country's real productive capacity

2. In an earlier paper (Harberger, 1953, pp. 156–7), I presented the hypothesis that the cyclical income elasticity of import demand was likely to be higher than the secular income elasticity. If correct, this hypothesis would modify the conclusions that have been drawn from Table 1. I have, however, come to question the merit of the hypothesis, which was based on the notion that the supply curves of import-competing industries tended to be stable over cyclical movements in aggregate demand but tended to shift to the right along with those of other industries in the course of secular growth. I now feel that cyclical shifts in the supply curves of import-competing industries will tend to be similar to those in other industries.

The process can best be envisioned as follows: aggregate demand declines, with wage rates remaining relatively rigid. Industries cut back production, and money prices fall (the industries move back along their shortrun supply curves, which express quantity as a function of absolute price for the given rigid level of money wages). However, the supply function of import-competing goods, from which the import demand function is derived, has as its price variable not the absolute price of the goods in question but that price relative to the general level of product prices in the economy. To see how this supply curve shifts in a situation of cyclical change, we may ask how the quantity of import-competing goods would change if, in response to the cyclical decline in aggregate demand, all final-product prices declined by, say, 10 per cent. All industries, then, would be moving back along those short-run supply curves which express quantity as a function of absolute price for a given level of wages. If these supply functions were all of unit elasticity, the quantities supplied by each industry would decline by 10 per cent. The relative prices of different kinds of goods, however, would not change at all. In particular, for import-

may have been concentrated in import-competing industries, or it may have drawn resources out of import-competing uses and into the export trades. A given increment in real output could thus have as its counterpart a wide variety of possible changes in the level of import demand. We should therefore expect that predictions of import demand obtained by applying what are essentially cyclical income elasticities to situations in which real income has grown secularly would fall rather wide of the mark. Nevertheless, I feel that the results of my extrapolations push one away from the belief that relative prices have little influence and toward the belief that they play an important role.

The error made in predicting 1954 imports on the basis of the change in income alone can be 'explained' by a price elasticity of plausible sign and magnitude in six out of eight cases. In the two cases where an implausible price elasticity is 'implied' by my calculations, it would have taken shifts of only about 10 and 0.7 per cent, respectively, in the import demand functions to produce this result if the actual price elasticity was negative and the income elasticity had the value estimated on the basis of Polak's work. In the case of Sweden, the positive value 'implied' by my calculations for the price elasticity could have been accounted for by an error of only 4 per cent in the estimated value of the income elasticity.

On the other hand, in the six cases in which a negative implied elasticity was found, it would take much more than a 10 per cent shift in the import function or much more than a small error in the

---

competing goods, the quantity supplied would be reduced by 10 per cent while relative price remained the same. More generally, so long as import-competing goods have, on the average, about the same production characteristics as goods in general, the amount of such goods supplied at a given relative price would tend to decline in a cyclical recession by about the same percentage as aggregate output in the economy. This conclusion holds even when the assumption of absolute wage rigidity is relaxed; all that is required is that wages not be completely flexible in the short run.

There is, of course, no necessity that cyclical shifts in the supply curves of import-competing goods should be of the same percentage as changes in aggregate output, but we cannot argue on *a priori* grounds that they are likely to be systematically different. Likewise, there are no *a priori* reasons why secular shifts in supply should fall dominantly in either category of industries.

estimated income elasticity to change the general tenor of the results.

Elasticities of Substitution and Export Demand

One of the most challenging contributions to the field of export demand is G. D. A. MacDougall's study of British and American exports (1951 and 1952). MacDougall began by comparing the relative inputs of labor per unit of output in the United States and the United Kingdom in different industries with the relative exports by the two countries of the products of those industries. He found a very close relation ($r = 0.8$), which showed that, for commodities for which American labor productivity was more than twice that of the British, the United States tended to dominate the export market, while, for commodities for which American labor productivity was less than twice that of the British, the United Kingdom tended to dominate. Then, abandoning the labor-input approach, MacDougall related the relative quantities of British and American exports to their relative prices. This was done separately for each of twenty years, using about one hundred commodities in each year. The results were amazingly good and consistent. In almost all years a price differential of 10 per cent between corresponding British and American exports tended to be associated with a quantity differential of from 20 to 30 per cent. That is, regressions of the form:

$$\left(\frac{\text{Quantity of U.S. exports}}{\text{Quantity of U.K. exports}}\right) = A\left(\frac{\text{Price of U.S. exports}}{\text{Price of U.K. exports}}\right)^{B}$$

gave estimates of B which ran from -2 to -3, with but few minor exceptions.

The fundamental objection to MacDougall's procedure is that it involves comparing incomparables. If all the quantities and prices used in making a given estimate referred to shoes, then we could call B the 'elasticity of substitution' of third-area importers between British and American shoes. We would also be on safe ground if the quantities and prices all referred to tires, or beer, or cigarettes. But what can one make of MacDougall's procedure, in which the relative prices and quantities of shoes, tires, beer, and a hundred other commodities are related to one another for a single year? Clearly, it is only under very special circumstances that onc could call a B estimated in this way an 'elasticity of substitution'. Yet one cannot dismiss easily a set of twenty regressions, yielding correlations in the neighborhood of 0.5 or better on a hundred observations, all telling pretty much the same story. If MacDougall has not estimated an elasticity of substitution, he has at least found a striking empirical regularity, for which there should be an explanation.

A first approach to explaining MacDougall's results is to ask under what circumstances his figures would, in fact, be estimates of an elasticity of substitution. They clearly would be if the separate elasticities of substitution between British and American exports of the commodities he compares tended to be the same, so long as the slopes of the individual-commodity substitution relations were not correlated with their intercepts. Then comparisons of prices and quantities of different commodities in the same year or of the same commodities in different years would all tend to yield estimates of the 'common' elasticity of substitution.

Recent work by Raymond E. Zelder indicates that this may be the case (Zelder, 1955). Using time-series data from the interwar period, Zelder estimated thirty-nine elasticities of substitution between American and British exports of manufactured commodities. His estimates clustered closely around the values MacDougall found in his many-commodity comparisons. Zelder's regressions of relative quantities of exports on relative prices yielded four estimated elasticities less than 1 and three greater than 4 in absolute value. Twenty-one lay between -1.5 and -3.5, and only two had an implausible sign. The correlation coefficients were, with few exceptions, between 0.5 and 0.9. Zelder's results are summarized in Table 2. The last column of this table presents a set of estimates of elasticities of substitution intermediate between those given by the regression of relative quantity on relative price (which tend to be biased toward zero) and those given by the regression of relative price on relative quantity (which tend to be biased away from zero).

Before drawing inferences from MacDougall's and Zelder's work, I should like to comment on the usefulness and relevance of measures of elasticities of substitution, since several recent discussions have been critical of their use under certain conditions (Polak, 1950; Morgan and Corlett, 1951; Morrissett, 1953). Consider a regression of the form:

$$\log \frac{q_x}{q_y} = A + B \log \frac{p_x}{p_y}.$$

One striking feature of such a regression is the absence of an income term. But if x and y are commodities with similar income elasticities, the ratio of their quantities will not be substantially affected by changes in income. Likewise, if another commodity, z, is closely related in demand to x and y, its exclusion from the relation will be unimportant if the cross-elasticities of demand for x and y with respect to the price of z are similar in sign and magnitude. Suppose, however, that a variable such as income or the price of z does not have an equiproportional effect on the quantities of x and y demanded. Such a variable will operate to 'shift' the relationship between the relative quantities and relative prices of x and y. But this will not prevent our obtaining an unbiased estimate of B, so long as the 'shift' variable is not significantly correlated with the ratio p_x/p_y.

On this basis, one would expect to obtain a poor fit but no bias when x and y have dissimilar income elasticities but their price ratio is not correlated with income. One would expect a spurious or biased estimate of the elasticity of substitution when x and y have dissimilar income elasticities and their price ratio is correlated with income. A case of this last type is illustrated in Polak's article on the subject, in which a possibly spurious elasticity of substitution is found between American exports of crude materials and British exports of manufactured products. I feel that it is extremely unlikely that bias of this type affected Zelder's or MacDougall's results. The commodities they compared were so closely similar in nature that one might reasonably expect the two components of each comparison (for example, British and American radios) to have similar income elasticities of demand and similar cross-elasticities of demand with other products. And even in the few cases in which this expectation may not hold, there is little reason to suspect a substantial correlation between the movements of the price ratio of the com-

Table 2

Elasticity of Substitution: Individual Commodity Exports of United States and United Kingdom (1921–38)

Commodity	*Regression of q_1/q_2 on p_1/p_2*	*Regression of p_1/p_2 on q_1/q_2*	*Correlation coefficient*	*Coefficient of variation of q_1/q_2 divided by coefficient of variation of p_1/p_2*
Chemicals:				
Aluminum sulfate[1]	−2.02	−4.36	−0.682	−3.0
Fertilizers	−0.55	−3.36	−0.404	−1.4
Ammonium sulfate[3]	−3.11	−9.81	−0.562	−5.5
Sodium compounds	−1.79	−2.64	−0.824	−2.2
Caustic soda	−1.22	−8.49	−0.380	−3.2
Iron and steel:				
Pig iron	−3.10	−3.86	−0.897	−3.5
Plates and sheets	−2.87	−3.80	−0.869	−3.3
Galvanized	−1.85	−3.12	−0.770	−2.4
Plain	−2.55	−3.68	−0.832	−3.1
Black	−2.41	−4.18	−0.760	−3.2
Tinned and terned	−4.07	−7.24	−0.753	−5.4
Pipes, tubes, and fittings	−3.17	−4.40	−0.849	−3.7
Railway materials[5]	−1.52	−2.51	−0.778	−2.0
Railway tracks	−1.14	−11.77	−0.031	−3.7
Razor blades[2]	1.95	27.46	0.267	7.3
Wire manufactures	−2.11	−4.55	−0.680	−3.1
Machinery and vehicles:				
Automobiles and chassis	−1.92	−2.63	−0.854	−2.3
Electricity generators[5]	−0.98	−1.41	−0.833	−1.2
Motorcycles	−5.52	−7.04	−0.885	−6.2
Radio sets[4]	−1.37	−14.02	−0.313	−4.4
Radio tubes[6]	−1.19	−1.44	−0.910	−1.3
Sewing machines[5]	−1.34	−2.64	−0.711	−1.9

Table 2 (*Continued*)

Commodity	*Regression of q_1/q_2 on p_1/p_2*	*Regression of p_1/p_2 on q_1/q_2*	*Correlation coefficient*	*Coefficient of variation of q_1/q_2 divided by coefficient of variation of p_1/p_2*
Non-ferrous metals:				
Brass tubes	−2.12	−8.66	−0.495	−4.3
Copper manufactures	−0.72	−49.90	−0.118	−6.0
Ingots and bars	−5.07	−32.12	−0.398	−12.8
Plates and sheets	−3.34	−4.57	−0.855	−3.9
Rods	−4.37	−6.84	−0.800	−5.5
Wire (bare)	−3.83	−12.49	−0.554	−6.9
Nickel[5]	−1.67	−3.02	−0.743	−2.2
Non-metallic minerals:				
Cement	−2.61	−3.01	−0.931	−2.8
Gasoline	−3.81	−16.97	−0.473	−8.0
Glass, plate and sheet	2.10	9.13	0.480	4.4
Lubricating oil	−1.95	−2.57	−0.872	−2.2
Textiles:				
Cotton cloth	−1.45	−3.71	−0.625	−2.3
Bleached and colored	−1.14	−4.34	−0.513	−2.2
Unbleached	−3.27	−4.56	−0.847	−3.9
Cotton yarn	−0.08	−89.31	−0.030	−2.6
Jute bags[5]	−1.85	−5.87	−0.562	−3.3
Woollen fabrics	−2.83	−6.00	−0.686	−4.1

1. 1925–38
2. 1930–38
3. Excluding 1926
4. 1931–8
5. 1922–38
6. 1927–38

pared commodities and the movements of income or of prices of other products.

Let us now consider what elasticities of demand for exports are implied by MacDougall's and Zelder's elasticities of substitution. The answer comes only after a little algebraic manipulation. Write the demand relations for x and y in logarithmic form, so that their slope coefficients are own-price elasticities and cross-elasticities of demand:[3]

$$\log q_x = A + E_{xx} \log p_x + E_{xy} \log p_y + E_{xz} \log p_z,$$

$$\log q_y = C + E_{yy} \log p_y + E_{yx} \log p_x + E_{yz} \log p_z.$$

The elasticity of substitution (B_{xy}) between x and y will be the same, regardless of whether p_x or p_y causes the price ratio p_x/p_y to change. Thus:

$$\partial \frac{\log q_x - \log q_y}{\partial \log p_x} = B_{xy} = E_{xx} - E_{yx}$$

or,

$$-\partial \frac{\log q_x - \log q_y}{\partial \log p_y} = B_{xy} = E_{yy} - E_{xy}.$$

When x and y are the only significant substitutes for each other (that is, where $E_{xz} = E_{yz} = 0$), we have, from the Hicksian 'law' that the effect on demand for x should be the same, regardless of whether the price of x is raised by 1 per cent or all other prices are lowered by 1 per cent: $E_{xx} = -E_{xy}$ and $E_{yy} = -E_{yx}$. Using the symbol v to represent total expenditure on the commodity in question, from the symmetry of this substitution effect we obtain $v_x E_{xy} = v_y E_{yx}$. Thus $E_{xx} + E_{yy} = B_{xy}$ and $v_x E_{xx} = v_y E_{yy}$, so that:

$$E_{xx} = \frac{v_y B_{xy}}{v_x + v_y} \quad \text{and} \quad E_{yy} = \frac{v_x B_{xy}}{v_x + v_y}.$$

When 'other commodities', here lumped together as z, are related in demand to x and y, this formulation is somewhat modified. Here the Hicksian 'law' requires that $E_{xx} + E_{xy} + E_{xz} = 0 = E_{yy} + E_{yx} + E_{yz}$. Applying this and the symmetry rule to the expression for B_{xy}, we obtain:

$$E_{xx} = \frac{v_y}{v_x + v_y} B_{xy} - \frac{v_x}{v_x + v_y} E_{xz}.$$

So long as x is a net substitute for 'other commodities' ($E_{xz} > 0$), E_{xx} will be underestimated in absolute value by the formula

3. Own-price elasticities and cross-elasticities are here defined with real income held constant, that is, excluding the Hicksian 'income effect'.

$v_y B_{xy}/(v_x + v_y)$. Similarly, E_{yy} will be underestimated by the formula $v_x B_{xy}/(v_x + v_y)$. By a simple extension of this line of reasoning it can be shown that E_{xx} will be underestimated by the formula:

$$E_{xx} = \sum_i s_i B_{xi},$$

where i ranges over all countries for which elasticities of substitution, B_{xi}, are available and s_i is the share of country i in the total exports of the group (including those of country x).

During the interwar period the United States exported roughly 45 per cent and the United Kingdom roughly 55 per cent of the total manufactured exports of the two countries. Hence, if we assume on the basis of MacDougall's and Zelder's work that the elasticity of substitution between British and American manufactured exports was about −3.0, we can estimate that the elasticity of foreign demand for British manufactured exports was at least −1.35 and that for American manufactured exports was at least −1.65. These estimates are subject to the following qualifications: (*a*) they contain a bias toward zero because in deriving them no account was taken of any substitution except that between British and American manufactured exports; (*b*) they contain a bias toward zero because the estimated elasticity of substitution (−3.0) on which they are based was derived from regressions of relative quantity on relative price; (*c*) they contain an aggregation bias away from zero. If the elasticities of substitution of British for American exports of all individual commodities were −3.0, the elasticities of export demand for British commodities would vary, being small where Britain supplied a large share of the total market and large where Britain supplied a small share of the total market. The use of Britain's share in the total export market to obtain an estimate of Britain's overall elasticity of demand for exports from the elasticity of substitution of British for American exports implicitly gives Britain's low-elasticity commodities a lower than 'proper' weight and Britain's high-elasticity commodities a higher than 'proper' weight in the overall average. MacDougall estimated the extent of this bias as applied to the elasticity of substitution rather than to the elasticity of export demand; his estimates differ from year to year according to the composition of trade, but, in general, his correction for aggregation bias involves reducing his estimated elasticity of substitution by about one-third.[4]

Applying MacDougall's correction for aggregation bias to our estimates of elasticities of export demand would yield new estimates, free from aggregation bias, in the neighborhood of -1. I suspect that the biases discussed in qualifications *a* and *b* probably substantially outweigh the aggregation bias discussed

4. This reasoning on aggregation bias can be supported as follows: Assume that the elasticity of substitution (B_{xy}) between British and American exports is the same for all individual commodities. Let v_{xi} and v_{yi} represent the values of British and American exports, respectively, of commodity *i*. The elasticity of demand for British exports of commodity *i* will, accordingly, be at least $B_{xy}v_{yi}/(v_{xi}+v_{yi})$. Aggregating these individual elasticities, weighted by value, over all British exports, we obtain:

$$E_{xx} = \sum \frac{v_{xi}}{(\Sigma v_{xi})} \cdot \frac{v_{yi}}{v_{xi}+v_{yi}} \cdot B_{xy}$$

as an estimate of the elasticity of demand for British exports. The alternative estimate obtained by neglecting the aggregation problem is:

$$E_{xx}{}' = \frac{\Sigma v_{yi}}{(\Sigma v_{xi}+\Sigma v_{yi})} \cdot B_{xy}.$$

This can be expressed as:

$$E_{xx}{}' = \sum \frac{v_{xi}+v_{yi}}{(\Sigma v_{xi}+\Sigma v_{yi})} \cdot \frac{v_{yi}}{v_{xi}+v_{yi}} \cdot B_{xy}.$$

The latter procedure will tend to give an overestimate of the elasticity of export demand, for in those cases in which Britain's share of the export market is small – i.e. where $v_{yi}/(v_{xi}+v_{yi})$ is large – the weight of $v_{yi}/(v_{xi}+v_{yi})$ will tend to be larger in the $E_{xx}{}'$ formula than in the E_{xx} formula. Conversely, in those cases in which Britain's share of the export market is large and $v_{yi}/(v_{xi}+v_{yi})$ is accordingly small, the weight of $v_{yi}/(v_{xi}+v_{yi})$ will tend to be smaller in the $E_{xx}{}'$ formula than in the E_{xx} formula.

The 'coefficient of correction' by which the $E_{xx}{}'$ formula must be multiplied to yield the E_{xx} formula is:

$$\frac{\Sigma[v_{xi}/(\Sigma v_{xi})][v_{yi}/(v_{xi}+v_{yi})]}{(\Sigma v_{yi})/(\Sigma v_{xi}+\Sigma v_{yi})}.$$

The corresponding 'coefficient of correction' for the estimate of the elasticity of demand for American exports is:

$$\frac{\Sigma[v_{yi}/(\Sigma v_{yi})][v_{xi}/(v_{xi}+v_{yi})]}{(\Sigma v_{xi})/(\Sigma v_{xi}+\Sigma v_{yi})}.$$

The weighted average of these two coefficients of correction is MacDougall's 'index of similarity', defined as:

$$\sum \frac{v_{xi}}{(\Sigma v_{xi})} \cdot \frac{v_{yi}}{v_{xi}+v_{yi}} + \sum \frac{v_{yi}}{(\Sigma v_{yi})} \cdot \frac{v_{xi}}{v_{xi}+v_{yi}}.$$

This index is derived from MacDougall (1951, appendix C and p. 494).

in *c*. If this is so, the estimates uncorrected for aggregation bias are closer to the truth than the corrected estimates.

On the basis of Zelder's work we can reasonably accept MacDougall's results as estimating the 'typical' elasticity of substitution between British and American exports. Accordingly, we can accept their implications for the values of export demand

Table 3

Elasticities of Substitution and Estimated Demand Elasticities for Exports (1928)

	United States	*United Kingdom*	*France*	*Germany*	*Japan*
Elasticities of substitution:					
United States	—	−2.6	−2.4	−2.4	−2.8
United Kingdom	−2.6	—	−2.2	−1.6	−1.6
France	−2.4	−2.2	—	−1.7	−2.2
Germany	−2.4	−1.6	−1.7	—	n.a.*
Japan	−2.8	−1.6	−2.2	n.a.*	—
Shares in exports of group	0.25	0.30	0.13	0.23	0.09
Estimated demand elasticity for manufactured exports	−1.90	−1.45	−1.85	−1.30	−1.47

* Not available

elasticities. However, MacDougall also estimated 'elasticities of substitution' between the exports of pairs of countries other than the United States and the United Kingdom; here we have no studies comparable to Zelder's to check the validity of the estimates. If we nevertheless take the bold step of accepting MacDougall's results in all cases, we obtain the estimates of export demand elasticities given in Table 3.

The elasticities of substitution given in Table 3 apply to the manufactured exports of the respective countries and were derived by MacDougall's method from 1928 data. The weights used to estimate export demand elasticities from the elasticities of substitution were rough averages of the shares of the respective countries in the total exports of the group in the interwar period. The estimated demand elasticities are subject to the biases previously discussed and are probably biased toward zero.

Effects of Devaluation

MacDougall's and Zelder's results suggest that price elasticities of demand for manufactured goods exports range upward in absolute value from a lower limit somewhere between −1 and −2. This conclusion is based on rather tenuous evidence, and one may reasonably inquire whether some other approach is available to confirm it. Another approach was used in an unpublished study of the 1949 devaluations, done by Michel Verhulst and myself at the International Monetary Fund in 1950. Our aim was to assess the effect of the devaluations on the pattern of international trade. Here was a case, unique to my knowledge, of a substantial repricing of the goods that enter trade, carried out in a short period of time, and not obviously the result of drastically changed demand conditions (as was the materials-price boom of 1950–51).

We compared the trade patterns of the first quarter of 1949 and the first quarter of 1950. In this way we avoided the speculative anticipation of devaluation, which is said to have influenced traders soon after the first quarter of 1949, and the substantial influences of recovery efforts in the European countries before 1949. We also avoided the effects of the Korean outbreak of June 1950. We compared similar quarters to eliminate seasonal influences.

Between the first quarter of 1949 and the first quarter of 1950 there were changes in income of as much as 5 per cent in some countries. We felt that their effect was sufficiently minor, compared with that of the international price adjustment, to warrant the use of a rather rough correction. Our assumption was that, although changes in income might have had an appreciable effect on the volumes of imports, their effects on the distribution of imports by source would be negligible. We therefore inquired into the effect of devaluation, not on a country's total imports, but only on its distribution of imports by source.

For each of fourteen major importing countries[5] we calculated the percentage distribution of imports by source for the first quarter of 1949 and the first quarter of 1950. Dollar values of imports from each source were deflated by an index of the dollar price level of exports from that source. Hence the percentage distributions of imports that we compared were distributions of import quantities, not values. If country *i* took 20 per cent of its total imports from source *j* in 1949, and 22 per cent from source *j* in 1950, we say that it made a net substitution of 10 per cent in favor of source *j* from 1949 to 1950. The average net substitutions for or against each source (with the net substitutions of individual importing countries or regions weighted according to the dollar values of their respective imports from each source), together with the first-quarter 1950 dollar price index of exports from each source, are shown in Table 4.

Table 4 shows a striking correspondence between the net substitution for or against particular sources and the changes in the dollar price levels of the exports of those sources. The rank correlation between the net substitutions and the 1950 price indexes is 0.85. This correlation suggests that the price mechanism was powerfully at work, but it does not provide estimates of the price elasticities of demand for the exports of the sources considered.

The key to such estimates is the identification of our concept of net substitution with the Hicksian 'substitution effect'. Hicks, in trying to isolate the substitution effect of a price change, conceptually holds the consumer's total budget at a level that will barely permit him to buy his 'old' bundle of commodities at the new prices. We, in isolating our net substitution, conceptually hold the importing country's aggregate spending on imports at a level that will barely permit it to buy its 'old' bundle of imports at the new prices. We thus fail to take account of any substitution that may take place between home goods and imports, but otherwise we follow in Hicks's footsteps. Our failure to take account of this substitution biases our estimates of demand elasticities toward zero.

5. The United States, Canada, United Kingdom, Sweden, Norway, Denmark, France, Italy, Belgium-Luxembourg, Netherlands, Germany, Switzerland, Australia, and India.

Table 4

Net Substitutions among Imports by Source and Indexes of Export Prices by Sources*

Source	*Average net substitution by 14 importing countries for or against exports of indicated source, 1st quarter 1949–1st quarter 1950 (per cent of 1st-quarter 1949 exports of source)*	*1st-quarter 1950 index of dollar price-level of exports from indicated source (1st quarter 1949 = 100)*
United States	−25.5	92
Latin America	−15.6	110
Rest of the world	−8.0	82
Canada	−7.2	91
Switzerland	−1.1	87
Outer sterling area	14.0	79
United Kingdom	14.1	72
France and Italy	15.8	82
Benelux	27.5	75
Scandinavia	27.6	69
Germany and Austria	53.1	73

* The basic data underlying this table were collected by the International Monetary Fund and the Statistical Office of the United Nations for their joint publication, *Direction of International Trade*. Export price indexes and indexes of exchange rates on the dollar were obtained from *International Financial Statistics*. Charts showing the net substitutions for or against each source by individual importing countries or areas were published in *International Financial Statistics*, August, 1950, pp. 2–5. These charts (labeled C_2–C_{11}) indicate that the average net substitutions shown here are typical of those for individual importing countries, except for Switzerland and perhaps Scandinavia. Our dollar price indexes of exports used to deflate the basic dollar-value-of-trade data are shown in *International Financial Statistics*, August 1950, p. 5. The deflation was done separately for twenty-seven export sources, which were later grouped into the eleven categories shown. In all cases except the outer sterling area and Latin America, the individual countries in a group had very similar percentage changes in the dollar price indexes of their exports.

Our counterpart of Hicks's consumer is a typical importer. Let dq_i measure the amount by which his imports from i would change as a result of a changed price situation, subject to the constraint that his aggregate quantum of imports remains unchanged. Let dp_i be the change in the dollar price level of i's exports, and let $\partial q_i/\partial p_j$ ($= X_{ij}$) measure the change in the quantity of imports from i occasioned by a unit rise in the price of j's exports, all other prices and the aggregate quantum of imports remaining unchanged. Since the dollar price levels of all export sources changed, our analytical representation of the situation must be as follows:

$$\begin{pmatrix} dq_1 \\ dq_2 \\ \cdot \\ \cdot \\ dq_n \end{pmatrix} = \begin{pmatrix} X_{11} & X_{12} & X_{13} \ldots X_{1n} \\ X_{21} & X_{22} & \ldots X_{2n} \\ \cdot & \cdot & \ldots . \\ \cdot & \cdot & \ldots . \\ X_{n1} & X_{n2} & \ldots X_{nn} \end{pmatrix} \begin{pmatrix} dp_1 \\ dp_2 \\ \cdot \\ \cdot \\ dp_n \end{pmatrix}.$$

This does not appear to help much. We are interested in estimating own-price elasticities, $p_i X_{ii}/q_i$, and we have data only on the dp_i and the dq_i. These data are not sufficient to permit us to estimate all the X_{ij}, yet it appears that we need estimates of the off-diagonal elements of the X-matrix to obtain the estimates of the diagonal elements that we want. Fortunately, the situation is not hopeless. A typical element in the preceding matrix equation is:

$$dq_1 = X_{11}dp_1 + X_{12}dp_2 \ldots + X_{1n}dp_n,$$

which can be written as follows:

$$\frac{dq_1}{X_{11}} = dp_1 + \frac{X_{12}}{X_{11}}dp_2 \ldots + \frac{X_{1n}}{X_{11}}dp_n.$$

I feel that it is grossly implausible that the exports of any pair of sources should be net complements in the typical importer's preference scheme. Hence I assume that all the off-diagonal elements in the X-matrix are positive. Since the diagonal elements must be negative, the ratios (X_{ij}/X_{ii}) must be negative. Furthermore, these ratios, as they appear in the last equation, must add up to -1, because the elements of any row or column of the X-matrix must add up to zero. Hence our typical equation can be simplified to:

$$\frac{dq_1}{X_{11}} = dp_1 - d\bar{p}$$

where $\bar{p}$ is an index number of the prices of the exports of sources 2 through n, with the individual prices weighted by (X_{1i}/X_{11}).

Once we have an estimate of $d\bar{p}$, it is a simple procedure to estimate the own-price elasticity, E_{11}. Since our prices are initially unity,

$$E_{11} = \frac{X_{11}}{q_1} = \frac{dq_1/q_1}{dp_1 - d\bar{p}}.$$

I have made two alternative assumptions in obtaining estimates of $\bar{p}$. The first postulates equal substitutability of imports from all other sources for imports from i, in the sense that a 1 per cent rise in i's export price level, leading to an E_{ii} per cent fall in i's exports, will carry with it a proportionate increase in the quantities of exports from all other sources. This assumption obviously does not hold precisely, for surely a 1 per cent rise in British export prices will help the United States export market more than it will the Latin-American export market. To allow for the obvious possibility that the degree of substitution among manufactured exports is substantially greater than the degree of substitution between manufactured exports and raw-material exports, I have made estimates based on the second assumption, that there is no substitutability at all between manufactured and primary exports. Under this assumption the United States, the United Kingdom, Scandinavia, France and Italy, Benelux, Germany and Austria, and Switzerland were regarded as exporters of manufactures. In estimating $\bar{p}$ under the second assumption, it was assumed that a rise in the export price level of any of the sources just named would bring about increases of equal proportions in the exports of the other manufacturing countries but would lead to no change at all in the exports of sources producing primary products. The first assumption thus estimates $\bar{p}$ for any export source as the value-weighted average of the export prices of all other sources, while the second assumption estimates $\bar{p}$ for any source of manufactured exports as the value-weighted average of the export prices of other sources of manufactured exports. I made no assumption comparable to the second for the primary product sources because I felt that only a few of the main primary exports of any one of these sources (Canada, Latin America, outer sterling area, and rest of the world) had important close substitutes among the main exports of the other areas in the group. The estimated elasticities are shown in Table 5.

I do not place a high degree of confidence in the individual estimates given in Table 5 for particular elasticities of demand for exports. I feel, however, that the results, taken as a whole, suggest that the price changes associated with the devaluations of

Table 5

Estimated Elasticities of Demand for Exports

Export source	*Estimated elasticity of demand for exports*	
	on first assumption	*on second assumption*
United States	−2.8	−1.1
Canada	−1.1	—
Latin America	−0.5	—
Outer sterling area	−1.5	—
United Kingdom	−0.8	−1.0
Scandinavia	−1.2	−1.4
France and Italy	−3.4	17.6
Benelux	−2.1	−3.2
Germany and Austria	−3.5	−4.9
Switzerland	−0.7	−0.2
Rest of the world	1.5	—

1949 had a substantial effect on trade patterns and that the price elasticities of export demand which produced this effect were significantly higher than earlier studies would lead one to believe.

A word of explanation is perhaps in order on the two positive price-elasticity estimates. When the second assumption was applied in calculating $\bar{p}$ for France and Italy, the result indicated that the dollar price level of French–Italian exports had risen by less than 1 per cent relative to the average export price level of other manufacturing countries. When this small rise was called upon to explain a net substitution of 15 per cent in favor of French–Italian exports, a large positive estimated price elasticity emerged. An error of only 1 per cent either in the French–Italian price index or in the estimated $\bar{p}$ could have created this result.

The positive price elasticity estimated for the rest of the world came from the attempt to explain an 8 per cent substitution in favor of that area's exports by a 5 per cent rise in the relative price of those exports. The estimate of the dollar price index of rest-of-the-world exports may be at fault. Unlike the other dollar price indexes used, this index was almost a pure guess, based on the fact that some of the neglected countries had followed the sterling area in devaluing, while others had not.

Related Research

Further evidence obtained from many different studies lends support to the conclusions that one would derive from the material already presented. Tinbergen (1946), estimating substitution elasticities between a given country's exports and those of the rest of the world, obtained estimates ranging typically between −1.5 and −2.5. These figures translate into 'typical' elasticities of export demand between −1 and −2. Kubinski (1950) estimated elasticities of substitution in Britain between different sources of similar imports. His mean elasticity of substitution was −4.5, his median −2.5. Translating once again into elasticities of export demand, we find that a typical elasticity of British demand for the exports of a typical supplying source lies in, or more probably above, the range −1.25 to −2.75. The study by Adler, Schlesinger, and VanWesterborg (1952) suggests that the United States demand elasticity for exports of finished manufactures from the United Kingdom is about −5.0, and from the Marshall Plan countries about −2.5.

Horner (1952) estimated elasticities of demand for Australia's exports of wool (−2.2), wheat (−5.9), and butter (−3.2), using a method deserving of much more extensive application. Recognizing that the demand for Australia's exports of a commodity is the difference between the rest of the world's demand and the supply of that commodity, he estimated separately the elasticities of demand and supply in the rest of the world. He then combined them appropriately with an adjustment for transport costs and tariffs, to obtain the estimates given above.

DeVries (1951) has estimated elasticities of United States import demand on the basis of the judgments of commodity experts asked by the United States Tariff Commission to estimate the effects of a 50 per cent increase and a 50 per cent decrease in the tariff rates on particular commodities. While these estimates undoubtedly vary greatly in quality, they do have the advantage of allowing somewhat more scope for long-run adjustments in the supply of import substitutes than is given by traditional time-series analysis. DeVries' weighted average elasticity of United States import demand for commodities subject to tariff is about −2.5; the median is about −2.0.

Conclusions

These pieces of evidence, taken together, point strongly to the conclusion that the price mechanism works powerfully and pervasively in international trade. I would hazard the rule-of-thumb judgment that in the relatively short run the elasticity of import demand for a typical country lies in or above the range −0.5 to −1.0, while its elasticity of demand for exports is probably near or above −2.

One should be wary about drawing long-range policy conclusions from these judgments, however. An elasticity of export demand of −2 implies that the country in question has substantial monopoly power; in particular, it implies that the country would, in the absence of retaliation, benefit from a 100 per cent export tax. I doubt that any country possesses this degree of monopoly power in the long run. To illustrate, take as an example Brazil, which produces roughly half the world's coffee. Assume that the elasticity of consumer demand for coffee is −0.5, while the elasticity of other producers' supply is 1.0. A 1 per cent rise in the price of coffee would entail a decrease in world demand of 0.5 per cent and an increase in non-Brazilian supply equal to 0.5 per cent of total world demand. Demand for Brazilian coffee would fall by 1 per cent of total world demand or by 2 per cent of Brazil's supply. Thus, in this example, the elasticity of world demand for Brazil's exports of coffee is −2. Actually, Brazil's experience in attempting to influence coffee prices suggests that she faces an even higher elasticity than this.

It is my judgment that there are few instances in which a country has as much monopoly power in the world market for a commodity as Brazil has for coffee. And where such instances exist, they are likely to cover only a small fraction of the country's total exports. I accordingly feel quite confident that long-run elasticities of export demand are substantially greater than 2, though I should hesitate to guess at a 'typical' magnitude. For this we need an accumulation of many more bits and pieces of evidence.

References

ADLER, J. H., SCHLESINGER, E. R., and VANWESTERBORG, E. (1952), *The Pattern of United States Import Trade since 1923*, Federal Reserve Bank of New York.

DEVRIES, B. A. (1951), 'Price elasticities of demand for individual commodities imported into the United States', *International Monetary Fund Staff Papers*, vol. 1, pp. 397–419.

HARBERGER, A. C. (1953), 'A structural approach to the problem of import demand', *American Economic Review*, vol. 43, pp. 148–59.

HORNER, F. B. (1952), 'Elasticity of demand for the exports of a single country', *Review of Economics and Statistics*, vol. 34, pp. 326–42.

KUBINSKI, Z. (1950), 'The elasticity of substitution between sources of British imports', *Yorkshire Bulletin of Economic and Social Research*, vol. 2, pp. 17–29.

MACDOUGALL, G. D. A. (1951), 'British and American exports: a study suggested by the theory of comparative costs', *Economic Journal*, vol. 41, pp. 697–724.

MACDOUGALL, G. D. A. (1952), 'British and American exports: a study suggested by the theory of comparative costs', *Economic Journal*, vol. 42, pp. 487–521.

MORGAN, D. J., and CORLETT, W. J. (1951), 'The influence of price in international trade: a study in method', *Journal of the Royal Statistical Society*, vol. 114, pp. 307–52.

MORRISSETT, I. (1953), 'Some recent uses of elasticity of substitution – a survey', *Econometrica*, vol. 21, pp. 41–62.

NEISSER, H., and MODIGLIANI, F. (1953), *National Income and International Trade*, University of Illinois Press.

ORCUTT, G. H. (1950), 'Measurement of price elasticities in international trade', *Review of Economics and Statistics*, vol. 32, pp. 117–32.

POLAK, J. J. (1950), 'Note on the measurement of elasticity of substitution in international trade', *Review of Economics and Statistics*, vol. 32, pp. 16–20.

POLAK, J. J. (1953), *An International Economic System*, University of Chicago Press.

TINBERGEN, J. (1946), 'Some measurements of elasticity of substitution', *Review of Economics and Statistics*, vol. 28, pp. 109–16.

ZELDER, R. E. (1955), *The Elasticity of Demand for Exports*, unpublished doctoral dissertation, University of Chicago.

8 B. Balassa

The Purchasing-power Parity Doctrine: a Reappraisal

B. Balassa (1964), 'The purchasing-power parity doctrine: a reappraisal', *Journal of Political Economy*, vol. 72, pp. 584–96.

I

The purchasing-power parity doctrine has had its ebbs and flows over the years. Interest in the doctrine arose whenever existing exchange rates were considered unrealistic and the search began for the elusive concept of equilibrium rates. It was first invoked – although in somewhat ambiguous terms – in the period of the Napoleonic wars (see Haberler, 1961, pp. 46–7), it received its christening at the hands of Gustav Cassel during World War I (Cassel, 1918), and it was resurrected after World War II (Hansen, 1948). It has also had its critics, among others Taussig (1927) after World War I and Haberler (1945) after World War II, but it has managed to survive nevertheless.

In recent years, new efforts have been made to clothe the purchasing-power parity doctrine in the garments of respectability, and a proposal has also been put forward to use this doctrine as a guide in establishing equilibrium exchange rates (Yeager, 1958; Houthakker, 1962). At the same time, new statistical material has become available that has a bearing on the relationship between purchasing-power parities and exchange rates. It may be of interest, therefore, to re-examine the claims put in for the validity of the purchasing-power parity doctrine.

The purchasing-power parity doctrine means different things to different people. In the following, I shall deal with two versions of this theory that can be appropriately called the 'absolute' and the 'relative' interpretation of the doctrine. According to the first version, purchasing-power parities calculated as a ratio of consumer goods prices for any pair of countries would tend to approximate the equilibrium rates of exchange. In turn, the relative interpretation of the doctrine asserts that, in comparison to a period when equilibrium rates prevailed, changes in relative prices would indicate the necessary adjustments in exchange rates.

II

Although his name has come to be associated with the relative interpretation of the purchasing-power parity doctrine, Cassel also formulated the absolute hypothesis by arguing that 'the rate of exchange between two countries will be determined by the quotient between the general levels of prices in the two countries'. (Cassel, 1916). Further, 'at every moment the real parity between two countries is represented by (the) quotient between the purchasing power of money in one country and the other. I propose to call this parity "*the purchasing power parity*". As long as anything like free movement of merchandise and a somewhat comprehensive trade between two countries takes place, the actual rate of exchange cannot deviate very much from this purchasing power parity' (Cassel, 1918, p. 413; Cassel, 1921, p. 36; Cassel, 1928, pp. 8–9).

Most recently, the absolute interpretation of the purchasing-power parity doctrine has been invoked by Hendrik Houthakker, who has expressed the opinion that the relative price levels of consumer goods provide an indication of the over- or under-valuation of individual currencies. Relying on purchasing-power parity calculations made by the German Statistical Office, Houthakker concludes that 'in terms of purchasing power the dollar is now (in March, 1962) worth 22 cents less than it is at the official exchange rate of 4 German marks to the dollar. This implies a very substantial overvaluation of the dollar which can certainly not be wholly attributed to statistical defects of the calculation.' (Houthakker, 1962, p. 297.) Houthakker also argues that, while the U.S. dollar appears to be overvalued as compared to the German mark, the mark itself is overvalued, and the Austrian shilling, the Danish crown, and especially the Dutch guilder, undervalued (Houthakker, 1962, p. 298).

If we were to apply this principle also to the less developed countries, their currencies would generally appear to be greatly undervalued. According to calculations made by M. F. Millikan, in comparison to the U.S. dollar, the ratio of purchasing-power parity to the exchange rate was 0.29 for southeast Asia and 0.27 for Africa in 1950 (see Kindleberger, 1958, pp. 2–3). Now, given that Houthakker proposes to correct the alleged overvaluation of the U.S. dollar by devaluation, the corresponding adjustment would entail a substantial appreciation of the currencies of the developing countries. Since this recommendation can hardly be taken seriously, the question arises what meaning can be attached to an international comparison of exchange rates and purchasing-power parities.

This question can be answered at various levels of abstraction. First, let us amend the traditional two-country, two-commodity model of international trade theory by introducing a non-traded good (services). Assume further, the existence of one limiting factor, labor, and constant input coefficients *à la* Ricardo, when one of the countries has an absolute advantage in the production of all commodities but this advantage is greater in regard to traded goods (agricultural and manufacturing products) than for the non-traded commodity (services). Under the assumption of constant marginal rates of transformation, the relative price of the non-traded commodity will thus be higher in the country with higher productivity levels than in the other.

Since the prices of traded goods are equalized in the two countries through international exchange, this proposition can also be formulated in terms of absolute prices, for instance, by expressing prices in terms of wage units. Correspondingly, whether or not we use the first or the second country's consumption patterns as weights, the purchasing-power parity between the currencies of the two countries, defined as the ratio of the price level of the second country to that of the first, will be less than the equilibrium rate of exchange, expressed in terms of the currency of the first country. Thus,

$$\frac{\Sigma p_2 q_1}{\Sigma p_1 q_1} < r_1^2, \quad \text{and} \quad \frac{\Sigma p_2 q_2}{\Sigma p_1 q_2} < r_1^2. \qquad \mathbf{1}$$

In other words, assuming that international productivity differences are greater in the production of traded goods than in the production of non-traded goods, the currency of the country with the higher productivity levels will appear to be overvalued in terms of purchasing-power parity. If *per capita* incomes are taken as representative of levels of productivity, the ratio of purchasing-power parity to the exchange rate will thus be an increasing function of income levels.

$$\frac{PP_1^2}{r_1^2} = F(y_2^1). \qquad 2$$

In a more general model, additional factors of production are introduced and the assumption of constant coefficients in production is relaxed. Still, the relationship shown under equation 2 can be obtained if we retain the assumption that international differences in productivity are greater in the sector of traded goods than in the non-traded goods sector. Assuming that invisibles and capital movements do not enter the balance of payments, the following reasoning can be applied.

(a) In the absence of trade restrictions, the exchange rate will equate the prices of traded goods, with allowance made for transportation costs.

(b) Under the assumption that prices equal marginal costs, intercountry wage-differences in the sector of traded goods will correspond to productivity differentials, while the internal mobility of labor will tend to equalize the wages of comparable labor within each economy.

(c) With international differences in productivity being smaller in the service sector than in the production of traded goods, and wages equalized within each country, services will be relatively more expensive in countries with higher levels of productivity.

(d) Since services enter the calculation of purchasing-power parities but do not directly affect exchange rates, the purchasing-power parity between the currencies of any two countries, expressed in terms of the currency of the country with higher productivity levels, will be lower than the equilibrium rate of exchange.

(e) The greater are productivity differentials in the production of traded goods between two countries, the larger will be differences in wages and in the prices of services and, correspondingly, the greater will be the gap between purchasing-power parity and the equilibrium exchange rate.[1]

These results can now be compared to those implicit in the absolute interpretation of the purchasing-power parity doctrine. According to the latter, purchasing-power parities calculated for any pair of countries would tend toward equality with exchange rates, while the above discussion points to the existence of systematic differences between purchasing-power parities and exchange rates. Were we to express exchange rates in terms of gold and calculate purchasing-power parities by using some standard system of weighting, the absolute interpretation of the doctrine would admit the possibility of purchasing-power parities being randomly distributed around exchange rates – at least in the short run. By comparison, the arguments of the present paper lead us to expect random deviations to occur around a curve indicating the relationship between the ratios of purchasing-power parities to exchange rates, on the one hand, and *per capita* income levels, on the other.

III

In attempting to provide an empirical verification of the above proposition concerning the relationship of purchasing parities, exchange rates, and income levels, some questions regarding the calculation of purchasing-power parities need first to be considered. By reason of intercountry differences in productive endowments and tastes, in these calculations we face the well-known index-number problem. The results will depend on the choice of weights – in the present case, the final bill of goods consumed in individual countries.

If differences in tastes do not counter-balance differences in productive endowments, there will be a tendency in each country to consume commodities with lower relative prices in larger quantities. Correspondingly, the purchasing power of country two's currency will be underestimated, if country one's consumption pattern is used as weights, and overestimated if the

1. This conclusion is further strengthened if we consider that services are relatively labor-intensive, since higher wages will raise the relative price of services in countries with high levels of productivity.

Table 1

Purchasing-power Parities for Gross National Production in 1960 (National currency per U.S. dollar)

Country	*Currency unit*	*Official exchange rate*	*At U.S. quantity weights*	*At national quantity weights*	*Geometric mean of cols. (3) and (4)*	*Purchasing-power parity as a percentage of exchange rate 100 × (5) ÷ (2)*	*Income per capita*
	(1)	(2)	(3)	(4)	(5)	(6)	(7)
United States	Dollar	1	1	1	1	100.0	2051
Canada	Dollar	0.996	—	—	0.921	92.8	1550
Belgium	Franc	50.0	44.4	36.5	40.2	80.4	1273
France	Franc	4.903	4.47	3.23	3.80	77.4	1152
Germany	Mark	4.171	3.86	2.73	3.25	77.9	1200
Italy	Lira	620.6	574	330	435	70.1	704
Netherlands	Florin	3.770	2.96	2.13	2.51	66.6	1166
United Kingdom	Pound	0.357	0.338	0.225	0.294	82.4	1212
Denmark	Krona	6.906	6.06	4.70	5.34	77.4	1269
Norway	Krona	7.143	6.81	4.84	5.74	80.4	1186
Sweden	Krona	5.180	—	—	4.66	90.0	1307
Japan	Yen	359.6	—	—	225	62.6	507

Source: All countries, excepting Canada, Belgium, and Norway: I. B. Kravis and Michael W. S. Davenport, 'The political arithmetic of international burden-sharing', *Journal of Political Economy*, August 1963, pp. 327–9; Canada: *Wirtschaft und Statistik* (1962), p. 445; Belgium and Norway: our estimate derived from Milton Gilbert and Associates, *Comparative National*

weights are the final bill of goods consumed in country two. This result has, in fact, been obtained in an investigation of several industrial countries. The estimates derived by the use of the two measures in a comparison of European economies and the United States are shown in columns 3 and 4 of Table 1. It is customary to use a geometric average of the two values in empirical work, although this average lacks a specific economic meaning.

Table 2

Purchasing-power Equivalents in Household and Personal Services in 1950: United States and Italy
(Lira per U.S. dollars)

	Purchasing-power equivalent		*Purchasing-power equivalent as a percentage of exchange rates*	
	U.S. quantity weights	*Italian quantity weights*	*U.S. quantity weights*	*Italian quantity weights*
Domestic services	136	136	21.8	21.8
Laundry, dry cleaning	628	628	100.5	100.5
Barber, beauty shop	176	176	28.2	28.2
Household and personal services, total	391	165	62.6	26.4

Source: Milton Gilbert and I. B. Kravis, *An International Comparison of National Products and the Purchasing Power of Currencies* (Paris: O.E.E.C. 1954), pp. 113–20.

The importance of weighing can also be seen in a comparison of the cost of household services in the United States and Italy for the year 1950, as given in a study by M. Gilbert and I. B. Kravis (Table 2). After conversion at exchange rates, domestic services in Italy appear to have cost one-fifth of the amount paid in the United States, barber and beauty shop services one-fourth, and laundry and dry cleaning about the same. At the same time, the purchasing-power equivalent for household services was 391 lira at U.S. weights and 165 at Italian weights, as against the exchange rate of 625 lira to the dollar.

Information provided by Gilbert and Kravis further provides evidence of the relatively high cost of services in countries with higher income levels that has been the cornerstone of my exposition. Ratios between purchasing-power equivalents and exchange rates for the year 1950 are shown in Table 3 with regard to groups of services for which information is available.

Taken in conjunction with available evidence on the tendency for interindustry wage equalization in individual countries (Kravis, 1956; Balassa, 1963, p. 238), the data appear to bear out my contention that international productivity differences in the service sector are considerably smaller than in the production of traded goods, raising thereby the cost of services in high-income countries. A uniform pattern is shown in comparison of the United States and Europe, and within Europe services are by and large cheaper in countries with relatively low incomes.

In Italy, the country with the lowest income levels among those considered, services cost, on the average, one-third of their cost in the United States in 1950, while for Germany and the Netherlands the corresponding figures were 38–43 per cent, and for the remaining group of countries (Belgium, Denmark, France, Norway, and the United Kingdom) 41–63 per cent.[2] At the same time, in comparison with the United States, the prices of all services were relatively lower than average prices indicated by G.N.P. (Gross National Product) deflators in the countries of western Europe, the only exception being recreation and entertainment in Belgium and Norway (Table 3).

I have suggested above that the higher level of service prices at higher income levels leads to systematic differences between purchasing-power parities and equilibrium exchange rates. To test this hypothesis, I have made a comparison for twelve industrial countries between the ratio of purchasing-power parities (calculated in terms of national currencies per U.S. dollar for the gross national product) to the rate of exchange, on the one hand, and *per capita* G.N.P., on the other. Data for 1960, shown in

2. An exact correspondence is not expected, considering that in various European countries, and especially in the United Kingdom, the postwar rationing and price controls still affected prices in 1950.

Table 3

Purchasing-power Equivalents for Services as a Percentage of Exchange Rates, 1950*

	Belgium	*Denmark*	*France*	*Germany*	*Italy*	*Netherlands*	*Norway*	*United Kingdom*
G.N.P. *per capita* ($)	956	989	831	650	418	798	929	995
Purchasing power equivalents:								
household and personal services	60.8	41.7	51.7	45.1	40.6	36.7	48.5	46.1
public transport services	53.2	63.4	47.7	51.3	42.4	42.8	64.0	43.9
recreation and entertainment	90.2	66.0	70.0	51.5	46.7	55.4	84.3	56.4
health	64.9	44.0	53.1	42.5	50.4	42.8	40.2	59.5
education	65.5	65.4	41.1	62.4	33.0	50.9	54.2	59.5
government administrative personnel	47.2	45.9	42.9	34.4	18.7	27.3	37.3	27.7
defense personnel	26.9	19.8	36.0	(20.0)	19.7	16.3	20.6	32.7
services, total	63.4	52.1	51.3	43.4	33.5	38.3	51.3	47.2
gross national product	81.3	71.1	75.4	71.7	69.6	61.2	68.2	70.1

* The original data are expressed in national currencies per U.S. dollar. All calculations have been made at U.S. and given-country weights, and a geometrical average of the results has been taken.

Source: Milton Gilbert and Associates, *Comparative National Products and Price Levels* (Paris: O.E.E.C., 1960), pp. 30, 75–80.

Table 1 and Figure 1, indicate a positive correlation between the two variables. The correlation coefficient is 0.92, statistically significant at the 2 per cent level.

The empirical results provide evidence for the validity of my proposition regarding the relationship between purchasing-power parities, exchange rates, and *per capita* income levels. And whereas the application of the purchasing-power parity doctrine is seen to give incorrect answers for determining equilibrium exchange rates, the observed relationship between purchasing-power parities and exchange rates may provide some clue as to the overvaluation or undervaluation of a currency. A consideration of information given in Table 4 points to the overvaluation of the French franc in 1955, for example, and indeed two devaluations followed in rapid succession in 1957 and 1958. Comparisons of purchasing-power parities and exchange rates will not, however, disclose under- and overvaluations of a few percentage points; hence the magnitude of the required revaluation.

IV

While the absolute interpretation of the purchasing-power parity doctrine appears unsatisfactory, it is a different question whether changes in the relative purchasing power of national currencies can provide an indication of the required degree of adjustment in exchange rates. Since the nineteenth century this proposition has been indorsed by several writers, who have suggested that comparisons be made with some previous period taken as a norm.

This formulation of the purchasing-power parity doctrine is independent of its absolute version and can be stated as a comparative-statics proposition: If we compare two equilibrium positions which differ only in regard to the absolute price levels prevailing in the two countries under consideration, the change in the equilibrium exchange rate will equal the change in the ratio of price levels between the two positions. In claiming that this proposition is applicable to the real world, the proponents of this doctrine emphasize the importance of the monetary factors and see the line of causation running from the money supply to prices and to exchange rates; at the same time, they neglect changes in income levels and in supply and demand relationships.

The relative interpretation of the purchasing-power parity doctrine has been advocated, for example, following periods of war when the normal channels of international trade had been disrupted. But even though monetary factors might have been of great importance during such periods, the occurrence of struc-

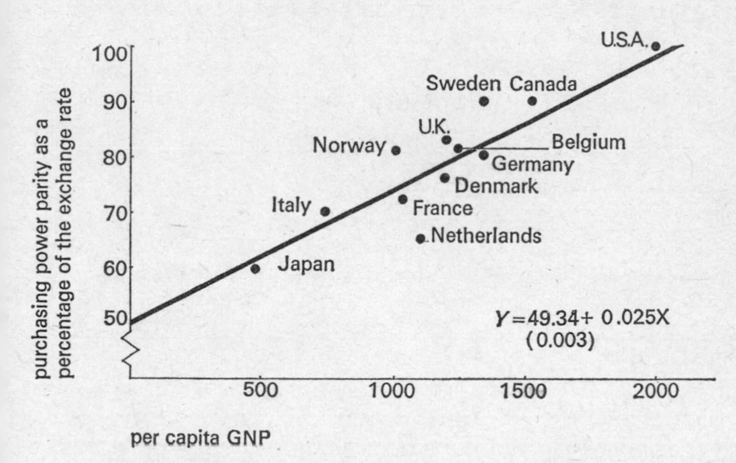

Figure 1 A comparison between the ratio of purchasing-power parities for twelve industrial countries in 1960

tural changes can hardly be excluded. Thus, especially in the case of moderate inflation, changes in demand and supply relations will give rise to errors in applying the purchasing-power parity doctrine for determining the new exchange rates.

Among the proponents of the purchasing-power parity doctrine, L. B. Yeager argues, however, that a correspondence between changes in purchasing-power parities and in exchange rates is indicated by a comparison of the interwar and post-World War II period. To support this proposition, he points to the fact that the 'actual-to-parity ratio fell inside the range 75–125 per cent for three-fourths of the [35] countries shown' (Yeager, 1958, p. 527). But Yeager's alleged demonstration is open to serious objections.

To begin with, it is not clear what degree of statistical significance this range represents. With changed emphasis, one may argue that the proposition is of little practical value since one-fourth of the cases do not even come within the 75–125 per cent range. Indeed, one could hardly rely on the relative interpretation of the purchasing-power parity doctrine for determining equilibrium exchange rates, if this were off the mark by over 25 per cent in one-fourth of the cases considered.

Table 4

Purchasing-power Parities for G.N.P. in 1955

(Units of national currency per U.S. dollar)

Country	*Currency unit*	*Official exchange rate*	*Purchasing-power parities*	
			U.S. quantity weights	*European quantity weights*
Belgium	Franc	50.2	44.9	37.6
France	Franc	350	394	287
Germany	Mark	4.20	3.51	2.54
Italy	Lira	625	605	337
United Kingdom	Pound	0.358	0.319	0.272
Netherlands	Florin	3.80	293	2.17
Denmark	Krona	6.91	5.94	4.57
Norway	Krona	7.14	6.58	4.78

Source: Milton Gilbert and Associates, *Comparative National Products and Price Levels* (Paris: O.E.E.C., 1958), p. 30.

At the same time, the calculated range will depend on the standard of comparison chosen. Yeager takes the United States as this standard, but there is no *a priori* reason for this choice. In fact, greater interest attaches to comparisons between countries that have a substantial amount of trade with each other, such as Belgium and the Netherlands. If the Netherlands is taken as the standard, the actual-to-parity ratio is calculated as 156.2 for Belgium – a result which can hardly be said to support Yeager's thesis.

It should further be noted that the cause-and-effect relationship between exchange rates and purchasing-power parities is not clear, since the postwar year chosen (1957) followed one or more devaluations in almost all of the countries under consideration. Actually, the problem of causation will arise in every practical instance where international commerce has not come to a standstill.

Yeager suggests that 'the causation ... run[s] much more strongly from price levels to exchange rates than the other way around' (Yeager, 1958, p. 522), and uses two arguments to support his proposition: that trade flows affect domestic prices only slightly, and that movements in the general price level are determined basically by changes in the money supply:

A minor reason is that, for many commodities, changes in the quantity shipped internationally amount to only a small fraction of the quantities appearing on markets at home and abroad, so that changes in trade flows may affect domestic prices only slightly. (Yeager, 1958, p. 520.)

The main reason for doubting that causation runs predominantly from exchange rates to prices is that the buying power of a country's currency is, above all else, determined by the quantity of money and the demand for cash balances. In the absence of changes in the money supply, exchange rates could hardly govern a country's whole general price level. (Yeager, 1958, p. 521.)

The first argument appears to reject marginal-cost pricing and to deny the possibility of commodity arbitrage that would lead to an international equalization of the prices of traded goods. There is a curious asymmetry here: while Yeager contends that high elasticities will bring about immediate adjustments in the case of international price differences due to differing rates of domestic inflation, the adjustment mechanism is assumed to be inoperative if the initial change was in the rate of exchange (Yeager, 1958, pp. 521 ff.).

The assumption that constancy of the money supply would check 'foreign-induced' inflation implies the acceptance of a simplified version of the quantity theory of money and appears to exclude the possibility of demand, as well as cost-push, inflation. But both of these types of inflation have relevance after a devaluation has taken place, since under conditions of full employment increased demand for the country's exports as well as the higher costs of imports is bound to lead to domestic price increases (Burtle and Liege, 1949; Fleming, 1958). Should the authorities be unwilling to increase the money supply, there is no reason to assume that velocity would remain unchanged.

The problem of causation is especially relevant if an international comparison of changes in wholesale prices is made, since wholesale price indexes are often heavily weighted with traded goods. Nurkse cites the case of Czechoslovakia in the 1920s when the degree of devaluation necessary to restore balance-of-payments equilibrium had been gauged by using a wholesale price index, and the exchange adjustment undertaken proved to be insufficient because this index was heavily weighted with traded goods, the prices of which reflected changes in the world market rather than domestic inflationary pressures (Nurkse, 1944). Further, with regard to the overvaluation of the British pound in 1925, Haberler quotes Keynes's remark that Churchill's experts 'miscalculated the degree of maladjustment of money values which would result from restoring sterling to its pre-war gold parity' by comparing the British and American wholesale price indexes (Keynes, 1931, p. 248).

According to Haberler, 'the moral may seem to be that we should use an index of domestic prices (cost of living) or of costs (wages) which do not adjust so quickly and would show a disparity if equilibrium has not been reached' (Haberler, 1945, p. 49). But Haberler adds that structural changes may greatly affect the balance of payments and calls for the use of a model incorporating traded as well as non-traded goods. Such a model has been used in section II, page 193, in connection with the discussion of the absolute interpretation of purchasing-power parity theory, and this same model will not be utilized for intertemporal comparisons.

V

Assume that in one of the countries a uniform increase in productivity takes place in the sectors producing traded goods, accompanied by a smaller rise in productivity in the service sector. The marginal rate of transformation and the price ratio between the traded commodities will then remain unchanged, while the relative price of the non-traded goods will rise. Now, since the latter does not enter international trade, purchasing-power parity calculations will incorrectly indicate the need for adjustment in exchange rates.

In fact, in present-day industrial economies, productivity increases in the tertiary sector appear to be generally smaller than the rise of productivity in agriculture and manufacturing. Data derived for the 1950s (shown in Table 5) indicate, for example, that in the seven major industrial countries examined, productivity increases in the service sector were in all cases lower than the rise of productivity for the national economy as a whole as well as for agriculture and industry taken separately.

In a more general model, the impact on the general price level of productivity improvements in sectors producing traded goods can be examined under alternative assumptions with regard to changes in money wages. Should money wages remain unchanged and productivity improvements be translated into lower prices, the prices of traded goods will fall but service prices will not decline proportionately, restricting thereby the decrease in the general price level.

Alternatively, we may assume that money wages (and profits) rise in proportion to the growth of productivity so that prices of traded goods remain unchanged. Competition among labor groups will now raise wages in the tertiary sector where increases in productivity are smaller, and hence service prices will rise. Finally, in intermediate cases, the growth of productivity in the production of traded goods will exert a downward pressure on the prices of exports and import-competing goods and an upward pressure on the prices of services.

The purchasing-power parity doctrine could still find application if productivity increases and wage adjustments were identical in every country, and if we also assumed neutral production and consumption effects. Under these, admittedly restrictive, assumptions, parallel changes in the general price level will take place and the doctrine will give the correct answer: there is no need for adjusting the rates of exchange.

But the purchasing-power parity doctrine is asserted to provide guidance in cases where prices in individual countries do not move in a parallel fashion, and such instances also have greater

Table 5

Annual Rates of Increase of Productivity in Individual Sectors, 1950–60

(Per cent)

	U.S.[1]	*Belgium*	*Germany*	*Italy*[2]	*Netherlands*	*U.K.*	*Japan*
Agriculture	5.9	5.0	6.5	3.7	4.5	4.0	4.7
Industry	2.9[3]	3.4	5.7	3.6	3.8	2.2	4.9
Services	2.3	1.2	2.9	1.5	2.9	1.4	3.4
Private G.N.P. per man	3.1	2.5	5.3	3.6	3.5	1.9	5.8

1. 1947–60.
2. 1955–6.
3. Manufacturing only.

Source: B. Balassa, *Trade Prospects for Developing Countries* (Homewood, Ill.: Richard D. Irwin, 1964), Tables A 2.3.1.–2.6.1.

practical interest. In view of our previous discussion, changes in the general price level would be determined in the process of technological improvements and wage adjustments, neither of which can be assumed to follow the same course in every country.

Table 6

Changes in Productivity and Prices in Selected Industrial Countries, 1953–61

(Index numbers for 1961; 1953 = 100)

	Manufacturing output per man-hour (*1*)	*G.N.P. deflator* (*2*)	*Wholesale prices of manufactured goods* (*3*)	*G.N.P. deflator as percentage of wholesale price index of manufactured goods* (*4*)
United States	124	117	111	105
Belgium	143	114	105	109
France	165	103	91	113
Germany	152	128	109	117
Italy	167	115	98	117
United Kingdom	122	127	116	109
Japan	197	115	91	126

Source: B. Balassa, 'Recent Developments in the Competitiveness of American Industry and Prospects for the Future', *Factors Affecting the United States Balance of Payments* (U.S. Congress Joint Economic Committee (Washington, 1962)), p. 38; W. Salant and Associates, *The United States Balance of Payments in 1968* (Washington: Brookings Institute, 1963), p. 73.

Correspondingly, an intercountry comparison of changes in the general price level cannot be used to indicate the need for modifications in exchange rate parities. At the same time, given the dual effect of productivity changes referred to above, we would expect productivity improvements in the sectors producing traded goods to be positively correlated with the ratio of the general price index to the index of the prices of traded goods.

To test this hypothesis, for seven major industrial countries I have compared changes shown by the index of output per man-hour in manufacturing, on the one hand, and the ratio between the G.N.P. deflator and the wholesale price index of manufac-

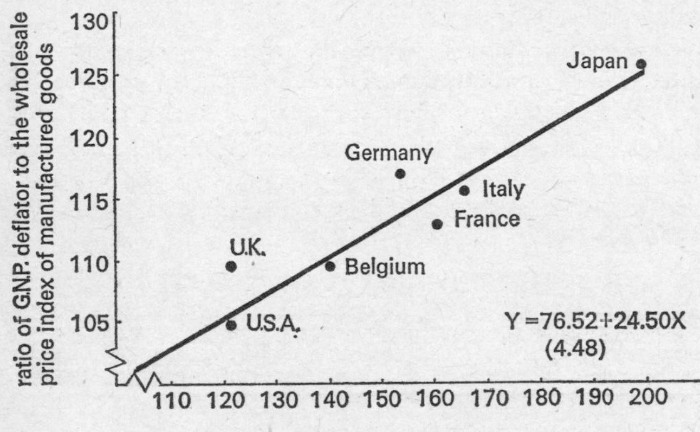

Figure 2 A comparison of changes shown by the index of output per man-hour in manufacturing and the ratio between the G.N.P. deflator and the wholesale price index of manufactured products, in seven industrial countries

tured products, on the other. Although traded goods include agricultural products too, I have chosen to restrict the investigation to the manufacturing sector, partly because productivity data for this sector are generally more reliable, and partly because agricultural prices are affected to a considerable extent by governmental policies. At any rate, the countries under consideration export chiefly manufactured goods. The results are shown in Table 6 and Figure 2, indicating a positive correlation between the growth of manufacturing productivity and the ratio of the G.N.P. deflator to the price index for manufactured goods. (The correlation coefficient is 0.91, statistically significant at the 5 per cent level.)

These results provide evidence for the importance of non-monetary factors in the process of price determination. In the presence of disparate changes in productivity and prices in the sectors of traded and non-traded goods, the reliance on general price indexes for deciding on exchange-rate adjustments appears to be misplaced. At the same time, for reasons mentioned above, price indexes heavily weighted with internationally traded goods will not appropriately indicate the need for modifications in exchange rates either.

This conclusion should not be construed as a denial of the sensitiveness of trade flows to changes in the prices of individual commodities. It appears likely, however, that more useful results can be achieved if, instead of attempting to rely on aggregate indexes, more attention is paid to the behavior of sectoral indexes with appropriate disaggregation.[3]

VI

While this paper has highlighted some of the inadequacies of the absolute and the relative versions of purchasing-power parity theory, its main contribution is a positive one: the emphasis on the need for amending the familiar models of international trade by giving explicit consideration to non-traded goods. The introduction of non-traded goods can enhance the realism of these models and may also offer new theoretical insights.

In the present instance I have shown that, by incorporating non-traded goods in the model, the existence of a systematic relationship between purchasing-power parities and exchange rates is indicated in intercountry as well as in intertemporal comparisons. These relationships can be of some help in judging the overvaluation or undervaluation of a currency, and changes in the degree of over-(under-)valuation, although they cannot indicate the magnitude of the required revaluation.

The observed relationship between purchasing-power parities and exchange rates also provides guidance for the international comparison of national incomes and living standards. In general, the use of exchange rates as conversion ratios will overstate the G.N.P. of high-income countries and understate that of low-income countries, with the degree of overstatement increasing as income levels rise (Balassa, 1961). Further, the conclusions

3. For a discussion of the effects of price changes on trade in manufactured goods, see Balassa (1962).

derived with respect to changes over time can be useful in interpreting disparate movements in the components of the G.N.P. deflators and the cost-of-living index as well as in projecting future developments.

Note, however, that, while in the above discussion we have assumed that services cannot be traded, this assumption will have to be modified if account is taken of international transactions in services. Tourism will affect service prices in the individual countries, and it will tend to reduce international disparities in these prices. But even if the cost of transportation involved in foreign travel is disregarded, tourism will not equalize service prices as long as it is restricted to periods of limited length, for example, those of annual vacations. An international equalization of service prices will, then, require the migration of labor in response to intercountry differences in living costs.

References

BALASSA, B. (1961), 'Patterns of industrial growth: comment', *American Economic Review*, June, pp. 394–7.

BALASSA, B. (1962), 'Recent developments in the competitiveness of American industry and prospects for the future', *Factors Affecting the United States Balance of Payments*, U.S. Congress Joint Economic Committee, Washington, pp. 27–64.

BALASSA, B. (1963), 'An empirical demonstration of classical comparative cost theory', *Review of Economics and Statistics*, August.

BURTLE, J. L., and LIEGE, W. (1949), 'Devaluation and the cost-of-living in the United Kingdom', *Review of Economic Studies*, vol. 1, pp. 1–28.

CASSEL, G. (1916), 'The present situation of the foreign exchanges', *Economic Journal*, March.

CASSEL, G. (1918), 'Abnormal deviations in international exchanges', *Economic Journal*, September.

CASSEL, G. (1921), *The World's Monetary Problems*, Constable.

CASSEL, G. (1928), 'The international movements of capital', *Foreign Investments, Lectures on the Harris Foundation*, Chicago University Press.

FLEMING, J. M. (1958), 'Exchange depreciation, financial policy, and the domestic price level', *International Monetary Fund Staff Papers*, April, pp. 288–322.

HABERLER, G. (1945), 'The choice of exchange rates after the war', *American Economic Review*, June.

HABERLER, G. (1961), 'A survey of international trade theory', *Special Papers in International Economics*, vol. 1.

HANSEN, A. H. (1948), 'A note on fundamental disequilibrium', in S. E. Harris, ed., *Foreign Economic Policy for the United States*, Cambridge, Mass.

HOUTHAKKER, H. S. (1962), 'Exchange rate adjustment', *Factors Affecting the United States Balance of Payments*, U.S. Congress Joint Economic Committee, Washington, pp. 287–304.

KEYNES, J. M. (1931), 'The economic consequences of Mr Churchill', *Essays in Persuasion*, Norton.

KINDLEBERGER, C. P. (1958), *Economic Development*, McGraw-Hill, New York.

KRAVIS, I. B. (1956), 'Wages and foreign trade', *Review of Economics and Statistics*, February, pp. 14–30.

NURKSE, R. (1944), *International Currency Experience*, League of Nations, Geneva, ch. 5.

TAUSSIG, F. W. (1927), *International Trade*, New York, ch. 26.

YEAGER, L. B. (1958), 'A rehabilitation of purchasing-power parity *Journal of Political Economy*, December, pp. 516–30.

9 W. Fellner

On Limited Exchange-rate Flexibility

W. Fellner (1966), 'On limited exchange-rate flexibility', in W. Fellner *et al.*, *Maintaining and Restoring Balance in International Payments*, Princeton University Press, pp. 111–22.

Recently twenty-seven economists signed a statement advocating two proposals. The first of these relates to so-called margin flexibility, that is, to an appreciable widening of the band around the parity levels of individual currencies. According to this proposal the upper support points, as defined in relation to gold, would be raised to 4 per cent or 5 per cent above parity levels and the lower support points reduced to 4 per cent or 5 per cent below parity. The second proposal would give each country the right to change, by unilateral decision, the parity level of its currency by no more than 1 per cent to 2 per cent per year. I shall refer to the first proposal as the *band* proposal and to the second as the *shiftable-parity* proposal.

The signers of the statement are listed below.[1] It should be added that economists known to be in strong support of the present system of adjustable pegs were not asked whether they wished to sign. Furthermore, about six academic colleagues who *were* asked declined to sign. Of these, two declined with the remark that they would have signed if the shiftable-parity proposal had not been included along with the band proposal. Two signers also commented that they would have preferred the statement without the shiftable-parity feature.

Only a very small proportion of the economists who are

1. The list includes the following economists from eight countries: Wilhelm Bauer, Richard E. Caves, Alan C. L. Day, William Fellner, Milton Friedman, Herbert Giersch, Gottfried Haberler, L. Albert Hahn, George N. Halm, Alvin H. Hansen, Arnold C. Harberger, Hendrik C. Houthakker, Bertrand de Jouvenel, Harry G. Johnson, Friedrich A. Lutz, Fritz Machlup, James E. Meade, Allan H. Meltzer, Lloyd A. Metzler, Fritz W. Meyer, Tibor Scitovsky, Arthur Smithies, Egon Sohmen, Ingvar Svennilson, Jan Tinbergen, Jaroslav Vanek, and Michel Woitrin.

believed to be in favor of these proposals were asked for their signatures. The sponsors – Professors Haberler, Machlup, Scitovsky, and myself – did not wish to get beyond the range of twenty-five to thirty signatories, since collecting the signatures of most experts who support the two proposals would have been an undertaking of a very different order, and once the number of signers exceeds twenty-five by an appreciable margin, readers get the impression that the sponsors were aiming for comprehensive coverage. It is worth mentioning also that, while it was clear to us from the outset that many who subsequently turned out to be signers had for some time been sympathetic to these proposals, the reaction of a good many colleagues whom we approached seemed quite unpredictable to us. The statement follows here.

The discussion of possible reform of the present system of international payments has been largely focused on the problem of 'international liquidity'. More specifically expressed, the discussion has been focused on the temporary financing of imbalances through providing additional reserves and borrowing facilities and on promoting the adjustment process through monetary and fiscal policies. The no less important issue of exchange rates has received little attention in official circles. The fact that, as the present statement shows, many professional economists can agree on a minimum program in that respect, would seem to demonstrate that there is a promising opportunity here for improving the international payments system.

Whatever the system of reserves, we believe that more exchange-rate flexibility is needed than exists under the I.M.F. [International Monetary Fund] rules now in effect. It has proved impossible, under the present rules, for many countries to maintain stable prices and high employment levels and at the same time to avoid the imposition of more and more controls on international payments. To achieve these domestic economic goals simultaneously with equilibrium in external payments requires more leeway for variations in exchange rates than exists now. This is why we favor two modifications in the I.M.F. rules.

Our first proposal is to widen the limits within which countries are obliged to keep the gold value of their currencies. This value should be allowed to vary up to four or five per cent on either side of parity, instead of the present one per cent. A spread of eight or ten per cent would thus be provided between the upper and the lower support points. This first reform would render possible day-to-day fluctuations in exchange rates sufficient to absorb many balance-of-payments disturbances without disrupting foreign trade and investment. The proposed system need not be applied to every country without exception; some could be permitted to peg their currency to another country's, or groups of countries could agree to keep the currencies of members of the group fixed in relation to one another.

The second modification we advocate is to allow countries unilaterally to change the par value of their currencies by no more than one or two per cent of the previous year's par value. This seems at first more restrictive than present rules, which allow changes up to ten per cent without prior approval by the I.M.F.; yet since the present permissible changes are based not on last year's but on the originally announced par values which in many cases are now hopelessly out-of-date, our proposal is, in effect, more permissive.

Our two proposals – to widen the range between the support points and to allow gradual adjustments of par values – do not go beyond what most proponents of the Bretton Woods Agreements had in mind. The need for this limited flexibility of exchange rates was generally recognized at the time, but the provisions that were formulated have proved impractical and therefore have not been used by countries even when their exchange rates had become clearly unrealistic.

The undersigned now join in advocating these reforms. While we differ among ourselves on what each of us considers the ideal set of rules and institutions, all of us hold that the alterations we propose would constitute a great improvement over the present situation. We submit that the increased flexibility of exchange rates under these rules would go far in solving the problem of adjusting future imbalances of payments. In addition, some of us believe that this flexibility might also reduce the demand for foreign reserves and would in this way contribute to solving the problem of international liquidity.

The alterations of rules which we propose are designed to deal with the long-run problem of preventing future disequilibria among the industrial countries. They are not suited for the elimination of large imbalances already in existence, nor for the problems of many less developed countries which need stronger medicine.

I will now turn to a few observations concerning the proposals. These will of course convey my personal views; other signers may or may not agree with them, or they may agree with some of my observations and disagree with others.

Let me begin by saying that it would of course be possible to define the band in relation to the dollar rate of the non-dollar currencies, instead of defining it – as does the statement – in relation to gold. This would have the consequence of reducing the flexibility of the dollar in relation to any other currency to one-half of the flexibility of any two other currencies relative to each other. Some difficulties of transition from the present system to limited flexibility might thereby be reduced; to some extent this would be achieved at the expense of the neatness of the new system but, in my opinion, without impairing its usefulness in any essential respect. Were such a variant adopted, one would presumably not want to introduce additional margins around the sterling parity of the sterling-block currencies (I mean in addition to the margin of the sterling rate around its dollar parity). However, I will here not go beyond pointing out the practical possibility of such a variant, and I will instead make the comments that follow here relate to the proposal as it was formulated in the statement.

In the Western industrialized world the ruling money-wage rates cannot be interpreted as competitive prices that would emerge in response to demand and supply in the labor market, and would tend to equate these. The bargaining process which establishes the wage rates in most of the important industries of the West is influenced by the state of markets, but not sufficiently to guarantee consistency of the bargaining results with employment objectives at levels of effective demand compatible with a stable general price level. It is true that wages actually paid depend not only on bargaining results but to some extent also on *subsequent* market developments (which may produce an upward 'drift' and may affect overtime as well as the classification of employees in plants and offices), but this introduces merely very limited responsiveness of hourly earnings to market forces, working rarely in the downward direction. Whether wage rates are compatible with economic equilibrium depends, therefore, in large part on whether other variables do or do not adjust to wages.

If in these circumstances exchange rates are held fixed, then economic systems have little leeway for adjusting to the changing requirements of external equilibrium. The line of least resistance is likely to be that described by upward adjustments in surplus countries, by means of a degree of monetary expansion that involves price inflation. Downward adjustment is difficult to impose upon countries unless it can be limited to squeezing out inflationary excess profits. If more than this is involved in a downward adjustment, then money-wage rates would have to be reduced, or the uptrend in money-wage rates should be slowed down appreciably. Balance-of-payments consultations of national representatives are unlikely to lead to this result. They are more likely to lead to some degree of coordination of national trends around an inflationary world trend and, in view of the incompleteness of such coordination, to recurrent use of discriminatory measures, including measures of exchange control.

Exchange-rate flexibility in free markets would introduce leeway which money costs do not give us. The exchange rates of deficit countries would tend to decline, relative to those of surplus countries, sufficiently to alter the relationship between exports and imports to an appreciable extent, unless offsetting movements of private capital should keep the rates nearly unchanged. Offsets of this kind will develop in cases where the disturbance is confidently expected to be of very short duration. Aside from such offsetting capital movements, the lowering of exchange rates in deficit countries relative to surplus-country rates would generate a powerful equilibrating tendency through the flow of goods and services. The elasticity assumptions implied in this statement seem safe assumptions in the Western context. The effect of speculative capital movements would (as was already said) be stabilizing at nearly the initial level of the exchange rates if a return to these levels were expected *very soon*; if a *slower* return to the initial rates were expected, then, during the period in question, speculative capital movements would presumably become stabilizing at somewhat lower deficit-country rates, namely, at rates that induce these capital movements in view of the expected gradual appreciation of the exchange rate *and* in view of the interest rates in deficit- and in surplus-countries. Expectation of a *long-run* ('permanent') lowering of the exchange rates of the deficit countries would tend to lead to stabilizing capital flows at the 'low' rates which are expected to continue, where again the proviso must be added that the question whether a given deviation from the assumed 'correct' exchange rates does or does not actually result in stabilizing capital flows depends on international interest-rate differentials.

In general, unless the market considerably overestimates the exchange-rate movements which would take place in the absence of speculation – unless this overestimate is such that feasible interest-rate policies cannot suppress its consequences – the role of speculation would be to prevent appreciable deviations of exchange rates from their justified levels. This is the sense in which speculation would normally have a stabilizing effect.

Those who trust the stabilizing effect of speculation completely usually favor unlimited exchange-rate flexibility with no support points and no monetary reserves. If for the time being these economists are willing to accept the band proposal, this is because in their view the proposal is a step in the right direction. Among the signers of the statement here discussed, there are no doubt some adherents of unlimited flexibility. Many of us, including the present writer, consider unlimited flexibility too risky, because we feel that while in most cases speculation would probably have a stabilizing effect, serious trouble could arise in instances where, under any feasible interest-rate policy, the effect happens to be destabilizing. A moment ago, these instances were described as representing situations in which the market considerably overestimates the exchange-rate movements that would take place in the absence of speculation. But it needs to be added that as a result of long-run changes occurring while speculative forces keep the exchange rate of a deficit country 'too low', overestimates of a swing *may* prove partly self-justifying, and if this should happen, then it becomes unclear just how much importance attaches to that level of the exchange rate which, in the absence of speculation, would have been the justified level.

What I have in mind is not so much that, for the duration of the speculative wave, bearish speculators can make short-run gains, and other speculators may expect to make further gains, even if the long-run level of the exchange rate in question should be higher than the increasingly low levels *to which* this activity may depress the actual rate. This possibility does exist, though one should perhaps not attribute too much importance to it because only exceptionally do substantial markets, of which producers avail themselves on a large scale, become dominated by phenomena which are 'purely psychological' in this sense. What may deserve more serious consideration is the fact that if temporary market forces lower the exchange rate of a country below the level which initially may be considered the long-run equilibrium level, and if for a while the rate stays lower because the market does not confidently expect a return to the higher level, then the prices of imports and of import-competing goods may rise, wages may rise, and the market may turn out to have been right in not expecting a return to the initial level.

Some would say that these misgivings are far-fetched, but I am among those who feel that speculation may occasionally cause severe disturbances, or may occasionally fail to eliminate exchange-rate movements which at the initial cost levels would prove temporary but which could affect 'irreducible' money costs without much delay. This is why I believe that our institutions should play safe by *prescribing* official intervention in the currency markets at the two limits of a band. Also, groups of countries whose intragroup imports possess, in one member country or in more, a very high weight as cost components could agree to keep their exchange rates fixed *in relation to each other*. This could reduce to insignificance the danger of lasting aftereffects such as could occasionally develop from otherwise temporary movements in exchange rates.

The possibility of these lasting aftereffects has considerably influenced Professor Triffin's attitude toward exchange-rate flexibility, and probably also the attitudes of several other contributors to this volume who, so far at least, have not expressed themselves in favor of limited flexibility;[2] but it is worth noting that in Triffin's appraisal, and possibly also in that of several other present contributors, the group arrangements here considered would reduce legitimate apprehensions quite a bit.[3] Speaking for myself, my apprehensions in this regard would at any rate have been weaker than those of some of my professional colleagues, yet I too would have felt hesitant about the statement of the twenty-seven economists if it had contained no provision for group arrangements (so-called currency areas). I am sure several other signers would have shared this hesitation.

2. Six of the contributors are among the signers of the statement.

3. See R. Triffin, *Princeton Studies in International Finance*, vol. 12, Princeton University Press, 1964.

As for the width of the band proposed in the statement, this would, I think, be large enough to create the required leeway. Most of the disequilibria in Western economic relations would be taken care of by movements of exchange rates in free markets, that is to say, by movements within the bands. This would in all probability reduce the demand for international reserves. Starting from the initial parities, the maximum distance which any two currencies could move relative to each other would be twice the 4 per cent to 5 per cent provided by the suggested reform. This distance of 8 per cent to 10 per cent would develop if one currency moved to the upper limit of the band, and the other to the lower limit (as defined in relation to gold). Subsequently, the maximum conceivable change in the relation between two currencies would be *twice* 8 per cent to 10 per cent, since subsequently one currency could move from the upper to the lower limit, while the other currency could move from the lower to the upper limit. What I am saying here relates to the band proposal alone; to the shiftable-parity feature I shall return presently.

I do not know how many signers would agree with my view that *within the band* there should be no official intervention at all. The *unmanaged* limited flexibility – that is, the unmanaged 'margin flexibility' – which I have in mind has many adherents. However, other adherents of limited flexibility are prepared to *permit* official intervention even at exchange rates that have not hit one of the limits of the band. To me it seems that under such a system of managed limited flexibility it would be very difficult to devise and enforce agreements which would exclude the danger of official actions at cross-purposes.

It is sometimes objected that the possibility of exchange-rate movements would create a great deal of uncertainty and that this would have a harmful effect on international economic relations. It is quite true, of course, that the public would be aware of the likelihood that exchange rates would continue to fluctuate and that this would introduce an element of uncertainty. Yet it needs to be emphasized that practically all exporters and importers, and a large proportion of the creditors and debtors, could cover themselves in forward markets. Properly organized forward markets give an indication of the market appraisal of the future worth of each foreign currency, that is, of its worth at dates of future payment on international transactions 'now' concluded. This argument does not in itself take care of the objection completely, because reliance on forward markets would become excessively costly – or even unmanageable – for types of investment abroad which, while they are likely to give rise to a future desire to reconvert funds into the creditor's currency, will create this desire at wholly unpredictable points of time and/or with respect to amounts which are unpredictable within wide limits. But such long-term investments are not free from exchange-rate risks even under 'fixed' rates, because we all know that a 'fixed' rate may become untenable, and adjustable pegs may in fact become adjusted. Nor are, under the present system, long-term international investments free from exchange-control risks. We should take into account also the reasonably strong presumption that, if in free markets the exchange rate of a foreign country should decline appreciably, this will happen as one element of a set of changes that will include an appreciable *rise* of the foreign country's asset values and income streams *as expressed in terms of its depreciating currency*.

When the arguments so far listed are considered jointly, the objections relating to the harmful effects of the uncertainty under limited flexibility lose their force. This, it seems to me, is all the more true because if we were to become single-minded in our desire to exclude the specific kinds of uncertainty that develop from the unpredictability of future prices in various markets, then we should generally favor fixing prices at levels chosen by policy-makers. Yet one needs to be a very extreme disbeliever in the functioning of markets to find such programs generally attractive. Arbitrary price-fixing causes inefficiencies and creates significant uncertainties of a different sort.

Within the band, the kind of uncertainty characteristic of systems of limited exchange-rate flexibility would work 'both ways' – though of course not in everyone's mind with the same force in the two directions – since the rate could decline, or rise, or stay unchanged. At the lower limit the rate could only rise or stay unchanged, at the upper limit it could only decline or stay unchanged, provided the possibility of the monetary authority's being unable to live up to the support commitment *and* the possibility of the authority's making use of the shiftable-parity feature were disregarded. If the possibility of default on the support commitment were not disregarded, then some weight would attach also to that kind of uncertainty which has existed all along under 'fixed' exchange rates and 'adjustable pegs' (that is, to uncertainty whether a currency will always be able to withstand the pressures to which it may become exposed). If the possibility of such a collapse *were* disregarded, but more than negligible probability attached to the shiftable-parity feature's coming into effect, then too the uncertainty would be two-sided at the limits of the band, but in one of the two directions only a *very small* change could be expected to occur in any one year. Even the widely shared expectation that the authority would make use of the shiftable-parity feature would cause no substantial reserve movements if the interest-rate policies of the countries concerned created the differentials that would make it unrewarding to speculate on a 1 per cent to 2 per cent appreciation or depreciation of a currency in terms of gold. Countries shifting their parity according to these provisions would presumably want to distribute the change in fine gradations over any year during which a shift takes place.

As was said earlier, not all economists in favor of the band proposal find the shiftable-parity proposal to their liking. I belong among those who feel that this provision could considerably increase the *credibility* of the support commitment, because in the long run the special structural or political problems of some countries may conceivably call for shifts of greater magnitude than would be permitted by the band provision.

However, I would expect that the forces of the market would usually keep most Western currencies at some distance from the limits of the band. Achieving this result may require corrections of some of the artificially fixed rates immediately prior to the adoption of the new system.

The system would almost certainly reduce the amount of inflation which, under the present arrangements, surplus countries need to accept in order to get themselves out of a surplus position, and in order to get other countries out of a deficit position. As for deficit countries, the new system would enable them to make a freer choice in the matter of balancing their various policy objectives. It is sometimes said that in the deficit countries this would in practice lead to a more inflationary course – and generally speaking to more irresponsibility – than is now observable. In some countries the change might, of course, have such consequences. However, it seems exceedingly unlikely to me that any of the advanced industrial nations – any of the nations possessing importance on the Western economic scene – would in the longer run adopt a policy line which would result in a consistent deterioration of its currency relative to the other currencies of the Western community. After all, exchange-rate movements are very clear and loud warning signals. They are much more readily noticeable by the public than are reserve movements. It seems reasonable to expect that, in deficit countries of major importance as well as in surplus countries, clearer signals would gradually *increase* rather than reduce effective pressures toward responsible behavior.

10 R. I. McKinnon

Optimum Currency Areas

R. I. McKinnon (1963), 'Optimum currency areas', *American Economic Review*, vol. 53 , pp. 717–24.

In a recent note (4), Robert A. Mundell has suggested that little in the way of a systematic attempt has been made to define the characteristics of an area over which it is optimal to have a single currency regime, or – what is almost the same thing – a fixed exchange-rate system with guaranteed convertibility of currencies. The extensive literature on the relative merits of fixed versus flexible exchange rates has been rendered somewhat sterile by this omission. Existing national boundaries have been implicitly used to define the single currency area to which flexible external exchange rates would or would not be applied. However, when different possibilities for the grouping of nations in single currency areas exist, as in the E.E.C., or when resource mobility is low within individual countries, Mundell demonstrates that it is necessary to ask what economic characteristics determine the optimum size of the domain of a single currency. I shall develop the idea of optimality further by discussing the influence of the openness of the economy, i.e. the ratio of tradable to non-tradable goods, on the problem of reconciling external and internal balance, emphasizing the need for internal price-level stability.

'Optimum' is used here to describe a single currency area within which monetary fiscal policy and flexible external exchange rates can be used to give the best resolution of three (sometimes conflicting) objectives: (a) the maintenance of full employment; (b) the maintenance of balanced international payments; (c) the maintenance of a stable internal average price level. Objective (c) assumes that any capitalist economy requires a stable-valued liquid currency to insure efficient resource allocation. Possible conflicts between (a) and (b) have been well discussed in the literature, especially by J. E. Meade (3), but joint consideration of all three is not usually done. For example, J. L. Stein (6) explicitly assumes internal price-level stability in his discussion of optimal flexibility in the foreign exchange rate. The inclusion of objective (c) makes the problem as much a part of monetary theory as of international trade theory. The idea of optimality, then, is complex and difficult to quantify precisely, so what follows does not presume to be a logically complete model.

'The ratio of tradable to non-tradable goods' is a simplifying concept which assumes all goods can be classified into those that could enter into foreign trade and those that do not because transportation is not feasible for them. A physical description of both tradable and non-tradable goods would correspond to that given by R. F. Harrod (1, pp. 53–6). This overly sharp distinction between classes of tradable and non-tradable goods is an analytically simple way of taking transportation costs into account. By tradable goods we mean: (a) exportables, which are those goods produced domestically and, in part, exported; (b) importables, which are both produced domestically and imported. The excess of exportables produced over exports will depend directly on the amount of domestic consumption, which is likely to be small when exportable production is heavily specialized in few goods. Similarly, the excess of importables consumed over imports will depend on the specialized nature of imports. Therefore, the value of exportables produced need not be the same as the value of importables consumed, even in the case of balanced trade where the values of imports and exports are equal. However, the total value of tradable goods produced will equal the value of tradable goods consumed under balanced trade. Thus, the expression 'the ratio of tradable to non-tradable goods' can apply unambiguously to production or consumption.

I. A Simple Model

Ideally, one would like to consider a large group of countries jointly and then decide how they should be divided up into optimum currency regions. The analytical framework for such a task does not exist, so it is necessary to consider a much narrower problem and hope it throws light on the general one – besides being of interest in itself. Consider a well-defined single currency area in which we wish to determine whether or not there should be flexible exchange rates with the outside world. The outside world is itself assumed to be a single currency area which is very large.

If the area under consideration is sufficiently small, we may assume that the money prices of the tradable goods in terms of the outside currency are not influenced by domestic exchange rates or domestic currency prices.[1] In actual practice, the domestic money prices of tradable goods will be more closely tied to foreign prices through existing exchange rates than will the domestic money prices of the non-tradable goods. Under this invariance assumption, i.e. fixed foreign-currency prices, the terms of trade will necessarily be immune to domestic economic policy. Some justification is given for this in R. Hinshaw (2), even for fairly large countries. We now inquire into whether external exchange-rate flexibility or internal fiscal-monetary expansion or contraction is most suitable to maintaining external balance, i.e. shifting production and expenditures between the tradable and non-tradable goods.

Case 1

Suppose exportables X_1 and importables X_2 together make up a large percentage of the goods consumed domestically. Suppose

1. If we apply this assumption to the standard elasticities model, then both the elasticity of foreign demand for home exports η_f and the elasticity of foreign supply of home imports ϵ_f, are assumed infinite. Thus a devaluation, i.e. a rise in the foreign exchange rate k, would always improve the trade balance, B, by an amount proportional to the sum of the home elasticity of demand for imports and the home elasticity of supply of exports, η_h and ϵ_h respectively, i.e.

$$\frac{dB}{dk} = Z(\epsilon_h + \eta_h)$$

where Z is the value of exports in the case of balanced trade. The trouble with this standard model is that η_h and ϵ_h depend on the amount of domestic absorption permitted in the course of devaluation as well as the openness of the economy; and it is difficult to make explicit what internal price repercussions may occur since the body of non-tradable goods does not enter explicitly in the model. Assuming both η_f and ϵ_f to be infinite is different from the usual simplification that both supply elasticities, ϵ_f and ϵ_h, are infinite, and in my opinion is more appropriate to the consideration of most small areas.

further a flexible exchange-rate system is used to maintain external balance. The price of the non-tradable good, X_3, is kept constant in terms of the domestic currency. Exchange-rate changes will vary the domestic prices of X_1 and X_2 directly by the amount of the change. Thus, if the domestic currency is devalued 10 per cent, the domestic money prices of X_1 and X_2 will rise by 10 per cent and thus rise 10 per cent relative to X_3. The rationale of such a policy is that the production of X_1 and X_2 should increase, and the consumption of X_1 and X_2 should decline, improving the balance of payments. Direct absorption reduction from the price rise in tradable goods may have to be supplemented by deliberate contractionary monetary-fiscal policy, if unemployment is small. Substantial theoretical justification for considering relative price changes between tradable and non-tradable goods to be more important than changes in the terms of trade for external balance is given by I. F. Pearce (5).

From Case 1, it is clear that external exchange-rate fluctuations, responding to shifts in the demand for imports or exports, are not compatible with internal price-level stability for a highly open economy, objective (c). In addition, such a policy by itself may not succeed in changing relative prices or affecting the trade balance. In a highly open economy operating close to full employment, significant improvement in the trade balance will have to be accomplished via the reduction of domestic absorption, i.e. real expenditures, which is the only possible way of keeping the price of X_3 constant in terms of the domestic currency. Thus, a substantial rise in domestic taxes may be necessary whether or not there is any exchange rate change. In the extreme case where the economy is completely open, i.e. all goods produced and consumed are tradable with prices determined in the outside world, the only way the trade balance can be improved is by lowering domestic expenditures while maintaining output levels. Changes in the exchange rate will necessarily be completely offset by internal price-level repercussions with no improvement in the trade balance.

To restate the core of the argument: if we move across the spectrum from closed to open economies, flexible exchange rates become both less effective as a control device for external balance and more damaging to internal price-level stability. In fact, if one were worried about unwanted speculative movements in a floating exchange rate in Case 1 of an open economy, a policy of completely fixed exchange rates (or common currency ties with the outside world) would be optimal. Blunt monetary and fiscal weapons which evenly reduced expenditures in all sectors could be counted on to improve immediately the trade balance by releasing goods from domestic consumption in the large tradable-goods sector. Exportables previously consumed domestically would be released for export; imports would be directly curtailed, and domestically produced importables made available for substitution with imports. The reduction of expenditures in the relatively small non-tradable goods sector would initially only cause unemployment which, depending on the degree of inter-industry resource mobility and price flexibility, might eventually be translated into more production in the tradable goods sectors, and possibly improve the trade balance in the longer run. The smaller this non-tradable goods sector, the smaller will be the immediate impact of reducing expenditures on employment and total production, and thus the more efficient this policy of expenditure reduction will be as a device for improving external balance (the surplus of production over expenditures).

Any region within a common currency area faced with a loss of demand for its products will be forced to cut its expenditures through a loss of bank reserves and regional income, thus eventually correcting the trade balance. A separate currency region with fixed exchange rates may have to carry out the cutback of expenditures more through deliberate policy if bank reserve losses are effectively sterilized. In either case, the immediate reduction in real income cannot be avoided if the trade balance is to be improved.

Case 2

Suppose the production of non-tradable goods is very large compared to importables and exportables in the given area. Here the optimal currency arrangements may be to peg the domestic currency to the body of non-tradable goods, i.e. to fix the domestic currency price of X_3 and change the domestic price of the tradable goods by altering the exchange rate to improve the trade balance. A currency devaluation of 10 per cent would cause the domestic prices of X_1 and X_2 to rise by 10 per cent, but the effect on the general domestic price index is much less than in Case 1.

The desired effect of the relative price increase in the tradable goods is to stimulate the production of tradable compared to non-tradable goods and thus improve the trade balance. On the other hand, if monetary-fiscal policy is primarily relied on to reduce domestic demand to maintain external balance, unemployment will be much higher. Much of the immediate impact of the reduction of expenditures will be in the extensive non-tradable goods industries. If there are any rigidities in resource mobility, the trade balance will not improve much in the first instance. Through this policy, it may be actually necessary to achieve a fall in the domestic money prices of X_3, the numerous non-tradable goods, before sufficient expansion in the production of X_1 and X_2 can be obtained. Since a major component of X_3 will be labor services, it may be necessary to lower wage costs *vis-à-vis* the domestic money prices of X_1 and X_2, which are fixed by the inflexible external exchange-rate system. Such a policy would contain all the well-known Keynesian difficulties of getting labor to accept a cut in money wages. In addition, a successful policy of lowering prices of the numerous X_3 goods would have a large impact on the average domestic price level. Effectively, we would have permitted the tail (tradable goods) to wag the dog (non-tradable goods) in pursuing restrictive monetary and fiscal policies, with fixed exchange rates to improve the trade balance, for a small proportion of tradable goods.

Our open economy of Case 1 somewhat resembles what Stein (6) has called a 'conflict' economy. In a conflict economy, export production is sufficiently large to dominate the generation of domestic income, and thus fluctuations in both are positively correlated. Therefore, with a fixed exchange rate, periods having low income will also have unfavorable trade balances, and vice versa. For income stabilization, objective (a), Stein concludes that a floating exchange rate will be optimal for a conflict economy in a Keynesian environment. The foreign exchange rate would then rise at the top of the cycle and fall at the bottom. These exchange rate changes will stimulate domestic production and income at the bottom of the cycle and damp them at the top. But it is precisely in this case of a highly open economy that exchange-rate changes will mean great fluctuations in internal price levels – sufficiently great, that any effects of exchange-rate changes on domestic production may be small. However, there may still remain a direct policy conflict between objectives (a) and (b) in the use of a floating exchange rate. Certainly, the liquidity value of the domestic currency will depend directly on the short-run fortunes of the export commodity(ies) for a floating exchange rate.

Qualifications

The sharp distinction between tradable and non-tradable goods makes the above model analytically much easier to work with; but in practice there is a continuum of goods between the tradable and non-tradable extremes. The relaxation of this sharp distinction does not invalidate the basic idea of the openness of the economy affecting optimum economic policies; but the empirical measurement of the ratio of tradable to non-tradable goods becomes more difficult. Some kind of weighting system for determing the total production in each category might be possible. Certainly, knowledge of total imports and exports would give one a good lead in determining total production of exportables and importables. In addition, the idea of openness would have to be modified when the area was large enough to affect external prices.

II. Monetary Implications of the Model

The above discussion has been concerned with the way by which relative price changes in tradable and non-tradable goods can be brought about, and the conditions under which monetary and fiscal policy can be used efficiently to maintain external balance. Minimizing the real cost of adjustments needed to preserve external balance hinged to a large extent on minimizing necessary fluctuations in the over-all domestic price level. Thus the argument is very much concerned with the liquidity properties of money, and it is worth while to look at some of the more general monetary implications of the model. Suppose X_1, X_2, and X_3 are classes of goods rather than single goods as in the Pearce model. One of the aims of monetary policy is to set up a stable kind of money whose value in terms of a representative bundle of economic goods remains more stable than any single physical good. Indeed, it is the maintenance of this stable value which gives money its liquidity properties. The process of saving and capital accumulation in a capitalist system is greatly hampered unless a suitable *numéraire* and store of value exists. It may be still more difficult if a more desirable money is available from another source, e.g. from a larger currency area. This latter possibility is discussed below.

If the area under consideration is sufficiently large so that the body of non-tradable goods is large, then pegging the value of the domestic currency to this body of non-tradable goods is sufficient to give money liquidity value in the eyes of the inhabitants of the area in question. It may not be sufficient from the viewpoint of potential investors in the outside world. However, if the area is large, what outside investors think need not be an overriding consideration. Efficient internal capital accumulation and full employment are more important than external capital movements. If, under these circumstances, trade patterns are so unstable that substantial relative price changes in tradable and non-tradable goods are required to maintain external balance and full employment, then flexible external exchange rates may well be optimal. Resulting internal price changes will not destroy the value of the domestic currency as money.

If the area under consideration is small so that the ratio of tradable to non-tradable goods is large and the prices of the former are fairly well fixed in the outside currency, then the monetary implications of pegging the domestic currency to the non-tradable goods are less satisfactory. Such a class of non-tradable goods may not constitute a typical bundle of economic goods. The class of importables may be more representative, and a currency pegged to maintain its value in terms of importables into a small area may have a higher liquidity value than one pegged to the domestically produced non-tradable goods. However, pegging a currency of a small area to maintain its value in terms of a representative bundle of imports from a large outside area is virtually the same thing as pegging it to the outside currency. Alternatively, if we have a number of small areas which trade extensively with each other, and each pegs its currency to a representative bundle of imports, then each currency will be pegged to the others. To maintain the liquidity value of individual currencies for small areas, a fixed exchange-rate system is necessary. In addition, capital movements among small areas are more needed to promote efficient economic specialization and growth than free capital movements among large, economically developed areas. Contractual arrangements for such movements are greatly facilitated by a common currency. These arguments give us some insight into why each of the fifty states in the United States could not efficiently issue its own currency, aside from the inconvenience of money changing.

If we have a small area whose currency is not convincingly pegged in terms of the currency of a larger area, and so on this account its liquidity value is less, then domestic nationals will attempt to accumulate foreign bank balances. This will occur even though the marginal efficiency of investment in the small area is greater than that outside. As long as the functions of savings and investment are specialized, savers will attempt to accumulate cash balances in the more liquid currency. The illiquidity of domestic currency may also reflect monetary mismanagement as well as small size. In either case, we would expect small countries with weak currencies to have a tendency to finance the balance-of-payments deficits of larger countries with more desirable currencies. Thus, we have capital outflows from countries where the need for capital may be rather high and which arise from 'monetary' rather than 'real' considerations. Authorities in such countries are generally forced to maintain rather strict exchange controls unless the currency can be pegged in a convincing fashion to that of the larger area.

The above argument is relevant to the use of uncontrolled floating exchange rates. This device of maintaining external balance will only work well when the currency in question has liquidity value of the same order as that of the outside world – or the world's major currencies. This condition was approximately satisfied in the case of the Canadian dollar up to 1961. However, a floating exchange rate for the Korean won may lead to less satisfactory results. If the official rate were made equal to the black-market rate and there were no further exchange restrictions, there would still be a capital flight out of Korea into currencies with superior liquidity value, aside from problems of political stability. A floating exchange rate in itself is not a sufficient control device and does not necessarily eliminate the need for exchange controls.

By contrast, short-term capital flows among currencies of approximately equal liquidity value are less likely with a floating exchange rate because of the exchange risk and the liquidity equivalence. The possibility of carrying out different degrees of easy or tight monetary policy in different countries is greater as capital flows would not be so responsive to interest-rate differentials. Once the world is divided into a number of optimal-sized currency areas permitting efficient internal capital accumulation, the desirability of short-term capital flows among areas well developed economically becomes less great, and it becomes desirable to insulate the monetary policies of the areas from each other in order that monetary policy may be used more freely to support full employment. However, it does not make any sense to advocate a floating exchange-rate system without first defining the optimal domains of individual currencies.

Suppose we look at the problem of a depressed subregion of a common currency area. Consider the case of West Virginia where non-tradable goods are largely labor services. We have an illustration of an excess supply of non-tradable goods and an excess demand for the tradable goods because of internal price rigidities. Thus, in this sense West Virginia has an *ex ante* balance-of-payments deficit even though in an *ex post* accounting sense there is a balance-of-cash flow in and out of the state. Would the adjustment of external balance and internal full employment be facilitated if West Virginia were incorporated as a country with its own currency? To the extent that the ratio of tradable to non-tradable goods was high, such a monetary system would have little chance of success. A devaluation would be associated with a large domestic price-level increase and hence money illusion would not be much help in getting labor to accept a cut in real wages (4, p. 663). Labor unions would still continue to bargain in terms of U.S. dollars. In addition, a West Virginian currency tied to a representative bundle of non-tradable goods would not be an entirely acceptable store of value. There undoubtedly would be attempts by West Virginians to accumulate U.S. bank balances. However, if the depressed area were substantially larger, with a small proportion of production in tradable goods, a separate monetary system might be preferable as a device for maintaining full employment and external balance in the absence of factor mobility.

III. A Concluding Note on Factor Mobility

The idea of factor mobility has two distinct senses: (a) geographic factor mobility among regions; (b) factor mobility among industries. I think it is fair to say that Mundell (4) had interpretation (a) primarily in mind. His discussion of optimum currency areas in large measure is aimed toward having high geographic factor mobility within each single currency area and using flexible external exchange rates to make up for the lack of factor mobility among areas. Thus, for a given amount of geographic factor mobility in the world, this method of division into currency areas would maximize the possibility of world income and employment, subject to the constraint of maintaining external balance. Of course, the currency arrangements themselves would affect factor mobility, so the extent of factor mobility has to be considered *ex post*. Once we consider problems of factor immobility among industries, it may not be feasible to consider slicing the world into currency areas along industrial groupings rather than geographical groupings. However, from our above discussion, an optimal geographic size still exists even when we are only concerned with interindustry factor immobility.

Consider the special but perhaps common case of factor immobility between regions, each with its own specialized industries, the case where it is difficult to distinguish geographical and interindustrial immobility. Suppose there is a rise in the demand for the products of region A and a decline in the demand for goods of region B. The value of the marginal products of the potentially mobile factors of production in region B in B-type industries will fall, and rise in region A in A-type industries. Now if the possibility of developing or extending A-type industries in B is feasible, then need for factor movement between A and B is not great. The existing immobility between regions can be accepted through monetary arrangements giving both regions their own currencies, thus permitting more flexibility in enabling each area to pursue monetary and fiscal policies geared to internal stability. But if B cannot easily develop A-type industries, then factor movements to A may be the only thing that will prevent a large fall in the unit incomes of potentially mobile factors of production in B. So a policy aimed directly at overcoming the immobility of factor movements between A and B may be optimal, and perhaps the two should be joined in a common currency area. This argument becomes stronger when one considers small areas trying to develop industries in which economies of scale or indivisibilities are very great instead of efficiently moving factors elsewhere.

In a world where trade patterns are not perfectly stable, there will always be the problem of changing the world pattern of resource use among various industries to preserve external balance, full employment, and efficient resource use. In the simple model given in section I above, we considered the optimum extent of a currency area in terms of its size and structure, i.e. the ratio of tradable to non-tradable goods, in promoting shifts in resources among various industries. The model accepted the degree of internal resource immobility among industries as an obstacle to be overcome as smoothly as possible. The arguments given there for applying flexible exchange rates to optimal-sized currency areas to efficiently overcome factor immobility hold in the main, whether the degree of internal mobility among industries is large or small. Such factor immobility among industries is a painful fact of economic life which has to be overcome as efficiently as possible. However, this criterion of size and openness of a single-currency economy in facilitating interindustry production shifts certainly has to be balanced with purely geographic factor-mobility considerations in determining the optimum extent of a currency area. All the above comments assume the absence of chronic differential rates of inflation. Freely floating exchange rates are always preferable to fixed rates in the presence of substantial monetary instability of the kind associated with, say, Latin America.

References

1. R. F. Harrod, *International Economics*, 5th edition, Cambridge, 1957.
2. R. Hinshaw, 'Currency appreciation as an anti-inflationary device', *Quarterly Journal of Economics*, Nov. 1951, *65*, 447–62.
3. J. E. Meade, *The Theory of International Economic Policy*. Vol. I, *The Balance of Payments*, London, 1951.
4. R. A. Mundell, 'A theory of optimum currency areas', *American Economic Review*, vol. 51 (1961), pp. 657–64.
5. I. F. Pearce, 'The problem of the balance of payments', *International Economic Review*, Jan. 1961.
6. J. L. Stein, 'The optimum foreign exchange market', *American Economic Review* vol. 53 (1963), pp. 384–402.

Part Three **Government Policy and Balance-of-Payments Adjustment**

The essays in Part Three shift the focus of attention explicitly to *policies* for dealing with imbalances in payments. In Reading 11 Harry Johnson underlines the identity between a current account imbalance and a discrepancy between aggregate income and expenditure, and he draws his celebrated distinction between expenditure-reducing and expenditure-switching policies to improve the balance of payments. W. M. Corden elaborates on this distinction and provides a geometric formulation of the trade-off between payments restrictions and demand reduction. The third reading in this part, by Marcus Fleming, compares the effectiveness of monetary and fiscal policy in influencing aggregate demand under regimes of fixed and flexible exchange rates. Reading 14, by H. G. Johnson again, provides a lucid survey of international monetary issues, including a discussion of the extent to which varying the 'mix' between monetary and fiscal policy may influence the balance of payments.

11 H. G. Johnson

Towards a General Theory of the Balance of Payments[1]

H. G. Johnson (1958), 'Towards a general theory of the balance of payments', *International Trade and Economic Growth*, George Allen and Unwin, pp. 153–68.

The theory of the balance of payments is concerned with the economic determinants of the balance of payments, and specifically with the analysis of policies for preserving balance-of-payments equilibrium. So defined, the theory of the balance of payments is essentially a post-war development. Prior to the Keynesian Revolution, problems of international disequilibrium were discussed within the classical conceptual framework of 'the mechanism of adjustment' – the way in which the balance of payments adjusts to equilibrium under alternative systems of international monetary relations – the actions of the monetary and other policy-making authorities being subsumed in the system under consideration. While the Keynesian Revolution introduced the notion of chronic disequilibrium into the analysis of international adjustment, early Keynesian writing on the subject tended to remain within the classical framework of analysis in terms of international monetary systems – the gold standard, the inconvertible paper standard – and to be concerned with the role and adequacy in the adjustment process of automatic variations in income and employment through the foreign trade multiplier. Moreover, the applicability of the analysis to policy problems was severely restricted by its assumption of general under-employment, which implied an elastic supply of aggregate output, and allowed the domestic-currency wage or price level to be treated as *given*, independently of the balance of payments and variations in it.

1. This chapter embodies ideas developed in lecture courses at Cambridge and elsewhere; part of the argument is reproduced from an earlier paper, 'Sketch of a generalization of Keynesian balance-of-payments theory', *The Indian Journal of Economics*, vol. 37 (1956), pp. 49–56.

The pre-war approach to international monetary theory reflected the way in which balance-of-payments problems tended to appear at the time, namely as problems of international monetary adjustment. Since the war, for reasons which need not be elaborated here, the balance of payments has come to be a major problem for economic policy in many countries. Correspondingly, a new (though still Keynesian) theoretical approach to balance-of-payments theory has been emerging, an approach which is better adapted to post-war conditions than the 'foreign trade multiplier theory' and 'elasticity analysis' of the pre-war period in two major respects: it poses the problems of balance-of-payments adjustment in a way which highlights their policy implications, and it allows for conditions of full employment and inflation.

The essence of this approach, which has been termed 'the absorption approach', is to view the balance of payments as a relation between the aggregate receipts and expenditures of the economy, rather than as a relation between the country's credits and debits on international account. This approach has been implicit to an important extent in the thinking of practical policy-makers concerned with balance-of-payments problems in post-war conditions. Its main formal development is to be found in the works of Meade (1951), Tinbergen (1952), and Alexander (1952), though many others have contributed (Stuvel, 1951; Harberger, 1950; Laursen and Metzler, 1950; Harrod, 1952).[2] The purpose of this reading is to synthesize and generalize the work of these writers, and to use their approach to clarify certain aspects of the balance-of-payments policy problem.

Let us first summarize the traditional approach to balance-of-payments theory. The balance of payments must necessarily balance, when all international transactions are taken into account; for imbalance or disequilibrium to be possible, it is necessary to distinguish between 'autonomous' international

2. The terminology of 'absorption' was initiated by Alexander; Machlup's criticisms of Alexander's argument (Machlup, 1955), though valid in detail, miss the main point of Alexander's contribution, a point obscured by Alexander's own emphasis on the contrast between the 'elasticity' and the 'absorption' approaches to devaluation and his attack on the former. The later argument of this paper attempts a reconciliation of the two approaches in a broader framework of analysis.

transactions – those which are the result of the free and voluntary choices of individual transactors, within whatever restrictions are imposed by economic variables or policy on their behaviour – and 'induced' or 'accommodating' international transactions – those which are undertaken by the foreign exchange authorities to reconcile the free choices of the individual transactors – and to define the 'balance of payments' to include only autonomous transactions. To put the point another way, balance-of-payments problems presuppose the presence of an official foreign exchange authority which is prepared to operate in the foreign exchange market by the use of official reserves so as to influence the exchange rate; and 'disequilibrium' is defined by changes in the official reserves, associated with imbalance between the foreign receipts and foreign payments of residents of the country, where 'resident' is defined to include all economic units domiciled in the country *except* the foreign exchange authority.[3]

The 'balance of payments' appropriate to economic analysis may then be defined as:

$$B = R_f - P_f \qquad 1$$

where R_f represents aggregate receipts by residents from foreigners, and P_f represents aggregate payments by residents to foreigners. The difference between the two constitutes a surplus (if positive) or a deficit (if negative); a surplus is accompanied by sales of foreign currency to the exchange authority by residents or foreigners in exchange for domestic currency, and conversely a deficit is financed by sales of domestic currency by residents or foreigners to the authority in exchange for foreign currency. To remedy a deficit, some action must be taken to increase receipts from foreigners and reduce payments to foreigners, or increase receipts more than payments, or reduce payments more than receipts; and conversely with a surplus (though the rectification of a surplus is not generally regarded as a 'balance-of-payments problem').

3. Where the central bank or other monetary authority also holds the foreign exchange reserves, it is necessary for the purposes of this paper to separate its functions conceptually into two parts, and to class its transactions as monetary authority (including those with itself as exchange authority) among transactions of residents.

The 'balance of payments' can, however, be defined in another way, by making use of the fact that all payments by residents to residents are simultaneously receipts by residents from residents; in symbols $R_f = P_r$. Hence the balance of payments may be written

$$B = R_f + R_r - P_f - P_r = R - P. \qquad 2$$

That is, the balance of payments is the difference between aggregate receipts by residents and aggregate payments by residents. A deficit implies an excess of payments over receipts, and its rectification requires that receipts be increased and payments decreased, or that receipts increase more than payments, or that receipts decrease less than payments; and conversely with a surplus. In what follows, however, surpluses will be ignored, and the argument will be concerned only with deficits.

The formulation of a balance-of-payments deficit in terms of an excess of aggregate payments by residents over aggregate receipts by residents constitutes the starting point for the generalization of the 'absorption approach' to balance-of-payments theory – what might be termed a 'payments approach' – which is the purpose of this chapter. It directs attention to two important aspects of a deficit – its monetary implications, and its relation with the aggregate activity of the economy – from which attention tends to be diverted by the traditional sectoral approach, and neglect of which can lead to fallacious analysis. These two aspects will be discussed in turn, beginning with the monetary implications of a deficit.

The excess of payments by residents over receipts by residents inherent in a balance-of-payments deficit necessarily implies one or other of two alternatives. The first is that cash balances of residents are running down, as domestic money is transferred to the foreign exchange authority.[4] This can, obviously, only continue for a limited period, as eventually cash balances would approach the minimum that the community wished to hold and in the process the disequilibrium would cure itself, through the mechanism of rising interest rates, tighter credit conditions,

4. Where monetary authority and exchange authority are one and the same institution, domestic monetary liabilities may simply be extinguished by sales of foreign exchange.

reduction of aggregate expenditure, and possibly an increase in aggregate receipts. In this case, where the deficit is financed by dishoarding, it would be self-correcting in time; but the economic policy authorities may well be unable to allow the self-correcting process to run its course, since the international reserves of the country may be such a small fraction of the domestic money supply that they would be exhausted well before the running down of money balances had any significant corrective effect. The authorities might therefore have to take action of some kind to reinforce and accelerate the effects of diminishing money balances.

This last consideration provides the chief valid argument for larger international reserves. The case for larger international reserves is usually argued on the ground that larger reserves provide more time for the economic policy authorities to make adjustments to correct a balance-of-payments disequilibrium. But, as Friedman has argued in criticism of Meade (1953), there is no presumption that adjustment spread over a longer period is to be preferred – the argument could indeed be inverted into the proposition that, the larger reserves, the more power the authorities have to resist desirable adjustments. The acceptable argument would seem to be that, the larger the international reserves in relation to the domestic money supply, the less the probability that the profit- or utility-maximizing decisions of individuals to move out of cash into commodities or securities will have to be frustrated by the monetary authorities for fear of a balance-of-payments crisis.

The second alternative is that the cash balances of residents are being replenished by open market purchases of securities by the monetary or foreign exchange authority, as would happen automatically if the monetary authority followed a policy of pegging interest rates or the exchange authority (as in the British case) automatically re-lent to residents any domestic currency it received from residents or foreigners in return for sales of foreign exchange. In this case, the money supply in domestic circulation is being maintained by credit creation, so that the excess of payments over receipts by residents could continue indefinitely without generating any corrective process – until dwindling reserves forced the economic policy authorities to change their policy in some respect.

To summarize the argument so far, a balance-of-payments deficit implies *either* dishoarding by residents, *or* credit creation by the monetary authorities – either an increase in V, or the maintenance of M. Further, since a deficit associated with increasing velocity of circulation will tend to be self-correcting (though the authorities may be unable to rely on this alone), a continuing balance-of-payments deficit of the type usually discussed in balance-of-payments theory ultimately requires credit creation to keep it going. This in turn implies that balance-of-payments deficits and difficulties are essentially monetary phenomena, traceable to either of two causes: too low a ratio of international reserves relative to the domestic money supply, so that the economic policy authorities cannot rely on the natural self-correcting process; or the pursuit of governmental policies which oblige the authorities to feed the deficit by credit creation. In both cases, the problem is associated fundamentally with the power of national banking systems to create money which has no internationally acceptable backing.

To conclude that balance-of-payments problems are essentially monetary is not, of course, to assert that they are attributable to monetary mismanagement – they may be, or they may be the result of 'real' forces in the face of which the monetary authorities play a passive role. The conclusion does mean, however, that the distinctions which have sometimes been drawn between monetary and real disequilibria, for example by concepts of 'structural disequilibrium', are not logically valid – though such concepts, carefully used, may be helpful in isolating the initiating causes of disequilibrium or the most appropriate type of remedial policy to follow.

Formulation of the balance of payments as the difference between aggregate payments and aggregate receipts thus illuminates the monetary aspects of balance-of-payments disequilibrium, and emphasizes its essentially monetary nature. More important and interesting is the light which this approach sheds on the policy problem of correcting a deficit, by relating the balance of payments to the overall operation of the economy rather than treating it as one sector of the economy to be analysed by itself.

An excess of aggregate payments by residents over aggregate receipts by residents is the net outcome of economic decisions taken by all the individual economic units composing the economy. These decisions may usefully be analysed in terms of an 'aggregate decision' taken by the community of residents considered as a group (excluding, as always, the foreign exchange authority), though it must be recognized that this technique ignores many of the complications that would have to be investigated in a more detailed analysis.

Two sorts of aggregate decision leading to a balance-of-payments deficit may be distinguished in principle, corresponding to the distinction drawn in monetary theory between 'stock' decisions and 'flow' decisions: a (stock) decision to alter the composition of the community's assets by substituting other assets for domestic money,[5] and a (flow) decision to spend currently in excess of current receipts. Since both real goods and securities are alternative assets to domestic money, and current expenditure may consist in the purchase of either goods or securities, the balance-of-payments deficit resulting from either type of aggregate decision may show itself on either current or capital account. That is, a current account deficit may reflect either a community decision to shift out of cash balances into stocks of goods, or a decision to use goods in excess of the community's current rate of production, while a capital account deficit may reflect either a decision to shift out of domestic money into securities or a decision to lend in excess of the current rate of saving.

The distinction between 'stock' and 'flow' balance-of-payments deficits is important for both theory and practical policy, though refined theoretical analysis has generally been concerned with 'flow' deficits, without making the distinction explicit. The importance of the distinction stems from the fact that a 'stock' deficit is inherently temporary and implies no real worsening of the country's economic position, whereas a 'flow' deficit is not inherently temporary and may imply a worsening of the country's economic position.

Since a stock decision entails a once-for-all change in the composition of a given aggregate of capital assets, a 'stock' deficit

5. With the community defined to include the monetary authority, a substitution of securities for domestic money can only be effected by drawing securities from abroad in exchange for international reserves.

must necessarily be a temporary affair;[6] and in itself it implies no deterioration (but rather the reverse) in the country's economic position and prospects.[7] Nevertheless, if the country's international reserves are small, the economic policy authorities may be obliged to check such a deficit by a change in economic policy. The policy methods available are familiar, but it may be useful to review them briefly in relation to the framework of analysis developed here.

To discourage the substitution of stocks of goods for domestic currency, the economic policy authorities may either raise the cost of stock-holding by credit restrictions or reduce its attractiveness by currency depreciation.[8] Under both policies, the magnitude of the effect is uncertain – depreciation, by stimulating destabilizing expectations, may even promote stock accumulation – while unavoidable repercussions on the flow equilibrium of the economy are set up. These considerations provide a strong argument for the use of the alternative method of direct controls on stock-holding, an indirect and partial form of which is quantitative import restriction.

To discourage the substitution of securities for domestic currency, the same broad alternatives are available: credit restriction, which amounts to the monetary authority substituting domestic

6. A temporary deficit of this kind must be distinguished from a deficit which is 'temporary' in the sense that the causal factors behind it will reverse themselves, leading to a later compensating surplus, e.g. a deficit due to a bad harvest.

7. The deficit involves the replacement of international reserves by stocks of exportable or importable goods and/or by holdings of internationally marketable securities, the change being motivated by private profit considerations. For this to constitute a deterioration from the national point of view, the alternatives facing private asset-holders must be assumed not to reflect true social alternative opportunities, or private asset-holders must be assumed to act less rationally than the economic policy authorities, or the national interest must be defined so as to exclude their welfare from counting. If any of these assumptions is valid, it indicates the need for a remedial policy, but not one conditional on the existence of a deficit or to be applied through the balance of payments. This point is argued more fully below, in connexion with import restrictions.

8. Stocks are built up by withholding goods from export or by increasing imports; depreciation makes both of these less attractive. A third policy might be increased taxation, either of stocks or of home-market sales of goods.

currency for securities to offset substitution of securities for domestic currency by the rest of the community; devaluation, which affects the relative attractiveness of securities only through expectations and may work either way; and exchange controls restricting the acquisition of securities from abroad. Considerations similar to those of the previous paragraph would seem to argue in favour of the use of controls on international capital movements as against the alternative methods available.

In both cases, evaluation of the policy alternatives suggests the use of control rather than price system methods. It should be recalled, though, that the problem is created by the assumed inadequacy of the country's international reserves. In the longer run, the choice for economic policy lies, not between the three alternatives discussed, but between the necessity of having to choose between them and the cost of investing in the accumulation of reserves large enough to finance potential 'stock' deficits. Also, nothing has been said about the practical difficulties of maintaining effective control over international transactions especially capital movements.

In contrast to a 'stock' deficit, a 'flow' deficit is not inherently of limited duration. It will be so if the monetary authority is not prepared to create credit, but this is because its existence will then set up monetary repercussions which will eventually alter the collective decision responsible for it, not because the initial decision implied a temporary deficit. If the decision not to create credit is regarded as a specific act of policy equivalent to a decision to raise interest rates,[9] it follows that the termination of a 'flow' deficit requires a deliberate change of economic policy. Further, a 'flow' deficit may imply a worsening of the country's capital position, providing an economic as well as a monetary incentive to terminate the disequilibrium.[10]

9. This assumption, which is slightly inconsistent with the argument above concerning the monetary implications of a deficit, is made here to avoid the necessity of repeating the analysis for the case where limited reserves prevent the authorities from allowing a deficit to solve itself.

10. Whether this is so depends on the use to which the finance provided by the deficit is put, which involves comparison with what would have happened in the absence of the deficit. If the deficit finances additional investment in productive domestic capital or income-yielding foreign assets

In analysing the policy problems posed by 'flow' deficits, it is convenient to begin by abstracting altogether from international capital movements (other than reserve transactions between foreign exchange authorities) and considering the case of a current account deficit. In this case, if intermediate transactions are excluded, the balance of payments becomes the difference between the value of the country's output (its national income) and its total expenditure, i.e.

$$B = Y - E.$$

To facilitate analysis by avoiding certain complications associated with the possibility of changes in the domestic price level, income and expenditure are conceived of as being valued in units of domestic output. A deficit then consists in an excess of real expenditure over real income, and the problem of correcting a deficit is to bring real national income (output) and real national expenditure into equality.

This formulation suggests that policies for correcting current-account deficits can be classified broadly into two types: those which aim at (or rely on) increasing output, and those which aim at reducing expenditure. The distinction must, of course, relate to the initial impact of the policy, since income and expenditure are interdependent: expenditure depends on and varies with income, and income depends on and varies with expenditure (because part of expenditure is devoted to home-produced goods). Consequently any change in either income or expenditure will initiate multiplier changes in both. It can, however, readily be shown that, so long as an increase in income induces a smaller change in aggregate expenditure, the multiplier repercussions will not be large enough to offset the impact effect of a change, so that an impact increase in output or decrease in expenditure will always improve the balance on current account.[11]

---

the net effect on the capital position may be favourable; if it finances additional consumption it is likely to be unfavourable, though even additional consumption may sometimes increase productive capacity.

11. Differentiating the equation in the text, we obtain $dB = (1 - e)dY + dE$, where e is the marginal propensity to spend out of income, dY is the total *increase* in output (including multiplier effects) and dE is the auto-

The distinction between output-increasing and expenditure-reducing policies may usefully be put in another way. Since output is governed by the demand for it, a change in output can only be brought about by a change in the demand for it; a policy of increasing domestic output can only be effected by operating on expenditure (either foreign or domestic) on that output. Given the level of expenditure, this in turn involves effecting a switch of expenditure (by residents and foreigners) from foreign output to domestic output. The distinction between output-increasing and expenditure-decreasing policies, which rests on the *effects* of the policies, may therefore be replaced by a distinction between expenditure-switching policies and expenditure-reducing policies, which rests on the *method* by which the effects are achieved.

A policy of expenditure-reduction may be applied through a variety of means – monetary restriction, budgetary policy, or even a sufficiently comprehensive battery of direct controls. Since any such policy will tend to reduce income and employment, it will have an additional attraction if the country is suffering from inflationary pressure as well as a balance-of-payments deficit, but a corresponding disadvantage if the country is suffering from unemployment. Moreover, since the impact reduction in expenditure and the total reduction in income and output required to correct a given deficit are larger the larger the proportion of the

---

nomous *decrease* in expenditure. If multiplier effects through foreign incomes are ignored,

$$dY = \frac{1}{1 - e(1 - m)} dA,$$

where dA is an autonomous change in demand for domestic output and m is the proportion of marginal expenditure leaking into imports. Splitting dA into two components, dO for output-increasing policies and $-hdE$ for expenditure-reducing policies (where h is the proportion of expenditure reduction falling on domestic output), gives the result:

$$dB = \frac{1 - e}{1 - e + em} dO + \left(1 - \frac{(1 - e)h}{1 - e + em}\right) dE.$$

Hence either an output-increasing or an expenditure-reducing policy will improve the balance, so long as e is less than unity. (Alexander has argued that since e includes induced investment it may well exceed unity; this possibility is ignored in the argument of the text.) Expenditure reduction will in fact improve the balance so long as multiplier stability is present.

expenditure reduction falling on home-produced goods, and since different methods of expenditure-reduction may differ in this respect, the choice between alternative methods may depend on the inflationary–deflationary situation of the economy. Finally, since the accompanying reduction in income may lead to some reduction in the domestic price level, and/or a greater eagerness of domestic producers to compete with foreign producers both at home and abroad, expenditure-reducing policies may have incidental expenditure-switching effects.

Expenditure-switching policies may be divided into two types, according to whether the policy instrument employed is general or selective: devaluation (which may be taken to include the case of a deflation-induced reduction of the domestic price level under fixed exchange rates), and trade controls (including both tariffs and subsidies and quantitative restrictions). Devaluation aims at switching both domestic and foreign expenditure towards domestic output; controls are usually imposed on imports, and aim at (or have the effect of) switching domestic expenditure away from imports towards home goods, though sometimes they are used to stimulate exports and aim at switching foreigners' expenditure towards domestic output.

Both types of expenditure-switching policy may have direct impact-effects on residents' expenditure. Devaluation may result in increased expenditure from the initial income level, through the so-called 'terms-of-trade effect' of an adverse terms-of-trade movement in reducing real income and therefore the proportion of income saved. Trade controls will tend to have the same effect, via the reduction in real income resulting from constriction of freedom of choice.[12] In addition, trade controls must alter the real

12. These arguments conflict with the assumption, more frequently made in connexion with trade controls than with devaluation, that the public will consume less because it cannot obtain the goods it prefers as readily as before. That assumption may well be valid in the case of a policy expected to be applied for a short period only, after which goods will become as available as before, or in the analysis of the short run during which the economy is adjusting to the change in policy; but it is invalid in the present context of flow disequilibrium, since it overlooks the effect of the policy change in reducing the future value of savings and hence the incentive to save. An example of this type of faulty reasoning is the assertion sometimes made that quantitative import restriction is particularly effective

expenditure corresponding to the initial output level if they take the form of import duties or export subsidies uncompensated by other fiscal changes; this case should, however, be classed as a combined policy of expenditure-change (unfavourable in the case of the export subsidy) and expenditure-switch.

Whether general or selective in nature, an expenditure-switching policy seeks to correct a deficit by switching demand away from foreign towards domestic goods; and it depends for success not only on switching demand in the right direction, but also on the capacity of the economy to make available the extra output required to satisfy the additional demand. Such policies therefore pose two problems for economic analysis: the conditions required for expenditure to be switched in the desired direction, and the source of the additional output required to meet the additional demand.

As to the first question, the possibilities of failure for both devaluation and controls have been investigated at length by international trade theorists, and require only summary treatment here.[13] Export promotion will divert foreign expenditure away from the country's output if the foreign demand is inelastic, while import restriction will divert domestic expenditure abroad if demand for imports is inelastic and the technique of restriction allows the foreigner the benefit of the increased value of imports to domestic consumers. Devaluation has the partial effect of diverting domestic expenditure abroad, via the increased cost of the initial volume of imports, and this adverse switch will not be offset by the favourable effect of substitution of domestic for foreign goods at home and abroad, if import demand elasticities average less than one half.

---

in under-developed countries because their economic structure allows little possibility of substitution for imported goods in either production or consumption.

One qualification to the argument of the text, which also applies to the final sentence of the paragraph, is that if the goods towards which domestic expenditure is switched are more heavily taxed than those from which expenditure is diverted (a type of complication which is ignored in the general argument of the text), real expenditure may fall rather than rise.

13. Impact effects on the level of expenditure from a given income level of the type discussed in the next-but-one paragraph preceding this one are ignored in this paragraph.

While the elasticity requirement for successful devaluation just cited is familiar, the approach developed in this paper throws additional light on what non-fulfilment of the requirement implies. From the equation $B = Y - E$, it is clear that, if direct effects on expenditure from the initial income level are neglected, devaluation can worsen the balance only if it reduces total world demand for the country's output. This implies that the country's output is in a sense a 'Giffen case' in world consumption; and that the market for at least one of the commodities it produces is in unstable equilibrium.[14] Neither of these ways of stating the conditions for exchange instability makes the possibility of instability as plausible *a priori* as their equivalent, reached through sectoral analysis, in terms of elasticities of import demand.

The second, and more interesting, analytical problem relates to the source of the additional domestic output required to satisfy the demand for it created by the expenditure-switching policy. Here it is necessary to distinguish two cases, that in which the economy is under-employed and that in which it is fully employed, for both the relevant technique of analysis and the factors on which the outcome of the policy depend differ between the two.

1. If the economy has unemployed resources available, the additional output required to meet the additional demand can be provided by the reabsorption of these resources into employment: in this case the switch policy has the additional attraction of increasing employment and income. The increase in domestic output may tend to raise the domestic price level, through the operation of increasing marginal real costs of production, and conversely the foreign price level may tend to fall, thus partially counteracting the initial effects of the switch policy; but such repercussions can legitimately be analysed in terms of elasticity concepts, since under-employment implies that additional factors are available at the ruling price.

2. If the economy is already fully employed, however, the additional output required cannot be provided by increasing

14. See Morgan (1955). Morgan's statement (p. 285) that instability requires 'very strong and perverse income effects' is fallacious – all that is strictly necessary is a preference in each country for home-produced goods.

production; it can only be provided through a reduction in the previous level of real expenditure.[15] This reduction may be brought about either by a deliberate expenditure-reducing policy introduced along with the switch policy, or by the inflationary consequences of the switch policy itself in the assumed full-employment conditions.[16]

If the increased output is provided by a deliberate expenditure-reducing policy, the nature of this policy will obviously influence the effects of the expenditure-switching policy, since the composition of the output it releases may be more or less substitutable for foreign output in world demand. Thus, for example, an expenditure-reducing policy which reduces domestic demand for imports and exportable goods will be more favourable to expenditure-switching than one which reduces domestic demand for non-traded goods. The analysis of the effects of an expenditure-switching policy supported by an expenditure-reducing policy must therefore comprise the effects of the latter in determining the composition of the productive capacity available to meet the increased demand created by the former, as well as the elasticity relations which govern the effects of the interaction of increased demand with increased production capacity on the prices and volumes of goods traded.

If the expenditure-switching policy is not accompanied by an expenditure-reducing policy, its effect will be to create an inflationary excess of aggregate demand over supply, leading to price increases tending to counteract the policy's expenditure-switching effects. Inflation, however, may work towards curing the deficit, through various effects tending to reduce the level of real expenditure from the full employment level of output. These effects,

15. Recognition of this point may be regarded as the fundamental contribution of the absorption approach, though none of the authors cited seems to have appreciated all its implications: Meade (1951), for example, analyses the case on the assumption that an appropriate expenditure-reducing policy is in effect, without examining the interdependence between the two policies or the alternative of inflation, while Alexander (1952) does not recognize that the effects of inflation on absorption could be achieved by policy.

16. For analytical simplicity, both the possibility of increased production through 'over-full employment' and of direct expenditure-reducing effects of a switch policy (discussed earlier in this reading) are ignored here.

which are familiar and have been analysed in detail by Alexander, include the effect of high marginal tax rates in increasing the proportion of real income absorbed by taxation as wages and prices rise, the possibility of a swing to profits increasing the proportion of income saved, and the effect of rising prices in reducing the real purchasing power of cash and government bonds held by the public, so reducing their wealth and propensity to consume. All of these effects, it may be noted, depend on particular asymmetries in the reactions of the sectors affected to the redistributive effects of inflation on real income or wealth, which may not in fact be present. The important point, however, is that these factors, on which the success of an expenditure-switching policy depends in this case, are monetary factors, and that the analysis required employs monetary concepts rather than elasticity concepts. As in the previous case, the elasticity factors are subordinate to the factors governing the reduction in aggregate real expenditure, in determining the consequences of the expenditure-switching policy for the balance of payments.

The argument of the previous paragraph – that in full employment conditions the success of expenditure-switching policies depends mainly on the effectiveness of the consequent inflation in reducing real expenditure – helps to explain both the prevalence of scepticism about, and hostility towards, exchange rate adjustment as a means of curing balance-of-payments disequilibria, and the fact that historical experience can be adduced in support of the proposition that devaluation is a doubtful remedy. The argument does not, however, support the conclusion frequently drawn from the analysis of devaluation in these circumstances, that import restrictions are to be preferred; this is a *non sequitur*, since import restrictions are equally an expenditure-switching policy. Rather, the proper conclusion is that expenditure-switching policies are inappropriate to full employment conditions, except when used in conjunction with an expenditure-reducing policy as a means of correcting the employment reducing effects of the latter.

But what of the choice between devaluation and selective trade controls, to which reference has just been made? So far, it has not been necessary to distinguish between them, since from the point of view of the balance of payments both can be treated as expenditure-switching policies. It is from the point of view of economic welfare that they differ; and the arguments on their relative merits have nothing to do with the state of the balance of payments, except that if controls are preferable a deficit may offer an opportunity for introducing them with less risk of foreign retaliation than if trade were balanced.

The welfare arguments for controls on a country's international trade may be divided into two groups, those centring on controls as a means of influencing the internal distribution of real income, by discouraging imports consumed by the rich and encouraging those consumed by the poor, and those centring on controls as a means of increasing the country's gains from trade through exploiting its monopoly/monopsony power in foreign markets. The former are of doubtful validity, both because the ethics of disguising a real income policy as a trade policy are suspect, and because both the efficiency and the effectiveness of trade controls as instruments for governing real income distribution are dubious. The latter are valid, to the extent that the country has powers to exploit the foreigner and can use them without provoking sufficient retaliation to nullify the gains.

This is the familiar optimum tariff argument. Its application to balance-of-payments policy depends on the level of trade restrictions already in force, as compared with the optimum level of restrictions (Alexander, 1951). If an expenditure-switching policy is required to correct a deficit, and the level of trade restrictions is below the optimum, restriction[17] is preferable to devaluation until the optimum level is reached; in the opposite case, devaluation is preferable. But it is the relation of actual to optimum restrictions, and not the state of the trade balance, which determines whether restriction is desirable or not.

This concludes the analysis of alternative policies for correcting a 'flow' balance-of-payments deficit on current account. To complete the analysis of 'flow' disequilibria, it would be neces-

17. Generally, optimum trade restriction entails restriction of both imports and exports; but if the country's currency is over-valued it may imply subsidization of some or even all exports, and if the currency is under-valued it may imply subsidization of some or even all imports. (These conclusions follow from the fact that a devaluation is equivalent to an all-round export subsidy and import duty.)

sary to relax the assumption that international capital movements are confined to reserve movements between foreign exchange authorities, and to consider alternative policies for correcting a deficit on current and capital account combined. The central problem in this case is to determine the level of current account surplus or deficit, capital export or import, at which economic policy should aim. This raises two further problems too difficult to pursue here: the optimum rate of accumulation of capital for the community as a whole, and the degree to which it is desirable to discriminate in favour of investment at home and against investment abroad.

In conclusion, the argument of this reading may be summarized as follows: formulation of the balance of payments as the difference between aggregate receipts and payments, rather than receipts and payments on international account only, has two major advantages. It brings out the essentially monetary nature of a deficit, which must be accompanied by dishoarding of domestic money or credit creation; and it relates the deficit to the operation of the economy as a whole. A deficit may reflect a 'stock' decision or a 'flow' decision by the community. The conditions which make a 'stock' deficit a policy problem indicate the use of direct control methods as against price system methods of correction. Policies for dealing with 'flow' deficits on current account may be divided into expenditure-reducing and expenditure-switching policies; in full employment conditions the latter must be supported by the former, or rely on inflation for their effect, which in either case cannot be analysed adequately in terms of elasticities. When capital account transactions are introduced into the analysis, the choice between policy alternatives requires reference to growth considerations not readily susceptible to economic analysis.

References

ALEXANDER, S. (1951), 'Devaluation versus import restriction as an instrument for improving foreign exchange balance', *International Monetary Fund Staff Papers*, vol. 1, no. 3, pp. 379–96.

ALEXANDER, S. (1952), 'The effects of a devaluation on a trade balance', *International Monetary Fund Staff Papers*, vol. 2, no. 2, pp. 263–78.

HARBERGER, A. C. (1950), 'Currency depreciation, income, and the balance of trade', *Journal of Political Economy*, vol. 58, pp. 47–60.
HARROD, R. F. (1952), 'Currency appreciation as an anti-inflationary device: comment', *Quarterly Journal of Economics*, vol. 66, pp. 102–16.
LAURSEN, S., and METZLER, L. A. (1950), 'Flexible exchange rates and the theory of employment', *Review of Economics and Statistics*, vol. 32, pp. 281–99.
MACHLUP, F. (1955), 'The analysis of devaluation', *American Economic Review*, vol. 45, pp. 255–78.
MEADE, J. E. (1951), *The Balance of Payments*, London.
MORGAN, E. V. (1955), 'The theory of flexible exchange rates', *American Economic Review*, vol. 45, pp. 279–95.
STUVEL, G. (1951), *The Exchange Stability Problem*, Oxford.
TINBERGEN, J. (1952), *On the Theory of Economic Policy*, Amsterdam.

12 W. M. Corden

The Geometric Representation of Policies to Attain Internal and External Balance

W. M. Corden (1960), 'The geometric representation of policies to attain internal and external balance', *Review of Economic Studies*, vol. 28, pp. 1–22.

This reading is concerned with the geometric representation of various relatively new ideas in international trade theory. These ideas deal with the interaction of income and price effects to attain internal and external balance, the ways in which objectives of policy conflict if a country limits itself to certain methods of adjustment, and what has become known as the 'absorption' approach. They have been embodied in numerous books and articles, and in particular Meade (1951). But it might be true to say that they have not yet become part of the corpus of generally understood and accepted economic knowledge. This seems to be borne out by the fact that clear statements of the relationships cannot be found in many of the international trade textbooks. It is not implausible that this may be due to the lack so far of a simple geometric summing-up.

What follows will not bc new to readers of Meade, Alexander, Nurkse, Johnson, and Harrod, apart from the geometry itself. It will only be of value to those who are assisted in their understanding by geometric exposition.

I. A Simple Diagram

Import restrictions and expenditure changes. A simple diagram

Hemming and Corden (1958) presented a diagram which showed how changes in expenditure and in import restrictions need to be combined to yield a balance-of-payments improvement at maximum real income. The diagram was used to distinguish the *partial equilibrium*, the *absorption* and (what was there called) the *real income* approach to the use of import restrictions. The diagram forms the starting point for our discussion here, and is reproduced as Figure 1.

Imports are shown along the *X* axis and home-produced goods other than exports along the *Y* axis. The quadrant *XOY* contains a map of community indifference curves. There is a fixed price ratio between imports and home-produced goods shown by the slope of the line *RJ*, and the initial income is *OR* in terms of home-produced goods or *OJ* in terms of imports. In

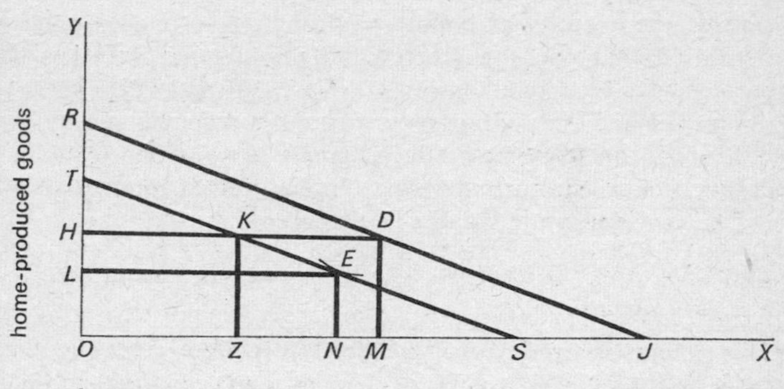

Figure 1 Import restrictions and expenditure changes (Hemming and Corden, 1958)

the absence of restrictions the volume of imports is *OM* and the domestic demand for home-produced goods *OH*. The foreign price of imports is assumed constant (the elasticity of supply of imports being infinite), so that the value of imports must change in the same proportion as the volume. No distinction is drawn between import-competing goods and other domestically-produced goods. They are all included in the general category of home-produced goods.

The key assumptions are that the volume and price of exports, and the value of other elements in the balance of payments (invisibles, capital movements), are given, so that the volume of imports required for external balance can be shown along the horizontal axis. Suppose that the import volume which yields external balance is *OZ*, so that imports have to be reduced by

MZ. And suppose, further, initial full employment without inflation, so that the domestic demand for home-produced goods required to maintain internal balance is *OH*.

It can then be shown that internal and external balance can be attained by a combination of deflation of expenditure and import restriction. A deflation from *OR* to *OT* will reduce the demand for imports to *ON* and the demand for home-produced goods to *OL*. Import restrictions which cut imports from *ON* to *OZ* will divert demand on to home-produced goods to the value of *LH*. Finally, the quantity of imports and of home-produced goods purchased will be *OZ* and *OH* respectively. External and internal balance have been simultaneously achieved. If part of the diversion of demand due to import restrictions had gone into savings rather than on to home-produced goods some of the required deflation of expenditure would have been attained automatically without any deliberate policy of deflation.

Development of the diagram. Expenditure-reducing and expenditure-switching policies

This simple diagram can be developed in two ways. Firstly, the effect on the value of exports of changes in expenditure and import restrictions can be taken into account. Even if we regard the quantity of exportable production as fixed, a reduction in expenditure may lower the domestic demand for exportable goods, and so free more goods for exports. Similarly import restrictions may divert demand towards exportable goods and so reduce the supply available for export. If these effects have to be taken into account the value of exports can no longer be assumed constant. This complication is necessary if the diagram is to illustrate economic policy problems in a country such as Britain, exporting the same type of goods which it also sells in large quantities on the home market and which are close substitutes for some of its marginal imports. Since the diagram was originally devised to study import restrictions in the United Kingdom, this complication was developed at great length in the original article, possibly at the cost of some clarity.

But it is a complication which may not be necessary when the diagram is used to illustrate short-term balance-of-payments policy in many of the world's primary product exporting countries. In Australia or Ceylon it may be reasonable to regard the value of exports as given, and to pose the balance-of-payments problem as the need to adjust imports to a given value of exports and capital inflow. Usually the supply of exportable goods is in the short-term quite unresponsive to changes in demand, while domestic consumption of exportables is either relatively unimportant (Australian wool, Ceylon rubber and tea) or is inelastic to changes in incomes and prices (Australian wheat and other foodstuffs). Therefore the value of exports can be treated as independent of expenditure changes and balance-of-payments policies.

Given the value of exports, and therefore the value and volume of imports the country can afford, it is possible to develop the diagram in another direction. It is possible to illustrate very simply the interrelationships between expenditure changes, price changes, and import restrictions necessary to attain simultaneous internal and external balance. It is possible to show how different situations require different combinations of price and expenditure changes, how import restrictions differ from exchange rate alterations, and both from tariffs, and how the *absorption* approach fits into all this. The author found the diagram useful in understanding parts of Meade (1951), and in particular in highlighting some rather paradoxical conclusions. It illustrates very explicitly Professor Johnson's (1958) distinction between *expenditure-reducing* and *expenditure-switching* policies and these terms will be used here. Finally, much of the inspiration comes from an unpublished paper by Professor Swan (1955). This is referred to in the appendix to this paper, page 286.

II. Zones and Sectors

The zones of economic unhappiness

We now return to Figure 1. We have seen that, with the given quantity and price of exports, there is internal balance if the total domestic demand for home-produced goods is *OH* and external balance if the demand for imports is *OZ*. Thus the point *K* represents a position of internal and external balance. Anywhere north of *K* there would be excess demand for home-produced goods and anywhere south of it, insufficient demand (unemployment). West of *K* there would be a balance-of-payments surplus and east of it a balance-of-payments deficit.

This then gives Professor Swan's four *zones of economic unhappiness*, shown in Figure 2. The zones are defined by the heavy straight lines drawn through *K*. In zone I there is a balance-of-payments surplus and excess demand for home-produced

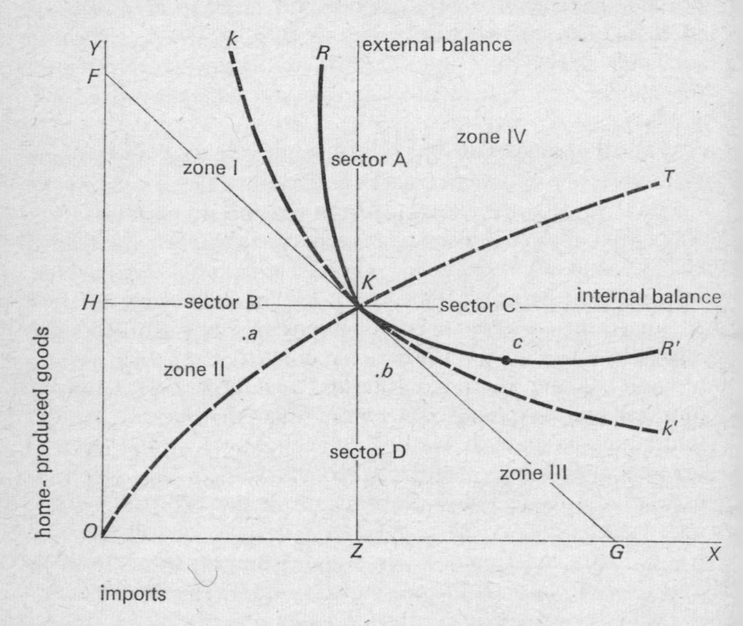

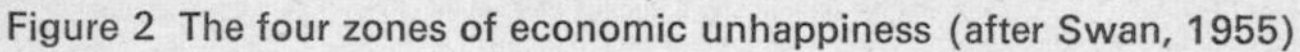
Figure 2 The four zones of economic unhappiness (after Swan, 1955)

goods. In zone II there is a balance-of-payments surplus and an insufficient demand for home-produced goods (unemployment). In zone III there is a balance-of-payments deficit and unemployment and in zone IV a deficit and excess demand. The vertical heavy line shows positions of external balance and the horizontal line, internal balance. At their intersection, at *K*, economic happiness is as complete as full employment without excess demand plus absence of a balance-of-payments deficit or surplus can make it.

The assumption of *excess demand* involves certain difficulties for we need to know what happens to that part of the demand for home-produced goods which cannot be supplied. For the moment it will be assumed that the excess demand is all saved involuntarily. This implies that when we refer to expenditure we mean intended and not actual expenditure. The various problems which are highlighted by the absorption approach to balance-of-payments policy are provisionally evaded with this assumption. It is an assumption which will be reconsidered later.

The policy sectors

The next step is to divide Figure 2 into *policy sectors.* Again, the point of internal and external balance, *K*, is our starting-point. It can be seen that a level of intended expenditure *OF* (in terms of home-produced goods) combined with a price ratio between home-produced goods and imports ruling in the home market, represented by the slope of the line *FG*, will yield both internal and external balance (without import restrictions). Given this level of intended expenditure and relative prices, consumers will settle at *K* where the indifference curve *kk′* is tangential to *FG*.

The various points on the indifference curve *kk′* all represent constant amounts of real expenditure. Thus this curve is one of the dividing lines for our policy sectors. At any point north-east of *kk′* real expenditure needs to be reduced, and at any point south-west of it, it has to be increased. An alternative approach might have been to use the line *FG*, which shows constant amounts of real expenditure in a more limited sense, in that expenditure is calculated at the equilibrium prices which would rule at *K*. The implications of the approach used here will be discussed later.

The line *OT* is the income–consumption line appropriate to the relative prices represented by the slope of *FG*. If the income elasticity of demand for imports were unity, *OT* would be a straight line. In Figure 2 the income elasticity of demand for imports is greater than unity. *OT* shows the various combinations of imports and home-produced goods which would be demanded if expenditure changed but the relative price ratio facing domestic consumers stayed constant. At any point south-east of *OT* the relative price of imports facing home consumers is lower than that represented by the slope of *FG*, so that, for any given level of real income, purchases of imports are greater than they would be if the price ratio appropriate to internal and external balance ruled. Similarly, north-west of *OT* the relative price of imports is higher. Therefore *OT* is the dividing-line for relative price policies. At any point south-east of *OT*, real expenditure has to be switched away from imports towards home-produced goods. There has to be a movement north-westwards along a given indifference curve. This could be brought about by raising in some way the internal price of imports in relation to the prices of home-produced goods or by increasing import restrictions. It is, of course, what a depreciating of the exchange rate would do, although it must be remembered that switching devices also affect real expenditure, and while they can bring the economy on to *OT* it is not necessarily done by staying on the same indifference curve. Similarly, at any point north-west of *OT*, expenditure has to be switched away from home-produced goods towards imports, an appreciation of the exchange rate being one way of doing this.

We thus get the four policy sectors defined by the indifference curve *kk′* and the income–consumption line *OT*, and shown in Figure 2. It should be noted that these policy sectors overlap the zones, so that (for example) a part of zone I and a part of zone IV are in sector A, and a part of sector A plus a part of sector B make up zone I. In sector A, which is the slice north of *K*, real expenditure should be reduced and switched *towards* imports. In sector *B* (west of *K*) expenditure should be increased but still switched *towards* imports. In sector *C* (east of *K*) expenditure should be decreased and switched *away from* imports, and in sector *D* it should be increased and switched *away from* imports.

Simple conclusions from the diagram

Although there are many types of switching policies, for the moment let us equate a depreciation of the exchange rate with a switch of expenditure away from imports and an appreciation with a switch towards imports. If exports were not assumed constant we would also have to remember that altering the exchange rate may switch foreigners' expenditure towards or away from our exports. We neglect at this stage the effect of exchange rate variations on real expenditure, and regard all changes in real expenditure as the result of deliberate policy measures. In fact alterations in the exchange rate may set up multiplier effects which create induced changes in real expenditure. But at this stage we assume that policy decisions determine whether these induced effects are to be allowed to work themselves out. If the policy decision is to keep real expenditure constant then the induced expenditure increases will be offset by policy decreases. In addition, alterations in the exchange rate may raise or lower real expenditure, depending on monetary assumptions. These effects are also disregarded at this stage. On this basis a number of simple conclusions can be drawn from the diagram.

a. To achieve both internal and external balance a combination of price (switching) and expenditure adjustment is necessary, unless the economy happens to be on *OT* or *kk'*.

b. This could be brought about by associating one instrument of policy with one aim and the other policy instrument with the other aim, in the way described by Professor Meade. Thus expenditure adjustments could be used to maintain internal balance and a flexible exchange rate external balance. For example, beginning in zone II, expenditure would be increased as long as there was any unemployment, while the exchange rate would be appreciated (i.e. expenditure switched south-east towards imports) as long as any external surplus remained. It can be seen that this policy might bring the economy into zone III, when the exchange rate would start depreciating. But a consistent application of the two policies would finally bring the economy to *K*, although (in this example) on balance the exchange rate might have had to appreciate or depreciate.

Similarly, internal balance could be brought about by flexible internal prices and external balance by changes in the level of real expenditure. This is the gold standard principle (Meade, 1951) and enables the exchange rate to be fixed.

But, as Professor Nurkse (Nurkse, 1956, p. 142; also Tinbergen, 1952) has pointed out, though it is quite possible to associate one policy with one aim and the other policy with the other aim, each policy does affect both the internal and the external situation. So it is purely arbitrary to link one aim with one particular policy. For example, beginning in internal and external balance at point *K*, a reduction in expenditure will create both unemployment and an external surplus. Similarly an appreciation would establish both unemployment and an external deficit.

c. The basic lesson taught us by Professor Meade is clearly confirmed by the diagram. In each zone the required direction of one of the policies is clear. In zone I an appreciation will bring internal and external balance closer. In zone III a depreciation will do this. In zone II an increase in expenditure is unambiguously the right policy, while in zone IV the need to decrease expenditure is clear. But if the other policy instrument were the only available one in each case, there would be a conflict of aims. For example, in zone III the aim of external balance would call for a decrease in expenditure and the aim of internal balance for an increase in expenditure.

d. So while the direction of one of the policy instruments is clear in each zone, the direction of the other is not. The diagram shows that the condition of 'economic unhappiness' does not in itself tell us the final net direction of both required policy measures. For example, unemployment (zones II and III) is compatible with three of the four policy combinations. At *a* it calls for appreciation and increased expenditure. At *b* it calls for depreciation and increased expenditure, and at *c* it calls for depreciation and reduced expenditure. *b* and *c* are both in zone III with unemployment and a balance of payments deficit. The policy recommendation at *c* seems particularly paradoxical. It would be difficult to convince a government that in a situation of unemployment expenditure should be reduced. It would have to be explained that the whole of the unemployment and more would be removed by a depreciation which was sufficient to restore external balance, and that the reduction in expenditure is needed to avoid the excess demand into which the depreciation would otherwise plunge the economy.

If we associate internal balance with expenditure changes and external balance with exchange rate alterations, we can say that the diagram shows us four *Paradoxical Segments*. In segment IB (zone I, Sector B) there is excess demand for home-produced goods and yet the policy prescription is for an increase in expenditure. In segment IID there is an external surplus and yet the prescription is depreciation. In segment IIIC unemployment appears to call for a reduction in expenditure. And finally, in segment IVA an external deficit is associated with a need for appreciation of the exchange rate.

It should be noted that all these conclusions will have to be modified once we cease to assume that excess demand for home-produced goods is saved. This is the modification introduced by the *absorption* approach and will be discussed later below.

III. The Assumptions of the Diagram

(*a*) First of all, what does it mean to assume a constant value of exports? It means both a constant volume and a constant price, this price being in foreign currency. The value of exports which we assume constant is in terms of foreign, and not necessarily domestic, currency. While a constant value of exports could result from an increase in volume combined with a fall in price, a change in volume has to be specifically ruled out for our diagram to work.

The volume and the price of exports must be constant only for the purpose of the analysis. Changes in them must not be induced by the switching and expenditure policies under discussion. But there can still be independent changes. An independent rise in the value of exports will shift *K* to the right (and with this alter the zone and sector boundaries). If it is associated with increased employment in the export industries (given the total work-force in the country) it will also move *K* downwards. Thus the diagram does not rule out fluctuations in the prices of exports on world markets. It shows what sort of policy adjustments such fluctuations call for.

A constant volume of exports means both a constant quantity of production of exportables and a constant quantity of domestic consumption of them. If domestic consumption of exportables is not significant then the second part of this assumption creates no difficulties. Otherwise we must assume specifically that both the price and the income elasticities of domestic demand for exportables are zero. The indifference curves in the diagrams then refer to the allocation of expenditure between imports and home-produced goods other than exportables, and are drawn on the assumption that there is a fixed consumption of exportables.

A constant foreign price of exports rules out the following two cases. Firstly, it rules out a direct link between purchases of imports and the foreign demand for exports. For example, reduced imports might lower incomes abroad and so cut the foreign demand for our exports. Here we must assume that the effect on foreign incomes is either offset or insignificant, or that even if there is an effect its further repercussion on the demand for our exports is not significant. Secondly, a constant foreign price of exports means that export prices must not be inflexible in terms of domestic currency, or fixed on a cost-plus basis. This possibility is relevant to devaluation in the United Kingdom and will be looked at later. Given then no direct link between imports and the foreign demand for exports, and given flexible market-based export pricing, the foreign price of exports must be constant as long as the volume is assumed constant. No specific assumption needs to be made about the elasticity of the foreign demand for exports.

These assumptions are not as limiting as might seem. They focus on the key factors in certain types of economies, though clearly the United Kingdom is not such an economy. More important, the main conclusions are not affected when the value of exports is allowed to vary provided one condition applies. A switching or expenditure policy which lowers imports must always raise the value of exports, and vice versa. If, for example, a switch away from imports also reduced the value of exports then the possibility exists that the balance of payments is worsened rather than improved. Such a case would upset our main conclusions.

(*b*) The foreign price of imports is assumed constant. So the elasticity of supply of imports is infinite. Taken together with the constant foreign price of exports, this means that we assume constant terms of trade. Again, it is only induced changes in import prices which are ruled out. An independent change in import prices would shift K, as well as altering the price ratio ruling in the domestic market with a given exchange rate. Later in the paper induced changes in import prices will be allowed for. It will be seen that such changes in no way affect any of the main conclusions.

(*c*) Some readers may have balked at the use of an indifference curve to define the policy sectors. But of course it is not necessary to know the precise path of the curve; all one needs to accept is the general idea of a curve sloping negatively through *K* which traces out combinations of imports and home-produced goods which are regarded, for policy purposes, as yielding the same amount of social welfare.

Alternatively, real expenditure might be calculated at the equilibrium prices ruling at the final position *K*, or at the initial price ratio. If the final price ratio is used then the line *FG* will replace the indifference curve *kk′* as one of the boundaries of the policy sectors. If, on the other hand, the equilibrium price ratio of the initial situation were to be used, we would have to construct yet another curve, *RR′*. This is derived as follows. Imagine *FG* to pivot on *K*. At each slope an indifference curve will be tangential to it at one point. The curve *RR′* traces out these points of tangency. Say the initial position is at *c*, which happens to be on *RR′*. The equilibrium expenditure line at *c* must pass through *K*, so that at the price ratio ruling at *c*, a change from *c* to *K* represents constant real expenditure.

The relationship between the three curves, *kk′*, showing constant real expenditure, *FG*, which is an approximation to constant real expenditure using final prices, and *RR′* which is a similar approximation using initial prices, illustrates the familiar index number problem. If the initial position falls between *RR′* and *kk′*, then a movement to *K* will require a fall in real expenditure, but the approximation using initial prices will suggest a rise. If the initial position falls between *FG* and *kk′*, it will require a rise in real expenditure, but the approximation using final prices will suggest a fall. And anywhere between *RR′* and *FG* real expenditure in terms of initial prices needs to rise and in terms of final prices to fall.

(*d*) Multiplier effects have been assumed away by supposing all changes in expenditure to be the result of deliberate policies. In fact policy changes in expenditure might be distinguished from induced changes. Suppose that in Figure 2 the economy is initially at some point on *OT* in zone II. The diagram tells us that an increase in expenditure unaccompanied by a switching policy is required. But it should be added that the increase directly induced by policy should only take the economy some of the way towards *K*, since the multiplier effect will do the rest.

Next, suppose that the economy is initially at a point on *kk′* in zone III; so real expenditure is the same as at *K*. The diagram tells us that a switching of expenditure, but no change in its total level, is required. The direct effect of a switching policy may raise or lower real expenditure; this depends on the particular policy used and on the monetary assumptions, and will be examined further below. For the moment let us assume that the direct effect keeps real expenditure constant and so moves the economy along *kk′*, a devaluation bringing it north-west towards *K*. But what about the further effect? Increased expenditure on home-produced goods raises domestic incomes; this induces an increase in real domestic expenditure; so incomes rise further, expenditure increases again, and so on. It seems therefore that switching policies have inevitable expenditure effects. The solution applied so far has been to assume that whatever the induced change in expenditure, it is offset by a policy change, unless the policy decision is actually to allow an increase in expenditure. In this way the switching effects of an expenditure-switching policy are isolated from its induced expenditure effects.

If induced expenditure effects are not to be assumed away, it must be remembered that a switching policy which initially moves the economy north-west along *kk′* to some point *x*, will further carry it north-east along the income–consumption line which passes through *x*. The initial effect is to lower imports and raise purchases of home-produced goods; the further effect is partly to restore the level of imports and to increase the demand for home-produced goods even more. In the special case where the marginal home leakage (marginal propensity to save less marginal propensity to invest) is zero, imports will return to their original level, and the induced expenditure effects will have reversed the beneficial effects of the switching policy on the balance of payments. But normally, with a positive home leakage, some part of the initial balance of payments improvement should remain. It follows that if the economy is originally on *kk′* in zone III and is to get to *K*, a policy decrease in real expenditure will have to offset the induced increase.

This multiplier complication arises only in zones II and III. Assuming at this stage that all excess demand for home-produced goods is saved, in zones I and IV the whole of an increase in expenditure goes on imports and savings; so the multiplier is unity and can be disregarded.

IV. Types of Expenditure-switching Policies

We will now illustrate various types of expenditure-switching policies – import restrictions, changes in the exchange rate, changes in the prices of home-produced goods, and tariffs. We will consider only the initial effects of these policies and not the induced changes in expenditure which they may bring about through the multiplier process. We begin with import restrictions because they are simplest to illustrate and are the most widely-used short-term switching policy.

We want to see how each of these switching policies initially affects real expenditure. But if the reader is prepared to accept the general proposition that all the devices switch expenditure away from imports while having varying effects on real expenditure, he may prefer to pass over this section of the paper. In all cases the answer depends on the monetary assumption which is made. One could of course assume that money expenditure is always so adjusted – through a perfectly elastic money supply or a flexible velocity of circulation – that real expenditure does not alter. In this case the only thing left to discuss here is the consequential change in the money supply or the velocity of circulation implied by various switching policies. Beyond this there are a whole range of possible monetary assumptions, only a few of which can be illustrated here. One of them is the extreme assumption that money expenditure is initially fixed, the value of which is that it indicates the direction of pressure on real expenditure when the money supply or the velocity of circulation are not entirely flexible.

It should be noted that the assumptions of the model cause most of the distinctions between the switching policies to vanish. Devaluation or a reduction in the prices of home-produced goods may achieve a balance-of-payments improvement not only by reducing imports but also by stimulating the volume of exports; while import restrictions and tariffs, on the other hand, act only on imports. But this distinction, on which so much of international trade theory focuses, disappears with the assumption of a constant value of exports. Again, the first two devices are more likely to worsen the terms of trade. But this distinction disappears since we assume the terms of trade as given. Import restrictions and tariffs allow the possibility of discriminating between different imports, while devaluation has a uniform effect. But we treat all imports as a single good here. Finally, the use of community indifference curves implies the disregard of distribution of income effects. So the distinction we are left with is that a given switching of expenditure, from an initial position to the income–consumption line *OT*, can have varying impact effects on real expenditure, depending on which switching device is used. In addition, if there is an element of flexibility in the money supply or the velocity of circulation, below full employment each of the switching devices will have a multiplier effect, and so induce a further expenditure change, as described above. But this effect will not be considered here.

Import restrictions

Suppose we start at point *D* (Figure 1) in internal balance and external deficit. This is in Sector C and calls for reduced expenditure and import restrictions. The process has already been described earlier in this paper. We could imagine that expenditure (at the initial price ratio) is reduced first, bringing the equilibrium to *E*, and is then switched by import restrictions, bringing it to *K*. Alternatively we may imagine that first import restrictions cut imports from *OM* to *OZ*, creating excess demand for home-produced goods equal to *ZM*, and then expenditure is reduced, eliminating the excess demand. In this latter case it must be remembered that the extent to which the restrictions keep imports below free demand (the excess demand for imports) is indicated not by *ZM*, the extent of the original import cut, but by *ZN*, since the free demand for imports will have been lowered by the reduction in expenditure.

Looking at import restrictions alone, if intended money expenditure stayed constant, real intended expenditure would be lowered since the indifference curve due north of *K* of *RJ* represents a lower level of welfare than that at *D*. Furthermore, import restrictions may even reduce intended money expenditure; unable to obtain the imports they want, consumers and investors may prefer to save some of the frustrated expenditure rather than try to spend it on the less desired home-produced goods. Finally, it needs to be remembered that at this stage of our analysis intended expenditure is not necessarily actual expenditure. If we start in internal balance and assume that any excess demand for home-produced goods is saved involuntarily, actual expenditure must fall to the level represented by the indifference curve through *K*.

Devaluation

In our model a devaluation of the exchange rate must switch expenditure away from imports and therefore must improve the balance of payments. In terms of the diagram it must move the equilibrium point north-west.

Two reasons are usually given why a devaluation may not improve the balance of payments, but the assumptions of the model here rule out both possibilities. First, a devaluation may fail to improve the balance of payments because it lowers the value of exports in terms of foreign currency more than it reduces the value of imports. Our assumption of a constant value of exports rules out this possibility. Secondly, the devaluation may create excess demand for home-produced goods which in turn either spills over into imports or causes the prices of home-produced goods to rise, so offsetting the effects of the devaluation. This possibility is assumed away at this stage by supposing all excess demand to be saved and the prices of home-produced goods to be constant.

A third possibility is that, starting in conditions of unemployment, the devaluation sets off a multiplier process which offsets the initial effect of the devaluation on the balance of payments. This has already been referred to. This process is only possible if monetary conditions permit the induced increase in real expenditure. But even given a flexible supply of money or velocity of circulation, the balance-of-payments effect will only be offset completely if the marginal home leakage is zero. Since this is probably an unrealistic assumption it is normally argued that below full employment (and ruling out an initial fall in the foreign currency value of exports) a devaluation must have the net effect of improving the balance of payments. At any rate here we are concerned only with the initial effect of the devaluation and not with the multiplier effect.

A devaluation can be analysed in two parts: the effect on imports and the effect on exports. We use Figure 3 to illustrate these effects. The initial position is at *L*, with expenditure in terms of home-produced goods of *OM* and in terms of imports of *ON*. The devaluation will switch expenditure to a point on the

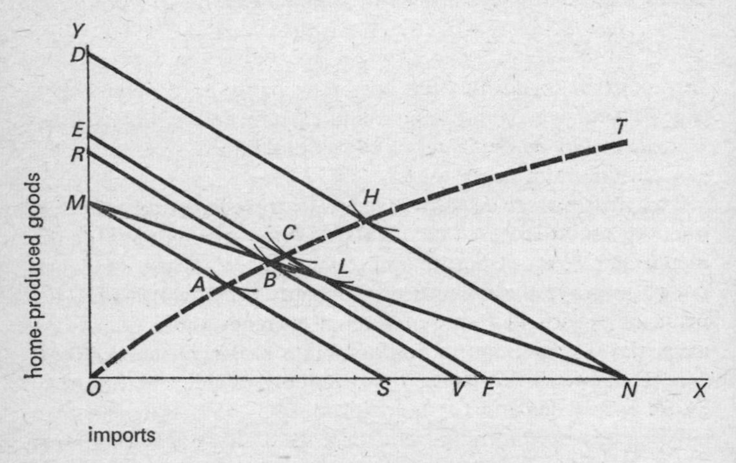

Figure 3 Devaluation – the effect on imports and exports

income–consumption line *OT*. The question is whether this point will be on an indifference curve higher or lower than that which passes through *L*. Will real expenditure rise or fall?

The devaluation raises the price of imports in domestic currency, the price in foreign currency being constant. With given expenditure in terms of home-goods of *OM*, expenditure in terms of imports falls to *OS*. The effect is the same as that of a tariff. Consumers' equilibrium at this stage moves from *L* to *A*. The increase in the domestic value of imports is shown by the vertical distance between *MN* and *MS*. The rise in the domestic price of imports has clearly reduced real expenditure.

This could be the end of the story, and indeed it would have to be if we assumed constant money expenditure in domestic currency. But an alternative (and not unrealistic) assumption is that money expenditure is equal to the domestic value of exports and other foreign currency proceeds plus a fixed amount in domestic currency. In this case the story must go on, and involves us in considerable complications.

The devaluation raises the value of exports in domestic currency, the value in foreign currency being fixed. This higher export income raises expenditure in terms of home-produced goods. For example, it might increase expenditure from *OM* to *OR*. Consumers' equilibrium will then move from *A* to *B*. Just as the rise in the domestic price of imports lowers real expenditure, so the rise in the domestic value of exports increases real expenditure.

Taking both the effect on imports and on exports into account, will real expenditure rise or fall on balance?

If exports are equal to imports initially the rise in the domestic cost of the initial quantity of imports is the vertical distance between *MN* and *MS* at *L*. Since a devaluation raises the domestic price of exports in the same proportion as the domestic price of imports, this vertical distance between *MN* and *MS* at *L* gives also the rise in the domestic value of exports; it is equal to *ME* in terms of home-produced goods or *SF* in terms of imports. So the final equilibrium will be at *C*.

It can be seen that in terms of the final price ratio (represented by the slope of *EF* or *MS*) real expenditure is the same at *C* as at *L*. Actually it has risen, since the indifference curve at *C* is above that at *L*. This is the familiar effect of an expenditure-compensated price change. The community could purchase the same combination of imported and home-produced goods as it did before devaluation – the combination represented by the point *L* – but due to the relative price change it chooses to purchase the preferred combination at point *C*.

If exports are initially less than imports, the aim of the devaluation being to bring them towards equality, we must see how the deficit is covered. It may be covered by capital inflow the value of which is fixed in terms of foreign currency, and thus rises in terms of domestic currency when the country devalues. The treatment required for capital inflow is then the same as that applied to exports, and in our analysis it can simply be included in 'the value of exports'. On the other hand, some part of the initial excess of imports over exports may be covered by capital inflow or a reduction in the country's reserves which is determined in terms of domestic, and not foreign, currency. In this case the devaluation will reduce the real value of the money expenditure equal to the original deficit. A constant amount of domestic money will purchase less imports than before. Whether the devaluation raises or lowers real expenditure depends now on the strength of two opposing considerations: on the one hand, real expenditure tends to rise since it has an effect similar to an expenditure-compensated price change; on the other hand, the expenditure compensation may be incomplete since the real value of the original deficit declines.

One special case is where imports are initially greater than exports (plus capital inflow fixed in terms of foreign currency), but where the devaluation brings them into equality. There must then be a fall in real expenditure. In Figure 3 the final equilibrium will be at *B*. The rise in the domestic value of exports is *RM*, which is equal to the vertical distance between *MN* and *MS* at *B*. Real expenditure when calculated in terms of the initial price ratio is constant, though in fact it has fallen. This is the reverse of an appreciation from initial trade balance, which – being an expenditure compensated price change – would raise real expenditure.

Generalizing, we can say that if the money supply is completely inelastic a devaluation must lower real expenditure. On the other hand, if it varies with the domestic value of foreign currency proceeds, but is otherwise inelastic, the story is more complicated. If initially the value of exports (defined to include capital inflow fixed in terms of foreign currency) is equal to or greater than the value of imports, a devaluation will raise real expenditure. But, if initially there is an excess of imports over exports, real expenditure may decline. The greater this initial deficit, the more likely it is that expenditure falls, and this must certainly be so if the devaluation brings imports into equality with exports. If there is some additional elasticity in the money supply or the velocity of circulation, the change in real expenditure, whether an increase or a decrease, will be less than indicated in this analysis. And if expenditure is actually fixed in real terms the problem discussed in this section disappears.

Decline in prices of home-produced goods

Now suppose that there is a reduction in local prices, with the exchange rate constant. This price reduction could be induced by a reduction in money expenditure. It cannot then be regarded as essentially a switching policy, although the switching of expenditure may indeed be an important by-product of it. Alternatively the price reduction could be induced by some factors other than the existence of excess supply of home-produced goods. It could be brought about, for example, by enforced wage cuts, or by monopoly control legislation. It is then the inverse of a cost, as distinct from a demand, inflation. This is the case which will be illustrated here.

Starting again at *L* (Figure 3), the price ratio will swing from *MN* to *DN*. If money expenditure does not change, expenditure in terms of imports – the prices of which also have not changed – must stay constant. Consumers' equilibrium is at *H*. Real expenditure has risen. If the elasticity of demand for home-produced goods is unity, *H* will be due north of *L* and the demand for imports will not alter. Imports will decrease only if the elasticity of demand for home-produced goods is greater than unity. If money expenditure had declined due to the fall in prices the equilibrium would have settled somewhere on *OT* below *H*. At the limit money expenditure might have declined in the same proportion as the prices of home-produced goods. Expenditure would then have stayed constant in terms of home-produced goods but declined in terms of imports. The equilibrium would have been at *A* and real expenditure would have fallen.

Tariffs

If the government does not spend the customs revenue, a tariff involves a reduction in real expenditure as clearly as a fall in prices of home-produced goods unaccompanied by a change in money expenditure involves a rise. The price ratio will now swing from *MN* to *MS*, the vertical distance between *MN* and *MS* indicating the revenue raised. Consumers' equilibrium will be at *A*.

If *A* is due west of *L*, the tariff will not have altered expenditure on home-produced goods. This means that the higher price of imports has not altered the proportion of total expenditure which goes on imports. In other words the elasticity of demand for imports is unity. If *L* represented an initial position of internal balance, there will still be internal balance at *A*. The tariff produces just the right combination of switching and expenditure reduction to attain external balance without disturbing internal balance. If the elasticity of demand for imports were greater than unity, *A* would be north-west of *L*, and a further cut in expenditure would be needed to maintain internal balance. If the elasticity were less than unity (*A* south-west of *L*), some of the customs revenue should be spent.

It is frequently assumed in the literature on tariff theory that the proceeds from the tariff are automatically redistributed, perhaps by a reduction in income tax. In this case expenditure in terms of home-produced goods will rise and the equilibrium will move to *B*. The increase in expenditure in terms of home-goods of *RM* is just equal to the tariff revenue (the vertical distance between *MN* and *MS* at *B*). Comparing the final position now with the initial position at *L*, while expenditure at initial prices has not changed, real expenditure has in fact fallen somewhat.

V. What Happens to Excess Demand?

So far it has been assumed that any excess demand for home-produced goods is saved involuntarily. In fact there are three possibilities and various combinations of them. First the excess demand may be saved. Second, it may spill over on to foreign trade goods. And third, it may raise the prices of domestic goods. Foreign trade goods include both imports and exportables. If there are tight import restrictions covering all imports the only possibility is that the excess demand absorbs exportables which would otherwise have been exported. This case was considered at length in the article by Hemming and Corden (1958). But if we assume the value of exports as given then the spill-over must be on to uncontrolled imports. A clear distinction needs to be made between the *spill-over effect* and the rise in the internal price-level. In the first case the excess demand is diverted, not eliminated. In the second case the excess demand should actually disappear in time.

The spill-over effect

Suppose we start in internal balance and external deficit at *L* (Figure 4). Then devalue, bringing the equilibrium north-west to *G*. In Figure 4, *G* and *L* are on the same indifference curve; in fact, as we have seen, *G* could be on a higher or lower indifference curve, depending on the monetary assumption and on the extent,

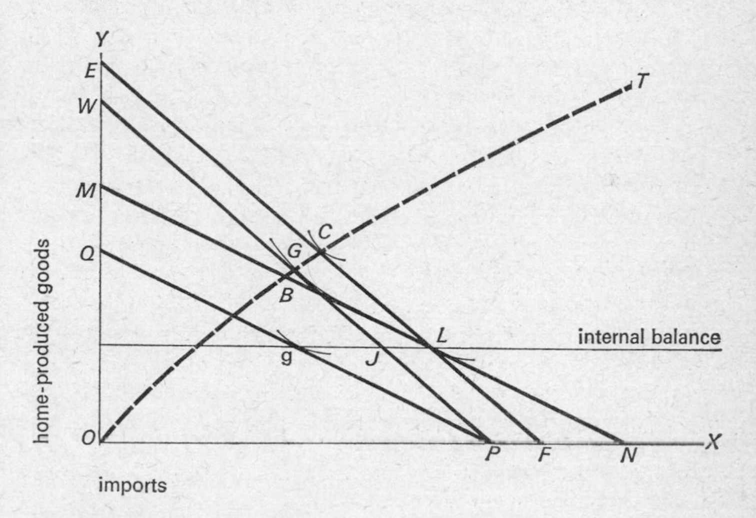

Figure 4 The spill-over effect

if any, of the initial balance-of-payments deficit. The movement to *G* represents the particular case where devaluation in itself does not alter real expenditure. There is excess demand for home-produced goods, equal to the vertical distance between *G* and *L*. We assume that all this spills over to imports. At the price ratio and expenditure given at *G*, imports, which had previously decreased from *L* to *G* will now increase to *J*. The new equilibrium is at *J*, where real expenditure is less than at *G* or *L*.

In this example the spill-over has partly but not wholly reversed the effect of the devaluation. It has only partly reversed it because when consumers cannot obtain the goods they really want, represented by the bundle of goods at *G*, and have to take more imports and less home-produced goods instead, their real expenditure falls even though their money expenditure stays constant.

It is possible that the spill-over completely reverses the effect of the devaluation. This could happen if the devaluation initially raised real intended expenditure. We saw above that if (*a*) money expenditure varies with the domestic value of foreign currency proceeds but is otherwise inelastic, and (*b*) imports are initially equal to exports, a devaluation will not alter real intended expenditure at final prices. In Figure 4, it would bring equilibrium to *C*, the equilibrium price line at *C* running through *L*. And this time the spill-over would return the equilibrium to *L*, completely reversing the effect of the devaluation.

If the initial cut in imports had been attained by import restrictions, the equilibrium (if such a term can be used to describe a situation sustained by import restrictions and involuntary savings) would have moved to a point such as *B* (Figure 4). If the whole of the excess demand then spilled over to (other) imports, the equilibrium would return to *L*, since the price ratio ruling at *B* is the same as that ruling at *L*.

All this assumes a money supply which is inelastic other than in response to changes in the domestic value of foreign currency proceeds. We see that even in this case the initial effects of a devaluation or of import restrictions may be completely reversed by spill-over. This result is certain if real expenditure is assumed to be constant. For example, in Figure 4 a spill-over may first bring the economy from *G* to *J*, but if this is then followed by a rise in money expenditure to restore real expenditure, the economy must return to *L*. In the case of import restrictions it will actually return to somewhere east of *L*, so that the restrictions will have worsened the balance of payments. Constant real expenditure requires a greater quantity of uncontrolled imports to substitute for a given amount of controlled imports since the uncontrolled imports are, after all, only the second or third preference.

How does this spill-over affect our sectors and zones in Figure 2? One approach is to say that positions of excess demand (zones I and IV) cannot be sustained. If the economy is temporarily in one of these zones, it will gradually slide southeastwards until it rests somewhere on the internal balance line. And yet this is not entirely satisfactory since excess demand for home-produced goods has not disappeared, but has only spilled over. There is not true internal balance.

Alternatively, assuming that spill-over does not affect real expenditure, we can say that every point on the indifference curve above *L* (such as *G*) represents in effect the same level of imports, and hence of external deficit, as *L* or any point due south of *L*. It follows that similarly every point on the indifference curve *kk′* (Figure 2) above *K* gives external balance, just as *K* itself and any point due south of *K* does. So the external balance line in Figure 2 has a kink at *K*. If full employment is not a definite point, there will be a gradual change in the slope of the external balance line. Or if 'internal balance' is interpreted as allowing for some unemployment, the kink will be somewhere north of *K*.

This adjustment means that a segment of the diagram in Figure 2 shifts from zone 1 (excess demand and external surplus) to zone IV (excess demand and external deficit). It means that, given initial internal balance and a certain level of real expenditure, an expenditure-switching policy cannot improve the balance of payments. Demand switched from imports on to home-produced goods will return to imports, even though these may now be a second-best.

Open inflation

So far it has been assumed that the prices of home-produced goods do not change. Excess demand spills over to imports at given prices. But in fact the excess demand is likely to raise prices of home-produced goods to some extent. This will both switch expenditure from home-goods on to imports and, if money expenditure is not increased at the same time, it will reduce real expenditure. Eventually the economy must settle somewhere on the internal balance line. Any position in zones I and IV is unstable since there is an automatic mechanism by which excess demand disappears.

Consider first the case where money expenditure is constant and return to Figure 4. We start again at *L* in internal balance, a devaluation bringing us to *G*. So prices of home-produced goods rise, the expenditure line swinging down, to the position shown by *PQ*. The diagram represents the special case where the new equilibrium is at *g*, due south of *G*. The elasticity of demand for home-produced goods is unity, so that demand for imports is not altered by the rise in domestic prices. Real expenditure has fallen sufficiently to offset the effect of switching, and the benefits of the devaluation on the external situation are not reversed. If the elasticity of demand for home-produced goods had been greater than unity part of the benefit would have been reversed since *g* would have been south-east of *G*. But as long as there is some reduction in real expenditure the whole effect of the devaluation cannot be reversed.

If on the other hand real expenditure is assumed to stay constant the whole effect of the devaluation must be reversed. Real expenditure will be maintained by increases in money expenditure whenever prices rise, and the equilibrium must eventually return to *L*.

It remains true that, starting in internal balance, a devaluation can improve the balance of payments only if real expenditure falls. But it is also important to remember that – provided the money supply or the velocity of circulation are not perfectly flexible – the rise in domestic prices can be the way in which the necessary decline in real expenditure is obtained and that this can be much greater than the decline in real expenditure which spill-over may bring about.

Complete price flexibility

In a neo-classical model internal prices would be flexible not only above but also below internal balance. Just as excess demand would disappear by a rise in prices, so unemployment would disappear through a fall in prices. Price flexibility would thus keep equilibrium somewhere on the internal balance line, while expenditure variations would determine just where on the line. If in addition we made expenditure responsive to foreign currency holdings (the gold standard mechanism), external balance would also be automatic, and price flexibility together with the gold standard mechanism would bring about internal and external balance.

A more intriguing situation would arise if we associated flexible internal prices with a flexible exchange rate. Say we start in zone IV with a balance-of-payments deficit and excess demand. The deficit will cause the exchange rate to depreciate and pull 'equilibrium' (if this is not rather stretching the term) north-west towards the external balance line. But excess demand will raise prices of home-produced goods, and pull the economy towards the internal balance line. If the increase in the prices of home-produced goods is allowed to reduce real expenditure, then after a period of depreciation and inflation the system will come to rest at internal and external balance (at K). But if real expenditure is maintained there can only be continuous depreciation and inflation.

The absorption problem

The important conclusion which emerges is that a fully employed economy cannot improve its balance of payments unless real expenditure is reduced. 'At a given level of productivity a fully employed economy has no possible way of closing a deficit in its foreign balance unless it can cut down its absorption of resources for domestic purposes' (Nurkse, 1956, pp. 137–8). In the early part of this paper it was assumed that excess demand for home-produced goods was saved. The cut in real expenditure (or 'absorption') was then achieved involuntarily but automatically. But if excess demand causes prices to rise or spills over to imports, a cut in real intended expenditure is needed. This may be the incidental effect of switching policies or of the rise in internal prices, or it may require a deliberate policy decision.

So the 'Simple conclusions from the diagram' on page 263 must be amended. Those conclusions followed directly from the zones and sectors in Figure 2 assuming that excess demand was saved. The amendments which must now be introduced represent the contribution of the absorption approach to balance-of-payments theory. They follow when excess demand is no longer saved, or, in terms of the diagram, when either the external balance line has a kink so that north of K it follows the indifference curve kk', or when positions in zones I and IV cannot be sustained.

All our earlier conclusions remain true for zones II and III where there is initial unemployment. But starting in internal balance or in excess demand the following amendments must be made. It remains true that expenditure increasing or reducing policy affects both the internal and external situation, provided we regard a change in the level of unsatisfied demand for home-produced goods as a genuine change in the internal situation. But it is no longer true that an expenditure-switching policy has any effect on the balance of payments unless it carries some expenditure reduction with it. Since an expenditure-reduction policy can affect both internal and external balance, while a switching policy can affect only internal balance, it would be possible to associate a switching policy with the aim of internal balance and an expenditure-reducing policy with the aim of external balance, but not vice versa. It is true that normally both policies are required to achieve both aims simultaneously, but it is also quite correct to say that expenditure changes are required to maintain external balance and switching policies are required to ensure that this is accompanied by internal balance.

So we must revise the earlier conclusion that it is quite arbitrary to link either of the two policies to either of the two ends. At or above full employment it is correct to link expenditure policy direct to external balance since it is the sole determinant of it. The interesting thing is that this link is not the one which (in the post gold standard age) is usually made when one of the policies is associated with one of the aims.

Suppose we start in excess demand and external deficit, somewhere in zone IV. The external deficit could only be removed by a reduction in real expenditure. Say that this is ruled out. Is there then any reason to alter the exchange rate? Since there is an external deficit the first idea might be to devalue (moving north-west on the diagram). But this will not reduce the external deficit. It means moving along a given indifference curve, and all it will do is to increase the excess demand for home-produced goods; less imports will be bought as a first preference and more as a second preference. In fact an appreciation (moving south-east on the diagram) would be preferable. It would not affect the external situation but at least would reduce the excess demand for home-produced goods.

Finally a familiar difference between the analysis of unemployment situations (zones II and III) and of excess demand situations (zones I and IV) can be noted. Assuming a flexible money supply, at unemployment an increase in the demand for home-produced goods creates induced expenditure increases; but at or above full employment it creates induced price increases. In the first case, if the marginal home leakage is positive, the induced expenditure increase will modify but not reverse the effect of a switching policy on the balance of payments; in the second case the induced price increase will completely reverse the effect of the switching policy. The difference in the two cases can be explained in terms of the absorption analysis. The balance of payments can only be improved to the extent to which saving is increased or investment decreased. Below full employment extra saving is generated in the multiplier process as real incomes increase. But at or above full employment there is no rise in real income. Savings are generated only if excess demand is saved; once it is assumed that it spills on to imports either directly or by means of a rise in the prices of home-produced goods the increase in savings disappears.

VI. Complications

A major limitation of our diagram is that it does not allow for induced changes in the volume of exports and the terms of trade. Though one hesitates to blur its simplicity by introducing complications, in this section three variations will be allowed for which can be introduced without much difficulty.

Induced changes in import prices

The foreign price of imports might decline as reduced quantities are bought. It is not difficult to incorporate such induced changes in import prices in the diagram. The general nature of the diagram and our earlier conclusions are in no way affected.

The simplest way is to draw a new *OT* curve (Figure 2) which shows how purchases of imports and of home-produced goods change as expenditure alters with a given exchange rate, but with import prices declining as one moves down the curve. Moving south-west on this curve, the slopes of the indifference curves at their intersections with it would get progressively flatter. This new *OT* curve would form the boundary for the policy sectors; it would cross the old *OT* curve at *K*, lie below it to the left of *K* and above it to the right. There would still be a unique volume of imports, *OZ*, which yields the value of imports required for external balance. But as one moved to the left along *OX*, the value of imports would now decline more rapidly than the volume.

An alternative approach is to stretch the *OX* axis and with it the indifference curve map. Moving to the right along *OX*, constant increases in import quantities would have increasing distances between them. Decreases in expenditure at a given exchange rate would continue to be represented by parallel price lines (even though the actual price ratio between imports and home-produced goods would be changing), and alterations in the exchange rate, but not in induced changes in import prices, would be reflected by changes in the slopes of the price lines. In this case the *OX* axis and the indifference curve map, and not the policy sector boundaries, change.

Home consumption of exportables

In certain circumstances, possibly applicable to Australia, or to Britain in the post-war period, it would be useful to hold the supply of exportables, but not of exports, constant. Thus allowance would be made for varying quantities of home consumption of exportables. Provided the foreign prices of exports and imports are given, which must mean that increasing quantities of exports could be sold without price reduction, there would be no difficulty in introducing this in the diagram. It is necessary only to define the *OX* axis as representing imports plus exportables, and the *OY* axis as specifically excluding exportables. A reduction in expenditure would cut both imports and home consumption of exportables, in a proportion depending on the income elasticities of demand for them. With given export prices and a given production of exportables, the reduced home consumption of exportables represents an equal increase in exports. Similarly a devaluation would switch domestic expenditure not only away from imports but also away from exportables.

If exportables are merged with imports along the *OX* axis it is no longer possible to show the effects of measures which affect only imports, namely import restrictions or tariffs. So a slight variation is to show exportables along the *OY* axis, producing the elaborations developed in Hemming and Corden (1958).

Cost-based export prices

Even with a variable domestic consumption of exportables, it is doubtful whether our diagram can be applied directly to an economy such as the United Kingdom's. In the long run the supply of exportables is certainly responsive to changes in the domestic prices of exports; and in the short-run, even though the supply of exportables may be fixed, their prices in foreign currency may well fall. It is this latter short-run case which will be considered briefly here.

In discussions of the United Kingdom devaluation of 1949 it is often said or implied that export prices tended to be inflexible in domestic currency – to be fixed on a cost rather than a market demand basis. With the supply of exports fixed, a devaluation will then mean a reduction in the foreign currency value but no change in the domestic value of exports. The foreign currency value of exports will fall in proportion to the devaluation. Whether a devaluation improves or worsens the balance of payments then depends only on the elasticity of demand for imports. If this is unity the value of imports in domestic currency does not change (and in foreign currency falls in proportion to the devaluation), and the balance of payments will not alter. Only if the elasticity of demand for imports is greater than unity will the balance of payments improve. This type of case is not generally provided for in formal international trade theory, which commonly assumes market-based pricing. It might be useful here (as also when there is excess demand for imports or for home-produced goods) to introduce a 'price flexibility factor'.

Cost-based export pricing can be represented in Figure 3. The initial position is at *L* and the increased price of imports shifts consumers' equilibrium to *A*. This time the domestic value of exports does not rise, so there is no increase in expenditure in terms of home-produced goods. Instead of the equilibrium shifting up to *B* or *C* (as in our earlier analysis), it stays at *A*.

The value of exports in terms of foreign currency falls in proportion to the devaluation. If *A* is due west of *L*, this means that the degree of external deficit originally represented by *L* is now represented by *A*. And in this case there has been no change in the balance-of-payments situation. But of course *A* may be north-west or south-west of *L*, depending on the elasticity of demand for imports, and then the foreign value of imports will have fallen more (north-west) or less (south-west) than exports.

Appendix: Alternative Diagrams

The inspiration for this article originally came from a paper by Professor T. W. Swan delivered to a meeting of Australian economists in 1955 (Swan, 1955). Professor Swan presented the

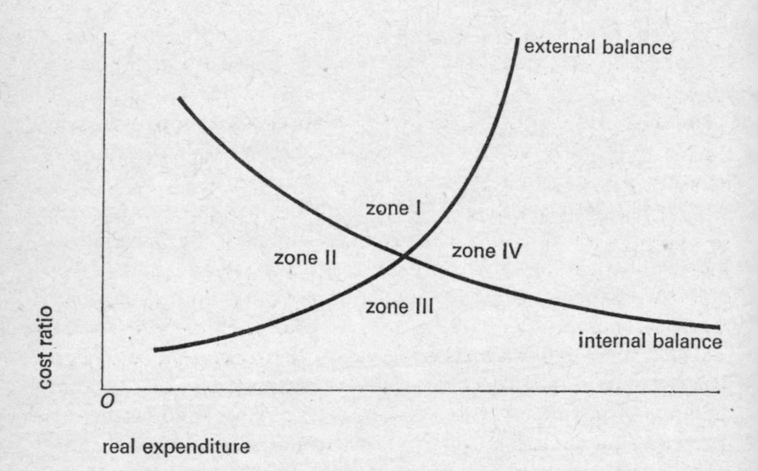

Figure 5 Real expenditure at constant prices (Swan, 1955)

diagram shown in Figure 5. On the vertical axis is the *Cost Ratio* which he described as 'some sort of index measuring the competitive position of Australian industries – e.g. the ratio of an index of international prices (prices of imports and exports) to an index of local wages, with weights reflecting the sensitivity of supply and demand for different commodities to changes in relative costs'. A devaluation, for example, is represented by an upwards movement. On the horizontal axis he showed *Real Expenditure* – domestic investment and consumption at constant prices. The two heavy lines show the various combinations of cost ratio and real expenditure which yield respectively internal and external balance. They 'divide existence into four zones of economic unhappiness' – the zones being defined as in our Figure 2. The steepening of the external balance line above internal balance represents the overspill effect.

Professor Swan made the key point which has been emphasized in this paper.

> . . . in each zone the necessary direction of adjustment of one of the two factors (Expenditure, Cost Ratio) is apparent, whereas the other may be either too high or too low, depending on our precise position in the zone . . . This is the source of many of the problems and errors of economic policy – if one factor is substantially out of line, the 'natural' indications for the other may be quite misleading (Swan, 1955).

Professor Swan assumed no import restrictions or tariffs, and held the terms of trade constant. But in fact the diagram could be generalized to show any kind of switching policy on the vertical axis. For a devaluation or a reduction in the internal cost level to be represented by a move northwards it is necessary only to assume that the elasticities in foreign trade are high enough – i.e. that, assuming away income effects, and no overspill, a devaluation does improve the balance of payments.

Basically Professor Swan's diagram shows the same things as Figure 2, but, while magnificently simple, it is a clock without a visible mechanism. It does not show how the internal and external balance curves are derived, and it requires our type of diagram to bring out the full meaning of real expenditure 'at constant prices'.

A diagram devised by Dr Salter (1959), very similar in conception to ours, enables the supply of exportables to vary by showing supply as well as demand reactions. His diagram (Figure 6) shows traded goods along the horizontal axis and non-traded goods along the vertical axis. Traded goods consist of importables and exportables. The production transformation curve shows the various combinations of traded and non-traded goods which can be produced at full employment. Dr Salter is able to show exportables and importables along a single axis by assuming constant terms of trade.

There is internal balance if the total demand for non-traded goods is equal to the supply and external balance if the demand for traded goods is equal to the supply. The price ratio and level of expenditure appropriate to internal and external balance are given by the point of tangency of an indifference curve to the transformation curve. In Figure 6, as drawn, there is unemployment and a balance-of-payments deficit. The pattern and level of

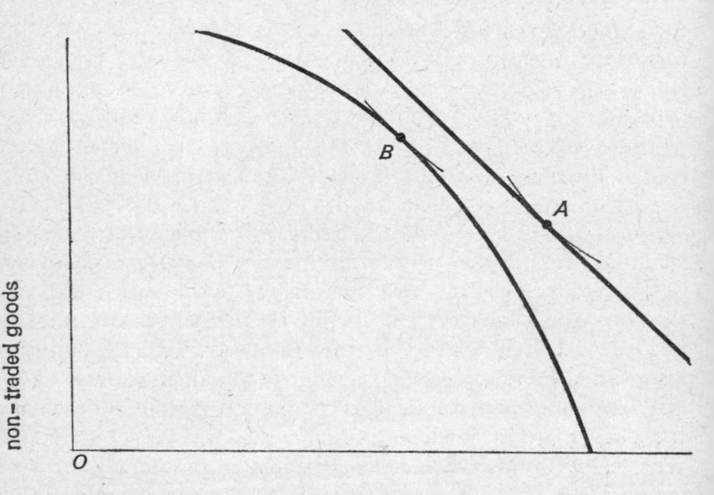

Figure 6 (Taken from Salter, 1959)

intended consumption is indicated by the point *A* and the pattern of potential production by *B*. The four possible *zones of economic unhappiness* are implied in the relationship between points *A* and *B*.

The advantage of this diagram (as also of Professor Swan's) is that it is not necessary to hold the volume of exports constant. It emphasizes that relative price changes alter not only the pattern of consumption but also the pattern of production. On the other hand it really requires that the two categories of traded and non-traded goods do not shade into each other.

Finally, a diagram published by Professor Meade (1949) takes into account not only the policies in one country but also in the Rest of the World. In all the models so far considered the foreign demand curve for exports is given. If country *A* deflates to remove an external deficit its imports fall and unemployment is created; but it is assumed that this would neither raise nor lower the demand curve for its exports. It is true that if the foreign elasticity of demand for exports is assumed to be infinite (as in Dr Salter's diagram) exports would increase, but this would be due to an increased supply and not to a shift in the demand curve. This neglect of a foreign repercussion can be based on the assumption either that country *A* is insignificant in relation to the rest of the world, or that the rest deliberately neutralizes the effects of *A*'s reduced imports, by not allowing the fall in its export income to have a multiplier effect.

One alternative to a *neutralizing* policy is a *neutral* policy. The reduced export income would then be allowed to reduce the rest's domestic expenditure and to multiply not only through the rest's economy but also to rebound back to *A* in the form of a reduced demand for its exports. Another alternative is for the rest to pursue an *offsetting* policy. The slack in its export industries would be taken up by increased demand for exportables brought about by a rise in its domestic expenditure. This would be a positive policy of internal balance. Thus, if our country deflates, so reducing its demand for the rest's exports, the rest will offset the effect of this on its own internal situation by inflating. This will raise the demand for our exports. So, if one country buys less from the other, the other's demand for imports will actually rise. Given this assumption, whether the initial deflation by country *A* leaves it with any unemployment which then has to be eliminated by a switching policy depends not just on the marginal propensity to import in *A* but on the sum of the marginal propensities to import in the two countries.

This is the type of model which has been represented diagrammatically by Professor Meade, and our Figures 1 or 4 could be regarded as half of his two-country Edgeworth box diagram. Professor Meade assumed policies of internal balance in both countries and compared the various switching policies which may then be needed to eliminate a balance-of-payments disequilibrium, but it would be possible to adapt his diagram to present our problems.

References

HEMMING, M. F. W., and CORDEN, W. M. (1958), 'Import restrictions as an instrument of balance-of-payments policy', *Economic Journal*, September.

JOHNSON, H. G. (1958), 'Towards a general theory of the balance of payments', *International Trade and Economic Growth*, Allen and Unwin, ch. 6. [Reprinted here as Reading 11.]

MEADE, J. E. (1949), 'A geometric representation of the balance-of-payments policy', *Economica*, November.

MEADE, J. E. (1951), *The Theory of International Economic Policy*, vol. I. *The Balance of Payments*, London.

NURKSE, R. (1956), 'The relation between home investment and external balance in the light of British experience, 1945–55', *Review o Economics and Statistics*, May.

SALTER, W. E. G. (1959), 'Internal and external balance – the role of price and expenditure effects', *Economic Record*, August.

SWAN, T. W. (1955), *Longer-run Problems of the Balance of Payments*. Paper given to the Congress of the Australian and New Zealand Association for the Advancement of Science. [Reprinted in H. W. Arndt and W. M. Corden, eds., *The Australian Economy: A Volume of Readings*, Cheshire, Melbourne, 1963.]

TINBERGEN, J. (1952), *On the Theory of Economic Policy*, Amsterdam.

13 J. Marcus Fleming

Domestic Financial Policies under Fixed and under Floating Exchange Rates

J. Marcus Fleming (1962), 'Domestic financial policies under fixed and under floating exchange rates', *International Monetary Fund Staff Papers*, vol. 9, no. 3, pp. 369–79.

The bearing of exchange rate systems on the relative effectiveness of monetary policy on the one hand, and of budgetary policy on the other, as techniques for influencing the level of monetary demand for domestic output, is not always kept in mind when such systems are compared. In this paper it is shown that the expansionary effect of a given increase in money supply will always be greater if the boundary has a floating exchange rate than if it has a fixed rate. By contrast, it is uncertain whether the expansionary effect on the demand for domestic output of a given increase in budgetary expenditure or a given reduction in tax rates will be larger or smaller with a floating than with a fixed rate. In all but extreme cases, the stimulus to monetary demand arising from an increase in money supply will be greater, relative to that arising from an expansionary change in budgetary policy, with a floating than with a fixed rate of exchange.

The Model

Let us assume a simple Keynesian model[1] in which (a) taxation and private income after tax both vary directly with national income, (b) private expenditure (on consumption and investment) varies directly with income after taxation,[2] and inversely with the interest rate, (c) the interest rate varies directly with the income-velocity of circulation of money (the ratio of national income to the stock of money), (d) the balance of trade (exports *less* imports

1. See Appendix (pp. 299–303) for a mathematical formulation.
2. It is assumed that the private marginal propensity to spend will always be less than unity with respect to income before tax.

of goods and services) varies inversely with domestic expenditure[3] and directly with the domestic currency value of foreign exchange, and (e) the balance of payments on capital account varies directly with the rate of interest. All magnitudes are expressed in domestic wage units, and wages are assumed to remain constant in domestic currency. No account is taken of any changes in the propensity to spend from real income changes that result from changes in the terms of trade. No account is taken, initially, of the effect of exchange speculation on capital movements.

Effects of an Expansionary Shift in Budgetary Policy

Let us first compare the effects of an expansionary shift in budgetary policy brought about by an increase in public expenditure, without any change in tax rates, under (a) a fixed exchange rate system and (b) a floating exchange rate system, respectively. (A decline in taxation, resulting from a reduction in tax rates, would have effects on expenditure, income, and the balance of payments similar to, though less powerful than, those resulting from an equal increase in public expenditure. No essential feature of the ensuing analysis would be altered if it had been concerned with the former rather than the latter type of budgetary expansion.)

Under fixed exchange rates, an increase in public expenditure will give rise to an increase in income which will be associated – if the economy was previously underemployed – with increases in employment and output.[4] The increase in expenditure will lead to a deterioration in the balance of payments on current account, owing, notably, to a rise in imports. The increase in expenditure and income will also enhance tax revenues, though not to such an extent as to equal the initial increase in public expenditure.[5]

3. It is assumed that the marginal propensity for the balance of trade to decline as expenditure increases is less than unity.

4. Since the marginal propensity to spend out of income is less than unity and since a fraction of each round of expenditure leaks abroad in additional net imports, the increase in income and expenditure will be limited, though possibly large. See Appendix, paragraphs 3 and 4.

5. The rise in tax revenue could exceed the initial rise in government expenditure only if the marginal propensity to spend out of private income after tax were substantially greater than unity. See Appendix, paragraph 5.

In order to isolate the effect of a change in budgetary policy, it is necessary to assume that monetary policy remains, in some sense, unchanged. In this paper, this is taken to mean that the stock of money is held constant.[6] To keep the money stock constant while the increase in government expenditure is pushing up incomes will necessitate economy in the use of money which is possible only if the interest rate is raised or allowed to rise. The rise in interest in turn will result in (a) a check to the increase in expenditure and income, though some increase will remain,[7] and (b) a favorable shift in the balance of payments on capital account, i.e. a decline in capital exports and/or an increase in capital imports.

Since the increase in public expenditure provokes an unfavorable shift in the current balance and a favorable shift in the capital balance, it is uncertain whether the balance of payments as a whole will deteriorate or improve. It is the more likely to deteriorate, and the less likely to improve, the higher is the marginal propensity to import and the greater the adverse effect on the value of exports as domestic expenditure increases, the less sensitive is the rate of interest to changes in money income and hence in the velocity of circulation, and the less sensitive are capital movements to changes in the rate of interest. See Appendix, paragraph 8.

To the extent that the increase in public expenditure gives rise to an improvement or a deterioration, respectively, in the balance of payments, the maintenance of a constant stock of money will call for a decline or an increase, respectively, in the rate of expansion of bank credit. More important is the fact that, if the policy of

6. The only clear-cut alternative would appear to be that of defining constancy of monetary policy as the maintenance of a constant rate of interest. In 'Flexible exchange rates and employment policy', *Canadian Journal of Economics and Political Science* (November 1961), Mr R. A. Mundell has compared the effects of monetary policy (defined as interest policy), fiscal policy, and commercial policy in a flexible exchange rate system and a fixed exchange rate system, respectively.

7. It is uncertain whether private expenditure, stimulated by the rise in income and depressed by the rise in interest, will increase or decrease. But expenditure as a whole, like income, will increase, except where income velocity is entirely inelastic. See Appendix, paragraphs 6 and 7. In this extreme case, not only expenditure but also income and the balance of trade will remain unchanged.

budgetary expansion results in a deterioration of the balance of payments, shortage of reserves may ultimately compel the authorities to abandon the policy and to renounce the associated expansion in income and employment.[8]

Suppose, now, that the increase in public expenditure takes place in a country where the balance of payments is kept in equilibrium through exchange rate adjustments. Then, if the parameters of our model – notably the sensitivity of capital movements to changes in the rate of interest – are such that a rise in public expenditure would have resulted, with a fixed exchange rate system, in a deterioration in the balance of payments, it will result, with a floating rate system, in a depreciation of the exchange rate, which will bring about a partial restoration of the trade balance. (This restoration will, in general, be only partial since some net deterioration of the trade balance, compared with the situation before the rise in public expenditure, must remain to offset the improvement in the capital balance.) To the extent that the current balance is restored, there will be an increase – over and above that discussed above – in expenditure, income, and output. In other words, the stimulus to income, output, and employment resulting from a given increase in public expenditure will be greater with a floating exchange rate than with a fixed exchange rate (see Appendix, paragraph 10). If capital movements were entirely insensitive to the rise in the rate of interest, the exchange rate would depreciate to whatever extent was necessary completely to restore the trade balance, and the stimulus to income and output would be of the same order as would have occurred in a closed economy.

On the other hand, if a rise in public expenditure would, with a fixed exchange rate, have effected an improvement in the balance of payments, it will, with a floating rate, lead to an exchange appreciation; and, to the extent that appreciation intensifies the deterioration in the trade balance, the net stimulus to income, output, and employment will be less than in an open economy with a fixed rate (see Appendix, paragraph 10). At first sight, the case in which a rise in government expenditure produces an exchange appreciation would appear to be an academic *curiosum*

8. It is assumed not only that the exchange rate will remain fixed but that there will be no resort to restrictions on international transactions.

without practical significance. However, as is shown in a paper prepared by Mr R. R. Rhomberg, expounding an econometric model of the Canadian economy, the responsiveness of international capital movements to changes in interest rates, and the responsiveness of interest rates to exchanges in money national income, have probably been sufficiently great in that country over a large part of the postwar period, relative to the marginal propensity to import, for a rise in government expenditure at a constant money stock to have tended to produce just such a result.

It is of interest to note that, if the flow of capital between the country and the outside world were infinitely elastic with respect to the interest rate, the appreciation of the exchange rate resulting from the inflow of capital would bring about a net deterioration in the current balance of payments large enough to offset completely the stimulating effect of the budget deterioration on national income. National income would not increase at all, and the interest rate would remain at the original level (see Appendix, paragraph 11).[9]

Effects of an Increase in the Stock of Money

Now, let us compare the effects of income, output, and employment of increasing the stock of money (a) with fixed exchange rates and (b) with floating exchange rates, respectively.

An increase in the stock of money will entail a decline in the velocity of circulation and lead to a reduction in the rate of interest which will stimulate an increase in private expenditure on investment and consumption, both directly and via the Keynesian multiplier. The rise in expenditure will be associated, as before, with a (smaller) increase in income and output and a deterioration in the balance of payments on current account (see Appendix,

9. A high sensitivity of the interest rate to changes in velocity of circulation, i.e. a low elasticity of velocity with respect to the interest rate, while it makes for a favorable balance of payments response to government spending, and while it therefore tends to make the income response smaller under floating than under fixed exchange rates, also tends to reduce the magnitude of that response under both exchange systems. If the velocity of circulation were completely inelastic, a change in government expenditure would have no net effect on income under either exchange system.

paragraphs 12 and 13). The rise in income will moderate the decline in the rate of interest but not to the point of eliminating it; otherwise, neither investment nor income could increase (see Appendix, paragraph 14). Since the monetary expansion, even after the rise in expenditure and income, lowers the interest rate, some deterioration will tend to occur in the balance of payments on capital account. In the case of a monetary expansion, therefore, by contrast with that of an increase in public expenditure, a deterioration in the balance of payments as a whole is bound to occur in all circumstances. It follows that the monetary expansion, and the associated expansion of income and output, could only be sustained indefinitely to the extent that in their absence the balance of payments would have been favorable.

It is easy to see that a monetary expansion must always exercise a more powerful effect on income and output when there is a freely floating rate of exchange than when the exchange rate is fixed. The initial tendency toward an adverse shift in the balance of payments will cause a depreciation of the exchange rate to whatever extent may be necessary to keep external transactions as a whole in balance. The favorable influence of the exchange depreciation on the trade balance must come to outweigh the adverse influence of the increase in income to whatever extent may be necessary to produce a net improvement in that balance equal to the deterioration in the capital balance. The stimulus afforded by the depreciation to the trade balance will also act, both directly and via the multiplier, as a stimulus to income, raising it above the level which would have prevailed with a fixed exchange rate.[10]

The expansive effect of a given increase in the stock of money under the floating exchange rate system will be the greater, the greater the responsiveness of the international capital flow to movements in the rate of interest. If there were no responsiveness whatever, the exchange rate would depreciate to the point at which, despite the monetary expansion, no change occurred in the current balance of payments. Income would expand to the same

10. See Appendix, paragraphs 15 and 16. However, in the extreme case where velocity of circulation is completely inelastic, money income will rise proportionately to the money stock under either exchange system. See Appendix, paragraph 17.

extent as in a closed economy. On the other hand, if the capital flow were infinitely elastic with respect to the interest rate, the exchange rate would depreciate to the point at which the balance of trade became so favorable, and income increased so much, that the rate of interest remained at its original level. This implies that money income would increase by the same percentage as the stock of money (see Appendix, paragraph 18).

Relative Effects of the Two Kinds of Financial Policy

It remains to be shown that the effect on income and output of a given monetary expansion relative to that of a given budgetary expansion will never be less, and will generally be greater, under a floating exchange rate than under a fixed rate, even where budgetary expansion has a tendency to cause a depreciation of the exchange value of the currency.[11] The simplest way to demonstrate this is to compare an increase in the monetary stock (Policy *A*) and an increase in public expenditure (Policy *B*) such that, under a fixed exchange rate, the two policies have equal effects in the aggregate on income, output, and employment, and to show that, under a floating rate, the effect of Policy *A* will never be less, and will in general be greater, than that of Policy *B*.

Since we have supposed that under a fixed exchange rate the two policies have the same aggregate effect on income and output, they will bring about approximately the same adverse shift in the balance of trade.[12] Since, with incomes the same under the two policies, the money stock will be greater and the velocity of circulation less under Policy *A* than under Policy *B*, the rate of interest will be less under the former than under the latter policy. If capital movements were totally insensitive to changes in the interest rate, the two policies would, under a fixed exchange rate, have the same effects on the balance of payments as a whole; and under a floating rate, they would require an equal exchange depreciation to restore external equilibrium. The consequent

11. To put the same thing in other words, the effect under a floating rate relative to the effect under a fixed rate will never be greater, and will generally be less, in the case of budgetary expansion than in the case of monetary expansion.

12. We have to neglect, as unknown, any effects on trade of the difference in the composition of expenditure under the two policies.

restoration of the trade balance and the associated further stimulus to income would be the same for the two policies. However, if capital movements respond in any degree to interest changes, the two policies will have different effects. Since Policy *A* reduces, and Policy *B* raises, the rate of interest, Policy *A* under a fixed exchange rate will occasion a more unfavorable capital balance than Policy *B*. It follows that under a floating rate, Policy *A* will require, to restore payments equilibrium, a deeper exchange depreciation, and will consequently bring about a greater improvement in the trade balance, and a greater stimulus to income and output, than Policy *B* (see Appendix, paragraph 19). The superiority of Policy *A* over Policy *B* as a means of increasing income and output depends notably, as we have seen, on the sensitivity of international capital movements to changes in the rate of interest. At zero sensitivity, there is nothing to choose between the two policies. If the sensitivity is infinite, the level of income resulting from Policy *A* will exceed that resulting from Policy *B* in much the same proportion as the money stock under *A* exceeds that under *B*.

The nature of the exchange regime has an important bearing not only on the relative effectiveness in influencing income and output of the two types of financial policy – monetary policy and budgetary policy – but also on their relative practicability or sustainability. Thus, under a fixed exchange rate (except to the extent that the external accounts were originally in surplus) monetary expansion can be sustained only as long as reserves hold out, while budgetary expansion, if capital movements are sufficiently sensitive to interest rates, may be sustained indefinitely.[13] Under a floating exchange rate, on the other hand, not only is monetary expansion, while it lasts, likely to generate more additional income than budgetary expansion, relative to

13. It should be noted, however, that the responsiveness of capital movements to interest rate changes is made up of two components: a relocation of existing capital and a shift in the location of the placement of new savings. Since the former component is nonrecurrent and the latter recurrent in character, it is probable that the sensitivity of capital movements to interest changes will be greater in the short run than in the long run. Consequently, the difference between the two policies with respect to effectiveness and sustainability is also likely to be less in the long run than in the short.

what would happen under a fixed exchange rate, but both types of policies can be sustained indefinitely, so far as the balance of payments situation is concerned.

The Exchange Speculative Element in Capital Movements

The foregoing argument has generally assumed the absence of exchange speculation. Under a floating exchange rate, the influence on exchange speculation varies according to whether it is equilibrating or disequilibrating. If it is equilibrating – as was generally the case, for example, in Canada in the 1950s – it will tend to mitigate the exchange rate variations resulting from variations in internal financial policy, whether that policy is budgetary or monetary in character. However, since the greater relative effectiveness which a floating rate gives to monetary policy, compared with budgetary policy, is attributable to the stronger influence that the former exercises on exchange rates, it is to be expected that equilibrating speculation, by damping down exchange rate effects, will tend to reduce the difference in effectiveness between the two kinds of policy. Disequilibrating speculation on the other hand, by exaggerating exchange rate variations, tends to accentuate this difference in effectiveness.[14]

Appendix

1. Let Y stand for national income
   T for taxation
   N for private income
   X for private expenditure
   S for public expenditure
   Z for total expenditure

14. Exchange speculation has a bearing not only on the relative effectiveness, but also on the practicability and sustainability, of the two policies. Under exchange rates that are fixed and are expected to remain so, exchange speculation would be absent. But if confidence in the fixed rate were less than complete, the fear of arousing disequilibrating movements of capital would tend to limit the magnitude and duration of the expansionary financial policies, particularly of monetary policy, the effect of which on the balance of payments is in any case the more adverse than that of budgetary policy.

Let B stand for exports *less* imports
M for stock of money
V for income velocity
R for rate of interest
C for net capital import and
F for domestic currency value of foreign currency.

2. Then

$$X \equiv X + S + B.$$
$$Z \equiv X + S.$$
$$V \equiv \frac{Y}{M}.$$
$$N \equiv Y - T.$$
$$T = T(Y). \qquad 1 > T_y > 0.$$
$$X = X(N,R). \qquad X_r < 0, \qquad 1 > X_n(1 - T_y) > 0.$$
$$R = R(V). \qquad R_v > 0.$$
$$B = B(Z,F). \qquad 1 > -B_z > 0. \qquad B_f > 0.$$
$$C = C(R).$$

[Consolidating these relationships and taking differentials yields the following three equations:

$$[1 - (1 + B_z)X_n(1 - T_y)]\,dY - (1 + B_z)X_rR_v\,dV - B_f\,d\mathrm{F} = (1 + B_z)\,dS$$

$$\left(\frac{1}{V}\right) dY - \left(\frac{M}{V}\right) dV = dM$$

$$-B_zX_n(1 - T_y)\,dY - (B_zX_r + C_r)R_v\,dV - B_f\,dF + dB + dC = B_z\,dS$$

The first equation refers to the real variables of the economy, the second equation is the monetary identity, and the third equation refers to the balance of payments. Applying Cramer's Rules yields most of following results. – Ed.]

3. Let $\left(\frac{dY}{dS}\right)_{00}$ signify $\frac{dY}{dS}$ under fixed exchange rates when $dF = 0$, and $dM = 0$.

Let $\left(\frac{dR}{dS}\right)_{00}$, $\left(\frac{dT}{dS}\right)_{00}$, $\left(\frac{dC}{dS}\right)_{00}$, $\left(\frac{dB}{dS}\right)_{00}$, $\left(\frac{dC}{dR}\right)_{00}$, $\left(\frac{dB}{dR}\right)_{00}$ be analogously defined.

Then $$\left(\frac{dY}{dS}\right)_{00} = \frac{1 + B_z}{1 - (1 + B_z)\left\{X_n(1 - T_y) + \dfrac{X_r R_v}{M}\right\}}.$$

4. Since $1 > -B_z > 0$,
$1 > X_n(1 - T_y) > 0$,

and $X_r < 0$,

$$\therefore \quad \left(\frac{dY}{dS}\right)_{00} > 0.$$

5. For the same reasons,

$$\left(\frac{dT}{dS}\right)_{00} = \frac{T_y(1 + B_z)}{1 - (1 + B_z)\left\{X_n(1 - T_y) + \dfrac{X_r R_v}{M}\right\}} < 1.$$

6. $$\left(\frac{dX}{dS}\right)_{00} = \frac{1}{\dfrac{1}{(1 + B_z)\left\{X_n(1 - T_y) + \dfrac{X_r R_v}{M}\right\}} - 1} \gtrless 0,$$

as $X_n(1 - T_y) + \dfrac{X_r R_v}{M} \gtrless 0$.

7. $$\left(\frac{dZ}{dS}\right)_{00} = \frac{1}{1 - (1 + B_z)X_n(1 - T_y) + \dfrac{X_r R_v}{M}} > 0.$$

8. $$\left(\frac{dR}{dS}\right)_{00} = \frac{R_v}{M}\left(\frac{dY}{dS}\right)_{00} > 0.$$

$$\left(\frac{dC}{dS}\right)_{00} + \left(\frac{dB}{dS}\right)_{00} = \left(\frac{dR}{dS}\right)_{00}\left\{\left(\frac{dC}{dR}\right)_{00} + \left(\frac{dB}{dR}\right)_{00}\right\}$$

$$= C_r + \frac{MB_z}{R_v(1 + B_z)} \gtrless 0,$$

as $\dfrac{C_r R_v}{M} \gtrless \dfrac{-B_z}{1 + B_z}$.

9. Let $\left(\dfrac{dY}{dS}\right)_{10}$ signify $\dfrac{dY}{dS}$ under floating exchange rates, when $dB + dC = 0$ and $dM = 0$.

Then $\left(\frac{dY}{dS}\right)_{10} = \frac{1}{1 - X_n(1 - T_y) - (X_r - C_r)\frac{R_v}{M}} > 0.$

10. $\left(\frac{dY}{dS}\right)_{10} \gtrless \left(\frac{dY}{dS}\right)_{00}$ as $\frac{-B_z}{1 + B_z} \gtrless \frac{C_r R_v}{M}$,

i.e. as $\left(\frac{dC}{dS}\right)_{00} + \left(\frac{dB}{dS}\right)_{00} \gtrless 0.$

11. As $C_r \rightarrow \infty$,

$$\left(\frac{dY}{dS}\right)_{10} \rightarrow \frac{1}{\infty}$$

$$\rightarrow 0.$$

12. Let $\left(\frac{dY}{dM}\right)_{01} = \frac{dY}{dM}$ at fixed exchange rates when $dF = 0$ and $dS = 0$.

Let $\left(\frac{dR}{dM}\right)_{01}$, $\left(\frac{dC}{dM}\right)_{01}$, $\left(\frac{dB}{dM}\right)_{01}$ be analogously defined.

$$\left(\frac{dY}{dM}\right)_{01} = \frac{-X_r R_v Y}{M^2}\left[\frac{1}{1/(B_z + 1) - X_n(1 - T_y) - X_r R_v/M}\right].$$

13. $$\left(\frac{dB}{dM}\right)_{01} + \left(\frac{dC}{dM}\right)_{01} = \frac{B_z}{1 + B_z}\left(\frac{dY}{dM}\right)_0 + C_r\left(\frac{dR}{dM}\right)_0 < 0.$$

14. $$\left(\frac{dR}{dM}\right)_{01} = \frac{-R_v Y}{M^2}\left[\frac{1 - X_n(B_z + 1)(1 - T_y)}{1 - (B_z + 1)X_n(1 - T_y) + X_r R_v/M}\right] < 0.$$

15. Let $\left(\frac{dY}{dM}\right)_{11} = \frac{dY}{dM}$ under floating exchange rates, when $dB + dC = 0$ and $dS = 0$.

Then $\left(\frac{dY}{dM}\right)_{11} =$

$$\frac{R_v Y(C_r - X_r)}{M^2}\left[\frac{1}{1 - X_n(1 - T_y) + R_v(C_r - X_r)/M}\right] > 0.$$

16.

$$\left(\frac{dY}{dM}\right)_{11} - \left(\frac{dY}{dM}\right)_{01} = \frac{R_v Y}{M^2}\left[\frac{C_r - X_r}{1 - X_n(1 - T_y) + R_v(C_r - X_r)/M} + \frac{X_r}{1/(B_z + 1) - X_n(1 - T_y) - X_r R_v/M}\right] > 0.$$

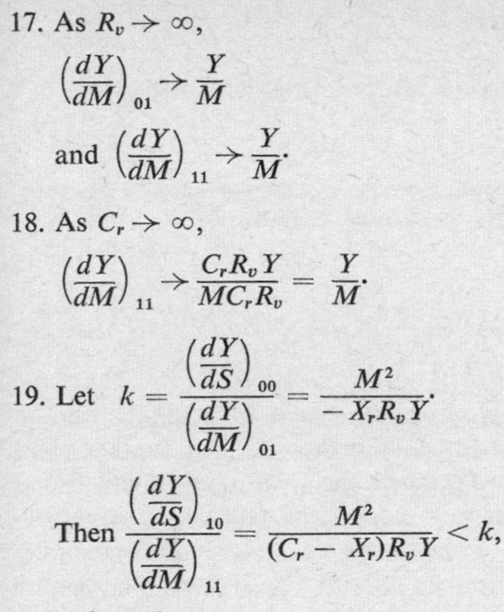

17. As $R_v \to \infty$,

$$\left(\frac{dY}{dM}\right)_{01} \to \frac{Y}{M}$$

and $\left(\frac{dY}{dM}\right)_{11} \to \frac{Y}{M}$.

18. As $C_r \to \infty$,

$$\left(\frac{dY}{dM}\right)_{11} \to \frac{C_r R_v Y}{M C_r R_v} = \frac{Y}{M}.$$

19. Let $k = \dfrac{\left(\frac{dY}{dS}\right)_{00}}{\left(\frac{dY}{dM}\right)_{01}} = \dfrac{M^2}{-X_r R_v Y}$.

Then $\dfrac{\left(\frac{dY}{dS}\right)_{10}}{\left(\frac{dY}{dM}\right)_{11}} = \dfrac{M^2}{(C_r - X_r) R_v Y} < k$,

unless $X_r = -\infty$

or $R_v = \infty$.

14 H. G. Johnson

Theoretical Problems of the International Monetary System

H. G. Johnson (1967), 'Theoretical problems of the international monetary system', *Pakistan Development Review*, vol. 7, pp. 1–28.

Introduction

Since 1958, international economists have been greatly concerned with the problem of international monetary reform. Research and writing on this problem has taken one or another of two broad forms. Those economists most concerned with policy have concerned themselves with emphasizing the need for international monetary reform and propounding workable (negotiable) schemes for achieving it. International monetary theorists, on the other hand, have been concerned with the theoretical policy problems of achieving and maintaining balance-of-payments equilibrium in the present international monetary system of fixed exchange rates. They have also become concerned with the problems of the system as a monetary system.

This paper belongs to the latter category. It seeks to outline the main propositions of the analysis of international economic policy and policy problems that have been developed by economists working in this field in recent years. Part I is concerned with the economic policy problems of maintaining both full employment and balance-of-payments equilibrium, first for a single country on a fixed exchange rate, then for two or more countries linked in a multi-country international monetary system. Part II is concerned with certain features of the present international monetary system, viewed as a monetary system. The analysis of Part I is Keynesian, that of Part II classical, in approach. Both parts draw heavily on papers presented at the University of Chicago Conference on International Monetary Problems organized by R. A. Mundell, held at Chicago in September 1966 (9).

I. Problems of Economic Policy in a System of Fixed Exchange Rates

The single economy in a world system

It is convenient to begin the analysis with the theory of economic policy in a closed economy, in which there is assumed to be price stability around the point of full employment, and on either side of full employment a rate of change of wages and prices that can be neglected for purposes of the present analysis. Left to itself, such an economy would come into equilibrium, as is well understood, at the interest rate and level of money (and real) output indicated by the intersection of the *IS* and *LM* curves, according to the familiar Hansen–Hicks diagrammatic analysis of the Keynesian system. If the government wishes to shift the economy to the equilibrium level of output corresponding to full employment, it has two alternative instruments at its disposal. Firstly, it could alter the money supply, shifting the *LM* curve so that its intersection with the *IS* curve yields a full employment level of income. As is well known, this policy will fail if the liquidity preference curve becomes perfectly interest-elastic at a rate of interest above the rate at which the *IS* curve *indicates* full employment.[1] Second, it could lower taxes or raise government expenditure, thereby – on the usual assumptions that lower taxes go only partly into saving and higher expenditure is only partly financed by additional saving – shifting the *IS* curve to the right and raising both output and employment and the rate of interest. For this analysis, the *IS* curve needs to be redefined as an $I + G$, $S + T$ curve, where G represents government expenditure and T total tax receipts, reflecting the conditions for equilibrium in the goods market that autonomous injections of demand from new investment and government expenditure must be equal to

1. As is also well known, the perfect interest-elasticity in question cannot be inferred from the speculative motive Keynes analysed, since in the long-run expectations must yield to the experience of sustained low levels of interest rates; also, the monetary authority could always absorb all the bonds held by the community, and extend its lending into direct finance of material investment, so lowering rates of interest regardless of the 'liquidity trap'. The exception therefore has to be regarded as the result of time and institutional limitations on central bank operations.

leakages from the circular flow of income in the form of private saving and taxation, the curve lying farther to the right the higher is government expenditure and the lower is taxation. The choice between the two alternative ways of achieving the single objective of full employment will presumably be made in the light of other objectives of economic policy, such as the desired rate of economic growth and the influence on it of the full employment interest rate, acting through its influence on the level of private investment.

Now consider an open economy, trading with the rest of the world at a fixed exchange rate. Given the exchange rate, the trade surplus (or deficit) of the country will be a decreasing (increasing) function of its level of national income and employment; and whichever choice of combination of policy instruments – fiscal policy and monetary policy – it makes to maintain full employment, the trade surplus (or deficit) will be the same. In consequence, it appears that a country on a fixed exchange rate that would have a deficit at full employment is faced with a conflict of objectives which it cannot surmount – either it must have full employment and a deficit, or it must have international balance and excessive unemployment.

To represent the policy problem of such a country, the *IS–LM* diagram must be revised, in so far as the *IS* curve is concerned, to transform the *IS* curve into an $I + G + X$, $S + T + M$ curve, where X represents exports and M imports at the assumed given exchange rate, X being assumed either constant or a decreasing function of national income (the latter on the assumption that a rise in income diverts production from the export to the home market), and imports being assumed to rise as national income rises. The trade balance must also be shown, in a separate quadrant, as a function of national income.

As mentioned, the situation of a country on a fixed exchange rate with a potential deficit in the trade account at full employment appears to pose a dilemma between full employment and a deficit, or international balance and abnormal unemployment. The solution provided in the immediate postwar period by James Meade (6) and other writers was to introduce the possibility of changes in the exchange rate. At a lower exchange rate (price of domestic currency in terms of foreign), given the satisfaction of certain elasticity or stability conditions, the trade deficit (surplus) associated with any particular level of income would be lower (higher). Hence, the country would achieve both objectives – full employment and a balanced balance of trade, or for short internal and external balance – by a proper combination of exchange rate adjustment and fiscal or monetary policy change. It should be noted that, if attention is concentrated on the fiscal and monetary policies required to maintain full employment of domestic resources, a devaluation designed to shift the relation between national income and the trade balance in a favourable direction would shift the $I + G + X$, $S + T + M$ curve upward. Consequently, to preserve exact full employment, a country seeking to correct an unfavourable trade balance by devaluation would have to counteract this shift in the trade-balance national-income relation either by a more restrictive monetary policy designed to shift the *LM* curve leftward to offset the rightward shift of the $I + G + X$, $S + T + M$ curve, or to correct the rightward shift of the $I + G + X$, $S + T + M$ curve by raising taxes or reducing government expenditure. In other words, such a country would have to accompany devaluation by a more restrictive fiscal or monetary policy. If it did not do so, the effect of its devaluation on its trade balance would be offset sooner or later by the inflationary consequences of the resulting excess demand for national output on domestic prices and therefore on the relative prices of the country's exports relative to its imports.

In the international monetary system as it has developed since the early postwar work on the theory of international economic policy, exchange rates have become for practical purposes virtually rigid, so that a country faced with the choice between balance-of-trade deficit and excess unemployment cannot resolve the dilemma by resorting to devaluation combined with some mixture of fiscal and monetary policy change. At the same time, the alternative to devaluation examined by the writers in question, the use of controls to foster exports and restrict imports has been ruled out – at least in large part – by the growing aversion to using variations in controls to correct balance-of-payments disequilibria. As a result, it again appears that countries will be faced with a dilemma between balance-of-payments deficits and abnormal unemployment.

This dilemma has been dispelled by recognition that the balance of payments comprises two elements, the current account and the capital account, and that while the current account balance can be taken as a function of the level of national income and employment, the flow of funds on international capital account is a function of the level of domestic interest rates relative to foreign interest rates and that this interest rate level is a function of the 'mix' of fiscal and monetary policy adopted to maintain full employment. Thus, while (in principle) the current account is determined by the exchange rate and the level of domestic activity, the capital account of the balance of payments can be adjusted to match the current deficit or surplus by a proper choice of the fiscal-monetary policy mix. A country that would have a current account deficit at full employment greater than its normal capital inflow, or surplus less than its normal capital outflow, can adjust the latter to the former by adopting a more restrictive monetary policy and a less restrictive fiscal policy; and vice versa. Thus the two objectives of policy – full employment and a balanced balance of payments – can be secured, despite the adherence to a fixed exchange rate, by a proper choice of the fiscal-monetary policy mix.

The problem and its solution are illustrated in Figure 1, which is drawn to depict the policy problem facing the United States in recent years, of a capital outflow greater than the current account surplus generated at the current exchange rate under full employment. In the Figure, LM_1 and IS_1 (actually $I_1 + G_1 + X_1$, $S_1 + T_1 + M_1$) represent the curves corresponding to an initial fiscal-monetary policy mix designed to secure full employment. At that level of income and employment, the current account surplus is T_1, less than the capital outflow K_1 generated by the equilibrium domestic interest rate r_1; the country therefore has an overall deficit of $K_1 - T_1$. By lowering taxes, or raising expenditure, or both, the government can raise the IS curve to $IS_2(I_2 + G_2 + X_1$, $S_2 + T_2 + M_1$, X and M being fixed by the full employment level of income); and by restricting the quantity of money it can raise the LM curve to LM_2; with this combination of policy changes, the interest rate r_2 corresponding to full employment is just such as to generate a lower capital outflow K_2 just equal to the current account surplus T_1, and the country achieves its two objectives of internal and external balance.

It is necessary to observe, however, that to continue to achieve these two objectives the country must continue to apply the fiscal and monetary policies represented by LM_2 and IS_2; by assumption, there is nothing in the situation to eventually restore a relationship between the domestic price level and foreign

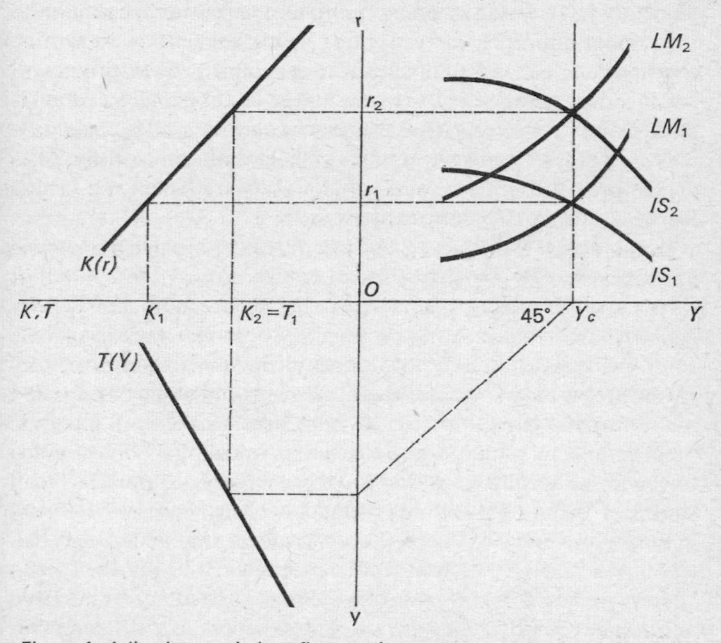

Figure 1 Adjusting capital outflow to the current account surplus at full employment

prices that will relieve the nation's policy-makers of the necessity of adopting this particular fiscal-monetary policy mix, regardless of any other policy objectives they may have. This is one of the major problems of the present international monetary system; it is possible to 'finance' international deficit and surplus positions by the choice of an appropriate fiscal-monetary policy mix, but this fact does not mean that there is any mechanism of adjustment present in the system. On the contrary, there may be the opposite of an adjustment mechanism, for two reasons. Firstly, presumably a country that would be in deficit at full employment gets that way because in fact at full employment its prices and wages rise faster than those of its competitors; hence if it succeeds by proper fiscal-monetary policy mix in maintaining full employment, its current account will tend to worsen over time and therefore it will be driven further into mixing fiscal expansion and monetary contraction, thereby piling up international debts (if it is a capital importer) or restraining its capital outflow at an increasing rate. Secondly, in so far as economic growth promotes international competitiveness, the higher level of interest rates it must maintain to keep its international accounts in balance will militate against a longer-run improvement in its competitiveness. (These propositions, however, obviously oversimplify the problem of restoring international balance.)

In the actual working of the international monetary system, however, there is a mechanism of adjustment at work, of the classical gold standard kind involving deflation in the deficit countries and inflation in the surplus countries. This is so because neither deficit nor surplus countries have been able, for various reasons, to operate the fiscal-monetary policy mix technique anywhere near perfectly. The deficit countries have in practice had to undergo more unemployment than they would like, and the surplus countries have been unable to prevent their surpluses from having inflationary consequences for their domestic price levels. Since the deficit countries have been unwilling to push deflationary policies beyond the point of preventing prices from rising, the resulting system of 'reluctant adjustment' (on this concept, see 5, ch. 3) operates via differences between deficit and surplus countries in their relative rates of inflation, with an average tendency to world inflation. Such an adjustment mechanism is bound to operate slowly, and to be vulnerable to temporary reverses associated with surges of inflationary pressure in the deficit countries such as have occurred in the United Kingdom and the United States in recent years.

The account of the problem of reconciling internal and external balance just outlined abstracts from two rather different aspects of the policy problem, which have figured in the literature of recent years. These may be termed 'the assignment problem' (8, pp. 70–77), and 'the welfare problem' (a problem which has been given birth, but not christened, by several writers).

The assignment problem follows from the observation that governments typically assign responsibility for the pursuit of policy objectives separately to separate governmental institutions which control particular instruments of economic policy; typically the Central Bank, controlling monetary policy, is given responsibility for external balance, and the Treasury, controlling fiscal policy, is given responsibility for full employment. The assignment problem is, which objective should be assigned to which agency, to assure the most efficient operation of policy. This problem raises some complex issues in economic dynamics, arising from what may be termed 'the feedback problem'.

This problem is that the pursuit of an assigned objective by one policy agency may disrupt another agency in pursuit of its own objectives, and so provoke policy actions by the second agency that disrupt the pursuit of the first agency's objectives, so that the pursuit of the objectives assigned to the agencies in fact leads away from rather than towards the attainment of the policy objectives sought. The solution to this problem, which has been provided by R. A. Mundell (10, pp. 227–57) is the 'principle of effective market classification' – that each agency should be assigned the objective on which the policy instrument under its control has relatively the greatest influence, as contrasted with other objectives. In a fixed exchange rate system, this means assigning external stability to monetary policy, and internal stability to fiscal policy.

The analytical essence of the assignment problem is illustrated by the two parts of Figure 2. For simplicity, fiscal policy is represented by the variable G, for government injections of expenditure into the economy, and monetary policy by the variable r, representing the rate of interest. In each case the YY curve represents the combinations of increasing fiscal laxity and monetary stringency that will preserve domestic full employment, and the FF curve represents the combinations of increasing fiscal laxity and monetary stringency that will preserve equilibrium between the current and capital accounts of the balance of payments. The FF curve must slope upward more steeply than the YY curve, because a movement rightward along the YY curve implies no change in the current account (since the level of output and employment is held constant), but an improvement of

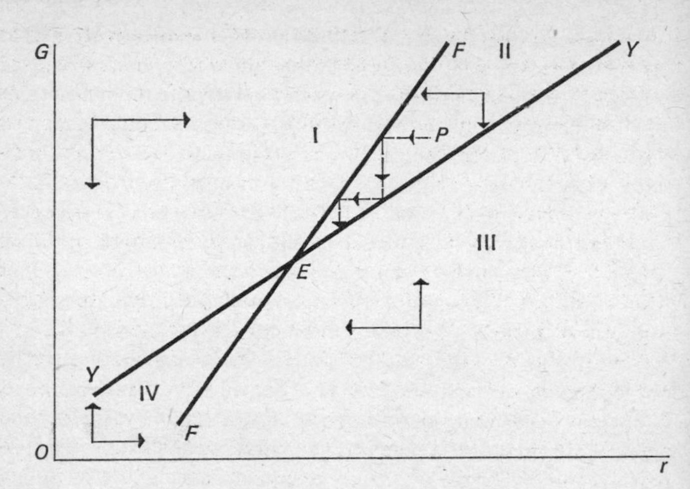

(a) fiscal policy for internal balance, monetary policy for external balance

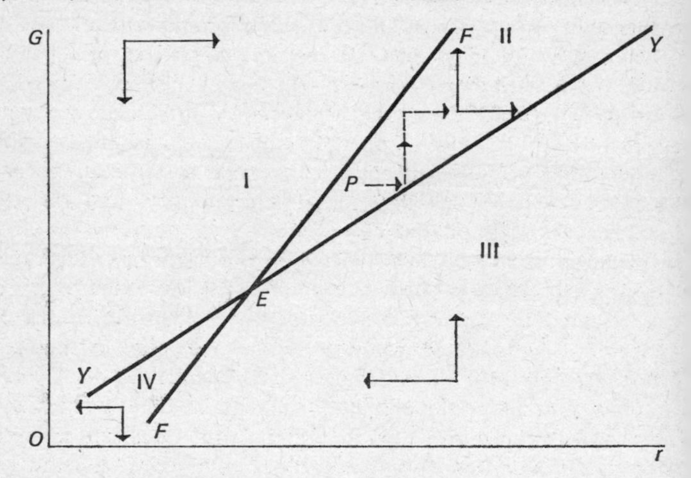

(b) monetary policy for internal balance, fiscal policy for external balance

Figure 2 The assignment of fiscal policy to internal balance and monetary policy to external balance, and vice versa

the capital account due to the increase in the interest rate. To offset this and keep the overall balance of payments in balance, government expenditure must be increased still more, to worsen the current account sufficiently to counteract the increased capital inflow. The intersection of the *YY* and *FF* curves at *E* shows the mix of fiscal and monetary policy required to achieve the two policy objectives of external and internal balance.

Now assume that the two objectives of economic policy are each assigned exclusively to one of the policy instruments, the controllers of the relevant instrument being instructed to operate their policy in the direction indicated by the relation between the actual state of the economy and the assigned target of full employment on external balance. Figure 2 depicts the two possible assignments, the internal balance to fiscal policy and external balance to monetary policy, and the converse. In each case, the horizontal arrows depict the direction in which monetary policy will be moving, and the vertical arrows the direction in which fiscal policy will be moving, for the four states of the economy into which the *YY* and *FF* curves divide the diagram. (I = deficit and overfull employment, II = surplus and overfull employment, III = surplus and deficient demand, IV = deficit and deficient demand.) For assignment (a), the arrows always point towards the policy equilibrium point *E*, indicating that under this assignment of targets to policy variables the operations of the policy authorities will converge on equilibrium. For assignment (b), however, the arrows point away from the equilibrium in regions II and IV, indicating that equilibrium may be approached only in an oscillatory manner, or may not be reached at all, depending on the precise nature of the policy responses to disequilibrium. (A crude way of appreciating the dynamic difference between the two assignments, easily manageable in diagrammatic terms, is to assume that the fiscal and monetary policy authorities take turns in changing their policies, each changing its policy instrument so as to bring the economy onto the *FF* or *YY* curve, whichever corresponds to the policy objective for which it is responsible; the dynamics of adjustment in the two assignment systems are illustrated by the dotted paths starting from the disequilibrium point *P* in region II.)

The assignment problem has occupied much attention in the

literature but it should be noted that the problem is created by the assumption that administratively efficient government policy-making requires the assignment of one objective to each controller of a policy instrument, and that the problem could be avoided by intra-governmental coordination of the use of policy instruments, all being used jointly in pursuit of all policy objectives.

The welfare problem, in its most basic sense, derives from the fact that under the fixed exchange rate system the international flow of capital, in the sense of real resources as contrasted with international security purchases and sales, is determined by the deficits (surpluses) on current account that result from the relative international competitiveness of the various countries, given their domestic price levels, employment policies, and exchange rates. Determination of international capital resource flows by these factors is to be contrasted with the classical mechanism of adjustment, under which domestic price levels (or exchange rates) would adjust so as to generate current account surpluses and deficits corresponding to desired international capital movements generated by the pursuit of maximum returns on investment. The resulting pattern of international capital movements obviously need not be anything like an efficient one, since there is no reason to expect that the real return on investment in countries with current account deficits is higher than that on investment in countries with current account surpluses; it may, on the contrary, involve a serious distortion of the allocation of new real investment resources, and a consequent welfare loss for the countries concerned and the world economy. Analysis of these welfare losses, however, has barely begun; and, indeed, the conceptual tools for dealing with the welfare aspects of investment problems remain to be developed (1, pp. 333–52, and 4, pp. 512–18). Given the fact that the international monetary system governs the international movement of real capital in this fashion, there arises a problem in the welfare economics of second-best (or perhaps third-best): whether the international flow of financial capital should be accommodated to the real capital flows by the fiscal-monetary policy mix technique analysed above, or whether the accommodation should be achieved by the imposition of interest-equalization taxes or other controls on international capital movements designed (at least partially) to insulate monetary and fiscal policy from being dominated by the obligation to maintain international balance, much as the United States and the United Kingdom have been imposing in recent years.[2] In the United States, at least, international monetary experts have an instinctive preference for freedom of international capital movements, and have tended to condemn the interest equalization tax and other interventions in international capital movements, as undesirable interferences with economic efficiency and violations of the purposes of the fixed exchange rate international monetary system.

This argument, however, is questionable on two grounds. Firstly, it can be objected that since private international capital movements are motivated by expected net private return, and since the relation of net private return to gross social return is heavily influenced by taxes and other governmental policies, there is no *a priori* reason for placing much confidence in the principle of freedom of private international capital movements as a guarantor of economic efficiency in the international allocation of world investment resources. Secondly, and more important, the argument for freedom of capital movements assumes an international adjustment mechanism capable of achieving the real international transfers private individuals and enterprises want to make. In the absence of such a mechanism, with the real transfers determined by countries' relative international competitiveness, the argument is essentially that countries' monetary-fiscal policies should be adjusted so as to induce the owners of capital to want to transact just the amount of international financial transfers that matches the predetermined real transfers. This entails adjusting each country's rates of domestic investment and saving to the level of interest rates at which financial and real transfers balance; and there is no reason to think that this procedure is superior to controlling capital movements and allowing the rates of domestic saving and investment to be determined by government policy, or by private decisions operating in the context of some agreed budgetary policy. (These alternatives allow for the two possibilities that the government may wish to

2. This part of the analysis draws heavily on a brilliantly reasoned recent paper by Franco Modigliani (7).

implement an overall growth policy by means of its fiscal policy, or that the population is content to fix budgetary policy by some criterion not related to growth, e.g. a cyclically balanced budget, and to let the rate of growth be determined by private saving and investment decisions.)

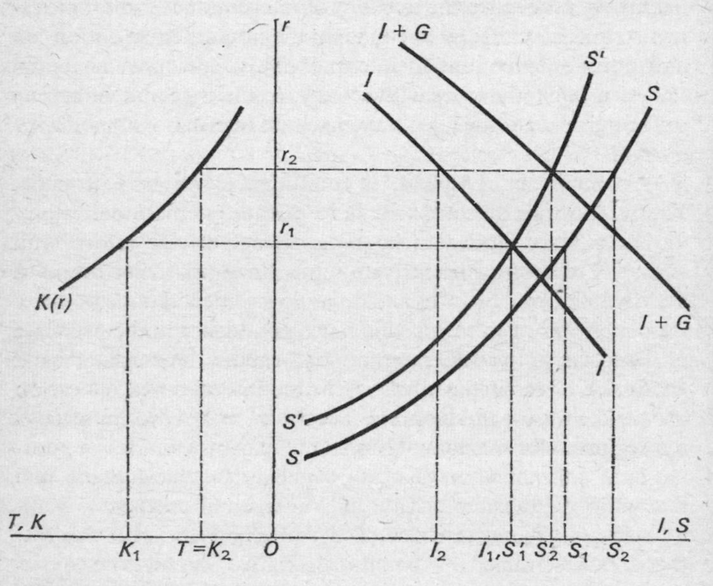

Figure 3

The problem is illustrated in Figure 3, which is again drawn to represent the United States' position of recent years; for simplicity, it is assumed that fiscal policy initially adjusted to some structure of taxes and expenditure considered socially optimal, and that in order to obtain the level of domestic interest rates required for international balance, the policy-makers increase government expenditure, financing it by additional borrowing and at the same time contracting the money supply to the extent required to prevent the increased government expenditure from raising aggregate income above the full employment level. On the right-hand side of the diagram, *II* represents the full-employment investment demand curve, *SS* the full-employment supply curve of private real saving, and $S'S'$ the full-employment supply curve of real saving less the real capital exports provided by the current account surplus. If there were no problem of balancing the current account surplus and the capital account deficit, equilibrium would be reached at the interest rate r, with rates of saving and investment respectively I_1 and S_1, corresponding to the desires of savers and investors and an equilibrium interest rate r_1. But at the interest rate r_1, as shown on the left-hand side of the diagram, desired exports of financial capital K_1 would exceed the current account surplus T. In order to balance its balance of payments while maintaining freedom of capital movements, the policy-makers would have to increase government expenditure by the amount G, contracting the money supply simultaneously, to arrive at the level of interest rates r_2 at which $K_2 = T$, in the process increasing private domestic saving to S_2 while cutting domestic investment to I_2.

In the new equilibrium, domestically-invested saving exceeds domestic investment by I_2S_2', this amount corresponding to purchases of government debt issued to finance increased government expenditure. This part of private domestic saving makes no contribution to increasing the future income of the economy, constituting merely the acquisition by savers of a future claim on income which has to be taxed away from the community at large; in fact, the real investment that contributes to future income has been reduced from I_1 to I_2. By providing an alternative asset (government debt) with a private yield to which there corresponds no social yield, the policy-makers have made private real saving larger and private real investment smaller than they would otherwise be.

If, on the contrary, the authorities used controls on the export of capital to restrict such exports to the level $K_2 = T$, the economy could be kept at the initial equilibrium position, without the wastage of private saving in financing government expenditure. In this situation, it would appear that the government was preventing private individuals from undertaking profitable foreign investments in the amount of $K_1 - K_2$; but since in any case they can only be allowed to undertake foreign investments in the amount of K_2, the real situation is that savers are forced to invest at home at the interest rate r_1, instead of being bribed to invest at home by the offer of government debt yielding at the rate r_2, this yield being obtained not from additional production but from additional future taxes on other income earners, at the expense of the reduction on potential future national income. This is a consequence of the reduction in real investment induced by the increase in interest rates to r_2. The issue is therefore primarily one of redistribution between savers and taxpayers; and so far as efficiency is concerned, it is a question not of efficiency *versus* inefficiency in the international allocation of capital, but of inefficiency *versus* efficiency in the use of the domestic saving potential, the fiscal-monetary mix technique wasting that potential in additional debt-financed government expenditure, and the control technique using it for investment in increasing future national income.

It should be emphasized, however, that this is very much an issue of second-best welfare economics. The first-best solution for a country faced with this policy problem – on the crucial assumption, which has been questioned above, that private-profit motivated international investment promotes efficient international allocation of new investment resources – would be a devaluation, to increase the current account surplus so as to permit the transfer of a large amount of foreign investment.

The international economic system

The analysis of the single country in the world economy in the preceding section assumed that the policy-makers in the individual country can take the situation in the rest of the world, and especially the level of foreign interest rates, as given. This assumption made it possible for the country to achieve internal and external balance simultaneously by resort to an appropriate mix of domestic, fiscal, and monetary policy. When the analysis is extended, however, to include the interactions of national economic policies in a world economy of two or more countries, the situation becomes more complex. In the first place, it is no longer possible for a country to secure its domestic objectives of internal and external balance by use of its own policy instruments alone; it can always be frustrated by inconsistent use by other countries of their policy instruments. In the second place, because the balances of payments of all the countries in the world economy must sum to zero ('Cournot's Law'), the external balance objective of all countries will be achieved if all but one of them achieve it. Hence, whereas in the single country case examined previously there were two policy objectives requiring two policy instruments to implement them, in the *n*-country case there will be $2n-1$

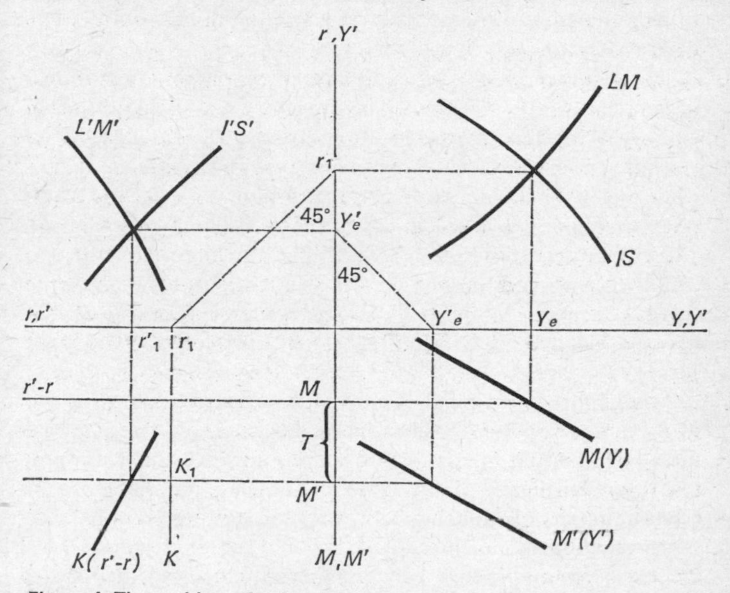

Figure 4 The problem of achieving external and internal balance in a two-country international system

objectives, requiring only $2n-1$ policy instruments. In other words, there will be one degree of freedom, or one spare policy instrument, in the system. This fact means that one country, and one country alone, can use one of its policy objectives for some other purpose; this poses the practical problem of which country will have this degree of freedom, or of how this degree of freedom can be used for some international purpose.

The problem of achieving external and internal balance in a two-country international system is illustrated in Figure 4; in the figure unprimed symbols refer to country 1 (again represented so as to conform to the recent situation of the United States) and primed symbols to country 2 (the rest of the world). Each country's imports are presumed to be a function of its national income, the *IS* curves being drawn to incorporate the full-employment level of imports by (exports to) the other country. The international flow of financial capital is assumed for simplicity to be a function of the interest rate differential between the two countries.

The figure represents one possible position of international economic policy equilibrium. The monetary and fiscal policies of country 1 inherent in the locations of the *IS* and *LM* curves generate full employment in that country with the interest rate r_1, while the policies inherent in the locations of $I'S'$ and $L'M'$ generate full employment in country 2 with the interest rate r_1'. The difference between the full employment imports of the two countries gives country 1 a current account surplus of T, while the interest rate differential r_1'-r_1 generates a financial capital flow from country 1 to country 2 of K_1, just equal to the trade surplus T.

Two important propositions are evident from the construction of the figure. The first is that the achievement of international policy equilibrium is possible only if countries 1 and 2 are prepared to harmonize their economic policies, in the sense of establishing the relationship between r and r' required to balance the international financial capital flow and the real resource flow, created by the difference between the full-employment imports of the two countries. To put the point another way, country 2 could always frustrate a fiscal-monetary policy mix adopted by country 1 in pursuit of internal and external balance, by adopting a laxer fiscal policy and tighter monetary policy than would produce an interest rate in that country consistent with the interest rate generated by country 1's policy mix. (In terms of the figure, such a policy would shift $I'S'$ and $L'M'$ to the left, maintaining their intersection at income Y_e'.)

Secondly, there is obviously an infinite number of combinations of fiscal-monetary policy mixes in the two countries that would balance the financial capital flow with the real resource transfer – because both countries could relax fiscal policy and tighten monetary policy in such a way as to preserve the required interest rate differential, and conversely. This means that one country could peg its interest rate level at any desired level, internal and external balance for the two countries together being preserved by an appropriate fiscal policy in that country and fiscal-monetary policy mix in the other. Alternatively it could fix its fiscal policy, for example, by insisting on maintaining a balanced budget for a fixed level of government expenditure, internal and external balance for the world economy being preserved by an appropriate fiscal policy in the other country and appropriate monetary policies in both.[3]

The presence of the degree of freedom associated with Cournot's Law gives rise to what has been termed 'the redundancy problem' (one redundant policy instrument). This problem, it should be noted, was absent from the classical gold standard mechanism, because the basing of national money supplies on an overall fixed total of world gold reserves prevented countries from pursuing independent monetary policies – the gold constraint absorbed the degree of freedom. It arises in the present international monetary system because national monetary policies have been cut free from the gold constraint.

There are two possible solutions to the redundancy problem, each of which raises difficulties that have been reflected in acrimonious disputes between surplus and deficit countries in recent years. One would be to allow one country to absorb the degree of freedom, and to govern one of its policy instruments by other objectives than external and internal balance; this was essentially the solution advocated by many Americans in the early years of the dollar deficit, when they pressed for U.S. monetary policy to be used for full employment while tacitly assuming that fiscal policy should go on being determined by congressional authority. The difficulty with this solution, as experience shows, is that other countries will want the freedom of policy that can by necessity only be allowed to one of them. The other solution would be to agree on an internationally desirable use of the one degree of freedom, for example, by agreeing on an

3. In a previous essay on this point, I erroneously implied that the country enjoying the degree of freedom could use it to achieve a desired structure of its balance of payments, e.g. size of current account deficit and matching capital inflow (3, chapter 8, p. 149). This is incorrect: the balances on trade account are fixed by the relative price levels of the countries.

average level of world interest rates desirable from the point of view of world growth. The difficulty with this solution, as experience also shows, is essentially the same: that countries differ strongly in their views of what is desirable. Specifically, there has been a persistent disagreement between the Americans, who have favoured low rates of interest, and the Europeans, who have favoured high rates of interest. Moreover, the dispute has been thoroughly entangled in a more basic dispute over who should bear the burden of longer-run adjustment to international disequilibrium, the Europeans favouring a more deflationary system that would throw a larger share of the burden on the deficit countries, and the Americans and British favouring a more inflationary international monetary system.

The redundancy problem is inherent in the logic of the international monetary system, given the assumption that countries have the objectives of internal and external balance and control of their monetary and fiscal policies. In practice, however, the system has been struggling in part with two problems that are the converse of redundancy. In the first place, not all countries have the capacity to use fiscal and monetary policy in the required mixes: the United States only adopted the principle of using fiscal policy for control purposes with the tax cut of 1964, and its ability to use fiscal policy is considerably restricted by the constitutional division of powers; similarly, Western Germany lacks the central authority to use fiscal policy in this fashion. Secondly, countries do not, in fact, confine themselves in their international economic policies to the objective of external balance, which all can pursue consistently. Instead, they have other balance-of-payments objectives, relating to the composition of their international accounts, which may well be inconsistent with those of other nations, and moreover impossible to pursue with the policy instruments they have available. As particular examples, both Canada and the Western European countries regard their current account deficits as undesirable – which means the adoption of an objective with respect to the size of other countries' current account surpluses is not necessarily consistent with those countries' objectives – and seek to correct these deficits by balance-of-payments policies (such as import-substitution). These are inappropriate to the problem (since a remedy requires increasing domestic saving or reducing domestic investment), but which may nevertheless aggravate the balance-of-payments problems of the countries with current-account surpluses matched by capital outflows. In addition, many countries are particularly averse to American investment within their borders, and seek to limit or prevent it by policies that are inconsistent with American policies towards foreign investment by U.S. residents and corporations.

II. Problems of the International Monetary System

The instability of the gold exchange standard

The present international monetary system is a gold exchange standard, that is, a system in which countries maintain fixed exchange rates by means of holding international reserves that include a national currency – specifically the United States dollar – in substitution for the basic international reserve, gold, which is in inadequate supply. The rate of growth of the stock of gold available for holding as monetary reserves (new gold production less private hoarding and other non-monetary usage plus Russian gold sales) has in the postwar period fallen substantially short of the rate of growth of demand for international reserves by countries other than the United States, and these countries have made up the difference by accumulating reserves of dollars, which are convertible on demand into gold. These dollars, in turn, have been supplied through the medium of a sustained United States balance-of-payments deficit.

An international monetary system of this kind is inherently unstable, in the sense that the passage of time inevitably erodes the foundation of the system on confidence in the convertibility of the dollar, by steadily reducing the ratio of the United States gold reserves to U.S. dollars held as international monetary reserves by other countries and, at least eventually, steadily reducing the absolute amount of gold reserves held by the United States. The reason is that, if other countries hold reserves of dollars and gold in a fixed ratio, and their demand for reserves increases more rapidly than the supply of monetary gold, their demand for additional gold reserves can only be satisfied by allowing them to absorb a disproportionate share of the new gold supplies, and if their demand for additional gold is large enough its satisfaction will require not only the new gold supplied but also a drawing on the United States gold reserves. Since dollars held by other countries as reserves are increasing faster than the world stock of monetary gold, while the United States gold

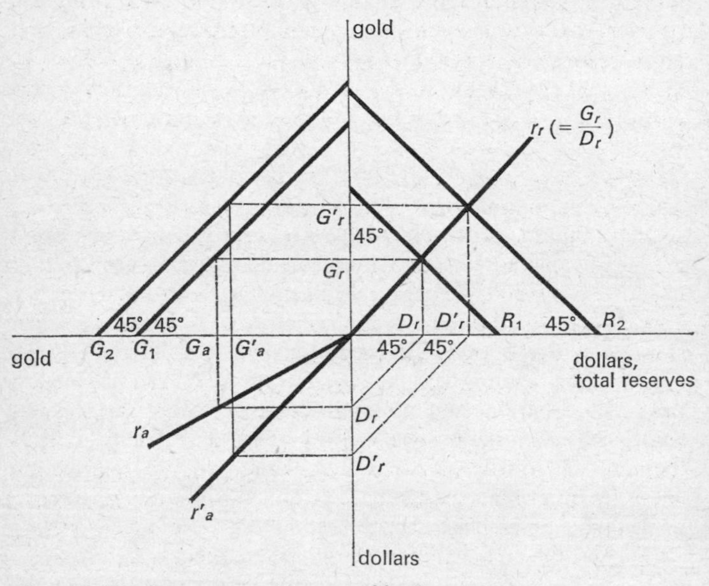

Figure 5 'The long-run confidence problem'

reserves must be increasing less fast or actually decreasing, the ratio of the United States gold reserves to U.S. dollar liabilities to the monetary authorities of other countries must be falling over time. That is, the international liquidity position of the United States must be steadily weakening, thereby undermining the objective basis for confidence by the rest of the world in the unlimited convertibility of their reserve dollars into gold.

This problem, which may be termed the 'long-run confidence problem', is illustrated in Figure 5. The north-east quadrant shows the international reserve position of countries outside the United States (the rest of the world). Initially, these countries hold R_1 of international reserves, divided between D_r of dollars and G_r of gold according to the desired international assets ratio r_r. The north-west quadrant shows the total world gold stock, initially G_1, divided between rest of the world holdings of G_r and the United States gold reserves G_a. The south-west quadrant (to which the dollars held by the rest of the world are transferred diagrammatically by means of a 45° line in the south-east quadrant) shows the international liquidity position of the United States; initially the United States holds G_a of gold reserves and has D_r of dollar liabilities outstanding, and hence has a ratio of gold reserves to dollar reserve liabilities given by the slope r_a with reference to the vertical axis.

Now suppose that, as a result of new gold production, the world monetary gold rises from G_1 to G_2, while as a result of world economic growth the total reserves demanded by the rest of the world rise by a greater proportion, from R_1 to R_2. If the rest of the world maintains the same ratio of gold to dollars in its reserves as previously prevailed, its dollar holdings rise to D_r', while the United States gold reserves fall to G_a' and the United States ratio of gold to reserve dollar liabilities falls to r_a'.[4] The United States international liquidity position would necessarily deteriorate; and it would continue to deteriorate so long as the rest of the world's demand for reserves grew faster than world gold supplies and it maintained its initial ratio of gold to dollars in international reserves.

The deleterious effects of the worsening of the United States international liquidity position on confidence in the convertibility of the dollar, and hence on the usability of the dollar as an international reserve currency, could be avoided in two ways. Firstly, this deterioration might be regarded as acceptable or even desirable by the rest of the world, on the grounds that the United States possessed a disproportionate share of the initial world gold stock. This was in fact the case up to about 1958. But for the rest

4. The United States gold reserves G_a' might initially rise rather than fall by comparison with their initial level G_a, if the rate of increase of reserves demanded by the rest of the world or the ratio of gold to dollars held by the rest of the world were sufficiently small; but ultimately, as the total reserves of the rest of the world increased relative to the world stock, the increase in the rest of the world's demand for gold would come to exceed the increase in world gold supplies and the United States reserves would have to fall.

of the world to accept a steady deterioration of the United States liquidity position while continuing to hold and use dollars as international reserves would amount to a deliberate decision to accept the progressive substitution of dollars for gold as the basic international reserve, since it would imply a decreasing expectation that dollars would be encashed into gold. Moreover, eventually the United States would run out of gold reserves from which to supplement the contribution of new gold supplies to the reserves of the rest of the world, and at that point the rest of the world would be forced to accommodate its gold–dollar ratio to the rate of increase of world gold supplies.

The second alternative would be for the rest of the world to progressively reduce its ratio of gold to dollar reserves held, so as to enable the United States to maintain its international liquidity position (ratio of gold reserves to dollar liabilities) intact. Since that would involve a steady reduction in the absolute level of gold reserves held by the rest of the world, it too would involve a deliberate decision to substitute dollars for gold as the basic international reserve. Moreover, eventually the United States would come to hold all the world's gold stock, and thereafter its liquidity position would deteriorate as a result of the disparity between the rates of growth of the rest of the world's demand for reserves and the world gold stock.

Thus both of the solutions to the long-run confidence problem just discussed involve the ultimate substitution of the dollar for gold as the world's international reserve money. This solution the rest of the world is not prepared to accept. The alternative, of which many variants have been proposed in recent years, and towards which the monetary officials of the leading countries have been working, is to develop a credit-money substitute for gold on an international basis, in place of the national credit-money substitute, the U.S. dollar, hitherto employed for this purpose.

Figure 5 can also be used to illustrate another aspect of the long-run confidence problem of the international monetary system, the problem as it has appeared to the United States policy-makers in recent years, in the form of the so-called 'dilemma of the deficit'. To provide the rest of the world with its desired increase in international reserves R_2-R_1, the United States must run the requisite deficit on its balance of payments (official settlements basis) of $D_r' - D_r + G_a - G_a' = R_2 - R_1$. The apparent dilemma is that if the United States runs this deficit its international liquidity position will deteriorate and its gold reserves fall, whereas if it takes policy measures to terminate the deficit to prevent these consequences, the result will be to prevent the reserves of the rest of the world from growing as rapidly as desired and therefore probably provoke policy changes injurious to world trade and economic growth. The apparent dilemma, however, is a spurious one, since the U.S. can create dollars for the rest of the world to hold as reserves not only by running a deficit but by purchasing foreign currencies with dollars, a procedure that would add equally to its international liabilities and assets and hence would not weaken (in fact, would arithmetically strengthen) its international liquidity position. This solution, however, might raise new problems, since to keep the system going the United States would have to sell gold as well as dollars for foreign exchange to be held in its own reserves, and the rest of the world might not regard foreign exchange backing of dollar reserves as being as good as gold backing; and it might distrust the power that large holdings of foreign currencies might give to the United States monetary authorities in the foreign exchange markets.

The foregoing analysis has been concerned with the long-run confidence problem of the present dollar exchange standard system, on the assumption that the system is working properly, in the sense of providing additional international reserves to the rest of the world at the rate at which demand for such reserves is increasing. In principle, this outcome could be secured by the pursuit of appropriate fiscal and monetary policies by the member countries of the international monetary system, on the lines analysed in Part I of this reading, interest rates in the United States and elsewhere being so aligned that the United States capital outflow exceeded its current account surplus by just enough to provide the rest of the world with the desired increase in gold and dollar reserves. Such close coordination of national economic policies, however, would be difficult to achieve in practice; and in fact in recent years the policy combinations adopted by the United States and Western Europe have resulted in an outflow of reserves from the United States larger than desired by the Western European countries. These countries have attempted to force the United States to change its policies to correct the situation, by taking a higher proportion of their reserve increments in gold rather than in dollars and so aggravating the U.S. loss of gold reserves. In essence, from the point of view of the European countries, United States policy has been led by the pursuit of domestic full employment into generating an increase in the world supply of international reserves that is inflationary for the world economy, and the European countries have reacted by using drawings of gold from the U.S. reserves to put pressure on the United States to desist from generating world inflation.

The situation resulting from this conflict of objectives may be termed 'the short-run confidence problem', or – because the method of disciplining United States policy by withdrawing gold if carried too far might produce an international liquidity crisis – 'the crisis problem'. Mundell has shown (9)[5] that the crisis problem is a particular case of the assignment problem, and that the present assignment of control over the amount of dollars outstanding to the size of the United States gold reserves and of the objective of world price stability to the rest of the world's (specifically, Europe's) control over the size of the United States gold reserves, entails a particularly unstable policy system, whereas the assignment of world price stability to the United States monetary policy and of the maintenance of the proper ratio of gold reserves to dollars outstanding to the rest of the world's control over the United States gold reserves would result in a stable world policy system.

The logic of this analysis is illustrated in Figure 6, where dollars outstanding are measured on the vertical axis and European (rest of the world) gold holdings are measured on the horizontal axis, a decrease in these holdings implying an equal increase in the United States gold reserves; *OR* represents the world stock of gold reserves. The curve *RR′* represents the relation between dollars outstanding and the gold stock available to the rest of the world when the United States maintains a fixed ratio of gold reserves to dollar liabilities. The line *SS′* (with a slope of −45°)

5. The diagrammatic analysis presented below is adapted from that of Mundell, who is the originator of it.

represents the fixed total of gold and dollars required to maintain world price stability; this line is to be interpreted as the sum of the United States domestic money supply required to circulate the maximum U.S. income consistent with price stability, and the

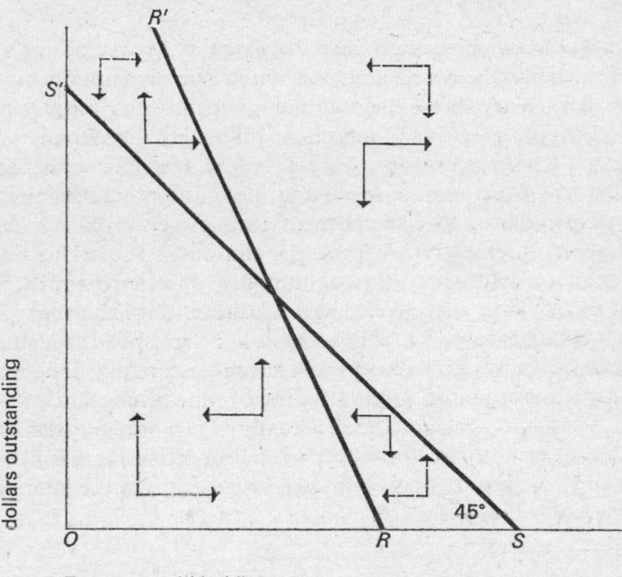

Figure 6 'The short-run confidence problem'

gold and dollar reserves required by the rest of the world to back a domestic money supply there consistent with price stability. (More generally, the total represented by the *SS'* curve can be considered the amount required as the United States domestic money supply and rest-of-world reserves required for world price stability on the average.) The solid arrows indicate the directions of motion of the international policy system in disequilibrium situations, when the United States monetary authorities respond to the U.S. gold reserve in controlling the supply of dollars and the rest of the world responds to the inflationary or deflationary implications of U.S. monetary policy by withdrawing gold from or depositing it in the U.S. reserves; the arrows indicate a possibility of instability in the north-east and south-west quadrants. The dashed arrows indicate the directions of motion of the international policy system when the assignment of instruments to targets is reversed; in this case the system must be stable.

As with the assignment problem discussed in the previous part, however, the analysis relies on the unrealistic assumption that each policy agency (here, each national monetary authority) acts in disregard of the effects of its actions on the problem facing the other, and therefore on the other's policy actions, in spite of the fact that both economic logic and practical experience will demonstrate the interdependence of their policy problems. In this respect, the assignment problem analysis is subject to the same criticism as the literature on duopoly problems that makes use of the reaction curve concept, a literature to which in fact it bears a close analogy. In reality, the gold reserve policies of the European countries in the recent past have been carefully designed to put pressure on the United States by threatening an international liquidity crisis without actually either bringing such a crisis about or running the danger of so doing; and there is little probability of such a crisis occurring, because it is in the interest of no country that it should.

New international reserve assets

As mentioned in the preceding section, many critics of the dollar exchange standard system have advanced proposals to reform the system by supplementing or replacing the reserve currencies – dollars and, to a far lesser extent, sterling – by a new international reserve asset to be created by an international credit operation; and the 'Group of Ten' leading industrial countries have for some years been working out the details of a scheme of this kind.

One of the major problems raised by the proposal to create new international credit money is that of how the new money is to be distributed, and how the member countries of the international monetary system are to share in whatever benefits result from the operation. (Other, more technical problems concern the mode of co-existence of the new reserve asset with gold and the reserve currencies, and the determination of the amount and rate of increase of the new reserve asset.) This problem, which raises some fundamental issues in monetary theory, has been termed (not altogether happily) 'the seigniorage problem', by analogy with the long-standing historical practice of royal mints of using the monopoly of the coinage to extract a profit from the coinage of bullion.

To appreciate the issues involved in the seigniorage problem, it is convenient to begin with the nature of the social saving involved in the substitution of credit money for commodity money. Consider first a commodity money system in which the monetary commodity is producible at constant cost in terms of other commodities in general. Such a system would have a stable price level; and as its output grew, it would have to devote a fraction of its real resources, equal to the product of the rate of growth and the ratio of money to income, to the production of commodity money. Now suppose that a monetary authority were able to substitute a non-interest-bearing paper money for the commodity money, the issue of paper money being assumed to entail negligible cost. There would be a once-over social saving equal to the real value of the existing stock of money, the resources embodied in which could be directed to more profitable uses, and a continuing social saving equal to the resources formerly used to provide the additional money required by economic growth. The once-over social saving could alternatively be represented by the flow of interest on the real resources initially embodied in the money stock; and the seigniorage accruing to the monetary authority from the use of paper rather than commodity money would at any point of time be equal to the interest on the existing money stock plus the rate of growth of that stock. The monetary authority could not, however, dispose of both these items at will. It could either use the interest on the existing money stock for its own purposes, investing the growth of the money supply in additional interest-bearing assets, or it could spend the resources put at its disposal by the issue of new money, sacrificing the growth of interest receipts on the money stock.

This analysis clarifies two aspects of the contemporary debate over the seigniorage problem. First, it is widely believed, especially among those who wish to tie international monetary reform to the provision of additional aid to the less developed countries, that the creation of a new international reserve asset involves the generation of a pool of real resources, which pool constitutes the benefit from international monetary reform that must be equitably shared. This would be true, if the alternative to international monetary reform were a commodity money system; but the actual alternatives lie among different systems of providing international credit money (including the present dollar exchange system), so that the problem is not to dispose of a social saving generated by the substitution of credit for commodity money, but to determine the distribution of the seigniorage generated by the issue of non-interest-bearing paper money.[6] This seigniorage arises from the transfer of real resources from the holders of money to the monetary authority; and it is obvious that it would always be possible to redistribute the seigniorage to the holders of money in such a way as to exactly compensate them for the real resources they surrender. This could be done in either of two ways: by paying interest on money equal to the yield on the investment of the real resources surrendered in return for money, and by giving money as a gift to those who demand additional quantities of it (that is, to those who desire additional money to hold as reserves – clearly not to those who would spend it).

The foregoing observation leads to the second point, that the seigniorage generated by the creation of new international reserve money could be distributed in two alternative ways: through the distribution of the interest proceeds of the investment of the new reserve asset, and through the gift of additions to the stock of the asset to members of the international monetary system. In concrete terms, the seigniorage could be distributed either by rules governing the distribution of the income derived by the authority responsible for managing the new reserve asset, or by rules governing the distribution of additions to the stock of the asset. Concretely, if it were desired to channel the seigniorage to the less developed countries, this could be done either by

6. It may be noted in passing that the Hart–Kaldor–Tinbergen proposal for an international commodity reserve money entails sacrificing the social saving from the substitution of credit, for commodity money, in return for the dubious gains of a price-support scheme for the producers of primary commodities. For a critique of this proposal, see (2, chapter 7).

investing the funds in commercial assets, paying no interest to holders and distributing the income from investments as grants to less developed countries according to some income-distribution rules; or by paying no interest to holders, and investing additions to the funds in non-interest-bearing perpetual loans to the less developed countries according to some loan distribution rule; or by some mixture of the two methods. Alternatively, if it were desired not to redistribute income among the member countries, this could be achieved by investing commercially and paying interest to holders of the new reserve assets, or by distributing new assets to those countries that wished to hold them, as described above.

The method adopted for handling seigniorage, however, would make an important difference to the efficiency of international monetary reform, for a reason not yet introduced into the analysis.[7] The holding of non-interest-bearing money involves the sacrifice of the yield on real assets in which the money could alternatively be invested, with the result that at the margin money-holding must yield a service of convenience sufficient to compensate for the loss of interest, even though the additional money holdings required to reduce the convenience yield to zero could be provided at no social cost. The extraction of seigniorage by the issue of non-interest-bearing international reserve assets therefore entails an unnecessary social loss, by restricting the holding of international reserves to less than the socially optimal level. It follows that the socially optimal system of international reserve creation should either pay interest at commercial rates on holdings of international reserves, or distribute new reserves free to would-be holders of additional reserves, rather than extract seigniorage by, in effect, taxing the use of international reserves and distribute this seigniorage according to some ethic of international equity.

In conclusion, it may be remarked that the analysis of seigniorage and the social saving from substituting paper for commodity money presented in this section explains the development

7. The ensuing argument depends crucially on the assumption that new international reserves are provided at a rate just sufficient to stabilize the world price level. A rising world price level would impose a tax, and a falling world price level yield a return, on holdings of non-interest-bearing money.

of the use of national currencies as international reserves. Such currencies compete with gold for the reserve role by offering an attractive interest-bearing substitute for non-interest-bearing commodity money; in so doing, they both suit the convenience of the reserve-holding countries and promote the optimization of international reserve holding. This suggests both that any attempt to return to the gold standard, as recommended by various European writers on international monetary reform, would be inevitably doomed to failure, since the incentive to find interest-bearing monetary substitutes for gold would remain; and that the creation of a new international reserve asset may not be successful in replacing dollars and sterling as international reserves, if the provisions for supplying the asset in question are too heavily dominated by the attempt to extract seigniorage.

References

1. J. Hause, 'The welfare costs of disequilibrium exchange rates', *Journal of Political Economy*, vol. 74 (1966), no. 4.
2. H. G. Johnson, *Economic Policies Towards the Less Developed Countries*, The Brookings Institution, 1967, Washington.
3. H. G. Johnson, 'The objectives of economic policy and the mix of fiscal and monetary policy under fixed exchange rates', in W. Fellner *et al.*, eds., *Maintaining and Restoring Balance in International Payments*, Princeton University Press, 1966.
4. H. G. Johnson, 'The welfare costs of exchange rate stabilization', *Journal of Political Economy*, vol. 74 (1966), no. 5.
5. H. G. Johnson, *The World Economy at the Crossroads*, The Clarendon Press, 1965.
6. J. E. Meade, *The Theory of International Economic Policy*. Vol. I. *The Balance of Payments*, Oxford University Press, 1951.
7. F. Modigliani, *International Capital Movements, Fixed Parities, and Monetary and Fiscal Policies*. Unpublished manuscript, 1966.
8. R. A. Mundell, 'Appropriate use of monetary and fiscal policy for internal and external stability', *International Monetary Fund Staff Papers*, vol. 9 (1962), no. 1.
9. R. A. Mundell, 'The crisis problem', *Monetary Problems of the International Economy*, University of Chicago Press, 1968.
10. R. A. Mundell, 'The monetary dynamics of international adjustment under fixed and flexible exchange rates', *Quarterly Journal of Economics*, vol. 74 (1960), no. 2.

Part Four **International Liquidity and International Capital Movements**

Part Four takes up two themes distinct from but related to the principal themes of earlier readings.

The last half of reading 14, in Part Three, shifts the focus from national balance-of-payments problems to the provision of international liquidity to the payments system as a whole. Fritz Machlup in reading 15 discusses the nature of international liquidity, some possible methods for creating convincing 'man-made' international money, and some principles for distributing the purchasing power so created. In the final reading Ragnar Nurkse contrasts long-term international capital movements in the nineteenth century with those in the twentieth, pointing out the fundamental differences both in their direction and in their character between the two periods.

15 F. Machlup

The Cloakroom Rule of International Reserves: Reserve Creation and Resources Transfer

F. Machlup (1965), 'The cloakroom rule of international reserves: reserve creation and resources transfer', *Quarterly Journal of Economics*, vol. 79, pp. 337–55.

The Cloakroom Theory of Commercial Banking

Older students of money and banking surely remember the cloakroom theory of commercial banking. It was a theory that gave bankers – shocked by the insinuation that the commercial banking system was able to 'create' credit and thereby increase the supply of circulating media – new confidence and a confirmed belief in their own innocence. They were convinced of their incapacity to do anything as wicked, tricky, or magic as create credit, let alone money. After all, did not every banker know that he stood to lose reserves in amounts equal to those by which he extended his loans or investments? Did it not follow that banks could never lend more than they had been able to borrow from their depositors who, having confidence in the bankers' probity and liquidity, had put cash at their disposal? Was it not therefore clear that banks were similar to cloakrooms[1] in that they received deposits of their clients' paraphernalia and were obliged to return them on demand?

Present-day freshmen and sophomores in elementary courses in economics who, after some effort, have comprehended the theory of bank credit creation feel quite superior to the innocent bankers of past generations. These bankers had not grasped the

1. See Cannan (1927). The difference, in Cannan's view, consisted only in the fact that 'money is more homogeneous than bags and their contents', so that depositors in a cloakroom insist on the *same* bag being returned whereas depositors in a bank are willing to accept other pieces of money in lieu of those they deposited. However, neither cloakrooms nor banks can create deposits. 'The most abandoned cloakroom attendant cannot lend out more umbrellas or bicycles than have been entrusted to him, and the most reckless banker cannot lend out more money than he has of his own *plus* what he has of other people's' (pp. 258, 259).

difference between storage and manufacture of money; in particular, they had not comprehended that the lending power of the commercial-banking system did not depend on money deposited with it but on the fact that the deposit liabilities of the banks had become money and could be increased by the act of lending.

Although one occasionally finds bankers who still believe the old cloakroom legend, the theory of commercial banking, in official as well as academic expositions, has safely freed itself of the stultifying effects of the old notion. Indeed, most countries, having understood the capacity of commercial banks to create money, have taken measures to control or limit the exercise of this power. These controls and limitations have generally been of a quantitative nature, usually in the form of requirements for banks to hold particular 'reserve assets' in certain ratios to their deposit liabilities.

A requirement of 100 per cent reserves would have eliminated the banks' power of credit creation. But one can imagine other forms of limiting this power, say, by measures reducing the general acceptability of deposits as circulating media. For example, depositories could have been prohibited from promising payment on demand and from transferring deposit balances to other accounts or other financial institutions; or all legal protection against fraud by checks could have been withheld. Alternatively, financial intermediaries could have been forbidden to accept deposits altogether, and thus be confined to receiving funds by selling shares of equity capital or of participations in particular investments. (As a matter of fact, limitations of these types have been proposed or even adopted in some countries with regard to thrift deposits or savings institutions, with the intention of down-grading the moneyness of bank liabilities and, thereby, the capacity of banks to create credit.) Another, rather fantastic restriction could have reduced financial intermediaries to the status of mere 'credit agents', neither borrowing nor lending, but receiving only the lenders' own cashier checks and passing them on to the borrowers.

These or other measures to hold commercial banks to a cloakroom function, to prevent them from graduating from warehouses of money to manufacturers of money, have not been adopted. According to the cloakroom theory commercial banks were unable to create credit; by a cloakroom rule they could be prevented from creating credit. No attempts have been made, however, since the cloakroom theory was exploded, to resort to a cloakroom rule of commercial banking. The authorities have been satisfied with quantitative limitations, controlling bank-credit creation but not preventing it.

The Cloakroom Rule for International Reserves

There has never been any serious doubt about the ability of national central banks to create national money. Regarding them, neither a cloakroom theory nor a cloakroom rule has been developed; their sight liabilities are money, without reservations. In order to limit the central banks' power of money creation many countries have adopted quantitative limitations, such as gold reserve requirements or minimum reserve ratios of gold and foreign-exchange holdings to bank note circulation or to both bank note and deposit liabilities. But countries have not tried to reduce the moneyness of such liabilities.

On the next higher level, however, in the case of international reserve, a cloakroom rule has been adopted for the foremost international monetary institutions. In full comprehension of the fact that an international money institution could be either a warehouse of existing money or a manufacturer of new international money, many or most central bankers of our time insist that an international institution such as the International Monetary Fund is and must be nothing but a warehouse and intermediary of currencies handed over to it; and they fight the idea that deposit liabilities of such an institution should be the accepted international reserve assets of national monetary authorities. The cloakroom rule for international reserves is strongly defended by a majority of practical experts and by many academic economists as well.

The Bretton Woods Agreements

The experts preparing for the Bretton Woods Conference in 1944 carefully studied the Keynes Plan (April 1943) with its full recognition of the principle of credit creation. The proposed

'International Clearing Union' was supposed to extend credit to countries in deficit and thereby create deposit liabilities accepted as international reserve by the central banks of member countries. This proposal was rejected by the United States, largely because of a fear that too much international money might be created and used to draw real resources from countries obliged to accept this fiat money in exchange for real goods and services demanded by overspending nations.

The plan accepted in lieu of a credit-creating Clearing Union provided for a credit-transferring Monetary Fund. The I.M.F. was to obtain national currencies by subscriptions from member countries and then to exchange limited amounts of such currencies against national currencies of countries in deficit. The 'sale' of currencies of countries in surplus, out of the Fund's holding, against currencies of countries in deficit, with the obligation of the latter countries to 'repurchase' their own currencies later with convertible currencies, is only a lending operation described in fancy terminology. In ordinary language, the Fund 'lends' currencies it has held as assets to countries that want to borrow in order to finance their deficits. By insisting that international payments be made only in national currencies (of key currency countries) or in gold, but *not* in deposit liabilities of the I.M.F., the signers of the Bretton Woods Agreements made the Fund a warehouse and transfer agent of national moneys and guarded against the possibility of its becoming a factory of international money.

The Cloakroom Function of the I.M.F.

One may be tempted to resort to another analogy in order to emphasize the essential contrast between credit transfer and credit creation. Savings banks and building and loan associations in the United States can only transfer funds received from depositors; they receive check-deposit balances in (deposit liabilities of) commercial banks and lend them to borrowers (exchange them against the borrowers' promises to repay); they can lend only what they have received. Commercial banks, on the other hand, viewed as a group, do not lend anything they have received and lose no liquid assets in acquiring the borrowers' promises to pay;

the borrowers or their payees receive deposit-liabilities of the commercial banks, deposits that are newly created in the process and constitute additions to the money supply.

Much of this contrast is analogous to that between an asset-lending I.M.F. and a liability-creating X.I.M.F. (if I may use Altman's code word for an 'expanded' International Monetary Fund). But the analogy fails in one important respect: funds deposited with savings institutions ordinarily come from the active income stream; they constitute current saving by income recipients choosing to let someone else do the purchasing that they themselves forego. Most of the funds paid into the I.M.F., on the other hand, are newly created liabilities of national monetary authorities, not previously existing moneys in active circulation. The currencies held as assets by the I.M.F. are therefore not the result of abstinence or saving by any person or nation; and when they are made available to countries in deficit for payments to other countries, these currencies become net additions to international reserves. The I.M.F. thus does play a role in the creation of international reserves, though this role is confined to putting into circulation the currencies created by national monetary authorities (Machlup, 1964a, p. 292; 1964b, p. 11). It remains true that the I.M.F. is a warehouse, transfer agent, and rental service for national currencies received from member countries.

The cloakroom function of the I.M.F. is not the result of a theoretical misunderstanding on the part of the experts assembled at Bretton Woods. It is rather the result of a deliberate limitation on the prerogatives of the I.M.F. The United States and other founding countries did not want the Fund to become a credit-creating institution and, hence, they anxiously avoided what would have been a precondition to the creation of a new international currency, namely, the acceptability of the Fund's deposit liabilities in international payments among national monetary authorities.

Expanding the Functions of the I.M.F.

For some fourteen years the world seemed well satisfied with the limitation on the Fund's functions to that of a rental service for currencies held in storage. This changed only when it was (slowly but increasingly) realized that the existing dual currency reserve and gold exchange system might not prove viable and that the continuous increase in dollar liabilities used as reserve assets of most of the nondollar world would cause trouble both if it went on and if it stopped. In the opinion of an increasing number of experts, the required reform or necessary evolution will take the form of extending the functions of the I.M.F. and, especially, of allowing its liabilities to become reserve assets for national monetary authorities. The chief protagonist of this view has been Robert Triffin. The principle, however, of I.M.F. deposits replacing or supplementing the present currency reserves is getting wide acceptance in academic circles and sporadic acceptance among official experts. In one form or another, the idea of I.M.F. liabilities serving as reserve assets of national monetary authorities has been incorporated in the Stamp Plans, the Harrod Plans, the Day Plan, the Angell Plan, the Maudling Plan, one of the Bernstein Plans, to mention only the best-known proposals (Machlup, 1964a, pp. 319–39; 1964b, pp. 39–61).

The idea of shifting the source of the lending power of the I.M.F. from the magnitude and composition of its *assets* to the acceptability of its *liabilities* is still resisted by many central bankers and government experts. Some of the objections focus on possible impairments of the Fund's own 'liquidity'. The expansion of Fund liabilities is viewed as dependent upon the Fund's 'resources' and as impinging on the Fund's ability to meet its obligations.

Even the officers and economists of the I.M.F. are exceedingly cautious in discussing the possibilities of creating 'unconditional liquidity on an international scale'. Thus in considering purchases of 'assets other than currencies', that is, investments by the Fund, they state that 'Any acquisition of assets by investment would tend to put a strain on the Fund's resources. . . . Investment would be likely to require an extension of the Fund's own resources derived from subscriptions or of borrowing by the Fund beyond what would otherwise be necessary.'[2]

2. See International Monetary Fund (1964), pp. 38–9. The extension of the Fund's resources by 'borrowing' is, of course, a correct legal description, since all deposit-liabilities are the logical legal correlative of 'borrowing'.

This emphasis on the Funds' 'resources' and on the composition of its assets calls for our critical attention.

Three Fundamental Propositions

The essential points will be understood more readily if we go back to some more general relationships that hold on different levels of the monetary system and can be formulated in three fundamental propositions:

1. For payments among customers of the same (commercial) bank, the assets (amounts, quality, composition, liquidity) of that bank are irrelevant; they become relevant only for payments to customers of other banks, that is, for *interbank payments.*

2. For interbank payments in the same country, the assets (amounts, quality, composition, liquidity) of the national reserve bank are irrelevant; they become relevant only for payments to persons or banks in other countries, that is, for *international payments.*

3. For international payments in the same world, the assets (amounts, quality, composition, liquidity) of the international reserve bank (or an appropriately organized I.M.F.) are irrelevant; they become relevant only for payments to persons, banks, or reserve banks on other planets, that is, for *interplanetary payments.*

Thus, as long as we are concerned only with international and not with interplanetary payments, there is no need to worry about the resources of an international reserve bank whose liabilities are accepted as reserve assets of national reserve banks. Some qualifications to this statement, however, are necessary. (And readers who are nervous lest the danger of inflation be disregarded may be reassured: this subject will be discussed presently.)

One qualification pertains to the first two propositions. They hold only if all payments are made by check or transfers from

---

From an economic point of view, however, it is the causal sequence that matters. Where certain liabilities enjoy acceptability as money and are transferred 'from depositor to depositor', the acquisition of additional assets need not wait for any prior act of borrowing but, on the contrary, the liabilities arise as a consequence of the acquisition of assets.

account to account. However, if there is also another kind of domestic money, say, coins or paper currency, some customers may wish to draw such money from their banks. The possible demand for nonbank currency is a factor to be taken into account. This demand may increase as the amount of bank money increases, because there are some things that cannot conveniently be purchased and paid for by check (for example, purchases of street-car tickets and of goods sold by coin automats). A second source of demand for nonbank money may be the primitive peasant's distrust of banks; he may wish to check periodically whether the bank still has 'his money', though he may leave it there once the teller produces enough currency from the till.

An analogous qualification is called for regarding the third proposition, which would be completely valid only if all international payments were made by transfers from account to account. However, if there is another kind of international money, say, gold bullion, some central banks may wish to add to their gold holdings. There is no increase in the demand for gold that can be explained by particular payments for which gold alone would be usable (as only coins can be used for automats). The sole source of demand for gold would be that of a distrustful national monetary authority wanting to check (like the primitive peasant) whether 'its gold' was still there.

Our three fundamental propositions relate only to the problem of liquidity and ability to pay. They do not relate to the problems of the danger of price inflations and induced redistributions of real income. Yet, these problems are involved in the banks' decisions about acquisition of assets. Through their selection of assets, banks – commercial, national, and international – can affect absolute and relative prices, the allocation of productive services, and the distribution of products among persons and among nations. These problems, rather than that of the liquidity of the international reserve institution, require attention.

The 'Correct' Rate of Monetary Expansion

The first of these problems, the danger of inflation, has been discussed so often that brief reminders of generally accepted conclusions ought to suffice here. Let us remember that the fear of illiquidity on the part of individual commercial banks through deficits in interbank balances of payments acts as a brake in the speed of credit expansion by the commercial banking system, and that this expansion is also controlled by such things as (legal or traditional) reserve requirements and circumspection in the supply of commercial bank reserves (government money or central bank money) by the national monetary authorities. Let us further remember that the fear of illiquidity on the part of central banks through deficits in international balances of payments acts as a brake in the speed of credit expansion by central banks, and that this expansion is also controlled by such things as (legal or traditional) reserve ratios (gold and foreign-exchange-reserve requirements) and by scarcity of supply of central-bank reserves (new acquisitions of gold and convertible foreign exchange).

An analogous brake would not exist for an International Reserve Institution, say, an I.R.I. or X.I.M.F. It would not have to fear illiquidity through deficits in the interplanetary balance of payments, and consequently the expansion of its assets (loans and investments) and, therefore, of its deposit liabilities (the new reserve assets of national central banks) could go on without limit unless agreed institutional constraints are imposed on it. If one distrusts the intelligence, wisdom, and character of those who will (by international agreement) make the rules and regulations for the institution or of those who will determine its policies, then one is justified in fearing that the rate of expansion of international reserves would be excessive. An excessive rate of expansion of central-bank reserves would in all probability lead to an excessive rate of expansion in commercial-bank reserves, which in turn would be liable to lead to an excessive rate of expansion in commercial-bank deposits.

On the other hand, there are those who believe that safe rules and regulations can be devised for the International Reserve Institution and that its management can be expected to pursue appropriate policies in determining the rate of expansion. They hold that the danger of inflation resulting from excessive creation of international reserves is greatly exaggerated. They hold that the annual increase of international reserves could be checked either by adherence to some rules of thumb or by discretion on the part of management correctly sizing up the total 'need' of additional international reserves, that is, the rate of increase that would avoid serious inflationary or deflationary mistakes.[3]

For the sake of a clear exposition of the second problem – of the induced redistribution of world output through the chosen distribution of newly created international reserves – we shall assume that the annual rate of expansion can be controlled and that an appropriate rate can be 'correctly' determined. This assumption, however, involves a serious complication for the amount depends on its distribution. If a larger portion of the new international reserves goes to national central banks with high propensities to expand credit in countries with high propensities to import, a given amount of new reserves will lead to a larger total of world demand and a stronger pull-up of prices and earning rates. If a larger portion of the new reserves goes to slowly expanding central banks in countries with low propensities to import, the effect of the reserve creation upon demand, incomes, and prices will be smaller. In addition, the effect will also depend on the form, terms, and conditions under which new reserves are obtained by central banks; that is to say, their marginal propensities to expand are likely to vary according to circumstances. It follows that a judgment of the 'correct' amount of reserve creation presupposes separate estimates of a large number of variables.

Despite all these complications we shall proceed to a discussion of the distribution effects of the 'correctly' determined, that is, noninflationary addition to international reserves.

Who Gets the Money First?

The new assets acquired by commercial banks may give an indication of who got the 'new' money first when it was created. 'Who gets the money first' may make a difference for various sectors of an economy. For if, with relatively full employment, the quantity of money increases over the years, the first spenders

3. Even if one is pessimistic concerning judgment and backbone of prospective managers of a prospective world reserve bank, one must not compare their prospective errors and failures with an ideal. It would be difficult to believe that even the worst managers of an I.R.I. or X.I.M.F. would have created nearly as much international reserve as was created under our present system from 1958 to 1963.

of the new money take real income away from others. This holds true whether productivity is constant or whether it increases. The first spenders of the new money obtain goods and services other members of the economy would have claimed; these others either suffer a net decline in 'real intake' or fail to get their full share in the increase of the total product made available through the rise in productivity.

The new assets acquired by the central banks will not give the relevant information if the expansion of its credit is largely in the form of loans to commercial banks or of open market purchases of government securities at a time the government is not enlarging its debt. For, in such instances, we do not know how the banks use the resulting increase in their lending power and how the sellers of securities (including banks) use their proceeds. The assets of the entire banking system would have to be examined to get some answer, however partial and ambiguous, to the question of the identity of the favored spenders. If business is the chief recipient of the new funds, a diagnosis of accelerated capital formation through 'forced saving' may be justified, though only with qualifications. For it is possible that business firms finance an increase in consumer loans, in which case the borrowing consumers encroach on those who merely spend what they earn.

If increases in bank assets are matched by increases in government debt and government spending, the diagnosis may be of an increase in government services, or perhaps an increase in transfer payments (to the old, the sick, the unemployed) at the expense of individual consumers' real purchases. If the increase in government spending is for a public investment program, future generations may be the beneficiaries of the enforced abstinence of present consumers. Other government programs may involve intersectoral transfers of potential intake. There may be even a geographic redistribution of national output if the new money is first spent by or for the benefit of particular regions within the economy. The number of possible combinations is large. It may be worthwhile for some economist to work through various models of 'redistribution through selection of first spenders of new money' and to search for operational indicators for the pertinence of particular models to particular situations.

On the international level the question is, in some ways, simpler because our interest is usually focused on the claims or drafts countries may make on one another's productive facilities. An international reserve institution, by providing new international money, enables the first spenders of this new money to obtain products from other countries. To the extent that the productive capacity of these other countries is fully utilized, involuntary abstinence is imposed on their nationals. Thus, we should not expect nations to be indifferent about the ways in which an international reserve institution uses its power to create international money and distributes it among various national monetary authorities. Power to create international money is power to take products from some countries and give them to others.

The case of underemployment in a country in which new international money is spent should be mentioned, chiefly because one may hold that such a country loses, to those that buy from it, little that it would have had without the additional foreign demand. On the other hand, such a country, had it been anxious to procure a higher level of employment, could have adopted internal policies to make sure that the output of the additional employment would go to its own nationals. Finally, the case of inflation in the exporting country deserves the comment that in this situation the international redistribution of output is combined with an intranational redistribution. In order to avoid complicating the problem, we shall assume that the increase in foreign demand does not imply price inflation. This assumption not only simplifies analysis; it also serves to drive home the fact that the problem of diverting a larger part of national output to the foreign spenders of the new international money is not merely an aspect of the phenomenon of price inflation.

Distributing the New International Money

Let us distinguish various ways in which the International Reserve Institution (I.R.I.) distributes, through its assets selection, its new deposit liabilities among different countries:

1. I.R.I. gives loans to countries in deficit or to countries that wish to increase their reserves. Such loans might be of short, medium, or long term; they might be conditional or uncondi-

tional. They might be the result of an exercise of agreed borrowing rights or of discretionary decisions by the management.

2. I.R.I. purchases from national monetary authorities currencies of other countries, within some limits, with or without commitments of the issuing countries to 'repurchase' their currencies within short, medium, or long periods of time, and with gold-value or exchange-value guarantees.[4]

3. I.R.I. purchases securities of the International Bank for Reconstruction and Development (I.B.R.D.), the International Development Association (I.D.A.), other international or national development aid institutions, or governments of developing countries.

4. I.R.I. purchases gilt-edged securities (especially medium-term or long-term obligations of trusted governments of affluent countries, but perhaps also I.B.R.D. bonds) regularly traded in the world's largest capital markets. These purchases might be subject to prior consent, perhaps even upon invitation, by the governments concerned, and resales might also be subject to agreement, perhaps limited to maximum amounts per month or year or permissible only when certain conditions prevail, such as a surplus in the country's balance of payments.

5. I.R.I. purchases national currencies (that is, obligations of national monetary authorities) in specified amounts and proportions fixed by some previously agreed formula. These currencies are not for resale or any use other than decorating the balance sheet of I.R.I. (that is, they will stay there until I.R.I. is liquidated or a member exercises a right to withdraw from the institution).[5]

4. There is no essential difference between the first and second technique, especially if the country that sells foreign exchange is not obligated in any respect. The possibility is listed here for only one reason: to disabuse readers of the belief that the surrender of 'gold and foreign exchange' is different from the surrender of one's own currency, that is, from the sale of a bank's own liabilities. Assume that I.R.I. was forbidden to purchase anything but 'gold and foreign exchange'; if only country *A* had gold, and no other country had any foreign exchange to spare, *A* could sell its gold to *B* in exchange for *B*-currency, *B* could resell the gold to *C* in exchange for *C*-currency, and so on, with the result that any number of countries would have acquired foreign exchange, which they could sell to I.R.I.

5. The essential difference between the first two and the last of the five techniques described here lies in the 'permanence' of the assets. Number 1

The First Round of Spending

What implications do the techniques of distributing the new reserves have for the speed with which the international buying power that they afford will actually be exercised? The reserves obtained by technique Number 1 are spent immediately ('today'), except in the case in which a country borrows only to show a larger gross reserve. The I.R.I. deposits obtained by technique Number 2 may replace foreign-exchange reserves received 'yesterday' for exports which, incidentally, the particular country might not have made had it not been assured of the exchangeability of the earned currency into I.R.I. deposits. The I.R.I. funds created by technique Number 3 and going – via I.B.R.D., I.D.A., etc. – to less developed countries will probably be spent 'tomorrow'. Thus, these three techniques of reserve creation have in common that the new money is probably spent without delay.

This is not so likely with regard to technique Number 4, which increases the reserves of countries where the sellers of the securities (acquired by I.R.I.) spend or hold their proceeds. If the sellers are highly liquid financial intermediaries or commercial banks in countries in surplus, the new reserves may long remain unused. The increased lending power of the liquid financial institutions and of the liquid central bank may not be exercised for the time being and no excess demand for foreign exchange may develop. If, on the other hand, the sellers have sold the securities in order to make loans urgently demanded from them, or if they are in countries suffering from balance-of-payments deficits, the reserves will not wait long before they are used for purchasing goods and services from abroad. In addition, the availability of these reserves may allow greater delays in the adoption of adjustment policies designed to remove the payments deficits of these countries. The probability that the new reserves will be spent quickly can be increased by selective open market purchases, that is, if I.R.I. makes its investments in deficit countries

---

provides for repayment by the particular borrower (of course, not of all borrowers taken as a group, if world-wide deflation is to be avoided). Number 2 may provide for repayment, depending on the agreed terms. Number 5 provides for nonrepayable loans, with or without interest.

(or if it increases its holdings of I.B.R.D. bonds, assuming that I.B.R.D. has prompt uses for its funds).

It should be understood that 'fast' and 'slow' use of the additional funds refers in all cases to the first round of spending. Received by surplus countries in exchange for 'real resources', the I.R.I. deposits come to rest in the foreign reserves of these countries; they have changed their character from 'unearned' to 'earned' reserves.[6] A second round of spending will come along only when the balance of payments of these reserve-holders turns and they become deficit countries. Since the adjustment mechanism has been slowed down almost everywhere, the second round may be long in coming.

Even the first round will come later, on the average, for reserves distributed by technique Number 5. If the formula used in the distribution includes such variables as present reserve holdings, national income, foreign trade volume, or I.M.F. quotas, a large part of the new I.R.I. deposits will go to surplus countries. These have no current use for more reserves – if 'use' means spending rather than holding (which may be poor semantics in the view of those who insist on reserves being what is held, not what is used up). If they are, moreover, conservative in their monetary policy – expanding domestic credit at a relatively slower pace than the fast-expanding and fast-spending countries – they will hold on to both earned and unearned reserves. It follows that only that part of the newly created I.R.I. deposits that goes to deficit countries will have a quick first round of spending and will then come to rest in the reserves of the 'thrifty'.

The Probability of an Early Turn-around

Countries in deficit receive from countries in surplus real resources (or claims to real resources) and pay for these resources with the newly created I.R.I. deposits. To be sure, the recipient countries hold their additional earned reserves as eventual counterclaims to real resources of other countries; but the actual return flow does not take place until the balance of payments

6. Reserves are 'unearned' if the nation obtained them without having to give up real resources, or claims to any of its real resources.

turns, and this may be many years off; indeed the time may never come.

The probability of an early turn-around is highest if the new reserves are created through short-term loans to deficit countries with the condition that effective adjustment policies be pursued. If all countries pursue policies resulting in quick and short swings from deficit to surplus to deficit and again to surplus, the transfers of real resources will likewise be for short periods only; no country, then, can be regarded as a long-term beneficiary at the expense of others. However, in this case it will be doubtful if the creation of new I.R.I. deposits will also serve the purpose of satisfying a growing world demand for international reserves, that is, for reserves to hold rather than to shuttle back and forth. If countries create domestic means of circulation at rates sufficient to avoid declining wage rates despite increasing labor force, and declining general price levels despite increasing outputs, they may want their foreign reserves to increase at approximately the same rates. Yet, a technique of reserve creation that regularly cancels most of any previous expansion will not achieve the desired continuous net growth. The erstwhile surplus countries, having now developed deficits, lose the reserves they have earned; and the erstwhile deficit countries, having now developed surpluses, repay their short-term loans to the international reserve institution. The reserves created by the loans are canceled as the loans are repaid.

Only if imbalances of payments increase over the years can the technique of short-term loans to deficit countries achieve a steady growth of international reserves. Assume that the first round of deficits is financed by loans of one billion dollars; if then the balance turns, the previous surplus countries swinging into deficit need not borrow except to the extent that their deficits are in excess of a billion. For example, if their deficits amounted to one-and-a-half billion dollars, a billion of I.R.I. deposits is wiped out and only one-half of one billion remains as a net increase in total reserves. This is why some economists do not regard reserve creation through loan expansion for the finance of payments deficits as an adequate system to take care of a growing demand for reserves. (The offer of short-term loans to countries that may be willing to borrow more reserves to hold rather than to spend would probably not be taken advantage of in amounts sufficient to secure the growth needed to avoid deflationary pressures.)

Reserve creation through I.R.I. investments in securities of development-finance institutions is different in that the probability of a return flow is slight. The first spending of the new funds by the beneficiaries, the less developed countries, draw real resources from developed countries. The I.R.I. deposits are likely to come to rest as permanent reserves of the countries that earned them through their exports, though they may occasionally circulate among these countries as they take turns in getting into short-term deficits with one another. The point is that it is not likely that the developing countries will earn back the reserves of which they had been the first spenders.

Little can be said with any degree of confidence about the future career of reserves created through open market policies. If the purchases of widely traded securities are undertaken at the initiative of the I.R.I., it should be possible for it to avoid a decline in its investment portfolio and hence in the volume of its corresponding deposit liabilities. But one cannot foretell whether these deposits would actively circulate among countries taking turns in swinging from deficit into surplus or whether they would stay inactive as owned reserves of countries with a steady (and steadily growing) demand for this 'backing' behind their national money supply.

With regard to I.R.I. deposit liabilities created and distributed by deposits of national currencies according to an agreed formula, we stated before that a large part of these unearned reserves would never be used in even a first round of spending. It would be moot to speculate on the probability of an early second round for that portion which, through deficits of the first recipients, has been transformed from unearned into earned reserves.

The Transfer of Real Resources to Developing Countries

The conclusion, undoubtedly, is that the creation of new international reserves can be instrumental in a transfer of real resources to countries in short-run deficit, to countries in long-lasting deficit, and to developing countries in perennial deficit. It is easy to understand the resulting conflicts of interest. Representatives of countries from which resources are withdrawn may object to the 'involuntary' philanthropy involved in such schemes, especially in the relief for slow adjusters and in the aid to late developers. Spokesmen for the underdogs may point to the hardships usually associated with adjustment in deficit countries and to the crying need for resources on the part of less developed nations.

Leaving aside the controversy about the 'proper' speed of adjusting imbalances of payments, let us examine the arguments for and against combining the creation of international reserves with the provision of aid to less developed countries. It should be understood from the outset: one may be genuinely impressed with the desirability of aiding poorer nations and with the desirability of providing for growing international reserves and may, nevertheless, resist schemes that try to do both these things in one process.

Any plan for reserve creation that is successful in avoiding deflationary pressures in developed countries will also benefit developing countries *indirectly* through its effects on the demand for primary commodities, supply of industrial products, and supply of capital. To insist on a 'rider' for the provision of *direct* aid to developing countries may seem gratuitous. Built-in development aid – by handing the new reserves first to less developed countries and forcing the more developed countries to buy back, as it were, these reserves, that is, to earn them by surrendering real resources – may seem to some a scheme designed to conceal or confuse, perhaps as an arbitrary squeeze play. If a group of industrial countries, used to holding 'tokens' for their financial settlements, want to increase their stocks of tokens because they want more to hold and more to hand back and forth among one another in settling temporary payments balances, why should they not be permitted to create such tokens for themselves without having to surrender real resources to poor countries? They may be willing to contribute most generously, they may even recognize a moral responsibility for aiding developing nations through liberal grants, loans, and investments – but they object to the arbitrary linking of matters that are inherently separate.

On the other hand, a very plausible argument can be made, on political as well as economic grounds, for combining development aid and reserve creation in one package deal. It may be politically difficult to obtain the appropriations for foreign aid that the governments may deem desirable; they may find it easier to get legislative approval for a plan establishing an international reserve institution whose investments will include securities of development-finance organizations. In political questions one cannot always insist on logical neatness and semantic clarity. The economic case for the package deal must rest largely on tradition: historically, international reserves have always been earned through the surrender of real resources and, to industrial countries, the cost of reserves under a plan of distributing new reserves first to less developed countries is not any higher than the cost of reserves under the gold standard.

The discovery that international money can be produced with cheap ink and paper, and need not be produced with hard work applied to metal dug out of the ground, affords a large saving. Should the holders of this cheap international money be the sole beneficiaries of the reduction in cost? If they are prepared to acquire additional gold reserves by surrendering real resources, one should think that they can pay the same price for a perfect substitute, for the deposits in the international reserve institution. The first spenders of the new deposits will be the beneficiaries of the technological progress in the production of international money, and these first spenders may 'just as well' be the developing nations.

When gold is the only international reserve money, some Africans, Australians, and Asians (and a few North Americans) must work in the mines to dig the stuff out of the ground. When credit entries in the books of an acceptable organization become substitutes for gold, work on highways, railroads, harbors, power plants, hospitals, and schools of developing countries can take the place of work in the gold mines[7] – provided the countries holding

7. The reader may wish to compare this thought with the famous Smithian remark about cheap paper currency being analogous to highways in the air. Here is the quotation: 'The gold and silver money . . . may very properly be compared to a highway, which, while it circulates and carries to market all the grass and corn of the country, produces itself not a single pile of either. The judicious operations of banking, by providing, if I may be allowed so

most of the international reserves are willing to pay for the 'perfect substitute' the same price they used to pay and continue to pay for gold reserves. Equal prices for perfect substitutes are the rule, rather than the exception, in competitive markets. The savings in the production of the low-cost substitute must be distributed somehow, and if the producer, in this case the International Reserve Institution, holds a monopoly, the distribution is for the owners of the company to decide. If they are so inclined, they may well let the developing countries have the lion's share.

Summary and Conclusion

The cloakroom theory of banking contended that banks were unable to create means of circulation. A cloakroom rule is adopted if the banks' power to create money is recognized and deliberately suppressed. The International Monetary Fund was advisedly reduced to a cloakroom function because the nations were fearful of excessive creation of monetary reserves. The contradicting governments confined the functions of the I.M.F. to that of a warehouse and rental agent for a collection of currencies, and prohibited it from becoming a manufacturer of circulating deposit liabilities.

This limitation can no longer be maintained in a world determined to maintain fixed exchange rates, to employ monetary expansion to promote economic growth, and to adhere to the rule that the supply of money ought not to expand much faster than the monetary reserves. In such a world the stock of international reserves will have to be increased year after year. The future need for international reserves can be met most cheaply and most efficiently by deposit creation of an international reserve institution. The danger of excessive reserve creation by such an

---

violent a metaphor, a sort of waggon-way through the air, enable the country to convert, as it were, a great part of its highways into good pastures and cornfields and thereby to increase very considerably the annual produce of its land and labour.' Adam Smith (1950), p. 246. The advantage of substituting paper for gold, by Smith considered from the point of view of one country, is regarded in the text as a saving to the world, with the benefit going to the less developed countries.

institution can be averted by explicit constraints and responsible management; reserve creation would surely be more rational than under the present gold-exchange standard. But the question of induced transfers of real resources to the first spenders of the new reserves calls for political decisions. The acquisition of reserves under the gold standard involved the surrender of real resources. If additional reserves under the new system can be created at no cost, the saving will benefit someone and its distribution must needs be arbitrary. If developing countries were made the beneficiaries, the cost to reserve holders would be no greater than under a gold standard. This may be proposed as an argument in support of schemes linking the creation of international reserves with aid to developing countries. On the other hand, the industrial countries may object to clandestine aid schemes and claim that they, as the chief holders of reserves, should be allowed to create additional reserves without having to 'earn' them through transfers of real resources to developing countries. Both arguments are persuasive and can be reasonably defended.

References

CANNAN, E. (1927), 'The difference between a bank and a cloak-room', *An Economist's Protest*, King, London, pp. 256–66.

INTERNATIONAL MONETARY FUND (1964), *Annual Report of the Executive Directors for the Fiscal Year ended April 30th, 1964*, Washington.

MACHLUP, F. (1964a), *International Payments, Debts and Gold*, Scribners, New York.

MACHLUP, F. (1964b), *Plans for Reform of the International Monetary System*, Department of Economics, Princeton University.

SMITH, A. (1950), *An Inquiry into the Nature and Cause of the Wealth of Nations*, Methuen, vol. 2, 6th edn (paperback edition, 1961).

16 R. Nurkse

International Investment Today in the Light of Nineteenth-century Experience

R. Nurkse (1954), 'International investment today in the light of nineteenth-century experience', *Economic Journal*, vol. 64, pp. 134–50.

To many Americans today the problem of international investment is doubtless a source of perplexity and even of some irritation. Ever since the last World War great expectations have been placed on the export of private American capital as a means of bridging the dollar gap as well as financing world economic development. In reality, private foreign investment throughout the period since 1945 has fluctuated at a low level and without any sign at all of an upward trend.[1] This is most disappointing. We suspect that the export of capital from Great Britain was one reason why the international economy of the Victorian era did not know of a chronic sterling shortage. We recognize, above all, that foreign investment was associated during that era with a tremendous spurt in world production and trade. There is in America a feeling of nostalgia for the nineteenth-century environment that made this flow of capital possible. The question is: why can we not re-create that environment?

The answer, I submit, must start from the fact that the circumstances in which overseas investment, and more especially British investment, went on in the nineteenth century (which I take to have ended in 1914) were in some ways quite exceptional. To realize this is of more than historical interest. So long as the peculiar features of that experience are not fully appreciated, memories of wonders worked by foreign investment in the past can only lead to false hopes and frustration.

Recent researches have made it possible to estimate approximately the percentage share of her national income that Britain used to lend abroad. Occasionally one finds the same proportions being applied to the present American national income as an

1. See *Federal Reserve Bulletin*, October 1953, pp. 1039–42.

indication of what the United States could or should do. Over the fifty years that preceded the outbreak of the First World War, it seems that Great Britain invested overseas an amount equal to about 4 per cent of her national income. In the later part of the period (1905–13) the ratio was as high as 7 per cent. If the United States today were to devote similar percentage portions of her national income to the same purposes, she would be exporting funds to the tune of $12 billion or, if we apply the higher percentage, some $20 billion each year. These figures are almost absurdly large and tend to confirm the view that there was something unique about Britain's foreign investment.

It was unique in that the greater part of it – roughly two-thirds – went to the so-called 'regions of recent settlement': the spacious, fertile, and virtually empty plains of Canada, the United States, Argentina, Australia, and other 'new' countries in the world's temperate latitudes. It was unique in that it went to these places together with a great migration of about sixty million people,[2] including many trained and enterprising persons, from the British Isles as well as Continental Europe. The conditions that made this flow of private capital possible do not exist to any great extent today, and probably cannot be re-created.

It was in the newly settled regions, which received two-thirds of the capital exports and practically all the emigrants, that nineteenth-century international investment scored its greatest triumphs. The remaining third of British capital exported (or more accurately a quarter, since some went to Continental Europe) was employed in a different type of area, where its achievements were much more dubious: tropical or subtropical regions inhabited, often densely, by native populations endowed in some cases with ancient civilizations of their own. The areas that formed a minor field for overseas investment before 1914 are the major problem today: the truly backward economies, containing now about two-thirds of the world's population. The empty and newly settled regions, from which international investment derived its brilliant general record and reputation, are today, in *per capita* income, among the most prosperous countries in the world.

2. This is a gross figure; some of the migrants returned.

Labor and capital are complementary factors of production, and exert a profound attraction on each other. The movement of labor to the new regions attracted capital to the same places at the same time. And the other way round: the flow of capital stimulated the migration of people to these places. To some extent, it is true, the parallel movements of capital and labor might plausibly be interpreted as two separate effects of a common cause; namely, of the opening up of the vast reserves of land and other natural resources. But the complementary nature of the labor and capital movements, based on the complementarity of the two factors, is equally plain. Any barrier to the transfer of one would have reduced the flow of the other. Labor and capital moved along side by side, supporting each other.[3]

In the twentieth century the situation is totally different. The capital exports from the United States can be viewed rather as a *substitute* for the movement of people. Capital and labor are still complementary, and still basically attract one another. But as things now are, restricting the movement of labor in one direction increases the need, if not the incentive, for capital to move in the opposite direction. Cheap labor, instead of being allowed to come to the United States to work with American capital there, is to some extent supplied with American capital abroad (supplied by the American government as in the years since 1945, if not by private profit-seeking investors, as in the 1920s). The underlying pressure – not necessarily the profit motive, but what we might call the global social pressure – is very strong for more capital to move out from the United States to work with the cheap labor in the world's backward economies. But notice that in this situation, in sharp contrast to the predominant nineteenth-century pattern, capital is being urged to go out to work with people that have not grown up in a capital-minded milieu, and may not be culturally prepared for the use of western equipment, methods, and techniques.

With this situation in mind, we can perceive what I think is

3. It is interesting to observe that the parallel nature of the two factor movements shows itself also, according to Professor A. K. Cairncross (1953, p. 209) in the close agreement with which capital exports and emigration from Britain varied from decade to decade between 1870 and 1910.

the basic rationale of the present American emphasis on direct business investment as a means of financing economic development. The advantages rightly attributed to it are, first, that it goes out with American enterprise, tied up with American 'know-how', and, secondly, that it is likely to be productively used, not swallowed up – directly or indirectly – by immediate consumption in the receiving country. Since, however, in the low-income areas the domestic market is small, this type of investment tends inevitably in such areas to concentrate on extractive industries – mines, plantations, oil wells – producing raw materials for export mainly to the advanced countries. This is, in effect, the so-called 'colonial' pattern of foreign investment, of which American oil operations abroad are now an outstanding example. It has its drawbacks as well as its virtues. But, in any event, the stress laid – even in the original Point Four program – on direct investments in economically backward countries should not, in my opinion, be dismissed as merely a product of conservative business ideology; it reflects in part an essential difference in the present-day environment of international investment as compared with the nineteenth century.

In the aggregate flow of capital in the nineteenth century, the 'colonial' type of venture played a minor role. Looking at Britain's foreign investment portfolio in 1913, we find that, of an estimated total of about £3,700 million outstanding at that time in nominal value, 30 per cent was in loans to governments, as much as 40 per cent in railway securities, and some 5 per cent in other public utilities, so that no less than three-quarters of the total was in public or public-utility investments. The rest includes banking, insurance, and manufacturing companies, as well as investments directly in raw-material extraction. The total should be increased by making some allowance (say, £300 million) for private holdings and participations not represented by securities listed on the London Stock Exchange; but that would make little difference to the proportions indicated. It is therefore far from correct to assume, as is sometimes done, that the 'colonial' form of enterprise in the extraction of mineral and plantation products for the creditor country was the typical pattern of foreign investment. To call it the 'traditional' pattern might be justified in view of its history in earlier centuries. But in the nineteenth century its total amount was comparatively small; and what little there was of it appears to have been concentrated, as one would expect, in colonial and predominantly tropical areas.

To the new countries, by contrast, capital moved chiefly through the medium of securities carrying a fixed return (i.e. bonds and preference shares) issued by public authorities and public-utility undertakings. To these countries, it appears, capital could safely be sent in the form of relatively untied funds, with a good chance that it would remain capital there, because the people in these places, having come from Europe themselves, knew what to do with capital and how to handle it. Cultural adaptation was no problem.

These countries – the 'regions of recent settlement' that absorbed the bulk of British overseas investment – were offshoots of European civilization.[4] For Britain, or at any rate for Europe as a whole, investment in these areas was essentially a process of capital widening rather than deepening. Indeed, when Britain sent capital out to work with Swedes, Poles, Germans, and Italians emigrating overseas, she may have done so at the expense of the deepening which her own economy is said to have needed in the period just before the First World War. But international investment in the nineteenth century was, of course, unplanned, and was determined by private rather than national advantages. French and German activities in Eastern Europe and the Near East were an exception in this respect. As Professor Viner (1952, p. 184) has remarked, 'the French loans to Russia . . . bore a close resemblance to the programme of military aid to Western Europe which we are now embarking on'.

Great Britain's national advantage, apart from the return flow of interest and dividends, seemed to be handsomely served

4. The precise composition of this group may give rise to some debate, though essentially the line is clear. It takes in Canada, the United States, Australia, New Zealand, and South Africa. In South America it certainly includes Argentina and Uruguay, rich farm and grazing lands in temperate latitudes settled predominantly by recent immigration from Europe. I would perhaps include also the southern tip of Brazil, to which the same description largely applies, and in which most of Brazil's productive capacity, including immigration as well as foreign capital, has been concentrated since the middle of the nineteenth century.

through cheaper food and raw materials, though this benefit was shared by other importing countries that had made no corresponding investments and, besides, as we now realize, was derived in part from *Raubwirtschaft*, through soil depletion and erosion in some of the rich new plains (for example, in the virgin grasslands of the Mississippi valley).

Production of primary commodities for export to the industrial creditor countries is characteristic of the 'colonial' pattern of direct investment in economically backward areas. In the regions of recent settlement foreign investment can also be said to have been induced essentially by the raw-material needs of the industrial centers – especially by Great Britain's demand for the wheat, wool, meat, and dairy products, which she decided not to try to produce for herself, and which these temperate regions were particularly well suited to produce. The capital that came into these regions did not, however, enter into primary production itself, but was employed above all in building up the costly framework of public services, including especially transport, which laid the basis for domestic industrial development, as well as for the production of raw commodities for export. These areas are now, and have been for some time, predominantly industrial (Hilgerdt, 1945, pp. 26, 39 and *passim*), a fact entirely compatible with the large or even preponderant share of primary products in their export trade.

Nineteenth-century foreign investment centered on the railway – that 'great instrument of improvement', in Lord Dalhousie's phrase. If account is taken not only of railway securities but also of the use to which many government loans were put, it seems that well over half of Britain's external investment before 1914 went into railway construction. The great bulk of this was in the newly settled countries. The Indian railways, though an important individual item, accounted for less than one-tenth of the total of overseas railway securities held by British investors in 1914. The United States and the Argentine alone accounted for more than half of that total. In the new countries the railway was important as a means of migration. The great pioneer lines – first in the United States, later in the Argentine and elsewhere – were deliberately planned and built *in advance* of current traffic needs; they themselves created the settlement and economic growth that eventually led to a full demand for their services.

Although individual promoters sometimes played the most conspicuous part, the railways in the new countries were built, as a rule, if not directly by governments, at any rate with extensive government assistance in the form of land grants, subsidies and guaranteed returns to the investors. In view of this fact, one can safely say that the bulk of international investment in the nineteenth century depended on government action in the borrowing countries. In French and German capital exports, some of which also went to the New World, the proportion of government loans and other public investments was even higher than in the British case.

It is true that the transport revolution, to which the cheapening of British food imports (especially in the years 1880–1900) was largely due, was a matter of steamships as well as railways. While railway construction overseas was a major object of international financing, British shipbuilding counted almost entirely as part of British home investment. Since ship and railway building had much the same effects on international trade and the terms of trade, the distinction between home and foreign investment appears in this case somewhat arbitrary. In the internal economic expansion of the new countries, however, the railways had, of course, a very special part to play, rather different from that of the ships. And so we hear, for example, that 'in the Argentine, the railway is like a magic talisman: for wherever it goes it entirely transforms the economic and productive conditions of the country'.[5]

Overseas railway investment became predominant from about 1870 onwards. But this does not mean that the earlier part of the century can be ignored. While the total of foreign investment was much smaller then, so was everything else. We should note that by 1870 Britain's overseas assets had already grown to about

5. See Martinez and Lewandowski (1911), p. 108. A statement such as this applies to a type of region with the particular physical and human characteristics already noted. It would not apply in the same way to a country like India, where, for reasons that cannot be entered into, the railway 'did not give rise to a flood of satellite innovations' and 'destroyed more employment opportunities (e.g. in traditional village industries) than it opened up'. See Jenks (1944).

the same order of magnitude as her annual national income. Capital imports were a prominent feature in the economic history of the United States for many years before the Civil War.

It is clear that the main flow of capital in the nineteenth century was not to the neediest countries with their 'teeming millions', which were indeed neglected, but to sparsely peopled areas where conditions for rapid growth along familiar western lines were exceptionally favorable. If we were to look round for similar opportunities in the twentieth century, I do not know where we should find them if not in the further development of the same regions of recent settlement; or else perhaps in Siberia – a vast area reputedly rich in natural resources, which may be longing for an injection of skilled labor from Europe and capital from the United States.

Once the main facts about the nineteenth-century capital flow are set out in something like their true proportions, it is curious to see how little they fit in with some preconceived notions that have been widely current. See Buchanan (1952), Ferns (1951), Hartland (1953), Imlah (1952), Jenks (1953), Rippy (1951), Salter (1951), and Thomas (1951). Bernard Shaw, for example, in Act I of *The Apple Cart*, made one of his characters talk about England sending her 'capital abroad to places where poverty and hardship still exist: in other words, where labour is cheap. We live in comfort on the imported profits of that capital.' Consider, more seriously, the summary which Mrs Joan Robinson gives of the views of Rosa Luxemburg:

> The capitalist nations are surrounded by primitive economies, each insulated from the others like a nut within its shell, waiting to be cracked. The capitalists break open a primitive economy and enter into trade with it, whether by enticing its inhabitants with commodities they have never seen before, by political cunning or by brute force. Now exports to the primitives provide an outlet for the product of the last batch of capital goods created at home. After a little while another nut is broken, a use for more capital is thereby found, and so on, as long as the supply of untouched primitive economies lasts . . . When the stock of unbroken nuts is exhausted, the capitalist system collapses for want of markets (Robinson, 1952, pp. 157–8).

This is one variant of neo-Marxist doctrine and, like others, it neglects some crucial facts. No pre-existing markets were conquered in the new countries. Markets were *created* there by labor, enterprise, and capital all drawn from Europe. In the industrially primitive countries markets were and have remained unattractive because of mass poverty. Why is it, for example, that in the 1920s Canada, Australia, and New Zealand, with already quite highly developed industries of their own and with a combined population of only 17.4 millions, imported twice as much manufactured goods as India with her 340 million people? (Hilgerdt, 1945, p. 84.)

The American public also, perhaps because it lives in one of the new countries itself, does not always appreciate the peculiar nature of the nineteenth-century investment experience. Some of us are too apt to forget – or to take for granted – all that went with it and to assume, from that experience, a 'simple equivalence of the pace of capital transfer and the pace of development' (Croome, 1953, p. 487). Keynes in 1922 made a remark that is worth recalling: 'The practice of foreign investment, as we know it now, is a very modern contrivance, a very unstable one, and only suited to peculiar circumstances' (Keynes, 1922, p. 161). He cautioned against extending it by simple analogy to a different set of circumstances. Private foreign lending in the 1920s can be viewed in part as a backwash of the great momentum which it had gathered before 1914. Was it because in Central Europe foreign investment was applied to a situation to which it was unsuited that it came to grief there? It might perhaps have worked; Hitler did not give it a chance. Yet the fact is that it did not work.

Will it work, and if so, how will it work, in the 'underdeveloped' areas of which we hear so much today? The preceding remarks have all been leading up to this question. My purpose here is to present the question, against the background of past experience, rather than try to answer it. In the time that remains I will only hazard a few brief comments on three general topics: direct business investment, public-utility investment, and governmental grants.

The assumption I am making here – that it is the low-income areas that constitute the main problem of international investment in the mid-twentieth century – may be challenged as arbitrary and not entirely justified. The most profitable opportunities may still be in the 'regions of recent settlement'. But having regard to their high income levels, these fortunate regions can, in the present discussion, be left to provide, by and large, for their own development needs.

For reasons mentioned earlier, direct investments by American business firms – usually financed from corporate reserves rather than security issues on the capital market – are thought to be particularly well suited to the economically backward countries. But they have their shortcomings also. In the life of an industrially primitive community they are apt to create not only a dual economy (Singer, 1950) but also a dual society, in which conditions for the diffusion of western technology may actually be the reverse of favorable. Foreign business investment is not always a happy form of encounter between different civilizations. Besides, if techniques are to be of wide and permanent use, they must be adapted to local conditions. The methods of giant corporations, whose foreign operations are sometimes only a side show, are often too standardized to favor such adaptation. And so the local economy may not get much help from the example they give; the example is often inapplicable. Let us remember that the Japanese acquired industrial techniques very effectively before they began to receive any substantial foreign business investments. Also the technical assistance programs now in operation remind us that there are other ways of spreading technical knowledge.

As a rule, when foreign business enterprise is attracted to economically backward areas, it is mainly for the production of raw materials for export markets, for the simple reason that the domestic market in such areas, even if protected by import restrictions, is generally too poor to afford any strong inducement to invest.[6] The natural result is a 'colonial' investment pattern,

6. From the latest comprehensive figures for American direct investments (*Survey of Current Business*, December 1952), it can be seen that of the total invested in Canada and Western Europe at the end of 1950, 23 per cent was in extractive industries, as much as 60 per cent in manufacturing and trade, 6 per cent in public utilities, and 11 per cent in miscellaneous activities, including cinemas and other entertainments. Of the investments outstanding on the same date in all other countries, which with a few exceptions are economically backward, 60 per cent was in extractive industries, mostly petroleum and mining, with 20 per cent, 17 per cent, and 3 per cent respectively in the other groups. This pattern is by no means new. We know that

open to the familiar criticisms that it tends to promote lop-sided rather than 'balanced' growth, and that it makes for instability due to high dependence on foreign demand for one or two staple products. If this type of direct investment is to take place in any considerable volume, it presupposes a long-run prospect of rapidly expanding demand in the industrial centers for the raw materials which it seeks to provide. Despite the forecasts of the Paley Report, there is no firm assurance of such an expansion except for certain minerals. Governmental purchase agreements alone cannot give this assurance in the absence of favorable basic demand conditions. A temporary stimulus might be got from the removal of United States tariff protection on primary products (such as sugar, copper, wool), but little can be hoped for in this direction.

In the last few years one of the chief economic obstacles to a greater flow of business funds to low-income countries has been the high level of business profits obtainable at home, from developing American natural resources and catering to the American mass market. Conditions may change. It is not inconceivable that business investment abroad might greatly increase in the future, and that it might bring substantial benefits to the poorer countries. Yet, on the whole, it seems unlikely that direct investment alone can become anything like an adequate source of international finance for economic development. It played, as we saw, a minor part in the nineteenth century. Can we rely on it to play a major part today? I doubt it.

What is most urgently needed today is a revival of the public or public-utility type of international investment that used to dominate the scene. The International Bank for Reconstruction and Development (the World Bank) has hardly begun to fill the gap left by the disappearance of this type of private foreign lending. If the past cannot be reproduced, it is all the more imperative to devise a new pattern suited to present needs and

---

in 1929 only one-fifth of total American direct investment was in manufacturing, and 84 per cent of this was in Western Europe, Canada, Australia, and New Zealand. 'Only to a very small extent, therefore, did American direct investments enter into manufacturing for the domestic market in under-developed countries' (United Nations, 1949, p. 32).

conditions. Critics have wondered how much of nineteenth-century foreign investment would have survived the tests and rules laid down by the World Bank. The Bank, being dependent on the private capital market for most of its loanable funds, inevitably reflects to some extent the attitudes of the private investor. And the private American investor is still waiting for a change in the weather, and remains unimpressed by statistics showing that only 15 per cent of the dollar bonds (not counting direct investments) floated in the 1920s by underdeveloped countries – that is, aside from Central Europe – have proved a permanent loss (see Gray *et al.*, 1950, p. 62).

It is said that there are not enough productive projects in the low-income countries to absorb much more money than is now going out. It is pointed out that the Marshall Plan, which accustomed the world to the sight of a large dollar outflow, was not a plan of new development so much as one of reconstruction, in an area where a solid industrial foundation and the 'know-how' of a skilled population already existed.[7]

No doubt this point has considerable force. But if there are not enough projects, can we not ask for international technical assistance to design them and to draw up the blueprints? Lack of basic services, such as transport, power, and water supply, is a particularly serious bottleneck in the poor countries. Because of this the *physical* environment – quite apart from the obvious difficulties arising from the political or social climate – is unfavorable to private investment. A large foreign firm producing raw materials for export may find it profitable to set up incidental facilities such as roads or waterworks, of which the local economy, too, can make some use. But the general utility of such things often depends in haphazard fashion on the technical features of the firm's main activity. It may be fairly high in the case of a railway built by a mining company from the interior of Peru to the seacoast. It is virtually zero in the case of the pipeline in which Arabian oil is pumped to the Mediterranean.

In the United States a hundred years ago public authorities, as

7. It will be remembered, however, that some of the Marshall Aid was in effect passed on to 'underdeveloped' countries (especially by way of the United Kingdom, whose over-all balance was in equilibrium in 1948–9 and in surplus in 1950).

well as private promoters, played a leading role in the drive for 'internal improvements', financed in part by foreign capital. There is no question that ample scope exists for international financing of public improvements in the poor countries today. Until these countries have acquired a skeleton framework of such facilities, conditions will not be particularly attractive for the more varied and smaller-scale business investments there. Even with such basic improvements, of course, the individual business investments, domestic as well as foreign, may fail to materialize, because of other obstacles. It is conceivable, therefore, that some of these public works would turn out to be white elephants. But the risk has to be taken; any form of capital investment is, in the last analysis, an act of faith. However hard it may be for the pioneering spirit that opened up the new countries to apply itself to the low-income areas today, not much can be achieved without that spirit, and no international organization concerned with development can remain untouched by it.

Apart from the distribution of the promoter-function, there still remains the question of finance. If the profitability of American business at home has kept down direct investments abroad, a simple comparison of bond yields does not explain why 'portfolio' lending cannot get started again. However, while the private investor has been standing on the sidelines, we may have witnessed the beginnings of a system of international grants-in-aid and low-interest loans from government funds. The reference to the principle of Equal Sacrifice with which Roosevelt defended the Lend-Lease program may some day appear significant in retrospect. I need not point to other signs and landmarks. Let me just quote a few recent expressions of opinion. The man who gave his name to the Marshall Plan, in accepting the Nobel peace prize last December, said that it was 'of basic importance to any successful effort towards an enduring peace that the more favoured nations should lend assistance in bettering the lot of the poorer' (*The Times*, 12 December 1953).

Dr Herbert Feis, the historian of nineteenth-century foreign investment, has expressed himself as follows:

A sense of obligation has won its way in the world to the effect that a wealthy country has a call of vague dimensions to provide means to assist poorer and suffering countries. To give free admission to (it) would bankrupt us and demoralise others; but to ignore the obligation wholly would be ... out of accord with the effort in which we are engaged, to bring together the nations of the world in peaceful and co-operative understanding (Feis, 1953, p. 59).

Even if we hesitate to accept the assumption that world peace can be bought or that material progress makes for contentment, the fact of growing pressures for international income transfers must nevertheless be recognized. It may be precisely because the problem of international investment is now, unlike what it was in the Victorian era, concerned in the main with the backward economies that the need for such transfers is felt to arise.

The difficulties which American trade policy encounters in following the British nineteenth-century example might also be taken to point to unilateral income transfers as more in accord with the underlying situation. With commercial foreign investment an adjustment of the trade balance to the return flow of interest and dividends cannot normally be long postponed, while gifts permit an export surplus indefinitely.[8]

The idea of international grants-in-aid is essentially a consequence of the increased gaps in living standards and of the closeness of contact that is creating at the same time an increasingly

8. However, I cannot fully share the view that, just because of the growing return flow to which it normally gives rise, foreign investment of the orthodox sort can be no more than a short-period remedy for international imbalance. When in support of this view it is said that the increase in Great Britain's foreign assets from 1880 to 1913 'was due wholly to the reinvestment of a part of the income derived from earlier investments' (Salter, p. 53), it seems to me that a somewhat arbitrary causal attribution is made between two items on opposite sides of the balance of payments, a procedure always of doubtful validity, and particularly so when one of the items represents payments on capital account, while the other belongs to the income account. That the individual British investor, on the one hand, was under no obligation to reinvest the interest he got from abroad is obvious. From the national viewpoint, on the other hand, all one can say is that the British current account, including foreign interest earnings as well as earnings from merchandise exports and shipping, showed a surplus, which was balanced by the outflow of capital. Britain had an excess of merchandise imports over exports throughout the period 1880–1913. Yet it is conceivable that if British foreign lending had come to a complete stop in (say) 1890, a disequilibrium in the international balance of payments – a 'sterling shortage' – might have been felt in the succeeding quarter of a century.

acute awareness of these gaps – a situation without historical precedent. This awareness is perhaps the most fundamental obstacle to the resumption of private international lending. In contrast to the position of the backward economies today, income per head in the principal debtor countries of the nineteenth century – the newly settled regions – can never have been far below European levels. Interest payments from poor to rich are now, it seems, not only basically unwanted by the rich countries but indeed are felt to be somehow contrary to the spirit of the age. And although public grants (for 'social overhead capital') and private foreign lending (for more specific investments) can ideally be looked upon as complementary rather than conflicting sources of finance, it is easy to see why in practice the two do not mix at all well. This applies not only to grants but also in some degree to international loans from government sources.

Persistent attempts in the United Nations organization to set up a system of international grants under U.N. auspices – from the U.N.E.D.A. (United Nations Economic Development Agency) proposal of 1948 to the S.U.N.F.E.D. (Special United Nations Fund for Economic Development) report of 1953 – have foundered on the rocks of American opposition. Yet American practices and pronouncements alike have kept world expectations alive, and this has continued to some extent under the Republican administration. Two notable declarations by President Eisenhower last year attracted wide attention: one was the statement in April about 'devoting a substantial percentage of the savings achieved by disarmament to a fund for world aid', the other being the so-called 'Atom Bank' proposal for the international provision of atomic energy for peaceful purposes.

It must be recognized that international unilateral transfers have no necessary connection with the subject of foreign *investment*. They may be for current consumption or for military use. Even if they are intended for, or tied to, particular capital projects, a net increase in the over-all rate of accumulation is not always assured. If they are to make an effective contribution to economic development, they call for domestic action in the receiving countries – fiscal, monetary, and other policies designed to withhold resources from immediate consumption and to direct them into capital formation.

But once the receiving countries are capable of devising the necessary controls for the productive use of outside aid, they should be equally capable of using such policies for the mobilization of potential *domestic* sources of capital (e.g. skimming off resources now absorbed by luxury consumption, making use of labor set free from the land through better farm methods or recruiting any surplus labor already existing on the land). It is far from my intention to suggest that in these circumstances foreign aid becomes unnecessary. Yet this consideration does shift the emphasis upon the need for domestic policies to insure that in the over-all use of resources, domestic as well as external, investment is given top priority (Nurkse, 1953). Here is the main criterion, and a body such as the World Bank has in this respect an even more vital role to play in the backward economies than that which the Economic Cooperation Administration and the Organization for European Economic Co-operation performed under the Marshall Plan.

These remarks on international grants and their possible uses may all be idle speculation, for which, perhaps, I should apologize. The practices alluded to may turn out to have been temporary devices related to particular emergency conditions. What I have said on these controversial matters should have been put in the form of questions – and extremely tentative questions at that. But they are, I think, questions which a survey of the present state of international finance inevitably draws to our attention.

References

BUCHANAN, N. S. (1952), 'International finance', in B. F. Haley, ed., *Survey of Contemporary Economics*, American Economic Association, Illinois.

CAIRNCROSS, A. K. (1953). *Home and Foreign Investment 1870–1913*, Cambridge.

CROOME, H. (1953), 'The dilemma of development', *New Commonwealth*, November.

FEIS, H. (1953), 'International economic outlook', *Proceedings of the Academy of Political Science*, May.

FERNS, H. S. (1951), 'The establishment of British investment in Argentina', *Inter-American Economic Affairs*, Autumn.

GRAY, G. *et al.* (1950), *Report to the President on Foreign Economic Policies*, U.S. Government Printing Office.

HARTLAND, P. (1953), 'Private enterprise and international capital', *Canadian Journal of Economics and Political Science*, February.

HILGERDT, F. (1945), *Industrialization and Foreign Trade*, League of Nations.

IMLAH, A. H. (1952), 'British balance of payments and export of capital, 1816–1913', *Economic History Review*, vol. 5, no. 2.

JENKS, L. H. (1944), 'British experience with foreign investments', *Journal of Economic History*, supplement 75.

JENKS, L. H. (1953), 'Railroads as an economic force in American development', in F. C. Land and J. C. Riemersma, eds., *Enterprise and Secular Change*, Homewood, Illinois.

KEYNES, J. M. (1922), *A Revision of the Treaty*, London.

MARTINEZ, A. B. and LEWANDOWSKI, M. (1911), *The Argentine in the Twentieth Century*, London.

NURKSE, R. (1953), *Problems of Capital Formation in Under-developed Countries*, Oxford and New York.

RIPPY, J. F. (1951), 'British investments in Latin America, end of 1913', *Inter-American Economic Affairs*, Autumn.

ROBINSON, JOAN (1952), *The Rate of Interest and Other Essays*, Macmillan, London.

SALTER, A. (1951), 'Foreign investment', *Essays in International Finance*, no. 12, Princeton.

SINGER, H. W. (1950), 'The distribution of gains between investing and borrowing countries', *American Economic Review*, Papers and Proceedings, May.

THOMAS, B. (1951), 'Migration and the rhythm of economic growth, 1830–1913', *The Manchester School*, September.

UNITED NATIONS (1949), *International Capital Movements in the Inter-war Period.*

VINER, J. (1952), 'America's aims and the progress of under-developed countries', in B. F. Hoselitz, ed., *The Progress of Underdeveloped Areas*, Chicago.

Further Reading

CLEMENT, M. O., PFISTER, R. L., and ROTHWELL, K. J. (1967), *Theoretical Issues in International Economics*, part 2, Houghton, Boston.

COOPER, R. N. (1968), *The Economics of Interdependence*, McGraw-Hill, New York.

FELLNER, W., *et al.* (1966), *Maintaining and Restoring Balance in International Payments*, Princeton University Press.

GRUBEL, H. (1966), *Forward Exchange, Speculation, and the International Flow of Capital*, Stanford University Press.

JOHNSON, H. G. (1958), *International Trade and Economic Growth*, Harvard University Press.

MACHLUP, F. (1964), *International Payments, Debts, and Gold*, Scribner, New York.

MUNDELL, R.A. (1968), *International Economics*, Collier–Macmillan, London.

MEADE, J. E. (1951), *The Theory of International Economic Policy*, vol. 1, *The Balance of Payments*, Oxford University Press.

NURKSE, R. (1944), *International Currency Experience*, League of Nations.

NURKSE, R. (1961), *Growth and Equilibrium in the World Economy*, Harvard University Press.

TEW, B. (1966), *International Monetary Cooperation, 1945–65*, Hutchinson University Library, London.

TRIFFIN, R. (1961), *Gold and the Dollar Crisis*, revised edition, Yale University Press.

TRIFFIN, R. (1966), *The World Money Maze*, Yale University Press.

Acknowledgements

Acknowledgements are due to the following for permission to reproduce the Readings in this volume:

Reading 2: Princeton University Press, International Finance Section and Professor R. Triffin.
Reading 3: University of Chicago Press.
Reading 4: University of North Carolina Press.
Reading 5: Kyklos-Verlag.
Reading 6: American Economic Association and Professor S. C. Tsiang.
Reading 7: University of Chicago Press.
Reading 8: University of Chicago Press.
Reading 9: Princeton University Press.
Reading 10: American Economic Association and Dr R. I. McKinnon.
Reading 11: George Allen and Unwin Ltd and Harvard University Press.
Reading 12: *The Review of Economic Studies* and Professor W. M. Corden.
Reading 13: International Monetary Fund.
Reading 14: Pakistan Institute of Development Economics and Professor H. G. Johnson.
Reading 15: Harvard University Press.
Reading 16: Royal Economic Society

Author Index

Subject Index